D1126080

CATHERINE COOKSON

By the same author

CATHERINE COOKSON

THE BIOGRAPHY

❖

Kathleen Jones

Constable · London

First published in Great Britain 1999
by Constable and Company Limited
3 The Lanchesters, 162 Fulham Palace Road
London W6 9ER
Copyright © Kathleen Jones 1999
ISBN 0 09 479370 0

The right of Kathleen Jones to be identified as the author of this work
has been asserted by her in accordance with
the Copyright, Designs and Patents Act 1988

Typeset in Linotron Sabon 11pt by
Rowland Phototypesetting Limited
Bury St Edmunds, Suffolk
Printed in Great Britain by
St Edmundsbury Press Limited
Bury St Edmunds, Suffolk

A CIP catalogue record for this book
is available from the British Library

For my grandparents Annie and Tom Sutherland,
whose stories of their own early struggles on Tyneside
made it possible for me to write this book.

'I can and I will' has always been my motto.

Catherine Cookson

CONTENTS

LIST OF ILLUSTRATIONS

ACKNOWLEDGEMENTS

Among the many people who have helped me to write this book, some of whom did not wish to be named, particular thanks have to go to John Smith, Catherine Cookson's former agent and friend, who generously allowed me to use material he had collected for a previous, unpublished, biography. Thanks also to the Trustees of the Estates of Dame Catherine and Tom Cookson, Anthony Sheil, Mark Barty-King of Transworld Publishers, Giles Gordon, Gill Coleridge, Tom Fenelli, Press Officer for South Shields Town Council, Alaisdair Wilson, curator of the South Shields Museum and Art Gallery, the staff of South Shields Library, the *Shields Gazette*, Tony Henderson and staff of *The Journal*, Andy Guy at Beamish Country Museum, the staff of Durham County Record Office, Lord Bragg, Mr Albert Knight and Corbridge Village Trust, Lord Ravensworth, Cliff Goodwin, all at Saraville, Ella and Harold Slight, Mr and Mrs A. Wilson, Leonard Cotterell, Andrew Dixon, Dr Lesley Gordon, Special Collections, University of Newcastle upon Tyne, Dr John Burn, Professor Ernst Honigmann, Ann Marshall, Father Ian Jackson, Margaret Lewis, Hastings Central Library, *Hastings and St Leonards Observer*, Hastings Museum, Josephine and Brian Austin, John and Margaret Charrot, Jan Dunlop and members of Hastings Writers' Group, Margaret Richards, Mr W. R. Lynch, the staff of Penrith Library for patiently obtaining so many books for me, Catherine Bainbridge at Appleby Library, Christopher Noble and the staff of the Mugar Memorial Library, Boston University, Boston, Mass., Gill Bilski and Helen McLelland. Personal thanks must go to Neil Ferber for research and unconditional personal support, Richard and Iris Gollner, Neil Hornick, Andy Marino and all at Radala, Carol O'Brien for being a marvellous editor, Alexandra Gruebler, Tara

Lawrence, Harriet Boston and all at Constable for their support and encouragement. Thanks to Transworld Publishers and Random House for permission to quote from Catherine Cookson's work, to Abacus for permission to quote from Catherine Cookson, People and Places. Permission to quote from Oneness and Separateness, by Louise J. Kaplan Ph.D is given by Simon and Schuster Inc. and quotations from Searching for Mercy Street by Linda Gray Sexton by permission of Little, Brown. Thanks to Dr Gottlieb at Boston University for permission to quote from unpublished manuscripts in the Catherine Cookson Collection, and Professor Ernst Honigmann for allowing me to quote from transcipts of his interview with Catherine in Newcastle University archives.

INTRODUCTION

Biography relies on written evidence and, for more recent lives, oral testimony. People who lived within the educated, literate levels of society, such as the members of the Bloomsbury Group who wrote to each other and about each other with such fluency, are a biographer's dream. Their lives are publicly documented and privately chronicled in numerous letters and diaries. But lower down the social scale, among the people who scrubbed their steps, emptied their chamber pots and delivered the coal, it was a different matter. Even if they had had enough education to read and write, paper and pen were not among their most frequently used possessions. Leisure to scribble down anything other than a shopping list was rare among people who worked twelve hours a day with only half a day off per week.

Literacy on the lower side of the upstairs/downstairs divide was actually discouraged. When the introduction of free education for everyone was debated in Parliament, there were many who feared that education would only foment social unrest and could even lead to industrial and economic decline. Theresa Rosier, the young educationalist in Catherine Cookson's novel *Katie Mulholland*, is discouraged from organising classes for working men and told by her parents, 'Child, do you think a miner would go down a mine if he could read and write correctly? Do you want your father's business to collapse? Do you want us to starve?' It also drove a wedge between neighbours. Those who wanted to better themselves were considered upstarts and treated with suspicion. Catherine Cookson describes the dilemma in her novel *The Black Velvet Gown*. Her heroine, Riah, living in a nineteenth-century northeastern community, is unusual because she has been taught to read and write by her husband. She is proud of the fact that her children are the only ones in the three rows of pit houses who can write their names. 'This alone had set them all apart. Seth could have taught lots of men in the rows to read and write, but they were afraid in case the pit keeker split on them to the manager, because reading was frowned upon, and, as some of the older men had pointed out forcibly to Seth, it got you nowhere except in trouble with those that provided your livelihood.'[1] Not only did education make them unpopular with their employers, it did nothing to improve their social conditions. As Catherine has one of her characters remark in *The Mallen Litter*, 'What are they after, them up there, eh, forcin' them to school? You can't fill their bellies with readin' an' writin'.'

In the first two decades of the twentieth century, despite the introduction of free, compulsory education up to the age of thirteen in 1880, adult literacy was still a big problem among the working classes. Most adults over thirty had grown up in families too poor to afford much in the way of schooling, and where earning a living took priority over education. Catherine Cookson's family, the McMullens, were no exception. The man who brought her up, her step-grandfather John McMullen, born in the 1850s, could not even sign his name. He collected his pension by putting a thumb print on the form. His wife Rose, Catherine's grandmother, could read but found writing a letter arduous. Her daughters Sarah, Kate and Mary had received rather more in the way of education, but were all working by the time they were twelve. They could read and write, but only at a fairly basic level. In later life Catherine's mother Kate would struggle to read books in order to better herself, even though they were full of words she couldn't pronounce or understand. Kate's attempts to use them were profoundly embarrassing for her daughter.

When Catherine was growing up, there were no books in the McMullen household. The daily *Shields Gazette* was purchased and read when there was a penny to spare, and weeklies occasionally found their way into the house – such publications as the *Happy Mag*, full of moral homilies and sickly verses, the whole having a sentimental tone that would have accorded well with the Victorian ethics of smiling through suffering and making a virtue out of poverty. When a literate lodger brought Shakespeare, Milton and Donne into the house, Catherine was told they were unsuitable. These were the days when Shakespeare's plays were produced in expurgated versions for family consumption.

The McMullen clan lived closely together. They rarely needed to write letters to each other, or to anyone else, and they didn't have the time or the privacy to keep diaries. Like millions of other working-class families, they left little record of their existence or the details of their daily lives and when they died they were buried in unmarked graves. If little Katie McMullen had not grown up to become a best-selling novelist, we would know nothing about them at all. The problem for the biographer is how to chronicle such invisible lives.

The only existing account of the McMullen family is the one written by Catherine herself and there is little corroborative evidence. Catherine wrote her autobiographical memoir *Our Kate* when she was in her fifties, recovering from a severe breakdown and trying to come to terms with her relationship with her mother. Autobiography of any kind must always be suspect. It is a species of fiction – in this case more than usually so. Catherine wrote more than eight drafts, gradually expunging from the text her bitterness and hatred for her mother and all the other people who had damaged her as a child. She freely confessed that she had 'used her novelist's guile' to construct a readable story and that she had not told the truth about her mother. 'I made her softer ... nicer ...' As she grew older she was more prepared to elaborate, either on the page or to interviewers, and at one point she even began to write another version of 'the truth' intending it to be published after her death. But she changed her mind. Most of this controversial material was destroyed, leaving only unpublished autobiographical fragments previously lodged with an American university and a number of taped interviews for whose use she refused permission until after her death.

The biographer researching her early life has only the various versions of her autobiography to go on, and the occasional testimony of people who knew her when she was young, but whose memories have been distorted by sixty or seventy years of time and the sudden gloss of celebrity that subtly colours or even changes people's recollections of times past. Childhood friendships become closer, intimations of genius were discerned where none had ever been detected and negative feelings and incidents are played down or omitted.

In Catherine's case, she became famous late in life, so there were few people still alive to remember her by the time journalists began to show an interest. Many of Catherine's close friends, the people who really knew her well towards the end of her life, are very protective towards her and reluctant to talk publicly. This is understandable. Catherine was an intensely vulnerable person whose privacy was important to her and she generated equally intense feelings of protection in those who cared for her. The biographer's task is further complicated by the fact that Catherine had little contact with her wider family in the forty years she lived in exile from the northeast, and there were no brothers or sisters or children to remember her intimately. Catherine Cookson is virtually the only witness to the details of her own extraordinary life. Reading her unpublished manuscripts or listening to the tapes that she made in the late 1980s when she finally decided to tell the truth about a number of episodes in her life is a sobering and sometimes shocking experience. Some of the material is so controversial that if it wasn't being told by Catherine herself, either in her own handwriting or the spoken word, it would be difficult to believe it happened. Comparing the different versions, picking out the inconsistencies, omissions and contradictions, is a considerable challenge and requires the skill of a lawyer. But the result is a story as fascinating, tragic and compelling as any of Catherine's novels.

During the last years of her life Catherine Cookson was virtually confined to bed. She was almost totally blind, had survived five heart attacks, had half her colon removed, and suffered daily haemorrhages caused by a genetic blood condition. Yet she still received visitors and journalists with unfailing courtesy and kindness, propped up in bed in her luxurious home in the Jesmond area of Newcastle. She continued to write, dictating her stories on tape, having the typescripts read to her and then editing them orally. She was looked after with total dedication by her secretary Ann Marshall, a nurse, and Tom, her husband of fifty-eight years, whose own health was equally precarious. They lived for each other, dreading the moment when one of them would die. That moment came in June 1998 when Catherine died peacefully a few days before her ninety-second birthday. Tom followed three weeks later.

At the time of her death, Catherine Cookson was one of the best-selling novelists of all time, outstripping Jeffrey Archer, Jackie Collins and Barbara Cartland. She was also one of the world's richest women, and had been created a Dame – the female equivalent of a knighthood – by the Queen. This was an extraordinary achievement for the woman who started life as Katie McMullen, an illegitimate girl brought up in one of the poorest communities of the Western world, whose mother had begged barefoot from door to door. At twenty-three, Catherine couldn't wait to leave the northeast and went to great lengths to conceal her illegitimate birth and her working-class origins. Later, when her status was secure, she actually emphasised the poverty and hardship of her childhood because it made her achievements more spectacular. Her life story became as carefully worked and edited as any of her fictions.

Although Catherine spent more than forty years of her life avoiding her roots in a wealthy neighbourhood in the south of England, she never really managed, mentally or emotionally, to leave the northeast behind. 'No matter how thick the veneer,' she confessed, that early environment had 'a way of kicking itself through the skin'. She wrote about it obsessively and at the age of seventy returned, as she thought, to die. She was happy, at last, to call herself 'a child of the Tyne'.

❖

PART ONE

A Child of the Tyne
1906–1918

I am still a child of the Tyne whose far horizons
reached only to Palmer's Shipyard in Jarrow
and the sands at South Shields.

Catherine Cookson

1

He pointed out the great smoking chimneys, the
mass of towering iron that was the gantries and
cranes, the ships in the river hugging the staiths, and,
of all things, a big, black looking boat sailing down
the river with the smoke pouring out of a funnel . . .
But . . . what she saw were rough looking people,
poor people, and lots of children, and mostly
bare-footed. The towns seemed full of poor
children . . .'[1]

The river Tyne is one of the great rivers of England and was as
inspirational for Catherine Cookson as the Thames was for Dickens.
She was born beside it, played beside it, once almost drowned in it,
and breathed the stench from its industries every day on her way to
school. Her family earned their living from the river – the very bits
of wood they burned on the fire were scavenged from it. When
Catherine opened the front door it was in front of her, glinting in
the steely northern light: 'the river . . . There, there it is, like a string
of herrings, all scaly and shiny', and 'far away in the distance . . .
the masts of the ships, disembodied things, seemingly borne on air'.[2]
On the hill overlooking the Tyne at east Jarrow was the street she
was brought up in, raised in the lively culture spawned by the river,
'Geordie culture' – as recognisable as Cockney or Liverpudlian. Catherine was, through her books, to give it an international identity and
a voice. It had so much vitality, she insisted, 'a vitality built on
struggle'.

The Tyne rises in the Pennines as two rugged mountain streams,
the north and south Tyne, which enclose the hill country where
Catherine chose to make her home during the last twenty years of
her life, and where she set many of her historical novels. As it nears

the sea, the Tyne grows in width and strength, becoming strongly tidal. It is a clean and beautiful salmon river now, but in the early years of the century when Catherine was young, it was fouled by the effluent from the mines, iron and steel foundries, dyemakers, shipyards, seven chemical works, glassworks, soap factories and tanneries that lined both banks, as well as the sewage discharged by one of Britain's biggest cities. The river was a major port for whaling and merchant shipping and a large North Sea fishing fleet went in and out of the Tyne. The quays were lined with fish markets and groups of girls whose job it was to gut and scale the fish. The night sky above the river was lit up by the arc furnaces of the steel works. The air stank with the reek from industrial chimneys, burning coal and coke, rotting fish and the salty edge of the raw North Sea wind. Sometimes it was so strong it burned the throat.

In 1906 – the year of Catherine's birth – the area was already in decline, its downward progress halted briefly during the First World War, to crash spectacularly afterwards during the slump of the twenties and thirties, becoming 'a graveyard of industrial hope'. Tyne Dock, where Catherine's grandfather and uncle worked, was still one of the biggest shipping ports in the world in the early years of the century. The ships and their cargoes made a kind of romantic litany – 'iron ore from Bilbao, black fine ore from Benisaf, the heavy ore from Sweden that made the steel, esparto grass for paper, prop boats from Russia . . .'3 But it was coal that was the foundation of its prosperity. Seven million tons of coal passed through it in a single year. Much of this coal came from the nearby collieries of Boldon, Harton, Jarrow, Birtley and Lamesley – all owned by Lord Ravensworth, one of the area's largest landowners. Jarrow colliery had such a terrible safety record that it was nicknamed 'the slaughterhouse' for the number of men who were killed there. Many of Catherine's relatives were miners in the Ravensworth collieries and she used them as the setting for some of her novels – most notably *Maggie Rowan*.

As the mines declined, so did the shipping trade, with huge debts of human misery. 'Most of the men on the Tyne had forgotten how it felt to carry a bait tin – in fact they doubted whether there had ever been a time in their lives when they had worked. The younger men didn't have to wonder about this; those born just prior to or during the 1914 war never knew what it was to be employed.'4 Geordie culture became synonymous with poverty, industrial decline and the growth of trade unionism. It is impossible to talk of Tyneside without thinking of the Jarrow marchers in the thirties. The history of Tyneside is part of the history of the Industrial Revolution and its social consequences – that is what makes Catherine Cookson's work universal rather than merely regional. The social and economic divide is global. Catherine was able, in her work, to fix a place and a time and a social class and make it universally applicable by the creation of heroes and heroines who are able to transcend the divide, rising, as she did, from poverty and humiliation to riches and respectability.

Jarrow and South Shields, the 'grim, grimy, dock-bound river towns' where Catherine Cookson grew up, have now been swallowed up in the urban sprawl of Newcastle – the major city of northeast England. They began as early settlements – fishing ports, boat-building and mining villages, around the mouth of the river Tyne – and gradually spread towards each other. On the north side of the river lie North Shields, Wallsend, Willington Quay and Newcastle itself; on the other side, South Shields, Jarrow, Hebburn and Gateshead. Now the whole area is divided up by motorways and a metro system and much of the industrial squalor Catherine knew has gone.

The air smells of the sea and the banks of the Tyne are lined by luxury flats and leisure developments. Most of the big shipyards are gone and the skyline is no longer crisscrossed by the masts of the sailing and steamships that moored in their hundreds at the beginning of the century. The coal staithes are gone, as are the pits that fed them. But the Jarrow timber slake is still there and so is the Tyne Dock. This is the area Catherine knew intimately and called 'the fifteen streets': a network of back-to-backs crammed in between Harton Colliery railway line and the sidings of the Tyne Dock itself. She herself lived on the other side of the railway arches, beside the timber slake; first in Leam Lane, now a dual carriageway, and then further up the river towards Jarrow in a development of three streets – William Black Street, Phillipson Street and Lancaster Street – always known as the New Buildings. Catherine passed under the arches of Tyne Dock almost every day of her early life. She would look up 'into the murky sky showing between them', imagining the brick viaducts as 'veins running from the ships, full of iron ore on its way to Palmers in Jarrow . . . wagons laden with pit props for the mines . . . carrying great green hands of bananas . . . or coming from inland

[11]

laden with coal heading for the staiths'. She knew that 'when the wagons were rumbling full-laden, men would be in work'.

Today there is a notice beside the road as you drive into the area bearing the name of Jarrow's most famous resident and in summer there is a month-long festival, sponsored by her to provide entertainment and diversion for tourists and residents alike. A whole section of the museum is devoted to her life, and the local tourist board markets the town as 'Catherine Cookson Country'. Ironically, in place of the docks, mines and factories that caused such misery for her family and their contemporaries, the biggest industry in Shields and Jarrow today is Catherine Cookson herself.

But in the first decade of the twentieth century, South Shields and Jarrow were places to be avoided. An elderly woman who grew up in some of the poorer streets north of the Tyne recalls a gulf between the two communities that was more than the width of the river. 'There was poverty . . . and then there was Jarrow.' There was little regular work and a lot of competition for any job that was going. There was always a queue of men outside the dock gates hoping to be signed on for a day's work. A man might be employed full time for a week and then be idle for six. It was a strongly Catholic area, settled by Irish immigrants, often with large families to feed. When the men were working, the local priest, Father Bradley, would stand outside the gates of the dock on payday and take 10 per cent of the men's money to support the church – and this in an area where people were not just 'clothes-poor', they didn't have enough to eat.

With deprivation and unemployment came other evils. Jarrow and Hebburn were not just regarded as the poorest communities on the Tyne, they had a reputation for lawlessness, violence and drink. There was little anyone could do to escape. Self-education was one means of betterment, but difficult to accomplish without guidance. With luck a pretty woman might catch someone's eye and marry up the social scale. The despair generated by the hopelessness of their situation is the driving force motivating the characters in Catherine's early novels. 'It was funny, but that was all life amounted to . . . working life out to keep it in – working for food and warmth; and when the futility of this was made evident, blotting it out with drink.'[5]

The area around the Tyne Dock where her family lived was dominated psychologically by the gloomy edifice of Harton Workhouse further up the hill on Harton Moor, the combined free hospital and asylum, last resort for unmarried mothers, orphans, the elderly, the physically or mentally handicapped, the insane, the homeless and the destitute. It was feared more than anything else. Inmates were strictly segregated and it was not always possible for families to see each other. Unmarried mothers would be strictly disciplined (sometimes beaten, sometimes denied food) if they attempted to meet or talk to their children. Lovemaking between married couples was a punishable offence since it might result in more mouths for the community to support. Those physically capable of doing so were forced to do hard menial work in return for their keep. In Catherine's novel *Kate Hannigan*, Kate's father dies of fright when he wakes up after an accident and finds himself in the workhouse hospital. Catherine's grandfather lived in constant dread of it. Families, however poor, tried to help each other avoid its humiliation. 'There was an unspoken feeling in these streets, which, if translated, would have implied . . . you save someone the workhouse and you'll never land there yourself.'[6]

For those who lived within the fifteen streets there was an unwritten but complex social code whose invisible boundaries were not to be crossed – much of it to do with pride and the prevention of a 'loss of face'. There was a hidden matriarchy with its own moral standards and traditions. Women might be beaten senseless by their husbands in the house next door, but it was never mentioned. Elaborate fictions were maintained to preserve each other's dignity. But it also meant the petty observation of minute degrees of respectability and social class – all that stood between them and the utter degradation of the workhouse. As Catherine wrote, 'Poverty is comparative. There were those who did not live in the fifteen streets who considered the people living there to be of one stratum, the lowest stratum; but the people inside this stratum knew that there were three different levels, the upper, the middle and the lower.'[7] Her family, the McMullens, prided themselves on belonging to the upper level, which was, Catherine said, 'the breeding ground of snobbery'.

Catherine's grandmother, Rose McMullen, had a reputation as a hard woman. Her broad, unsmiling face above the tightly buttoned blouse, hair drawn severely back into a bun, stares joylessly back from her photographs. Hers was a toughness born from bitterness and tragedy, where every ounce of optimism or humour had been beaten out of her by experience. Rose had been born into a relatively comfortable home, to parents who had a smallholding and were in regular work. Her first husband, William Fawcett, was a kind, deeply religious man who died of tuberculosis in his early thirties, leaving her with five daughters to support. Rose was forced to move back in with her parents and go to work at the Jarrow Pudding Mills while her mother looked after the children.

Employment for women on the Tyne was more abundant than for men, because they had the option of domestic service as well as industrial labour. But as Mary Wollstonecraft had remarked a century earlier, most of the work available to women was degrading and often physically harmful as well. Women contracted lung diseases in the cotton mills or coal mines, suffered lingering deaths from phosphorus in match factories, and lost their sight sewing in darkened rooms. The women of the urban poor around the Tyne were strong, determined and often subversive. They worked until they dropped. 'Poverty could not defeat them, men could not command them, and society could not subdue them. Hard work remained their lot and however much society changed, one fact remained unalterable; [they] worked all their lives.'[8] This was the culture in which Catherine grew up.

In the Puddling Mills, where Rose McMullen worked, scrap iron was heated in a furnace before being pounded by the steam hammers to remove impurities. People laboured in searing heat and highly dangerous conditions. They died from injury, lead poisoning or exhaustion. The work was physically draining, even though the owners gave the workers free beer to keep them going through the day. This gave rise to a local expression, 'being puddled', which means to be the worse for drink.

Catherine often speculated why her grandmother had married John McMullen, an illiterate Irish jack-the-lad, whose main claim to distinction was that he was one of triplets. He had just been demobbed from military service in India and still had some of the glamour of the uniform about him. Rose was lonely, disliked losing her independence and, above all, hated the daily drudgery of the Puddling Mill. To Rose, John seemed quiet, had a reputation as a hard worker, was prepared to take on five children not his own, and his army gratuity was still in his pocket.

Neither the gratuity nor the initial optimism lasted long. Rose was never good with money – she was wasteful and could somehow never 'make an inch go a mile', as the saying was. Work was scarce in Jarrow and, because so many men were desperate for what was available, wages were pitiful. For a ten-hour shift, working thigh-deep in cold and filthy water to unload iron ore from the boats, John McMullen could earn only three shillings and sixpence – in 1971 the equivalent of seventeen and a half pence. When he couldn't get any other work he was forced to break stones at the workhouse for a shilling voucher which could be exchanged for food at a local shop. And there was soon another mouth to feed when Rose gave birth to a son, John – named for his father but always referred to as Jack. Gradually everything decent in the house, from furniture and kitchen utensils down to the bedding and the clothes from their backs, went to the 'In and Out' where they were pawned to pay the rent. When they needed something back, something else was taken in to redeem it. You could pawn the bread knife after dinner and take the bed-clothes in to get it out for breakfast.

When two of the daughters died before they were thirteen, the three remaining Fawcett sisters – Sarah, Kate and Mary – regarded it not as a tragedy so much as a blessed release. Now there would be more for everyone else. The girls received little schooling, since school cost a penny a week each and that was enough money to buy a meal. The family lived on a kind of stew made from vegetables, beans, barley and what were called 'pieces' – assorted bits of meat and offal swept from the butcher's floor. 'What did it matter if there was sawdust sticking to the black congealed blood on the meat . . . it made a dinner.'

If times were very hard, Catherine's mother, Kate, would be sent out begging. It was generally Kate who had to go, because she was likely to arouse more sympathy. She had been born with a foot turned inwards, leaving her all her life with a swollen ankle and a slight limp. Barefoot, her legs split and bleeding from cold sores, she went to better-off neighbourhoods to knock on doors and ask for bread. The shame of it stayed with Kate all her life. Her older sister Sarah was put into service when she was only twelve years old. She was paid very little, but at least she had her board and lodging. Sarah was glad to get out of the house. She hated her stepfather. As the eldest she had had to bear the brunt of his violent and abusive behaviour. Once, when she had gone to visit an aunt in Newcastle before coming home for her day off, she stayed overnight because she'd missed the last tram home, and John McMullen beat her black and blue with the buckle end of his leather belt because he didn't believe her story. Almost any employer was preferable to this.

Kate, who, despite her docile nature, was not a favourite with her mother, was already working before she was tall enough to see over a washtub. She went out on a daily basis, to work for a butcher's family; six thirty in the morning until late evening doing the laundry and all the household cleaning for a family of six. The butcher's wife had a stool made so that Kate could reach the poss-stick to do the washing. This was a colossal job even for a fully grown woman. It involved heaving heavy linen and work clothes in and out of boiling water with a stick – possing, bleaching, rinsing, mangling – and then all the work of drying and ironing. Kate had half a day off every fortnight and was paid two shillings and sixpence a week – every penny of which went to Rose McMullen. As soon as Mary was old enough she had to do the same. It was a kind of child slavery still widely accepted in late Victorian England.

Despite the fact that her mother was so hard on her, Kate grew up into a warm-hearted, pretty girl with a beautiful ivory skin and soft brown hair. She was much loved in the community for her spontaneity and kindness and perhaps it was these qualities that made her mother dislike her. Like other girls of her age, Kate hankered after nice clothes and romantic love, and she had a strong sense of fun that had little opportunity for expression. Catherine remembered that Kate would suddenly be caught by a kind of spring madness. She and her sister Mary would dress up in men's clothes and dance out of the house, giggling and calling other women in the street to follow them in a mad frolic round the houses, beating tin cans and singing the Kerry piper's song – its words singularly appropriate:

> O, for the days of the Kerry dancing,
> O, for the lilt of the piper's tune,
> O, for one of those hours of gladness,
> Gone alas, like our youth – too soon.

When Kate was nineteen, she got a live-in job working behind the bar in a country inn, the Ravensworth Arms, in Lamesley – a small hamlet now on the fringes of Gateshead. Lamesley was not so much a village as a scattering of farms and cottages, a parish church, a blacksmith's forge and the inn – all of which served the estate of Ravensworth Castle, a Gothic pile which was the principal residence of the Earl of Ravensworth. Unconfirmed local gossip related that Kate had been in service at the castle before she got the job at the Ravensworth Arms. Mary, three years younger, was also employed there as a housemaid. Kate's warm and lively personality was very popular with the customers at the inn and she seems to have become a good friend of the owners' daughter, Jenny Hardy.

Kate was invited to the staff dances at Ravensworth Castle, where she raised eyebrows by dancing first with the butler and then with one of the guests.[9] It may well have been this gentleman who began to visit the saloon bar of the inn whenever he was in the area expressly to see Kate – the man she was to enter on Catherine's birth certificate as 'Alexander Davies'. This unknown man had, according to Mary, the manners of a gentleman and was handsomely dressed in a gentleman's black coat with an astrakhan collar, black hat and gloves. He was also very well-spoken. The inference was that he was in some way connected with the castle – that he worked there, had business there or was a visitor. If he was visiting Ravensworth Castle he would certainly have been dressed in black, since two of the earls had died in quick succession during 1903 and 1904 and the entire household was in mourning. The deaths, and the fact that there were no male heirs in the direct line, generated a great deal of estate business. There had also been a terrible scandal when the first Lord Ravensworth's 59-year-old widow (amply provided for under his will) married her 28-year-old footman James William Wadsworth, described as 'a steward, son of an estate agent'. And there were disputes to be settled between the two dowager countesses and the new earl about the ownership of heirlooms and furniture. There was considerable activity and large numbers of visitors from London and Devon, where the younger dowager countess was living.

Whatever Kate's lover's connection with the castle, he was totally unlike any of the rough young men Kate had known around the Tyne Dock. Kate's family thought him a gentleman, but there was later speculation that he, like Lady Ravensworth's new husband, was only a footman. But even this would have been a considerable step up the social scale for Kate. The facts are very difficult to disentangle from the rumours. Some sources seem to suggest that it was a brief affair; others that he came to see Kate spasmodically over a period of about two years, sometimes timing his irregular visits to coincide with her precious day off. For Kate he didn't come often enough, and she seems to have known little of his background. Was he already married? Certainly Kate, although deeply in love, seems to have kept him at a distance. Her daughter Catherine felt that 'she knew from the beginning that it was hopeless and therefore she kept him in his

[17]

place'. Catherine believed her mother when Kate told her that only once, when she was twenty-three, did she allow herself to weaken and be carried away by her emotions. Unfortunately for Kate, 'once was enough'. Was this wishful thinking on Catherine's part? If she became pregnant from a single episode of lovemaking, then Kate was certainly not one of the lucky ones.

Kate didn't tell her daughter anything about what had happened to her until Catherine was almost thirty, and then only the barest details. Everything Catherine knew about her elusive father was gossip she heard as a teenager from Kate's sister Mary ('a bitch of a woman') or from the village blacksmith's wife. Neither was able to give an accurate or unbiased account. They couldn't tell Catherine whether the unknown gentleman knew about Kate's pregnancy, or whether he melted away as soon as he became aware of it. He either couldn't, or wouldn't, marry her.

Whatever the truth about her lover's behaviour, Kate spent nine months in torment. She told Catherine later that if the baby in her womb had been aware of what she suffered during those months, it 'would have been born mental'. Catherine used Kate's words in her novel *Maggie Rowan*. Surely, she wrote, the baby must have been contaminated, in the months during which it lay 'in her turbulent womb, fed by her blood, that in itself must have borne the poison of her mind, poison she manufactured daily with thoughts of bitterness and recrimination mostly levelled against herself'. Kate's situation was made worse by the fact that her sister Sarah had had an offer of marriage and wrote to Kate asking whether she should accept. His name was Mick Lavelle and he was a coal miner. Sarah's wavering seems to have had to do partly with his lowly occupation (miners had a reputation for being rough and lazy and treating their wives badly) and partly with his size – he was smaller than she was. Kate's reply was emphatic. Marry him, she told her sister, even if you have to live in poverty for the rest of your life. Marriage, any marriage, was better than what she was having to endure.

Kate worked as long as she could before the pregnancy became obvious. Then, 'sick to the depths of her soul', Kate went back to Jarrow to tell her family that she was having an illegitimate child. Her stepfather had to be restrained from beating her to a pulp for bringing such shame on them all. He had horse-whipped her sister Sarah for a much lesser offence. It is difficult for us, now, to understand just how terrible the stigma of illegitimacy was. Women were

expected to be sexually pure; the most innocent acts could be miscon-
strued and it was all too easy for a woman to get a reputation for
loose behaviour. As the heroine of Catherine's novel *Maggie Rowan*
remarks, 'It's funny what little things it takes to make a lass into a
bad woman.' To conceive a child outside marriage was an unforgiv-
able sin, a sullying of moral purity that could never be redeemed. A
woman who did so was irretrievably 'fallen', and the sin was also
visited on the child, who was marked a bastard for the rest of his
or her life. The injustice of it was later to be a factor in Catherine's
loss of faith. A God who could sanction such cruelty against Kate
and herself could not also be 'a benevolent father . . . someone who
has our welfare at heart'.

A family story was told to Catherine by Mary that, shortly after
Kate's return, a man called Alec had once come to the house asking
for her. Just before Kate died she told Catherine that, after she had
left Lamesley, the father of her child came to seek her out at the
McMullens' house in Jarrow. He took her out for the day, promised
to return and marry her as soon as he could make the arrangements,
gave her the address of a house in Newcastle where she could contact
him and told her that he would come back for her shortly. She never
heard from him again. When Kate went to the house, she found that
he was not known at that address.

Years later, 'overcome with a longing to see his face and hear his
voice',[10] Catherine went to Lamesley to look for her father. She
already had the name given to her by Mary and when she enquired
in the village and talked to the blacksmith's wife, she was apparently
told that this man had been dismissed by his employer in 1906 and
had returned to the south of England, where he came from. If she
was given other details of his identity, Catherine didn't admit to it.
She always maintained that she didn't know for certain who her
father actually was. The way was left open for her to fantasise about
her paternity and create for herself the dream of a landed gentleman
who would one day reclaim her and restore her to her rightful position. When one of her biographers suggested that Kate had been
seduced and abandoned by a footman, Catherine was not amused.
Asked by another interviewer whether she knew the truth about her
parentage, she replied enigmatically that if she did, it would go to
the grave with her and Kate.

If the story of 'Alec's' return and his subsequent cowardly
behaviour is true, his deceit put Kate through even more torment

before she finally realised that she had been abandoned. The rich could afford to send their daughters away and have the child quietly adopted without loss of face, but the poor did not have that option. As Catherine later observed, 'the cruelty of the bigoted poor has to be witnessed to be believed. It has to be lived with to be understood.' If a girl's family would not help her, her only resort was the workhouse, where she would be physically punished by hard labour and have her child taken away from her to be brought up as an orphan, unloved and overdisciplined. 'Fallen' women were obliged to remain for fourteen years, until their offspring were deemed to be old enough to leave and earn their own livings.

For Kate's predicament, the solution was more humane. The child was to be left with her grandmother and step-grandfather and brought up as theirs. It was a fiction often adopted by families in order to preserve a veil of respectability – one that was used frequently in the twentieth century. Kate's daughter would be brought up as her sister.

2

Move your eyes and look there, right across the
valley. Don't look at the jumble of new red roofs,
look past them . . . Go on, lift your lids, look right up
. . . high up. There it is, the fortress of pain wherein
you were a child and you learned to laugh, only it
looks nothing like a fortress, it's just a solitary little
street.[1]

Kate Hannigan, Catherine's first and most autobiographical novel,
opens with the birth of an illegitimate baby girl. A young doctor,
who does not expect to get paid, is shouting at a drunken, light-
fingered midwife while begrudging, unhelpful grandparents wait in
the room below. In Catherine's case there was no upstairs room; she
was born in a crowded two-roomed dwelling – kitchen and bedroom
– already occupied by Rose and John McMullen and their sixteen-
year-old son Jack. In the poorer streets of Jarrow, babies were usually
delivered by local midwives, who had no professional qualifications
and were often paid 'in kind'. Doctors were summoned only as a
last resort. It was small wonder that the infant mortality rate was
twice the national average – Catherine was lucky to survive. She was
delivered by a popular local physician, Dr McHaffie, who had been
called in for Kate's difficult labour and who gave his services free.
Before the NHS, doctors had to be paid. In poor areas, most doctors
ran a club where patients paid so much a week – usually only a few
pennies – to cover themselves for medical emergencies. The McMullens were too poor even to afford the club. For families like them,
if the doctor wasn't willing to treat them free of charge, there was
only the workhouse infirmary or the chemist, who would offer advice
and recommend patent medicines, for which they also had to pay.

The child who eventually became Catherine Cookson began life with several different names. Christened Catherine, she was generally known first as Katie, then Kitty, McMullen – her step-grandfather's name. But she later learned that because her mother was unmarried, her real surname was Fawcett – a name she never used. Her birth certificate gives her name as Catherine Ann Davies, the child of Alexander Davies, commission agent, and Catherine Davies, née Fawcett. Kate Fawcett risked being found guilty of a criminal offence to try to give her daughter legitimacy and avoid having her described on her birth certificate as a 'bastard child'.

In the days before doctors were obliged to write out a certificate giving the date and time of birth as well as the mother's name and the sex of the child, it was easy to falsify details before a registrar. Many births went totally unrecorded. Either too ill or too confused after Catherine's birth to go to the register office within the legally specified time, and unwilling for reasons of her own to allow anyone else to go, on 13 August, Kate gave a false date of birth for her daughter – 27, rather than 20 June 1906 – so that she would not be guilty of late registration. She also described herself as a married woman, giving her husband's name as Alexander Davies, occupation 'commission agent' – the modern equivalent would probably be 'businessman'. This was a bold and courageous act. Perhaps Kate was still hanging on to the belief that Catherine's father would return and marry her, making their daughter legitimate – in which case the name on the birth certificate would be her real name in anticipation of a future reality.

To be a bastard was a terrible thing. It meant not only a social slur, but people believed that in some obscure way the moral taint was passed on from mother to child. An illegitimate person was barred from certain types of 'respectable' employment. It might also affect the prospects of matrimony – there were many men who were not prepared to marry an illegitimate girl. There were also legal barriers which discriminated against children born outside marriage, and many of these were not removed until relatively recently. There is a fiction that at some point in time, Kate's lie was detected and the record altered. But this is not the case. Catherine's birth certificate does not even have a marginal note. Unfortunately she did not know until quite late in her life that she was, as far as the official record existed, legitimate, and often went to great lengths to avoid having to produce her birth certificate.

Kate was ill after Catherine was born, suffering from painful, engorged breasts and what was known as 'milk fever'. John McMullen was credited with saving her life by sucking the excess milk from her breasts to give her relief. When she grew up, the thought of it filled Catherine with disgust, since she knew that, in his sleazy, lascivious way, he would have enjoyed doing it.

When Catherine was born, the McMullens were living in Leam Lane, just beyond the railway arches and the entrance to the Tyne Dock. Number 5 was next door to a notorious public house known as the Twenty-Seven. The buildings were demolished in the 1970s and a filling station erected on the site. The area had once been country, overtaken by nineteenth-century industrial development, but the lane still led upwards to the houses of the better-off and the open countryside of Simonside – 'a few fields with hedged lanes between. If you didn't turn round and look back you could imagine there were no docks, no pits, no drab grey streets; and if you could stretch your imagination you could visualise these fields with their straight rows of tender green going on for ever.'[2] On the other side of Leam Lane, the grey dome of the gasworks rose and fell, filling the air with the fumes of burning coke, and further along the river-bank was the tidal backwater – the 'slake' – where timber was left to season in the water. Here at low tide people scavenged across the mud for driftwood to fuel their fires. It was a dangerous place and the deep mud was heavily polluted by the chemical works which dwarfed the ruins of the Venerable Bede's monastery further along the bank. Children were allowed to roam around at will; Catherine remembered going down to the dock gates alone at the age of three.

Kate went back to work as soon as possible after Catherine's birth, leaving the baby to be cared for by her mother. This was no easy task. Rose was in her fifties, worn out by hard work and disappointment, suffering from 'women's complaints' and a heart condition. The energy required to look after a small and lively child drained her last reserves. Kate worked for a baker in Chester-le-Street – a small town in County Durham – and came home once a fortnight on her day off with a bag of groceries and her wages, which she 'tipped up' to Rose. Neither of her sisters contributed to the family economy, but then neither of them had 'a sin' at home that needed to be clothed and fed.

Catherine grew up believing Rose and John were her mother and father. She called them Ma and Da. Rose was a jealous 'Ma' to

Catherine. One of her earliest memories was of Kate coming home and picking her up to cuddle her, and of being snatched from Kate's arms by Rose. Kate's maternal instincts were withered at source by her own mother's ungiving personality, and her feelings towards her child were ambivalent from the beginning. The baby was a source of shame and disgrace, a constant, bitter reminder of all she had lost. Even as a small child Catherine sensed this, and believed all her life that Kate had rejected her.

When Catherine was five the McMullens, feeling the financial benefit of both old John and young Jack being in work, as well as Kate's fortnightly contributions, moved up the hill to William Black Street and a group of houses known as the New Buildings. They were divided into what we would now call maisonettes or apartments; locally they were called upstairs houses and downstairs houses, each with their own front door. The McMullens moved first into an upstairs house and then very quickly into a downstairs house in 10 William Black Street, where they had three rooms, their own back yard – where they could keep poultry in wooden cages, or 'crees' – and an outside privy. Although the yard was back to back with another street of houses, at the front there were fields accessible through the broken-down fence across the lane. From the end of the street Catherine could see right across the river and watch the ships come and go from the docks.

These streets were demolished in the 1970s as part of a slum-clearance programme, and the site became part of the Bede Industrial Estate – something the local council now bitterly regrets. But to please the increasing number of visitors from all over the world who came to Jarrow to see Catherine Cookson's house, the local authority built a replica of the street in South Shields Museum. With Catherine's cooperation, they tried to make it as accurate a representation as possible. The door opened into the front room – a kind of parlour for visitors, which had an alcove accommodating the double bedstead where John and Rose slept as well as a three-piece suite, a pedestal table, assorted chairs and a 'desk-bed'. This was a single fold-out bed that closed up into a desk during the day and was used by Catherine when she was small.

Just inside the back door was a small scullery, big enough for a backless chair with a tin basin on it – used for washing hands and faces – and a shelved cupboard that was used as a pantry. There was no water in the house; it all had to be carried from a tap in the yard which often froze in winter. There was no bath. People washed, both 'up and then down', in the scullery basin, and bathed infrequently in a tin bath in front of the fire. The scullery opened into the kitchen, which was the heart of the house where the family lived and all the work was done. It was there, in the kitchen at William Black Street, that Catherine claimed all her novels were born. She had only to close her eyes to be back there. Everything she heard and saw was burned into her memory, to be relived and retold in her fiction.

> The kitchen was bright and gleaming. From the open fireplace the coal glowed a deeper red in contrast with the shining blackleaded hob, with the oven to its right and the nook for pans to its left. It sent down its glow on to the steel-topped and brass-railed fender, where its reflections appeared like delicate rose clouds seen through a silver curtain. The fire glinted on the mahogany legs of the kitchen-table and on the cups spread on the white, patched cloth ... The hard, wood saddle, standing along the wall to the left of the fire-place, took on an innocent deception from the glow; its flock-stuffed cushions looked soft and inviting ... Even the sneck of the door that led to the front room had glints of white along its black handle.[3]

The huge, burnished steel range had to be kept alight winter and summer for cooking and hot water. In front of it there was a good kitchen table with a leather top – a relic of better times – which was used for family meals. To one side of it, almost the width of the kitchen, was a piece of furniture known as the saddle – sometimes called a settle – a hard wooden sofa upholstered with flock cushions. It served as seating during the day and as an alternative bed at night for Catherine's uncle Jack, who otherwise slept in the bedroom. On the other side of the fireplace was the wooden chair occupied by John McMullen, and the floor was covered by what was called a 'clippy mat' – a heavy rug made from cut rags pulled through hessian. Catherine and Kate spent many a winter's evening cutting up old clothes and 'progging' them into rugs on a wooden frame. Once the floor covering of the poor, these rag rugs are now, ironically, much sought after as collector's items.

Under the kitchen window was another table, made of plain wood, which was used for baking and food preparation. The kitchen was so crowded with furniture that it was possible to sit on the saddle only by climbing over the end of it or moving the table, and the bedroom could be reached only by edging your way along the wall behind the table and the saddle. The bedroom contained a washstand made from a wooden box with a curtain in front, the small three-quarter iron bedstead in which Catherine had been born, and an old treadle sewing machine. There was no wardrobe or cupboard. Clothes were hung on wooden pegs behind the door. Kate slept in the room when she came home, sharing the bed with Catherine, fighting the nightly attack of fleas which swarmed from the old feather mattress. Later the room was occupied by lodgers, who shared it with Catherine's uncle Jack.

For a young child the move was fun, since Catherine was allowed to ride on the coalman's flat cart with the furniture and there was all the excitement of the new house. But the McMullens had done a 'moonlight flit' from Leam Lane and neither Kate nor her sisters had been told of the move. Kate had a dreadful shock when she came home on her day off and found the house deserted. She panicked, fearing the worst – that they had all been taken to the workhouse. A neighbour put her right and told her where they'd gone, though she didn't know the exact address, and Kate set off up the hill in the dark to find them.

It was one of the significant moments of Catherine's childhood. She remembered being outside, playing the usual street game where children tied a skipping rope to the lamppost and spun themselves round and round it until they were dizzy, singing, 'When I went down to Strawberry Fair, singing, singing, buttercups and daisies.' She remembered vividly looking up and seeing Kate coming towards her down the street. 'I stopped dizzying and stared at her, while the rope went limp in my hand. To me she looked beautiful – tall, dressed in a grey costume, with beautiful hair on which was perched a big hat. She took hold of my arm and shook me from my daze, saying "Where are they?"' Catherine couldn't understand the violent emotions Kate displayed as she dragged her daughter into the house, tearing into Rose with words, tears running down her face. Rose was defensive. She told Kate she couldn't afford the paper or the stamp to send the letter and besides, she was too busy to write.

A family the McMullens called Romanus lived upstairs and they epitomised the strict codes that operated in the street. The man was a docker, his wife an unhappy 'woman of better class' who was slowly drinking herself to death. When Jim Romanus came home to find his wife drunk, he beat her senseless. Every word, every blow, could be heard in the rooms below, but nothing was ever said or done. These were things that were none of anyone's business. One day there was a tremendous thud on the floor while Jim Romanus was at work. His wife had suffered a stroke and died a few hours later.

There was an extraordinary mix of people living in the New Buildings – some on their way up, others on the way down. The former owners of the Barium Chemical Works lived in two large houses on Phillipson Street, almost next door to the Kanes, who were so destitute that their daughter Mary Ellen had to borrow Kate's boots to go into town. So much of their household was in pawn that they even had to borrow the McMullens' bread knife to cut their bread.

Among the fifty families in the New Buildings, private lives were public property, but it would have been very bad manners to acknowledge this. Turning a blind eye was the only privacy people had. When a neighbour crippled a child's thumb with a flat iron, or cut off her dog's tail in a temper, no one was willing to inform the cruelty inspector. It was better to ignore these things. 'Mind your own business and leave others to mind theirs' was the catch phrase. Everyone was in the same boat and the slightest rocking might spell disaster for them all. This didn't mean that there was never any gossip. Tales were whispered from one house to another until a few threads had been twisted into a rope and finally 'into a hawser'. But there was rarely any action. Occasionally a man would be beaten up for 'interfering' with someone else's wife or child. Rarely, a woman would be driven from the street by a group of other women, but this was often, as Catherine recalled cynically, to protect themselves rather than any moral standard – if eyes were turned one way, they wouldn't be looking another. Appearances were everything.

Kate's pleasant job at the bakery ended when her mother's health broke down completely and she had to come home to look after her parents, her half-brother Jack and her six-year-old daughter. It was the end of Kate's limited freedom and, for Catherine, the beginning of a long period of financial hardship and humiliation. Kate had now not only to earn enough money to support the household, she had to do all the work as well. Almost a hundred years ago it was a full-time job. There were no labour-saving devices and little in the way of ready prepared food. For those with money, bread, cakes and pies could be bought at the bakery; for the poor they had to be made. There was no electricity or central heating in the houses – all methods of lighting, cooking and keeping warm were dirty and labour-intensive. Candles left grease stains that were difficult to remove, oil lamps had to be cleaned and filled, and the flues of stoves and ovens regularly swept out. All the water had to be carried from the yard, and cleaning was done with steel wool, scrubbing brushes, a mop, bucket and carbolic, or a cheaper caustic lye soap made from animal fat and wood ash.

Before she went out in the morning Kate had to clean and light the fire in the big range, take out the ashes and bring in coal and wood. Then there were the slops to take out, beds to air, the kitchen to scrub and a midday meal to prepare and leave on the hob. The invalid Rose had to be washed and dressed for the day, and Catherine had to be got ready for school. In the evening when Kate got back she had the dishes to wash, rooms to clean, Rose to put to bed and then there was the baking of bread and cakes to be done for the next day. There was always a pile of ironing and mending waiting for a free moment.

Despite the fact that old John was now out of work with a bad leg and his son Jack was laid off or on half time, it would have been unthinkable for them to have done any domestic chores. As Catherine explained, 'a man's rightful standing in his home was a thing to be guarded, to be fought for. It lowered a man's prestige if he so much as lifted a cup. The lower down the working class scale you were, the more this rule applied.' The McMullen men would have 'let the clothes go rotten on their backs' before they would have stooped to the kitchen sink. They didn't even mend their own boots. So they sat by the fire in the evening after a day's idleness, drinking beer, while Kate, who had been up since dawn and had already done double a full day's work at home and elsewhere, baked and ironed and then mended shoes.

Kate took any work that came her way, decorating, repairing window frames, cleaning and washing. Laundry was a huge task in those days and any woman who could afford it paid someone else to do it for her. Not only were there vast numbers of heavy linen sheets, pillowcases and tablecloths, women and children wore long, full skirts with several petticoats made of cotton, flannelette and wool, as well as complicated cotton underwear. Then there were the men's shirts and their heavy moleskin work trousers. Catherine remembered standing on a chair to help Kate by prodding the clothes in the washtub with the poss-stick, while Kate turned the handle on the huge mangle in the yard. The wash-house floor ran with water; the walls ran with condensation; lines of washing stretched across the alley; and in the kitchen, clothes horses stood around the fireplace festooned with damp sheets waiting to be ironed. Kate's hands were raw and her arms ached so much she couldn't sleep and she would be forced to get up in the night to 'burn them into numbness with raw liniment'. Catherine suffered too. It was her job to take the washing back in the laundry basket, which was too wide for her to get a proper grip on the handles and so heavy that she would have to drop it every ten paces to have a rest.

The work and the hopelessness of it all affected Kate's spirits. There seemed no end to the cycle of work and debt, nothing to look forward to except more of the same, and little love, happiness or comfort. Her life, she told Catherine, was 'running out fast through a dark alleyway' like the dirty water from the washing tubs. But it was not all drudgery. Once, when Catherine was coming back from an outing with Kate along the banks of the river on a windy, moonlight night, watching the reflection of the moon on the water, 'she looked down at me and laughed, and clutching not so far back to the spirit of her childhood, she grabbed my hand, crying "Come on, let's race the moon".'

Until Kate's return, Catherine's life had followed a certain pattern within secure boundaries. She believed that she had a ma and a da, as well as three older sisters and a brother, and there was a larger extended family of great-aunts and cousins who all lived in the neighbourhood. Kate's sister Sarah, her husband Mick and their children lived a tram ride away in the mining village of Birtley. Catherine's great-aunt Lizzie, Rose's sister, lived nearby, as did John McMullen's niece and her husband George. Rose's other sister, Maggie, lived a few doors up in William Black Street. When Kate's younger sister Mary married, she moved into the same street.

This caused complications in the family, undercurrents Catherine was only dimly aware of. She knew that Mary and Kate were often on bad terms and didn't speak to each other for months on end, but she didn't know why until she was older, blaming it on Mary's hot temper and difficult disposition. She thought Mary was jealous of Kate because everyone liked her – Mary was less popular. But Mary's boyfriend Alec had been 'sweet' on Kate and there was some speculation that he might have asked her to marry him eventually. Having any kind of romantic involvement was difficult for Kate after she returned home. She wasn't allowed to look at a man, never mind 'walk out' with him – a tyrannous punishment for her one fall from grace, enforced by John McMullen's belt buckle. Alec came to the house with Mary and was attracted to Kate and she to him. Who knows what might have happened if Mary, after years of sneering and looking down her nose at her disgraced sister, had not become pregnant herself and obliged Alec to marry her. Catherine created a scene like this for her fictional character *Kate Hannigan*, when Patrick Delahunty, although engaged to Kate, is seduced by another girl in a moment of drunken weakness and has to marry her when she conceives a child.

Catherine's little cousin Alec, named for his father, was a great favourite with Kate, allowed to run free in the McMullens' kitchen. Catherine was an equally frequent visitor to Aunt Mary's. When Mary and Kate were on speaking terms, Catherine was often asked to baby-sit. Mary's house was very different from the McMullens'. Not only was her husband in regular work, but Mary had saved up her wages to buy decent furniture. She had a proper bedroom suite and a dressing table with triple mirrors. Catherine used to stand in front of them and admire herself whenever she went to baby-sit. There was good contemporary furniture in the parlour (no need for it to double as a bedroom in this house) and an antique dresser in the kitchen. Catherine went through all the drawers and cupboards out of curiosity, marvelling at the luxuries that Mary could afford. Mary was often generous to her niece. Once, for Christmas, she bought Catherine a beautiful china doll with real hair and a silk dress. It was one of Catherine's most treasured possessions – kept until she was nineteen. It became a major source of resentment between Catherine and her mother when Kate gave it away, without permission, to one of Catherine's young cousins, who ripped it to pieces.

At four and a half Catherine started school at Simonside, a Protestant school where she was extremely happy. But two years later, something happened to throw Catherine's education off course. Afterwards, she blamed John McMullen for insisting that she went to a Catholic school, but this may not have been entirely true. It was about this time that an incident occurred in the street. As Catherine played 'knocky-door-neighbour' around the New Buildings, an irate woman whose knocker had been banged once too often, came out and berated Catherine with a word she had never heard before. Foul-mouthed as John McMullen could be, it had certainly never been used at home. 'You're a bastard,' the woman said. 'Inside and out you're a bastard.' Catherine came home and asked Kate what the word meant. John McMullen was all for going round to the woman's house and having it out with her, but Kate managed to placate him. 'We want no rows. She'll hear more than that afore she's finished.' The meaning of the word was never explained.

Catherine became even more confused when she stood on the steps of the school listening to Kate explaining to the headmistress that as she was a Catholic, she would have to go to a Catholic school. Then she heard Kate telling the teacher something that seemed totally inexplicable. 'McMullen's not her name,' Kate said. 'It's Fawcett.'

3

Pray, Father, I've killed the cat.
Ah, my child, you'll suffer for that!
But, pray Father, 'twas a Protestant cat,
Oh! Then, my child, it doesn't matter about that.[1]

'How do you assess the agonies of childhood,' Catherine wrote. 'As a child you have as yet acquired no words to fit the pain.' In the twin towns of Shields, both North and South, feelings between the Catholic and Protestant members of the community ran high. Older residents still remember the taunting and physical bullying of Catholic children in the school playground and the gangs of children who fought each other in the streets.

Catholic, Catholic, ring the bell,
When you die you'll go to hell.

That was the Protestant gang call and the Catholic response was:

Protestant, Protestant, dirty lot,
Your backside's blue and your nose all snot!

The violence and cruelty, masquerading as religious zeal, unleashed on such occasions as St Patrick's Day are described by Catherine in many of her novels, but with particular vividness in *The Fifteen Streets*, where the relentless persecution of any kind of 'difference' almost ends in a death. The gangs gathered at street corners carrying 'innocent-looking paper balls' each with a hefty stone in the centre and chanting the hymn 'Oh glorious St Patrick look down in thy love'. 'The ending was the signal for the advance, both sides moving slowly towards each other. Then, with a rush, there was a swirling of balls, and there were screams, and cries of "Long live Ireland!" "Up the shamrock!" in which were mingled "England for ever!" and "God save the King!".' Sometimes individuals would be singled out, chased down the black, oozing horror of the Gut before being beaten senseless. 'Mick . . . yelled out to the crowd . . . "Give him a chance . . . Let him away! . . ." The boy was shivering in stark terror; he knew what this chance meant; it meant running, running, running until his whole body sobbed and his trousers became wet. And he knew that long after the fear would have passed the feeling of his wet trousers would remain. But it was either running or being stoned here.'[2]

Catherine had been brought up, like her mother and her grand-parents, as a 'wooden Catholic' – baptised into the church, but not practising. When she played in the streets she mixed with both Catholic and Protestant children and she went to a Protestant school. The need for her to be properly educated as a Catholic was the reason given to Catherine to explain why she had to be taken away from the primary school she loved and eventually sent to a Catholic school where she experienced 'mental and physical torture'. As well as being bullied by some of the teachers, she was also taunted and beaten by other Catholic children. One boy, she remembered, used to hold her against a lamppost and bang her head against the steel until she screamed.

At home Catherine's life was dominated by the strict, Irish Catholicism of her step-grandfather, free with his hands and always ready to enforce the priest's words, although he never used his leather belt on Catherine. This brand of primitive Catholicism would disturb the highly strung and imaginative child – intellectually, spiritually and emotionally – for the rest of her life, contributing to the severe breakdown she experienced in middle age. When she was sent to the Catholic school she was delivered into the hands of the church. 'God came into my life . . . And with God came priests, and the confessional, and nightmares, purgatory and repentance – and fear.' Paradoxically, Catherine's grandfather never went to church himself, boasting that he had only gone there twice in his life – to be christened and married. Catherine described herself as 'a sort of liaison officer running between him and God', imagining that she was going to church to save his soul. She was too young to see through his hypocrisy.

John McMullen, as head of the household, was always known as 'the Father' – the first syllable pronounced with the short, flat northern 'A'. He was illiterate, foul-mouthed, moody, and violent in drink. Catherine and Kate dreaded the times he came home 'mortallious' and began singing Irish songs. He would stand in the middle of the kitchen brandishing a three-foot steel poker, raising his voice with 'Sing us an Irish Comallya, Sing us an Irish tune', attacking the 'dirty Protestants' with the poker, smashing the pictures off the walls, the legs off the chairs. He attacked his son Jack, also given to coming home fighting drunk, and sometimes threatened his wife and stepdaughter.

He rarely threatened Catherine and, once he'd become quieter, her help would be enlisted. 'Many were the nights I have been woken out of a deep sleep by our Kate and me grandma standing over me and Kate whispering "Katie, come on, get up, do you hear? Get up and go and get him to bed." '[3] The sleepy child would drag herself out of the warm blankets and stagger into the kitchen to wheedle and plead with the old man she still believed to be her father, 'sprawled in his chair, alternately singing and swearing'. It also fell to Catherine to assist him into the front room, undress him to his long-johns – soiled and stinking – and then put him to bed. Only then was it safe for Rose to creep in reluctantly beside him. These early experiences provided rich material for Catherine's novels and certainly contributed to her sexual inhibitions as an adult.

In the days before proper sex education and contraception, sexual intercourse for many women was something to be feared and avoided. In *The Fifteen Streets* Mary Ellen, pregnant with her twelfth child at forty-five, observes the failing strength of her husband. 'Drink and hard work and wet clothes that were often frozen to his skin were at last taking their toll. He seemed to retain his strength for one thing alone . . . if only that would slacken with the rest . . . Then God, let it be soon.'[4] Catherine's novels are littered with women who refuse their husbands 'conjugal rights'. She had first-hand experience of the consequences of this as she lay in bed at night and heard Rose's voice in the front room saying repeatedly, 'Leave me alone, will you?' In her autobiographical first novel, *Kate Hannigan*, the young child wakes in the night to hear 'her granda's voice, low and terrible with menace . . . causing the little body to stiffen on the bed; then her grandma's voice, thick and full of something that struck greater terror into Annie's heart, had cried, "Don't! Oh, don't! I won't! I won't!".' Like the young Katie McMullen, the child in the novel sits up and shouts, 'Leave her be, granda! leave her be!' In the morning she observes her grandmother's bruised arms, but nothing is ever said. Rose McMullen suffered from poor health, which was her excuse for refusing physical contact. But given her barely disguised disgust for her husband, this may simply have been a convenient excuse. As she grew older, Catherine magnanimously recognised that it was her grandfather's sexual frustration that drove him to get drunk and indulge in licentious behaviour with other women in the street. In Catherine's novel, this frustration also leads the grandfather to masturbate in front of his grandchild, but there is no evidence that John McMullen was ever guilty of this. Catherine retained an enduring affection for him all her life.

Changing schools completely disrupted Catherine's childhood equilibrium. One reason for suspecting that it may not simply have been the desire for a Catholic education that precipitated Catherine's removal from Simonside Protestant school is the fact that she was sent first to another school, known locally as the Meases. Like Simonside, this had a mixed attendance of both Catholic and Protestant children – mainly the latter – but it was situated in a poor area called Bogey Hill and was regarded as run-down and 'slummy'. It made Catherine realise how much she had loved Simonside. She didn't stay at the Meases long. Soon afterwards Kate sent her to the Catholic school at Jarrow – a halfpenny tram ride away, and too far for Catherine to come home for her dinner in the middle of the day. She often walked the two miles to school and saved her halfpenny to tuck into a secret hoard of savings in the timbers of the lavatory roof. These halfpennies she used to buy comics, sometimes *Tiger Tim's Weekly* or *Comic Cuts*, but her favourite was the *Rainbow* with the Bruin Boys on the cover and inside 'the little girl who was really a fairy and worked magic'.[5]

Catherine hated Jarrow school. Within a short time she had begun to complain about feeling tired, then she started to pretend to be sick in the mornings, hoping that Kate would let her stay at home. Soon the sickness and the tiredness were genuine. Catherine witnessed a train crash on the way to school. The crowded early-morning Newcastle train had become derailed and Catherine came on the scene just as the dead and dying were being brought out of the carriages to be lined up along the side of the road for the ambulances. Catherine had never seen anyone dead before. At the time she was not distressed, merely fascinated, but the local priest comforted her, and insisted on giving her a rosary as a memento. Catherine was bewildered by the gift. Perhaps, she speculated, 'he intended that I should pray for the souls of the dead'. The experience came at a bad time, and somehow or other, from then on, the realities of death became confused in Catherine's highly developed imagination with religious fear and guilt.

At Jarrow school Catherine was being prepared for her first communion. The prospect of death and a descent into hell were made very real to the children by the priest Father Bradley, whose stern manner and hellfire Catholicism struck terror into their hearts and minds. Catherine later wrote about him as Father O'Malley in *Kate Hannigan*, and has the local doctor remark, 'I've had three cases of hysteria in children during the past month. And I've traced it all to the fear of Hell and Purgatory that damned priest has put into their little heads.'[6]Catherine, in her unpublished autobiography, asserted that Catholic children were brainwashed in the same way as young Russians in a collective.

Catherine's first confession was a terrifying experience. Confused and unsure what she had to do, she went into the wrong side of the confessional and found herself fumbling at the priest's knees. She was hauled out and thrust into the penitent's cubicle – a black box with a grille through which she could see a profile dimly illuminated which she felt bore more resemblance to the Devil than the priest. She had only the vaguest notion of what she was supposed to say, knowing only that she had to tell the priest how wicked she was.

Like her fictional character Kate Hannigan, Catherine began to have nightmares. 'After my first confession at the age of seven, I had the idea that hosts of people in Heaven were watching my every move and would report to God on all my misdeeds, and so I would be sent to Hell. I used to placate them, one after the other – the Virgin Mary, Joseph, St Anthony, St Catherine, St Agnes – and instead of getting relief by going to confession Father O'Malley made it worse, a thousand times worse.'[7] Catherine repeatedly dreamed that she had died and was falling 'struggling and groping' into a bottomless pit of darkness – an absence of light so tangible, so thick that her hands could feel it. 'I knew I was going straight into Hell.' She woke up screaming, tangled in the blankets, with Kate bending over her saying, 'Wake up and stop that noise. No more late suppers for you.'

On one occasion she found that she had got out of bed during the dream and was standing by the front door.

Catherine became increasingly disturbed. When she looked in the dressing-table mirror at Aunt Mary's house, the face of the child who looked back at her wore, as she later remembered, 'a quiet look – a rather lost look'. In the end Catherine's unhappiness at Jarrow school was acknowledged and Kate sent her daughter to St Peter and Paul's school in Tyne Dock, a short walk away. If the aim of moving schools had simply been to give Catherine a Catholic education, why hadn't Kate sent her there straight from Simonside? Why send her daughter on an expensive journey every day to a different area? With money so tight, the halfpenny a day was very precious. The answer soon became apparent. At Tyne Dock school everyone knew who Catherine was. Kate's struggle to conceal her daughter's illegitimacy would soon all be for nothing.

Catherine remembered Tyne Dock school as an ordeal. 'I learned very little and my days were filled with fear.' The headmistress, Miss Caufield, terrified her pupils into submission with sadistic zeal by the use of the cane and the lash of her sarcastic tongue. From the beginning, she singled Catherine out for the largest share of correction, perhaps because she knew of her illegitimacy and was 'beating the sin' out of her, as Miss Flynn did to Rose Angela in *Colour Blind*.

All the children in the class knew that Miss Flynn didn't like Rose Angela Patterson . . . Even the motion of Rose Angela's walk was enough to arouse a deep feeling of resentment in Miss Flynn. As she watched the child thread her way among the desks towards her she wanted to dash at her and shake that quiet, maddening poise out of her. She did not question herself as to her reason for hating this child; consciously she told herself that the child was the outcome of a sinful union . . . She stared down on Rosie and wet her lips, one over the other, as she arched the cane back and forward between her two hands – she'd knock some of the sin out of her![8]

Miss Caufield focused first on Catherine's hair – her most beautiful feature. It was a soft, wavy auburn which Kate twisted up with rags every night and carefully brushed out into ringlets in the morning before Catherine went to school. As soon as she got there, Miss

Caufield would call Catherine out in front of the class and insist that she put her hair in plaits. Every day Kate would send her to school with long curls and every evening Miss Caufield would send her home again with her hair braided. Kate's small rebellion marked Catherine as a target.

Miss Caufield nicknamed her 'Grandma' and the whole class laughed every time she used the word. Thereafter she never missed an opportunity to humiliate Catherine. Monday mornings were the worst. Catherine would be asked to stand on her chair so that everyone could see her and then she was subjected to an inquisition. 'Well, Grandma, and were you at Mass, yesterday?' Catherine had rarely been to Mass. Kate's pride wouldn't allow her to go in her weekday clothes, so if Catherine's Sunday coat or her only pair of decent shoes were in pawn (and they usually were), she couldn't go to Mass. Catherine was so afraid of Miss Caufield that she would ask the other children what the priest had talked about so that she could try to pretend that she had been. She rarely succeeded.

'You have made another mistake, Grandma. Father Bradley did not speak of Lazarus. You weren't at Mass, were you?'
'N . . . No, Miss Caufield.'
'Why do you lie? Were you at Confession on Thursday?'

The questions went relentlessly on and on, but they always ended with Catherine being caned. 'Even the first switch of the cane splaying its agony across my hand was enough to knock me backward. Usually I got three, sometimes more.'

Being late for school was also a grave sin meriting extreme punishment. Catherine became so afraid that she would walk to school, using the tram fare to buy flowers in the hope of bribing the headmistress. But she never succeeded. It was against this background of terror that Catherine heard Miss Caufield instruct the class that in a few weeks they must all bring in three yards of flannelette material in order to learn to sew a nightdress. When Catherine relayed the request to Kate, it was met with stony silence. No one in the house had any work at the time – Kate didn't even have the money for the rent.

The weekend before the sewing lessons were supposed to begin, Catherine was beside herself with fear at the thought that on Monday morning, she would be the only girl in the class to have no material.

All through Friday night and Saturday she wept and nagged until, on Saturday evening, Kate suddenly cracked. She dragged Catherine out of the house by the hand and they walked the two miles to Jarrow in the dark. 'I don't remember to which shop we went, but I do remember that my eyes nearly sprang from their sockets when I saw her pick up part of a bale of flannelette that was standing on display in the shop doorway and walk away with it. I scrambled after her into the back lane where she pushed it under her coat, and then we both ran.' Catherine was physically sick on the way home.

The family economy was at its lowest point. They had so little money Catherine had to go out scavenging on the local rubbish tip. She took a sack with her to collect cinders and any other combustible material she could find. At that time the largest part of the household rubbish collected was ash from fire grates – the refuse carts were referred to as ash-carts. In the poorer houses the grates were raked out in the mornings and only the powdered ash put into a bucket. This would be put either down the privy outside or into the bin. The cinders were separated out to make a 'bottom' for the new fire. They would be used and reused until they became dust. In better-off households the cinders were raked out with the ash and ended up on the tip, where the poor dug them up and carried them home to supplement their own fires. The adults in the McMullen household had too much pride to be seen scavenging, so Catherine was sent instead.

Like many other children, she took to following the coke carts that fuelled the gasworks. She carried a sack and picked up the pieces of coke that fell from the carts as they bumped over the tram lines. She was also sent to the slakes to look for driftwood and lumps of coal carried by the river's tidal current from the staithes where the boats were loaded. Catherine was proud of her success at finding things. It was her contribution to the family economy. 'There was the joy at night of watching it, piled high in the grate, making blue and orange flames.' Part of the joy was in the knowledge that she was pleasing Kate, and if she pleased her enough, Kate might love her more.

Sometimes Catherine's enthusiasm tempted her to stray out of the slake towards the Gut – a deeper channel where the river Don ran across the slake to join the Tyne. Here there were treacherous crosscurrents and deep, black, sucking mud. Catherine went out to it using the network of posts and rotten planks, lashed to each other and then to the posts, that crossed the slake to provide access to the rafts of timber that were there for seasoning. 'Sometimes I would find myself clinging on to a post terrified to return the way I had come.' On one occasion she saw a really good piece of sound timber that had once been used to tether the floating wood, but had come adrift. After a long struggle, she pulled it out of the water and left it on the bank to collect after she had taken her sack of sticks home. When Catherine returned, her great-aunt Maggie was carrying the wood up the road. There was an argument when Catherine laid claim to it, but in the end, no doubt knowing the family need, Maggie surrendered the plank and Catherine dragged it home. John McMullen declared that it was too good to burn and used it to repair the hen house in the back yard, where it was seen by the local policeman. As a result John McMullen had to appear in court accused to stealing timber from the slake. The magistrate refused to believe that a small child could have carried the wood home and imposed a fine, which Kate had to pay.

The rent – four shillings and sixpence – had not been paid for many weeks and there was a debt of almost five pounds. Money was so tight that there was nothing to pay into the usual Christmas clubs. So on Christmas Day, when Catherine eagerly began to unwrap the parcels in her bulging stocking, she found, instead of the usual *Chatterbox Annual*, sweets and stocking fillers, only a single small present at the top. The rest of the stocking was filled with the pot vegetables she had bought in the market for Kate the day before, wrapped up in paper. 'When I reached the bottom of the bag I was overcome by a colossal sense of disappointment and disgust ... Disgust that our Kate could have been so silly as to wrap up all these vegetables ... which would be used for the dinner.'

With no one in work, Catherine was often denied the penny pocket money she got from Jack or Kate on a Saturday. It paid for her matinee at the cinema and bought her favourite comic. She found it very hard to go without. One day, sent to the corner shop for a newspaper, she was tempted into theft. Although she referred to it in later interviews and unpublished manuscripts, she didn't write about the incident in her published autobiography. A full account of it is given to Katie in *The Fifteen Streets*.

His search took him into the back shop, and Katie was left alone standing before an assortment of comics. They were arrayed on a sloping counter: *Rainbow, Tiger Tim's Weekly, Comic Cuts*, and others. Her eyes dwelt on them longingly. It was weeks since she was able to buy a comic . . . there stretched before her the rest of the afternoon and the long, long evening . . . Her eyes darted to the back shop. All she could see was Mr Powell's feet on the top of a pair of steps. Her hand went up and touched the *Rainbow*. It hesitated for a second, then with one swift movement, the *Rainbow* was inside her coat and for the first time in her life she found herself wetting her knickers. The combined horror was too much for her. She ran out of the shop . . . She did not stop to look inside her coat; her sin had already obliterated the joy of the comic. She was a thief! She had stolen! . . . Standing over the gutter, under the high, bleak arches, she vomited, and the comic slipped down from beneath her coat and became fouled with the sick.[9]

In her unpublished manuscripts Catherine describes how she became an accomplished thief and would hide other comics under the one she was paying for in order to get two or three for the price of one. She only desisted when a visiting missionary priest made her realise that she was in danger of losing her soul.[10] When Catherine confessed her sins to the priest, she left the confessional staggering under the weight of his wrath. She was almost irredeemably bad: 'It's a wonder you're not in hell's flames burning, child.'[11] The priest's assessment added to Catherine's sense of worthlessness.

Every week something else went to be pawned. All the good things had already gone and now it was 'bits of underwear still damp from the wash' or Kate's only good blouse. Sometimes Catherine was sent to borrow a suit from a neighbour to put in pledge. Kate's pride would not allow her to be seen going to the pawnshop herself, so Catherine had to go instead and she would often be kept away from school to make the journey – once or twice a week. Young as she was, Catherine was aware of the humiliation. Occasionally she would refuse to go; 'I hate going. It's awful. Everybody looks at me.' But when Kate began to cry or – worse – collapsed silently at the table with her head buried in her hands, Catherine always relented. Kate was skilled in emotional blackmail.

Outside, the neighbours knew all too well where she was going, and she felt 'real agony' when she had to pass the rows of men lined up outside the Tyne Dock hoping for work. These men all knew who she was. Sometimes, if she had a halfpenny, she would jump on the Shields tram to conceal her destination, travel two stops and then walk back through the alleys to the pawnshop. Once there, she would stand outside looking in the shop windows, pretending that she'd been sent to buy something. When there was no one to see her, she slipped into the pawnshop. The proprietor, Bob Gompertz, was a kind man, but Catherine still had to go through the humiliation of having the parcel unwrapped in front of her and Kate's poor items of clothing held up for everyone to see while Bob said 'Well, this has seen its last days, hinny,' and offered less than half what Catherine had been told to ask for. Being under fourteen, Catherine couldn't sign the pawn pledge herself, so she would have to wait until Bob was able to ask an adult to sign it for her, and another penny or two would have to be paid to the person who signed.

Catherine developed a horror of being looked at. In the street when she saw someone she knew, she would walk sideways and turn her face to the wall. 'I knew that if I couldn't see them, they couldn't see me.' Gradually she began to create a world of her own to escape into. Her refuge was the outside privy, locally referred to as 'the netty'. It was the only place in those crowded houses where an individual could lock themselves in and be sure of privacy. Annie, the child in *Kate Hannigan*, explains the feeling of security it gave Catherine. Once she was inside, with the door bolted, 'the safe feeling crept over her, the feeling she always had when she was in here. No one could get at you here, it was quiet, like a little square house, all red and white, and you were tight locked in.'[12]

Like the others in the street, it was an earth closet – a broad wooden plank with a circular hole in it over a brick pit. When it was not in use, another piece of wood was put over the hole as a lid. At the back of the pit there was a hatch which opened into the back alley where the night-soil collectors came along with their carts to shovel out the contents. It was very embarrassing to be caught on the privy when they came. Catherine remembered leaping from the seat to hide her face against the back of the door, her knickers around her ankles, hot with shame. When the carts didn't come often enough, the contents oozed out into the back alley through the ill-fitting hatches, creating an insanitary slick along the cobbles. Families who were 'particular', like the McMullens, kept their toilets clean and sweet-smelling by daily scrubbing with carbolic soap and by putting ash down the hole to deodorise the contents.

Whenever she was upset or needed privacy, Catherine would head for the privy at the bottom of the yard, bolt the door and sit on the wooden lid. 'It was a wonderful place for musing and meditation. Here you were shut in and became lost in a world apart, a secret world.' Catherine would put her fingers over her eyes to diffuse the light, peer through the cracks and fantasise about a different way of life where there were no debt collectors or pawnshops, where everyone had beautiful clothes and enough to eat. She did this throughout her childhood, whenever she wanted to avoid a particularly difficult reality; 'I would turn my face to the wall and I would see a picture, which became the focal point of my striving, because it presented to me a different way of life. It showed me a big house peopled by ladies and gentlemen, and surrounded by cars, horses and servants.' And, of course, Catherine was always in the picture, 'dead centre'.

Her fantasies were fed by the early cinema. If she was given a penny she would go to the matinee at the Crown in Tyne Dock on a Saturday afternoon. If there was no money, it was sometimes possible to pay in kind, by collecting glass bottles or jars. At the cinema, Catherine stared 'wide-eyed and open-mouthed into the wonders of another world', a world filled with gracious houses and beautiful people 'exactly like the pictures I conjured up on the wall'. Her favourites were *The Perils of Pauline* and romantic films like *The Sheikh*, starring Rudolph Valentino. She disliked the Keystone Cops and 'daft people like Charlie Chaplin'. Chaplin's pathetic creations were far too near reality. 'The poor, desolate creatures he portrayed were too near to something inside myself.'

Emerging from the Crown one Saturday afternoon, dazzled by the sunlight and still rapt in her imaginary world, Catherine was aware of Kate coming towards her down the street. Except that it didn't seem like Kate. Her eyes were clouded, she was walking with an exaggerated lurch, laughing and talking 'thick and fuddled'. It came to Catherine suddenly 'in a sickening revelation' that Kate was drunk. The morality of the time was merciless to women who drank. Men like John McMullen and his son could drink as much as they liked – were expected to. But if women did so, they were branded as sluts. Catherine comforted herself all the way home 'with the thought that . . . well she's only our Kate, she's not me Ma, for I knew that the greatest disgrace in life was to have a Ma who drank.' But although she did not consciously know then that Kate was her mother, from that day onwards, a shadow fell over her relationship with Kate and Catherine began to get a 'sick feeling' inside her, a sensation that didn't leave her until long after Kate died.

4

Why was life like this? No little joy or happiness
lasted; only the fears and hurts lasted, and the feeling
of inferiority.[1]

There were no books in the McMullen household. The first stories
Catherine heard were read aloud from penny papers or borrowed
volumes. Mostly she listened to the 'crack' around the fireplace – the
northeast, particularly the Irish community, had a strong tradition of
oral storytelling. It was a gift she inherited and as a small child she
would often tell stories, not always able to distinguish facts from the
realities of her imagination. Like her child character Mary Ann in
A Grand Man, she told children and teachers at school that her
family were rich and had a car, describing in detail the wonderful
furniture they had at home.

> 'And besides the great big house,' she said, her eyes moving from
> one to the other, like revolving saucers, 'we've got three servants
> and two cars and two horses ... galloping ones.' She curved her
> arms into what she considered was the shape of the horses' legs,
> and she jerked them at a great speed to indicate the velocity of
> the steeds. 'And,' she finished in a voice weighed with awe, 'some
> day I'll show you them; and our house, and the car besides, some
> day when I have a party.'

Mary Ann, she explained later, was herself as a child.

For Catherine it wasn't telling lies, 'it was more in the nature of
a story'. There was a big difference between 'making on' and the sin
of untruth. Telling stories was allowable, so long as the audience
entered the fictional conspiracy too. 'To partake in the make-believe

world of childhood is not to lie unless the word lie is actually uttered, but once it is then make-believe is wrong; it immediately becomes a sin – another weight to be carried on the head until the priest removes it in confession.' Sometimes Catherine's fantasies got her into trouble. She always remembered John McMullen telling her, 'You know what you are, Katie McMullen, don't ya? You're a stinking liar. But go on, go on, don't stop, for begod! it will get you some place . . . Either into clink or into the money.'

Catherine's first experience of poetry came through the colloquial rhymes chanted by children in the street. Litanies, witching spells, work shanties, skipping songs and proverbial lore.

> Now you're married I wish you joy,
> First a girl and then a boy.
> Seven years over,
> Seven years after,
> Now's the time to kiss and give over.

The first real poem she encountered was Longfellow's 'The Children's Hour', which was presumably read to her at school and deemed suitable for young minds. But its dark and haunting imagery frightened Catherine and its meaning eluded her: 'I did not connect it with love.' When she was an adult it became an intimate evocation of her confused feelings towards her family, particularly Kate, and was used as the powerful central motif in her novel *The Round Tower*.

> I have you fast in my fortress
> And will not let you depart,
> But put you down into the dungeon
> In the round-tower of my heart.
>
> And there will I keep you for ever,
> Yes, for ever and a day,
> Till the walls shall crumble to ruin,
> And moulder in dust away!

Then there was the Scottish lodger who had books of poetry on the cupboard in the bedroom – Shakespeare, Chaucer, Donne and Milton. Catherine had tried to read *Venus and Adonis*. To her child's mind it was all about 'kissing without ever getting anywhere'. She was told off because it was 'mucky poetry' and was forbidden to read any more.

But it was a teacher at Tyne Dock school who was really responsible for stimulating her delight in literature. Although two hours of every day were given over to religious tuition, there was still time for the three R's. The English classes were Catherine's favourites. 'I learned the beauty of words, words I couldn't spell, or even understand. But there was the sound of them, the lilt of them, the pictures they conjured up in my mind.'[2] Miss Barrington, a large, motherly woman who taught with a great deal of kindness, would write a poem on the blackboard and give a penny to the first child who could learn it by heart. It was usually Catherine who came home with the penny.

In her novel *The Fifteen Streets*, the child Katie entertains her family in the evening by standing in front of the fire and reciting the verses she had learned at school. Catherine too, as a child, entertained the McMullens on long winter evenings. The mat would be rolled up in front of the fire and she would dance for them, sing the songs she was rehearsing for the Christmas concert, recite the verses she could still remember word for word forty years later. It was her first experience of public approval. When Catherine's teacher awarded her a china ornament filled with chocolates for the best performance in the concert, Catherine was amazed. It was the only school prize she ever received.

Catherine's first instincts were towards poetry and from the age of eleven onwards she began to scribble verses as well as stories and plays. Poets feature in many of Catherine Cookson's novels, from the posturing poetess of *Kate Hannigan*, whose poetry is totally dishonest, to the struggling Jack in *Pure as the Lily*, whose gift is stillborn amid poverty and family conflict. Catherine herself wrote a lot of poetry, using this medium as an emotional safety valve. Although it is of great interest as an insight into Catherine's personality, it is not of a very high literary standard and very little of it has been published.

The first book to come into Catherine's possession was a source of guilt and shame. The *Chatterbox Annual* had been borrowed from the caretaker's daughter at Simonside school and Catherine became so attached to it that she couldn't bear to give it back. When she left Simonside she kept the book, but – as with the stolen comics –

guilt for the dishonest act gradually spoiled her enjoyment. Later, Kate tried to make sure that Catherine was given the *Chatterbox* for Christmas, but there were years when the money wasn't enough and the longed-for annual would not be there. Catherine's first proper book of her own was bought by a generous neighbour. Mr Romanus upstairs had married again, this time a young woman who wore gaudy clothes and make-up. Her attempts at housework attracted the scorn of the neighbourhood, but she was good-natured and full of fun. Mrs Romanus took Catherine into a shop in South Shields and allowed her to choose the book herself. Catherine chose Grimms' fairy tales and was ecstatic. 'I loved her for buying me that book.' The stories were read over and over again until she knew them by heart and the pages were in tatters. She was always being scolded for being a bookworm and sometimes Kate blamed books for Catherine's nightmares and tried to stop her reading so much.

If Catherine escaped reality between the pages of a book, Kate was drowning her unhappiness at the bottom of a whisky bottle. Most of the time she drank at home where it could be concealed, but sometimes, if she had money, she went out, down to the Alkali, named for the chemical works, or to the pub known as the Twenty-Seven where the men drank when they finished unloading the twenty-six staithes of Tyne Dock. Women who went to public houses on their own and drank with the men were considered 'no better than tarts'. Sometimes Catherine was taken with her and made to stand outside in an agony of apprehension, dreading the moment when she would come out, drunk, and they would have to walk home together. Like the child Rose Angela in *Colour Blind*, fear of Kate's whisky drinking began to dominate Catherine's life. 'For a long time now it had seemed to [her] that she had been gathering to herself different kinds of fear. There was the fear of going home and finding her ma crying, sometimes with her head on her arms on the kitchen table, sometimes lying across the bed upstairs. At these times the fear would paralyse her limbs and she would want to be sick.' For Catherine, as for her child character in *Colour Blind*, this fear could be dispelled 'if, as sometimes happened, her mother put her arms blindly about her and there was no smell of whisky from her'.[3]

Catherine focused all her resentment towards her mother's drinking on a heavy stoneware jar of a type known locally as a 'grey hen', which could be taken to local pubs and beer shops to be filled. When the McMullens drank at home, one of Catherine's most hated tasks was being sent out to queue for the beer. Again it was family pride that delegated this job to a child, and it was noticed and commented on by the neighbours, loudly enough for Catherine to overhear. 'A bloody shame, sendin' that bairn for the beer with that great jar.' Almost every evening Catherine would walk all the way down to Tyne Dock, sometimes as far as the Stanhope Road, carrying the jar which held about a gallon of liquid, have it filled with beer until it was almost too heavy to lift, and then bring it back on the tram. She had to carry it wedged on her hip and walk with a curious, crablike action. This heavy task – too heavy for a small, fine-boned child – repeated night after night for years on end, may well have contributed to the spinal problems she had later in life.

The shame and disgrace that Catherine felt at having to go for drink was compounded by the fact that there was hardly any money for anything else. Young as she was, she knew that if John McMullen and Kate had stayed sober the rent would have been paid and many of the trips to the pawnshop could have been avoided. Yet the times of real poverty were preferable to times when everyone was in work and Kate had money for 'the hard stuff'. Then she drank whisky and Catherine dreaded the consequences. She had a terrible, apparently irrational fear of her mother drinking whisky. Just two or three glasses were enough to work a change in Kate. 'It is impossible for me to describe the sick terror that filled me when Kate took whisky . . . she became another being, the colour of her eyes seemed to change, her mouth did actually take on a different shape . . . she also wanted company and gaiety.' Catherine couldn't conceal her disgust and Kate would turn on her and say, 'Don't look at me like that, I'm telling you. Haven't I enough to put up with?' Sometimes her mood would become quarrelsome. But at other times she would become maudlin and affectionate, trying to hug Catherine's stiff, resisting body as she turned her face away from the hated smell of whisky, which nauseated her as it did the child Constance in *Fenwick Houses*. When Christine bends over her daughter and says 'somewhat thickly, "Hallo there, dear, kiss Mummy good night"', the child pushes her mother's face away saying 'I don't like you, I hate you, you smell nasty', just as Catherine said she did to Kate.[4] Catherine never forgot the expression on Kate's face when she pushed her away – the utter desolation she saw in her eyes.

Catherine's dread at seeing her mother drunk on whisky was the cause of Kate losing her job. She had begun to work at a pub near Palmer's shipyard. It wasn't particularly well paid, but it was regular work. It also provided an easy source of spirits. Most of the time Kate would bring a small bottle back home with her, but at other times she would send Catherine. Catherine would pray all the way on the tram, 'Oh Holy Mother, let them be run out. Dear Sacred Heart of Jesus . . . will you not let there be any stuff for her.' On this particular occasion, Catherine handed over the usual note from Kate, and watched the requested half bottle of whisky being wrapped up. But as she watched, 'I felt all the blood draining from my body, I wanted to be sick . . . I remember hearing myself imploring them not to give it to me, to say they were sold out. And I remember the man and woman sitting side by side in front of me, looking at me with the most strange expression on their faces.' Catherine's distraught appearance must have taken them both by surprise – Kate was a good worker and they had had no reason to think badly of her character. Horrified and filled with pity, the publican's wife comforted Catherine, stroking her hair and exclaiming, 'Dear God, dear God!' Her husband took Catherine by the hand and assured her that Kate would never get another drop of whisky from them. Filled with relief but also afraid of the consequences of what she had done, Catherine went home. Kate lost her precious job at the end of the week.

Catherine was seven when what little security she had was brutally torn apart. Until then, hard though her lot was, she saw herself as no different from any of the other children in the street, who shared her games or went down to the timber slake to jump across the rafts of wood. Her best friend was a girl called Belle who lived at the corner of Phillipson Street. One day, when Catherine and Belle were playing shops with some of the girls at the end of the street, using broken pieces of china and glass to represent the merchandise, someone cheated and slipped a particularly pretty piece of coloured glass out of Catherine's pile when she wasn't looking. Catherine turned to the girl she suspected of stealing the glass and said, 'I'll go and tell me ma about you, so I will!' Belle took no notice and with a great air of self-importance made a series of shattering statements: 'She's not your ma. If you want to know, she's your grandma . . . your Kate's your ma and she drinks and –' shouting in Catherine's face – 'YOU haven't GOT NO DA, me ma says so.' The other children took up the shout. 'You haven't got no da! You haven't got no da!'

That moment was burned into Catherine's consciousness for ever. Sixty years later she wrote that 'no-one [who] has had the security of parents wrenched from him, can have any idea as to the force of this impact. How it shatters for always the whole world of childhood and reverberates through the rest of life.' A television programme broadcast in July 1998 interviewed a number of children – some still in their teens – who had been brought up, as Catherine had, to believe that other family members were their parents. Some had even been formally adopted. For some of them, the trauma of discovering that someone they believed to be a sister or an aunt was actually their real parent, was overwhelming. First was the bitterness of betrayal. 'I'll never forgive them for lying to me,' one of them said. Then the loss of any solid foundation for their lives: 'I became totally insecure. How could I believe anything they told me ever again?' Most of them had needed counselling or therapy in order to come to terms with feelings of rejection. They all looked back to their childhood, searching for memories of loving behaviour from the natural parent, which had rarely been forthcoming. As happened between Rose and Kate, new relationships were jealously defended, and the lack of any close emotional bond between child and birth mother was interpreted by the child as rejection. 'She never gave me any special attention,' one girl said. 'So she can't have wanted me very much.' For Catherine, these feelings may well have been magnified by the actual physical suffering inflicted on her by Kate. Every trip to the pawnshop or the pub left an emotional wound as deep and tangible as if she had been caned.

Catherine's first reaction to the news was to run back to her own back yard and lock herself in the privy, where she sat picking the loose whitewash off the wall and tried to make sense of what she had been told. How could our Kate be her ma, when she wasn't even married? She came out of the privy, intending to go into the house and ask Kate the truth. She could see Kate through the kitchen window laying the tea and Catherine stood for a long time watching her going to and fro. In that moment, some kind of emotional truth pierced her confusion; 'as I looked at her, I knew our Kate was me ma'.

It was the pivotal moment that changed the course of Catherine's life. In her unpublished autobiography, Catherine told how, from this day on,

> I first became acquainted with the lost feeling, the feeling of alone-ness. Over the years this feeling has grown, this feeling that is cold and impersonal and unconquerable. It has grown into a vacuum which at times sucks me into itself. I have reasoned with it, I have talked to it, as one separate being to another, but it still remains aloof. It will not cooperate, it will not be comforted; . . . for it has a life of its own, an all-knowing, desolate, universal life.[5]

Over the next few days Catherine wrestled with another problem. Everybody had to have a father. Even Jesus had a father. Somewhere, somehow she must have a da. This was the moment when her child-hood fantasy of living in a big house with servants and cars became something more serious. If John McMullen was not her father, she was free to create one for herself. At first she scanned all the men she knew, but none of them seemed a likely candidate until she thought of Dr McHaffie. He was young and attractive and he had a car – he had once given her a lift to school in it, to the envy of her friends. 'Then the solution came; like a streak of dazzling light it flashed into her mind, bringing with it the remedy.'[6] Dr McHaffie would be her father.

The seven-year-old child sensed an underlying sympathy between Dr McHaffie and Kate; on Kate's side liking and deep respect, on the doctor's 'he must have had compassion for her from the moment he brought me into the world, and he must have pitied her as he watched what could have been, or was still then, a beautiful woman both in looks and nature disintegrating under the pressure of hard continuous work, poverty and inner shame and loneliness'. Catherine did not for a moment think what the consequences of her innocent make-believe might be – what damage she might have done to Kate or to the doctor's reputation if it had been believed.

As time went on, the fantasy of the doctor was replaced by another. Catherine came to believe that her unknown father had been a gentle-man. That would explain why she had this sense of difference, of not belonging, these fantasies of big houses, servants and cars. She was really a gentleman's daughter, and one day he would come to reclaim her and she would be dressed in beautiful clothes, sent to a proper school and surrounded by luxury. The theme of the young, innocent girl from a poor background, seduced by the rich gentleman and then abandoned, runs through many of Catherine's novels. Sensitive children, carrying the genes of nobility, are brought up in squalor and poverty until they fight their way out of it. This was how Catherine saw herself.

In Catherine's first novel, *Kate Hannigan*, the street game, the children's quarrel, the revelation and the scene in the lavatory are written just as Catherine remembered the real-life incident. But the make-believe is taken a stage further. The young doctor is secretly in love with Kate and at the end of the novel they marry, providing the child, Annie, with the father she had chosen. For seven-year-old Catherine the knowledge of her illegitimacy was like a bereavement. She had suddenly lost her parents and been presented with Kate, 'someone of whom I was deeply ashamed, who in my early years I came to fear, then hate; then wish dead, yet all the time loved, loved because she was the only thing that was mine; even while I disowned her in my mind I loved her'.

When Kate was drunk Catherine hated and feared her. But then there were the times when they raced the moon together along the bank of the river, and there were other times when they sat beside the fire on a winter afternoon with the mat frame stretched between them across the table and Kate would sing songs. On one afternoon, Catherine remembered, Kate had begun to sing her favourite song, a popular sentimental ballad called 'Thora' which Catherine disliked because it was Kate's party-piece when she was drunk. The last two lines were:

> Child of my dreams, love of my life.
> Hope of my world to be.

Something of Kate's real emotion must have infused her voice as she sang these lines; their eyes met over the hessian frame and Catherine began to cry. Kate comforted her awkwardly and then there was a single moment of real understanding and mutual feeling. 'On that day in the kitchen ... we became close, we became one. At rare moments in our lives we touched like this.'

Most of the time their relationship was a turbulent roller coaster of anger, love, fear and a chasm filled with unspoken questions. They clashed regularly, but they never talked. Catherine never asked about her father and Kate never spoke of him. Only once, when Catherine stood staring at her accusingly, did Kate say, in drink, 'Don't stand there looking at me with his eyes!' And Catherine knew she had inherited at least something from her unknown father.

A lot of small incidents now made sense to her when she looked back. She now knew the meaning of the word 'bastard' and what its consequences were likely to be. One event in particular brought it home to her. A girl called Cecilia Waller, daughter of one of the better-off families in Phillipson Street, was having a birthday party and everyone had been invited. They were promised games and cakes and sweets. Although Catherine had not been specifically asked, it didn't occur to her that she wasn't supposed to go – all her friends were going. On that Saturday afternoon she made Kate dress her hair, tie on a new ribbon and a clean pinafore, and then she went out into the yard. She could see the girls running to and fro behind the curtains and she jumped up and down to attract attention, but no one came to the door to let her in.

Kate was standing at the kitchen door, her face twisted by an expression Catherine didn't understand. 'It's no use, you know, hinny. It's no use,' she said. Catherine went out into the back lane – empty because everyone had gone to the party – and she felt the sudden misery of exclusion. 'There descended on me a feeling of desolation, of aloneness' that was too great to be borne. She still could not believe that she was deliberately being left out. They must have forgotten her. She ran across the lane, through the yard and knocked at the door, only to be told that she wasn't allowed to come in. 'Me ma says you can't . . . me ma says you haven't got no da.'

When Catherine dragged herself back, Kate was standing in the kitchen, her face set. For seven years she had tried to protect her child from the consequences of her own fall from grace. Now Catherine would have to fight her own battles. 'Never you mind, lass,' she told Catherine. 'You'll see your day with them. By God, you will.' Catherine never forgave Cecilia. More than fifty years later, when she came to a book-signing and asked Catherine if she remembered her, Catherine denied ever knowing her. When a bewildered Cecilia insisted that they had been best friends and played together as children, Catherine turned her back. She also ignored Belle in similar circumstances and would later admit that she had 'a sort of talent for hatred'. She tried very hard as a good Catholic to forgive people for what they did to her, but there were some things she could not either forgive or forget completely.

From this time on, Catherine's nightmares came more frequently. The descent-into-hell dream had a new sequel. After she'd stopped falling into darkness she would find herself at the bottom of a long staircase. As she walked up she could see Kate standing at the top with a strange man. He was very tall, but Catherine couldn't see his face. When she reached them they picked her up by the arms and legs as if to swing her to and fro in play. Then suddenly they would throw her down the stairs. Catherine told Rose about the dream, although she didn't tell her that the woman in it was Kate. Rose, always superstitious, told her that she would be all right as long as she woke up before she touched the bottom; otherwise she would be dead. 'I always woke up before I reached the bottom.'

Catherine became much more aggressive. In her unpublished autobiography she recalls that 'it was as if I had said to myself, "All right, I'm different, and by God I'll show them I'm different." So it became a matter of great importance to me that I should boss all those with whom I played.'[7] At school, always a natural leader, she became disruptive and combative. Catherine lashed a neighbour's child with a skipping rope she had refused to lend. Other children were threatened with violence unless Catherine was allowed to have her own way. Often, just the words 'Aa feel like a fight' were enough to make someone back down. If they didn't, they were likely to take a beating. On one occasion Catherine swung a little girl round so hard she pulled her arm out of its socket. Catherine bullied, pummelled and kicked her way towards respect, with total disregard for the 'skelping' she would get from Kate when she went home.

The climax came when she pushed a small boy into the muddy water of the slake and held him under until he almost drowned. A major tragedy was averted by a man on a passing tram who saw what was happening, jumped off and hauled the boy out just in time. The father came round later to see Kate. He was apologetic but purposeful. If it hadn't been for the man's intervention, 'wor Billy would be up the Gut this minute ... Ya'll hev to do somethin' with her, Kate, ya just will.' Catherine overheard this conversation from the bedroom and locked herself in the privy until she was coaxed out by her grandfather and persuaded to 'take her medicine' in the form of a beating.

Just how serious the incident was is difficult to judge at this distance, based on the recollections of the child. But Catherine thought herself 'capable of doing the worst things possible'. In later years she would have to struggle, physically and mentally, to restrain herself from killing her mother and, on another occasion, a baby. 'All of us are capable of the highest sacrifice or the lowest crime,' she said. It all depended on the circumstances. The violent abuse of children has in several recent cases resulted in those children violently abusing others to the point of death.

Catherine always asserted that she had been emotionally and physically abused as a child. Her accusations about her mother's rejection and harsh treatment of her are well documented in *Our Kate*. In her unpublished autobiography she says that she also experienced what she considered serious sexual abuse on three occasions, although she was unable to describe what happened to her with any clarity because she found the recollection too painful. Two instances are lightly touched upon, one in childhood and one as a teenage girl, but the third is never disclosed. If she was sexually abused, it would explain why Catherine, in her published autobiographical work, having previously described herself as a lively extrovert, begins to draw a picture of herself as a very disturbed child. She was vomiting frequently, experiencing feelings of bodily shame, fear, guilt, having nightmares and sleepwalking, as well as becoming 'dissociated' and withdrawn during the day. These are all danger signs that teachers and social workers are taught to look out for as indicators that a child is being abused.

Whatever was happening at home, Catherine vented her feelings of anger, grief and violence on other children. She said that she felt desolate and totally alone. 'Shame is the fire that cleanses the soul ... But my shame didn't cleanse my soul, it burnt it up, shrivelled it up like fried bacon skin.'[8] As she grew older, she learned to control her violent impulses and not to lash out at other children. But once this outlet was denied, the feeling of difference and isolation continued to grow. There were two people inside her head now – two utterly different personalities.

I would be confronted by another being, to whom I would talk and reason, for this being had a kind of cold aloofness I couldn't get at. It would not co-operate, it would not be comforted, it would not be drawn into the warmth of my real character for it was developing fast a life of its own, an all-knowing desolate life, a negative life that told me there was nothing of any value, nothing worth striving for.

Only the fighting spirit she had inherited from Kate kept her from being completely swamped by this second self. But this other dark being was always there and would eventually have to be dealt with.

5

Certainly my women characters are strong, they
always come through, but that is because they are
me. I have had to be strong all my life, from the time
I was a child I have had to contend with fear . . .[1]

Although everything had changed for Catherine after her friend's revelation, for everyone else the world went on in the same way. The house in William Black Street was full of lodgers, five of them sleeping in the front room – two on the double bed, one on the sofa, one on the desk-bed and one on the floor. John and Rose slept in the bedroom, Jack on the saddle in the kitchen and Kate and Catherine went up the street to Mary's. These men were only there for a short time, installing new boilers at the timber yard, so the family felt it was worth the inconvenience for the money it brought in. At other times there would be one or two lodgers sharing the bedroom with Jack, while Kate slept on the saddle and Catherine went back into the front room with her grandparents, to sleep on the desk-bed. Taking lodgers meant a certain amount of disruption in the cramped rooms, but it was one of the only ways to earn money when there wasn't any other work. The lodgers varied from dockers working with Jack on the unloading staithes, to itinerant seamen.

One of the men had the works of Shakespeare, which he allowed Catherine to look at. Kate assured her she wouldn't be able to understand them, but Catherine read one of the sonnets at the end and understood enough to feel awed by it. Another man had an incontinent son and had to be asked to leave. A philandering sea captain told Catherine not to believe in either heaven or hell – 'it's only imagination. Everything's imagination.' His personal creed and most important advice to Catherine was 'Have one aim in life . . . Happiness!' A lodger called Billy Potts, who worked in the docks, kept the hens fed by filling his trouser legs with grain at the end of his shift. When he came home he would undo the strings tied below his knees and allow the corn to cascade to the ground. He left hurriedly after Catherine almost frightened him to death when she let off a firework in the yard and it went through the half-open bedroom window and exploded!

More than one of the men made a play for Kate. Catherine remembered her flirting with them, particularly when she'd had a drink or two, but there was always John McMullen's threatening presence in the kitchen and every moment of Kate's time to be accounted for when she was out. Gossip already blackened Kate's reputation with her drinking and her illegitimate child. She had to be doubly careful of her behaviour.

Shortly afterwards, despite all these difficulties, Kate became engaged to an Irishman who lodged with the next-door neighbours. Perhaps his nationality won favour with old John, and the man was young, attractive, always full of laughter and kind to Catherine. There was no possible reason to distrust him. But one night when Kate went out to fetch something to drink and this man and Catherine were alone in the kitchen, he picked her up, first to put her on his knee – which she was used to – but then he carried her over to the big armchair and began to kiss and fondle her in an urgent and disturbing way. This was the first of Catherine's allegations of sexual abuse. She tried to write about the incident fully in her unpublished autobiography, but was unable to do so, even after a gap of more than forty-five years. She writes, 'my mind baulks at what followed'. Then there is a space and another attempt to describe her ordeal, but 'it is no use, I find I cannot describe what followed'. She can say only that she was close to being raped, but that at the last moment 'something burst in me' and she began to scream, 'Don't do bad things. Let me go . . . I'll tell our Kate . . .' Catherine always believed that 'but for my guardian angel I would have been crippled by that beast . . . physically and mentally crippled'.[2]

Catherine describes how she opened the door to Kate later, knowing 'with an absolute certainty' that she must never tell Kate or John McMullen what had occurred. But somehow, Catherine believed, they must have found out, because later, when her grandparents returned, there was a terrible fight, 'the worst row that had ever happened in the house'. Rose was knocked clean under the table when she tried to intervene and Catherine found herself kneeling on the floor trying to get her grandmother up 'in the midst of stamping, screaming, bashing and yelling'. The Irishman was thrown out. Kate was no longer going to marry him. The child blamed herself. It was all her fault. She was sure that Kate blamed her for the loss of her chance of marriage and respectability. Guilt and fear were a permanent feature of Catherine's complex relationship with her mother.

Most girls growing up experience some kind of sexually threatening behaviour from male adults, and Catherine was no exception. The old man who served in the shop where Catherine was sent for her grandfather's Woodbines was fond of coming round the counter and refusing to give her the change until she had kissed him, which she hated and feared, but knew that she mustn't tell anyone 'or there'd be murder done'. And there were other, darker scenes nearer home, to which she was, on her own testimony, only a witness, not the recipient. Catherine blanked these memories out until she was an adult.

When she came to write her third novel, *Colour Blind*, still working through much autobiographical material, she included an episode in which a brother has incestuous designs on his sister. Kate, who was staying with Catherine at the time, read the proofs of the novel and was amazed at the accuracy of the story. The heroine, Bridget McQueen, is the recipient of unwanted attentions from her brother Matt, witnessed by her young daughter. The child is too young to understand what is going on, but is still consumed with a fear 'that caused her to wake up, trembling and sweating, in the night, and cry for her mother, but being aware as she cried that her mother could lift this fear from her did she so wish, that hers was the power to say to Uncle Matt, "Don't come into this house any more!"'[3]

'What a memory you have, lass, and how well you've put our Jack over,' Kate said when she read it. Catherine was puzzled. 'But Jack's not in the book,' she replied. Kate looked back at her and said 'Matt, he's Jack, isn't he?'[4] She proceeded to tell her daughter something Catherine already knew, but had pushed so far down in her subconscious as to obliterate it. Only then did Catherine remember waking in the night when she slept with Kate in the feather bed to see Jack bending over Kate, holding her down, pleading with her, 'his voice thick', and Kate fighting him off before she ran out of the bedroom, barefoot and in a thin cotton nightdress, to lock herself in the privy for the rest of the night. Incest, the invisible sin, was prevalent in the overcrowded dwellings of the poor – a crude local joke defined a virgin as 'a lass that can run faster than her brother'.

There were other incidents Catherine's memory suddenly yielded up, things she had 'pushed into the dark cupboards of my mind'.[5] Kate on her hands and knees raking the ashes from the grate one Good Friday when Rose and John had gone out, and Jack shouting at her and threatening her with his fist before running into the bedroom. Catherine remembered Kate wearily giving her sixpence and sending her out to get beer from the Twenty-Seven, without understanding why.

There were a lot of questions in Catherine's mind. Why hadn't Kate said anything about it at the time? she asked her mother. And the answer both saddened and angered her. 'Aw, lass, if I had brought this thing into the open who would have got the blame?' In the morality of the time it would certainly not have been the man. Jack was known as a 'good fellow'; everyone knew he was shy and didn't go after women. So the blame would have fallen on Kate, whose reputation had already been ruined. Kate had reasoned it all out in her mind. 'Jack would never have dreamed of anything like that on his own, they would have said. Not unless he was enticed. If I had showed him up life would have really been unbearable.' To leave was also impossible, with her mother sick and a roof to keep over her daughter's head. 'I had to keep my mouth shut and sleep light.'

The threat of incest was a motive Catherine used in another of her early novels. Christine Winter, the pretty unmarried mother at the centre of *Fenwick Houses*, feels increasingly uneasy about her brother's outwardly innocent visits to her room at night. The instinctive fear of a threat the child feels but is too ignorant to identify is brilliantly conveyed in her writing.

There had lately come into me a fear when I heard our Ronnie speaking my name like that, and he was doing it more and more, for he was always wanting to talk to me in the night. He had never touched me or sat on my bed. He just squatted on his hunkers by the side of the bed and talked and talked in whispers. Yet fear of his visits was growing in me and I was terrified lest my mother should find out, for somehow I knew she would blame me. Yet I kept asking myself, why, why should she?

When she talked to Kate about it, Catherine suddenly realised 'that all I had written in the previous four years – not just some of it – came from my childhood, and were things I had buried deep in my mind'. The pages of her first novels were 'pages from my subconscious'. It is hardly surprising that these novels so often portray violently abusive families.

In 1913, Jack brought two friends back from the docks to stay. They were both from Maryport in Cumbria, had been at sea for two years and had been given their voyage money. They stayed for four days of eating and drinking on a scale Catherine had never seen before. It also amazed her that, although they consumed a great deal, they remained peaceable and jolly and there was no fighting. One of the men, David McDermott, was already married, but his brother-in-law Jack Stoddard was attracted to Kate right from the beginning. Somehow, around the kitchen table, an understanding was reached between the two of them.

For a while, money ceased to be a problem. John McMullen injured his leg in the docks and was no longer considered fit for work. With the help of the union, whose dues Catherine queued up at the union office to pay for him every week, he negotiated compensation of £100 – quite a generous amount at the time. The money could have made all their lives more comfortable, but it was squandered by Rose 'in dribs and drabs' – some of it on drink. John, Jack and Rose had new clothes, which would eventually find their way to the pawnshop, and Rose bought an imposing chest of drawers for the front room. It impressed the neighbours, but the drawers were largely empty. Catherine remembered bitterly that nothing came Kate's way at all, despite the fact that almost everything Kate earned went into the family kitty and she was working herself to death looking after them all. Catherine was promised a bicycle, but that never materialised either.

Eventually the money was gone – the last five pounds vanishing from John McMullen's pocket. The house was turned upside down and there were accusations and recriminations, but the money did not reappear. John McMullen fumed and raged. Catherine heard Kate say under her breath 'Devil's cure to it', which she translated to mean 'serves him right'. Catherine thought that Kate had taken the money as a small payment for her daily drudgery, or as an insurance against her daughter's future.[7] The sum of five pounds was to appear again without explanation after Rose's death.

The conversation in the kitchen of number 10 began to centre on the deteriorating relationship between England and Germany.

Catherine was aware of a new feeling 'of bustle and urgency'. Kate read aloud each evening from the newspapers and the situation was so often argued over by old John and his son Jack that when war was finally declared, Catherine went down to the slake expecting to see warships entering the Tyne with their guns blazing. She was disappointed to find that very little changed except that now she had to stand in queues for food.

Jack got drunk with some of his friends and enlisted under the influence of alcoholic bravado, an act which pleased John McMullen. The family fell prey to jingoism. John McMullen became convinced that the German pork butcher in Tyne Dock was a spy. Children were taking money to school to buy war savings stamps. Catherine hated the girls who were able to take two shillings – the amount allegedly required to kill a German; 'my tuppence wouldn't have given him a limp'. Mary's husband Alec was turned down as being unfit for military service and this became another source of friction between Kate and her sister. Jack too lost no opportunity to lord his superiority over his mild-mannered, more peaceable brother-in-law. The night Jack went off to France they all went to Newcastle station to see him off; Kate got very drunk on whisky and wept uncontrollably. That was the thing that Catherine afterwards remembered most clearly – Kate 'bubbling away' loudly, and her own feelings of shame at her mother's lack of restraint.

Rose died in 1917 while Jack was in France. For a long time she had not been well enough to leave the house. Finally she was bed-ridden, her swollen body propped up as the fluid began to fill her lungs. On the night she died, Catherine was sleeping in the desk-bed in the same room. All Rose's family were there, her sister Maggie and her three daughters, Sarah, Mary and Kate. No one explained to Catherine what was happening; when she asked, she was simply told to go to sleep. She lay awake listening to her grandmother's spasmodic, tortured breathing, heard it falter, rattle and then stop. No one thought to give Catherine comfort or to move her to another room. When she woke in the morning, Rose, the woman who had given her the only mothering she had known, and who had loved Catherine very much in her own hard fashion, was laid out on the brass bedstead across the room.

Catherine's grief was enormous, but she had no means of expressing it. Kate forced her to take one last look at Rose three days later before she was screwed down in the coffin. The fluid-distorted flesh had already begun to decompose and 'the sight of this blue-black, terrible looking face frightened me to death . . . I ran out of the room, out of the house.' Over the next few days Catherine was ill and vomited frequently. Kate was puzzled, but the neighbours interpreted it correctly as being connected with the loss of Rose – 'the bairn's missing the old girl'. It was a pattern that would be repeated throughout Catherine's life. Strong emotions, particularly those generated by fear and guilt, would make her physically sick. She could even make herself vomit to order.

There wasn't enough money for a decent funeral. Catherine was outraged by this, and by the fact that the neighbours all had a whip-round for flowers, as they usually did when someone died, and the money – which could have given Rose a proper funeral – was wasted on floral decorations that wilted and died. Rose was buried in Jarrow cemetery on a bitterly cold December day, raw with snow flurries. 'Kate's crying at the graveside was like the howling of a dog, and I was stiff with cold and loneliness and shame and I wished I was dead too.' Although Rose's death should have made it possible for Kate to develop a relationship with her young daughter, this didn't happen. Instead, the eleven-year-old child focused all her feelings of loss and anger on her mother: 'Why hadn't our Kate died instead of me Grandma?'

After Rose's death there was open war between Kate and her stepfather. Now it was John McMullen who came into the bedroom and made sexually explicit advances that had to be fended off. The fact that Kate slept with Catherine should have provided some pro-tection, but still when he came in to wake her in the morning he would put his hand in Kate's groin, gripping her upper thigh until she pushed him off. John had a war job in the docks and was once more earning money and drinking it. Eventually the situation reached a climax. He came in drunk and violent one evening and began to shout at Kate and threaten her until she turned on him with a cast-iron pan. For three days afterwards, she and Catherine lived with Mary until Kate could stand Mary's temper no more and moved back to number 10 and an uneasy truce. Mary urged Kate to leave old John to fend for himself, but Kate couldn't do it.

At the outbreak of war Kate had agreed to marry Jack Stoddard. Catherine liked Jack very much. He was what was known as a 'canny man' in Tyneside dialect; kind and good-natured. Catherine wrote letters to him when he was posted to France and he used to write back to her. When he was taken prisoner of war soon afterwards, Kate stopped writing to him and announced that they were no longer going to be married. Catherine was puzzled and hated Kate even more for what she felt was a betrayal. To ditch a man while he was being held prisoner halfway across Europe was cruel and she blamed Kate for this inexplicable act.

Kate's sister Mary seems to have played a part in the mystery. Some time later, when Catherine was baby-sitting at Mary's and going through the dressing-table drawers, as she often did, she found a bunch of letters from Jack, addressed to Kate, which Mary had stolen. Did Mary steal the letters so as to create a rift between Jack and Kate? According to Catherine, she was such a jealous woman that there was no mean act she wasn't capable of. When the young man next door was on night shift and sleeping during the day, Mary used to make as much noise as she could around the house to annoy him, and she once raked out his mother's fire in the wash house because it wasn't strictly her day to use it. Catherine never really explained why there should be such bad feeling between Mary and Kate at this time, but as well as the accusations about Alec's reluctance to serve his country, there was also a disagreement over an allotment plot which the McMullens paid for out of their £100 windfall, were then denied by the owner on a pretext and which was subsequently given to Mary and her husband Alec. The two families were not on speaking terms for quite a while. Mary could quite easily have vented her spite on Kate.

Whatever the truth about Mary's involvement, Catherine gives the impression in her memoir *Our Kate* that her mother broke off her engagement to Jack because David McDermott's wife had died. She telescopes the period of time between the breaking of the engagement and the time that Kate announced she was going to marry David in order to make this plausible. But Kate did not 'take up' with David McDermott until 1920 – six years later – and there had been another lodger in the picture before then.

Catherine felt later that Kate bought her a piano as a form of compensation for what she had suffered, but it was a ridiculous thing to do when the family were so deeply in debt. It was a dramatic, illogical and extravagant gesture to assuage Kate's guilt towards her daughter. Rather than buy a second-hand piano – it was possible to pick them up for almost nothing – Kate went to one of the best shops in Sunderland and bought a brand-new rosewood instrument for £100. In order to get credit, Kate had to put down a five-pound deposit. When she wrote *Our Kate*, Catherine said she didn't know where her mother could have got such a sum of money from – they were behind with the rent as usual, Kate still owed money for Rose's funeral and Catherine was visiting the pawnshop at least once a week. In her unpublished autobiography, Catherine suggests that it was the five pounds so mysteriously taken from John McMullen a year or so before.

Catherine was sent for lessons to a Mrs Dalton, recommended by Bob from the pawnshop, who sent his own daughter there. But it was books, rather than pianos, that Catherine craved. It was Kate who was musical, loved singing, and perhaps had secretly longed to have a piano herself for the late-night family singsongs. Learning the piano was also something the children of the better-off did, a necessary accomplishment for the young lady she wanted her daughter to be.

In other circumstances, Catherine would have enjoyed it. She had an innate need for musical expression that emerged later in life in compositions and secretly taped songs. But the purchase of the piano – such an enormous burden of debt – weighed heavily on Catherine and the fear of it froze her fingers to the keys. 'It was fear and fear alone that paralysed my learning.' She was afraid that Kate would get into arrears with the weekly payments, or would not be able to afford the lessons, and above all she was afraid that she herself would be a failure and Kate's wonderful gesture would be for nothing. Catherine's misery increased as her first predictions became realities. Soon Kate was paying off the lessons in pie and pea suppers which Mrs Dalton's sons came up the hill to collect. Catherine fell behind with her practising, stumbling over the elementary exercises to the exasperation of her teacher. But what was the point of learning when the piano and the lessons could not be afforded and would be bound to vanish like everything else?

When the preliminary examination came, everyone was sure that Catherine would fail. She remembered the examiner being very kind to her and talking to her for a long time after she had finished playing. Catherine passed with honours, but by the time the certificate came it was quite irrelevant, as the piano was being repossessed for non-payment of the instalments. 'When I heard the van come I hurried down the yard and into the lavatory, and there I sat with my head bowed and my hands as usual pressed tightly between my knees, telling myself over and over again it didn't matter, it didn't matter.'

It was around this time, after Rose's death and the incident of the piano, that Catherine began writing in earnest. A story called 'The Wild Irish Girl' was begun in an exercise book that her uncle Jack had stolen from a school where he was billeted. It featured a young girl being pursued through a wood by a man but was never completed because Catherine had no idea why the man was pursuing the girl or what would happen if he caught her. She confessed that it was written as a kind of 'relief' after the death of Rose. Catherine told an interviewer that she had known she was a writer from very early in her life. 'Inside myself, I knew it. I knew I could see things about people that others couldn't.'[8]

Catherine's uncle Jack was in France with his regiment and had become a crack shot. In recognition of his skill as a sniper he had been offered a lance corporal's stripe. Against John McMullen's advice he took the promotion and was with the regiment when they advanced across the river Ancre towards the German-held ridge of Miraumont during August 1918. The McMullens received notification from the regimental chaplain that he had been wounded in the offensive and was at a casualty clearing station waiting to be transported back to England. Kate went off to Jarrow to buy new bedlinen and other domestic necessities for his return, but while she was out a telegram arrived. John McMullen was illiterate, so it was Catherine who opened it and read the news that Jack had died from wounds received in action on 5 September. When Kate came back she wept, partly from relief. Later in the evening, fortified by drink, she told Catherine that her half-brother's death was 'the best thing that could have happened, for there'd be no place for me or you here if he'd come back. One of us would've had to go and it wouldn't have been him.' It was thirty years before Catherine understood what her mother had been saying.

From that time on John McMullen got a war pension, claiming that he had been dependent on his son's earnings. When Jack's belongings were sent home, Catherine was given Jack's old pocket watch to keep and she used it to try to get her uncle out of purgatory. She knew that if she didn't, he would go to hell for his sins. Apart from drinking and fighting, he had been lazy and Kate had had trouble getting him up in the mornings to go to work. Catherine had no reason to love Jack – he had once thrown her violently into the street in a drunken brawl – but he was part of her family, loved whether it was deserved or not. She held his watch in her hand in bed at night and prayed for his soul. 'Night after night I would drag him a little further out of the black depth.' Hell and purgatory were the only religious realities to Catherine – 'Heaven was a closed shop.'

The links between the health of the body and the mind are complicated and still not completely understood. Catherine was thirteen when she had a complete mental and physical breakdown. For years she had been living with fear and shame and guilt, suppressing anger and other violent feelings towards her mother. The deaths of Jack and Rose coming within nine months of each other, her growing sense of religious confusion, together with the onset of puberty, created a tension within her that could not be contained. Kate had never told Catherine the facts of life. When she went to the privy and found her knickers stained with blood, she ran screaming up the street to her aunt Mary, convinced that she was dying. The knowledge that Kate had failed to give her even this elementary information was yet another instance for Catherine of her mother's unkindness and neglect.

All these pressures began to tell on the highly strung, oversensitive girl. Catherine began to feel increasingly tired and lifeless – 'funny tired' – something that she later attributed to anaemia, though her blood disorder would not manifest itself for another five years. She also suffered from odd pains in her arms and legs. She was sick a lot. What finally precipitated a complete collapse was a playground injury. Another girl – ironically one with a withered arm – pushed Catherine over and she fell heavily, bruising her hip on a ridge of concrete. Although it didn't seem too serious at the time, her leg was intermittently painful over the next few days. Sometimes it would be all right and she would be able to play with her friends in the street, but at other times, usually when she had to go for beer with the grey hen, or when it was time to go to school, it would ache unbearably and Catherine would be forced to limp.

According to Catherine, Kate 'acted with utter callousness'. For years she had witnessed Catherine making herself ill in order to avoid school or the trips to the pawnshop, and now she thought that Catherine's aching leg was simply another excuse. She offered no sympathy. Catherine was by now seeing everything through a haze of physical and emotional pain. Carrying the grey hen was impossible, stumbling to school on icy mornings a nightmare. She became increasingly ill. One Monday morning Kate forced her to go to school despite the fact that she was sobbing from cold and the pain in her hip. It took Catherine an hour to reach the school and when she got into the classroom she collapsed and lost the use of her legs. She was carried across the road to the doctor's house. He looked at her leg and said that it must be rested; she must not walk on it. A neighbour carried Catherine home and soon she was tucked up on the hard cushions of the saddle.

After two days' rest she was well enough to sit up and play cards with the lodger, but during the card game she began to hallucinate. 'The kitchen disappeared and I began to see funny things. Funny things like the ladies and the gentlemen in my picture on the wall, but now they were moving about and the horses were galloping and I saw a pony and trap coming right through the kitchen . . .' Other chimeras materialised from the dark corners of the room, including 'the man who stood at the top of the stairs and helped to throw me down; and there was the Devil, and Miss Caufield, and the Irishman who had been going to marry our Kate'. All these nightmare figures were talking and laughing with each other. In lucid moments Catherine was aware of Aunt Mary and Uncle Alec standing anxiously in the middle of the kitchen talking to John McMullen. Kate was drinking whisky and Catherine could smell it on her breath when she bent over her.

For more than twelve hours Catherine was in this condition, floating in and out of consciousness. Then she remembered waking in the middle of the night in pain and total darkness and crying out for her mother. When Kate came out of the bedroom and shouted at Catherine to shut up, it was as though she had struck her a physical blow. It severed one of the last emotional threads between Catherine and her mother and caused 'a festering resentment' that surfaced again during Catherine's second breakdown, where she again lost the use of her legs.

Another doctor was sent for in the morning, not Dr McHaffie but a young black doctor new to the area. In *Our Kate* Catherine writes that the doctor diagnosed torn sinews and inflammation of the joint, prescribed complete bed rest and gave dire warnings of what would happen if his treatment wasn't carried out. But this was not the case. In her unpublished autobiography, the doctor didn't know what to make of Catherine's illness. He certainly prescribed rest. But the idea that she had torn all the sinews of the joint and might have lost her leg came from a conversation Catherine overheard in the kitchen.

Kate was talking to a friend who told her that Catherine's case was just like a young boy who had fallen in the docks – he had torn all the sinews in his leg, but it had been neglected and in the end he had to have it amputated. The imaginative child, listening in the back bedroom, took this experience as her own and decided that, if Kate had not been made to notice her pain, she too would have had to have her leg amputated.[9]

Catherine spent several weeks tucked up comfortably in the back bedroom, where Kate tried to tempt her appetite with such treats as grapes and kippers. Catherine's mind wandered in and out of reality for a long time. She remembered only isolated events: Kate bringing her the grapes, still flecked with sawdust; the patch of sky through the bedroom window; Kate whispering to visitors in the kitchen. Sometimes Catherine thought that Rose was in the bedroom with her, lifting her up, comforting her. 'It must have been my need of her and her presence still strong in the house that made me imagine this.' The death of Rose had robbed Catherine of the only person she felt she could rely on to protect her. All those around her, who were supposed to have her welfare and security at heart, either neglected her, abused and threatened her or actively tried to harm her. There was no one left she could trust to take care of her. She was constantly humiliated, and suffered the terrible betrayal of the abused child, where the very people the child looks to for security and protection are those who are perpetrating the abuse. In her more lucid moments Catherine prayed that the hated Miss Caufield would die before she had to go back to school. But unknown to Catherine, Miss Caufield had cancer, and when she died shortly afterwards, Catherine was racked by guilt that she had actually caused her teacher's death. She began once more to have nightmares about Hell.

As Catherine grew stronger and was out of bed again, she was well enough to start helping Kate with the housework, make trips to the pawnshop and the ash tip, and she should really have gone back to school. However, Catherine refused to go and the 'school-board man' became a regular visitor. At first Kate pleaded Catherine's health, then her own health. The attendance officer didn't press very hard. The authorities often turned a blind eye when children of poor families left school early in order to go to work. One of the reasons Catherine didn't want to go back was that she had somehow contracted head lice, which were very difficult to eradicate in her beautiful long auburn hair. She was determined not to have it cut off, but her scalp was covered in sores and scabs. Washing it with carbolic and combing it through with a fine-tooth comb every day was agony and it made Catherine feel dirty and ashamed. In her unpublished autobiography she describes this incident as being the main catalyst in creating what she referred to as 'a fetish for personal cleanliness',[10] which she retained for the rest of her life. Contributing episodes she remembered from her childhood were the struggle with the fleas in the feather mattress and an occasion when, as a small child of three or four, she had wet her knickers with fright.

The breakdown and her subsequent long absence from school altered Catherine. She said that she became aware that a change had taken place inside her head. During her illness she had grown up. As she watched her former schoolfriends playing outside in the alley, a question was forming itself in her mind. 'I remember saying to myself "What are you going to do?"' The answer was predictable. Kate had sworn that her daughter would have a better life than she had had. But what else was there for a young, poor, uneducated girl from the New Buildings to do except go into service?

Catherine's resolve to leave became stronger after she was stopped by one of their better-off neighbours while on an errand for Kate and given some urgent advice. 'Get yourself away from that house as quick as you can,' the woman said. 'You'll never do any good for yourself there, my dear, and you could make something of yourself.' She was putting into words something Catherine had sensed for a long time, that underneath their friendly behaviour towards her, everyone was waiting for her to go the same way as Kate. She should 'make a break from them', the neighbour said, before she too was dragged down like her mother. The woman nodded towards the house where Kate was peering through the window to see whom Catherine was talking to. That it was Kate she was being urged to get away from was implicit in the conversation.

PART TWO

A Question of Belief
1919–1939

The word 'impossible' is black.
'I can' is like a flame of gold.

Minnie Aumonier

6

I will succeed. I simply cannot fail.

Catherine's first job was with a neighbouring family she called John-son in her autobiography, though this was not their real name. It is hard to understand why she altered it – most of the characters in *Our Kate* are referred to by their real names, unless, as with Belle and Cecilia, there are unpleasant associations. Perhaps in later years, she didn't want people in the wider community to know whom she had drudged for. The father of the family was a foreman carpenter at the docks, a skilled trade that put him in a higher social bracket than the McMullens. They lived on Simonside Terrace in a six-room house which had separate sitting and dining rooms. One of Cath-erine's friends had worked there and when she was asked to leave, the woman, a Mrs Sowerby, whose sister was the mayoress of Jarrow, asked Catherine if she'd be interested in the job. At first Catherine enjoyed it. She was paid ten shillings a week to work from eight o'clock in the morning until six at night, cleaning the house and doing the washing for the couple and their three sons. Catherine had a teenage crush on the eldest, but although he liked her, he thought her much too young.

Gradually the gloss of having a job and earning her own money began to wear off. Catherine wasn't cut out for domestic service: 'there was always the question of who was the mistress and who was the maid!' Catherine had egalitarian ideas bred in her by John McMullen, who once told her, 'Well pet, no matter who they are, they've all got to gan to the netty!' Ideally she would have liked a job in the chemist's shop, as this was considered very 'ladylike', but she knew that her education and her home background made that unlikely.

A friend from the Catholic church, whose father was a sea captain, offered to give her lessons in pen-painting on fabric. They cost a shilling each, which Catherine could not afford. After some negotiation she got 'half a lesson for sixpence'. In that half-hour she realised that she had a natural aptitude for this kind of art. She decided to set up her own business painting silk or satin cushions, tray cloths and decorative frills for the mantelpiece – which were all the rage at the time. She canvassed for subscribers and soon had twenty people willing to pay a shilling a week to get one large or two small black satin cushion covers hand-painted with flowers. Catherine used transfers for the mixed bouquets and the gilded baskets of fruit on the covers, putting the finishing touches in freehand. The peacocks for the mantel frills were very intricate and took longer. Catherine had to work long hours to get them finished and rarely earned more than nine shillings profit a week. But she felt that it was better than domestic drudgery and there was pride in the thought that she was working for herself and not skivvying for someone else. She also loved the colours and found that painting gave her 'the exalted feeling of being an artist'.[1] The main drawback was that she was living at home and in the kitchen all day under Kate's feet.

There are revealing gaps in her published autobiography – between her illness and leaving school in the autumn of 1919, and the time when she went to Harton Workhouse laundry in October 1924, there are five years. Yet she claims to have spent only two at home painting cushion covers and a few months on either side of this in her two domestic posts. At one point in *Our Kate* she tells the reader that she began pen-painting only a year before her mother's marriage in 1923. This leaves about two years to be accounted for. Either Catherine spent longer in domestic service than she admitted, or much longer at home painting cushions, or there were other jobs she didn't think worth recording. A great deal has been edited out, but this is hardly surprising. The teenage years are difficult ones for any child and Catherine's were particularly so. All the indications are that at this time, Catherine was a turbulent and troubled young woman.

Strengthened by religious conviction and her new sense of adulthood, Catherine was beginning to stand up to Kate. Like many teenage girls, she first rebelled over clothes. Rose had always dressed Catherine in plain, serviceable dresses, often patched and faded, but unexceptional. Kate had very little taste in clothes and even less money. She bought Catherine a second-hand jacket in the market which had once been part of a lady's tailored costume. It was black and made of thick, durable serge with large, feather-shaped buttons. Much too big for Catherine, it came almost to her knees and had spectacular sleeves, very narrow at the wrists, Edwardian style, and then ballooning out towards the shoulder. 'When I lifted my arms I must have had the appearance of a flying bat from behind and an odd bird from the front.' It also had a braided collar which stuck out, no matter what Catherine did, 'like a cock's angry ruffle'. On the day she refused to wear it any more, Kate promised to get her a new one. But the new coat was of cheap, poor fabric, a sickly green colour with garish orange stripes. Catherine tried it on, declared it hideous and threw it back at Kate. It eventually went to the pawn-shop and Catherine later saw another girl wearing it in the street. Catherine also refused to go for beer any more, or to the pawnshop. Kate would have to go herself. There were constant, violent rows and on one occasion when Kate lashed out – as she was apt to do – Catherine hit her back. They were both horrified. It was the last time Kate would raise her hand to Catherine.

Although Catherine tended to remember only the bad times, Kate did struggle to give her treats. She regularly paid sixpence into a weekly club so that she and Catherine could go on one of the horse-drawn 'brake' trips organised every summer by a neighbour. Catherine gave Kate little credit for it. She saw these expeditions into the countryside as occasions for Kate to let her hair down, have a few drinks and behave badly. Catherine would be sick with apprehension. Once, after a picnic, when everyone went for a walk through the wood beside the river, Catherine was conscious of 'the sunlight flickering over the grass' but not in a pleasurable way.

> The sunlight as always emphasised my shame. For our Kate was acting the goat. She'd got a load on early in the trip and now she was having fun, laughing and singing and being boisterous, and drawing to herself looks of disdain . . . it pierced me in every part of my body. I hated our Kate for being the cause of it and I hated those who dared to look down on her.

But although Catherine tended to allow her feelings for her mother to colour her recollections of the past, this was also a very sociable period for Catherine and there were many, many good times she omitted to describe when she wrote *Our Kate*. In her unpublished memoirs, Catherine described how, from the age of thirteen, she went to a weekly club at her old school, organised by one of the teachers for girls who had left early. There were dances and other activities, including netball, which Catherine played very well; at fourteen she became captain of the girls' netball team. She played tennis regularly too – so forcefully that she was told she played like a man. Catherine began to blossom. After she left her domestic job and began working for herself, the proceeds of her pen-painting bought good clothes and the big hats she always loved. She had an ambition to be the smartest girl in the area and this 'brought eyes both male and female to me'. At the youth club dances Catherine met Lily McGuire, a meeting recalled forty-eight years later; 'I still think of it as a great event, for I loved Lily McGuire.'² But it was a very innocent girlish crush and they became inseparable. At weekends either Lily would stay at Catherine's house or Catherine at Lily's, sharing a double bed and talking far into the night. Catherine wrote plays which she and Lily would act out in the front room, 'self consciously I would play the part of the hero until I broke down with giggling'.³

Although most of her new earnings went to Kate for her keep, Catherine was able to buy some things for herself. One of the first was a bicycle, bought – like everything else – on the tally system. She paid for it in weekly instalments, always having to fight Kate for the money. Kate would try to persuade Catherine to let the payments slide so that she could borrow the money for drink or the rent or some other debt she needed to pay. But Catherine held firm until the bicycle was paid off. On fine evenings, she and Lily would cycle up to the moors into the clean air. Her friendship with Lily was her first adult relationship with someone outside the family. It eventually foundered when Lily acquired a boyfriend. Catherine told Lily some unpleasant gossip she had heard about him and Lily accused her of trying to split them up out of jealousy. Lily broke off their friendship and Catherine was very hurt. But for two or three years they were very close. When Lily confided to Catherine her horror that her mother was going to have yet another baby, Catherine talked about her own problems for the first time. She told Lily how she longed to be able to get away from home, but all the nice things she managed to get for herself ended up in the pawnshop to fund Kate's drinking. Although it was a relief to be able to tell someone, she was afterwards ashamed because she felt she had betrayed her mother. Despite the neighbour's warning words two years earlier, Catherine believed, naively, that everyone liked Kate and thought well of her, and that she was the only person who really knew of her drinking and her debts. But Kate's behaviour had long been gossiped about in the New Buildings; though most people found her likeable and good-natured, she had a reputation as a drinker.

After the death of Miss Caufield and her own intense guilt, Catherine became more deeply religious. Like many teenage girls, she had a love affair with the Catholic church. Her pubescent crisis coincided with the visit of a Catholic mission to Jarrow and the stern admonitions of the missionary priest, to whom she confessed her deepest sins, made her more determined than ever to be a model Catholic and achieve salvation. Like Kate Hannigan in her first novel, Catherine 'had the idea that hosts of people in Heaven were watching my every move and would report to God on all my misdeeds, and so I would be sent to Hell. I used to placate them, one after the other.'[4] She bought a font for holy water and statues of St Joseph and the Virgin Mary, purchasing them from the church a few pennies at a time, and set up an altar on the mantelpiece in the bedroom. Here she made her daily devotions, morning and evening. At one point she even decided to become a nun – an ambition quickly knocked on the head by Father Bradley, who, in Catherine's opinion, considered himself 'cousin to God'. She went to both Mass and Benediction on Sunday, visited the Holy Family on the way to the cinema and knelt regularly at the feet of Our Lady whenever she passed the church. When she confessed, as she now did every week, she went to Father O'Keefe, a kinder and more approachable priest than Father Bradley. But there were also niggling religious doubts, which she tried to put down to the action of the devil on her conscience. She worried about her Protestant friends. Would they all go to hell? 'I saw most of the neighbours in a state of undress being forced to sit on hot grid irons ... and my mind protested and said it wasn't right.'

Her new concerns were reflected in her writing. One of her first completed stories was one entitled 'On the Second Floor' – a story about Christ coming to earth again and living anonymously in a slum. When finished it was over 16,000 words long and she couldn't afford to have it typed. Her best friend Lily had a younger sister Maisie who prided herself on her clear printing. So Catherine paid

[79]

her two shillings and sixpence to print it out. She had no idea what to do with it and there was no one to give her advice. Her first thought was to send it to the local paper. The editor was scathing. A journalist who worked on the paper later told Catherine that he'd walked out of his office flourishing the hand-printed bundle and said, 'Some so and so fool has sent at 16,000 word story to a penny daily, can you beat that?' He threw it back on the junior's desk and it was returned the following day, obviously unread. Catherine was mortified and it was a long time before she risked showing any of her work again.

Once the war was over, David McDermott reappeared in Kate's life, first as a lodger when he was on shore leave, and then as a prospective husband. When he came off his voyage in 1923, the question of marriage was seriously discussed. David's wife had died, and Kate's relationship with his brother-in-law Jack Stoddard had fizzled out during the war. There had been other suitors for Kate, but nothing had come of these affairs. David McDermott was not a particularly good match. He was a ship's stoker, eight years older than Kate and, like most of the men in her life, he drank. But Kate was forty and her looks were going quickly with hard work and drink. Her hands were reddened with washing soda and soap, her face bloated with beer and whisky and she had put on a great deal of weight elsewhere. But David McDermott had been staying comfortably at number 10 on his shore leaves for the past ten years; Kate was good company, she cooked for him and washed for him. It was already a marriage in all but name. Perhaps local gossip persuaded them to regularise the arrangement. Kate may well have felt that his offer was as good as she was going to get. If so, it was something in the nature of a defeat. Was this where all her hopes had brought her?

Catherine was horrified by the idea that Kate might marry Davie; she thought about running away from home. Though she was never really clear about the source of this repugnance, one of the things she feared was that Kate would have another baby and that she would be kept at home to look after it. Eventually Catherine was sent to the register office to collect the forms for the licence and to arrange the date. There was to be no proper ceremony for Kate, no priest, no blessing, though since neither was divorced they could have a had a church wedding. Davie was, apparently, a Catholic, since he came from a family of Irish immigrants to west Cumbria, and he would certainly not have been tolerated in the house by John McMullen if he had been Protestant.

Catherine portrays their wedding day as 'cold, soulless and drab', but this may well have been the projection of her own inner feelings on to the event. On Saturday 30 June 1923, a seventeen-year-old Catherine 'bowed down with a nameless shame and the feeling of betrayal' went with them to Shields Register Office to witness their marriage. Catherine was the only member of Kate's family at the wedding and there was no family party afterwards. It was, like Rory and Janey's in *The Gambling Man*, a 'shabby wedding'.

> Fleas in your blankets,
> No lid on your netty,
> To the poor house you're headin',
> Shabby weddin', shabby weddin'!

After the ceremony Catherine mounted her bicycle and went to spend the weekend with her aunt Sarah in Birtley.

Soon after the wedding, people fell into the habit of referring to Davie as Catherine's father and she loathed it. She was even spoken of as Catherine McDermott, as if she had taken his name too. 'Davie my father! Davie was the last man I'd choose for a father. Davie was only a stoker, the lowest form of sea-going life.' And yet she admitted that she had nothing against him. He was a 'quiet, absolutely unassuming man' – good-natured to a fault and willing to let John McMullen reign as boss at his own fireside. He was no match for Kate's temper either and Catherine felt that Kate would have been better with a stronger man who could have curbed her excesses.

Kate's marriage and Catherine's rejection of Davie as a stepfather bred in Catherine a great longing to know who her real father was. Unable to ask Kate, she talked to Aunt Mary and it was then that she heard the story of the anonymous gentleman with the silver-topped cane, 'a toff' who 'talked la-di-da',[5] who had come to the saloon bar on irregular visits and seduced Kate. Mary was unsure about his occupation, telling Catherine that he might have been a brewer or a broker. Mary's words created in Catherine's mind 'an inordinate pride, a sense of fake superiority and a burning desire to meet this wonderful creature'. The gentleman father she had fantasised about suddenly gained flesh and blood. People might treat her like dirt under their feet, but she was a gentleman's daughter and, like all those princesses in disguise in the Grimms' fairy tales she had learned by heart as a child, she would show them what she was made of.

In order to show people her true qualities, it was necessary to better herself. Catherine developed a strong desire to be a nurse, but had no idea how to go about it. She knew it was possible to train in the hospital wing of Harton Workhouse, and that Father Bradley was on the Workhouse Board. So she went to visit him and asked whether he would give her a reference. Catherine took his brusque refusal badly – interpreting it as yet another rejection because of her illegitimacy and her family background. But Catherine was still very young, only seventeen at the time, and did not have the required standard of education for the training school. Father Bradley explained all this to Catherine, but she nursed his refusal as a grievance throughout her life.

Catherine's relationship with her mother continued to deteriorate. The fact that Davie and Kate were now officially a couple made her feel even more excluded and alien than she had before. And where was Catherine to sleep when Davie was home on leave and occupying the featherbed with Kate? On the saddle in the kitchen? Or in the front room with her grandfather? There was no room for Catherine now at number 10. Her rows with Kate often ended with her screaming, 'I'm finished, I'm getting out!'

Both Lily and Catherine went to the Catholic youth club which ran weekly whist drives and dances at the school, chastely supervised by the priests. Catherine found to her surprise that she was very popular with the boys. She went out with two or three young miners and was troubled by her awakening sexuality. Catherine dealt with these situations by blanking them out. 'I was brought up in a strange kind of innocence, made possible by my imagination which built walls around myself to shut out things that under our conditions of living were hard to ignore.'[6] She knew nothing of the biological facts of sex at this stage – only confused longings and guilty thoughts that she felt compelled to confess to the priest. She must keep her thoughts pure, he told her, but Catherine retorted, how could she help what came into her mind when she was in bed at night? One thing she was sure of, she would never go the way of her mother. She knew, as she grew older, that the neighbours fully expected her to do so. That Catherine did not step over the line accidentally was something of a miracle given her total ignorance on sexual matters. Until she

Catherine, aged six, in the doorway of number 10 William Black Street.

Kate Fawcett, Catherine's mother, aged 23.

Rose and John McMullen, Catherine's grandparents, with their son Jack.

Children playing in the back streets of Shields.

The river front – looking across the mouth of the Tyne.

South Shields Street Carnival. Catherine won a prize
'for causing most amusement en route'.

The drink shop in Cuthbert Street. Fetching beer in the 'grey hen' was one of Catherine's most hated tasks.

The Jarrow tram outside the entrance to Tyne Dock.

Leam Lane, where Catherine was born. The little girl is standing opposite the notorious 'Twenty Seven' public house, which is next door to number 5.

The daunting edifice of Harton Workhouse.

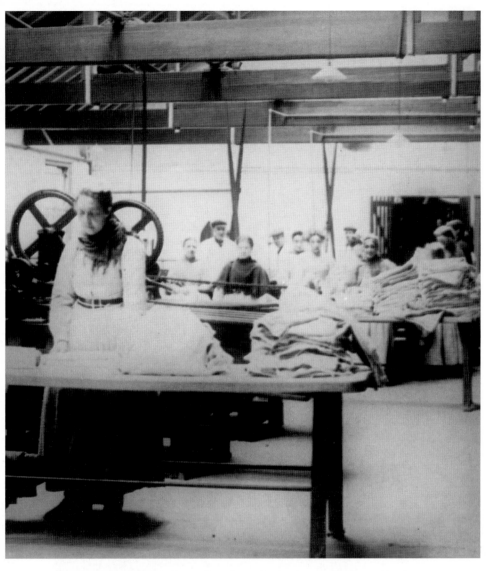

Harton Workhouse Laundry where Catherine worked as a checker
in the glass booth at the back on the right of the photograph.

Catherine, aged about 19, reclining on the grass
in a happy, relaxed moment.

was eighteen and began to read books on anatomy and physiology, she believed that you could become pregnant simply by kissing someone. Ignorance of sex and its consequences is a constant theme in her books. If girls had known the mechanics of it they could have protected themselves better. Catherine told an interviewer, 'I do wish I'd known more about sex . . . I imagined that if you opened your mouth while you were kissing you'd had it, so I must have been the closest-mouthed kisser in the North . . .' In her unpublished autobiography, Catherine says that 'the agony I suffered after first succumbing to a real kiss, was never enlarged upon until I was forty'.[7]

But Catherine's innocent dream world was increasingly under threat. In her unpublished autobiography she tells how a woman who lived in the street behind the house 'tried to corrupt me'. The bedroom window could be seen from the kitchen of number 10 and the curtains were often closed on Sunday afternoons, arousing Catherine's curiosity. The woman took great pleasure in telling Catherine what went on between her husband and herself behind them, which Catherine refused to believe. She also lent Catherine a book called *The Awful Disclosures of Maria Monk*, a salacious account of a young girl who becomes a nun, is seduced by a monk and has a child. This was being passed furtively from hand to hand among teenage girls at the time and it was rumoured to contain graphic descriptions of orgies in a monastery. Catherine was shocked by it. She said it was a 'dirty' book and not anything that a good Catholic girl should be reading. But when a dockland prostitute called Bluebell rented the flat upstairs, Catherine was confronted with the realities she had refused to look at between the pages of a novel. Bluebell's tenancy was terminated when her permanent 'gentleman friend' visited unexpectedly and found her entertaining another client. Catherine was to use the experience in her future novels *The Glass Virgin* and *Katie Mulholland*.[8] These incidents disturbed Catherine. Her adolescent attitude to sex was a mixture of ignorance and prudery contrasted with an increasing tendency to sexualise all her relationships. She saw sexual advances everywhere and was terrified of them. If someone showed Catherine that they liked her, she believed that they were sexually attracted to her, and both her published and unpublished autobiographies list so many instances when she claimed that inappropriate physical advances were made to her, it is difficult to believe that they were all true. Although claiming to have no knowledge of the subject, she was also very much aware of women who were interested in her sexually. Her first experience of what she called 'unnatural women' came as a teenager and she certainly knew enough to differentiate between ordinary female affection and its sexual counterpart.

The situation at home was resolved when Catherine once again became ill. She wasn't eating properly and was suffering from extreme lethargy, probably either from anaemia or depression. In *Our Kate* Catherine writes that her mother took her to Dr McHaffie, who told them that the lead in the paint Catherine was using on the cushion covers had got into her system and was slowly poisoning her. But in her unpublished autobiography Catherine tells how she heard Kate talking about the Pudding Mills where Rose had worked, and how people died of lead poisoning. When Kate was describing the symptoms, 'it was only then it struck her what might be wrong with me'.[9] Catherine became convinced that she was suffering from lead poisoning. The painting had to be given up, and Catherine was too tired and depressed to care. She went to all her customers and gave them back the money they had paid her, and began to worry about what she was going to do next. There was another angry row with Kate, which resulted in Catherine going up the hill to borrow a shilling from Lily's mother in order to put her name down on the domestic register. 'I was determined I was going to make a break.'

At the registry there was no shortage of situations. Catherine was sent first to a woman who wanted someone to help her care for her four-year-old son while the family were in Italy – not a nursemaid, but a girl still young enough to be able to play with him. Catherine could hardly believe her luck. She had no particular desire to work with children, but the woman was pleasant and Catherine longed to travel. The job had been offered and accepted when there was suddenly an obstacle. Catherine realised that she would be required to care for the child occasionally at weekends. Would this mean that she would sometimes be unable to attend Mass on Sundays? John McMullen and Father Bradley had done their work too well. Catherine told her prospective employer that it would be impossible; she must go to Mass every Sunday. 'It is a mortal sin to miss Mass . . . under pain of everlasting damnation I must not miss Mass.' The dream of Italy was given up. Catherine's strength of will, particularly when it came to self-denial, was implacable.

Instead, Catherine became 'companion maid' to a cultured middle-aged woman in Harton village who lived in 'a gentleman's residence' surrounded by substantial gardens. Catherine was at first awed by the quiet opulence of the big, airy rooms filled with beautiful old furniture, pictures, carpets and silverware. It was the kind of lifestyle she had imagined for herself. There was a great need inside Catherine for beauty, and when she stood in these rooms, feeling the thickness of the carpet under her feet, or ran her fingers over the rich patina of the antique furniture she was supposed to dust, she felt a burning sense of injustice. What had this woman done to deserve all this, while Catherine lived in such ugliness?

The job description turned out to be fraudulent. Catherine was to be a maid of all work, not a companion. From six in the morning until nine o'clock at night she cooked, washed, cleaned and waited at table. At the end of the week she had to open the door to her employer's wealthy friends, holding a silver tray to receive their cards, before serving tea for her afternoon 'At Home'. Catherine hated the whole charade. When she pushed the trolley into the drawing room she felt everyone's eyes were upon her: 'like a cow in the cattle market I was under appraisal'. The servility they seemed to expect of her, as of right, stung her rebellious skin raw. When her employer complimented her on her demeanour later in the day and told her that she had seemed 'born to it', Catherine was almost too angry to speak. When she had imagined herself among ladies and gentlemen in a big house as a child, 'I had never seen myself as a servant in the picture'. Catherine would probably have given in her notice then and there if she had not just borrowed five pounds from one of the local clubs organised by Lily McGuire's mother, in order to buy her uniform. The money was supposed to be paid back at a few shillings a week out of her wages. How was she to manage?

At home on her half-day off, she went with Lily to the Catholic youth club's weekly dance, and there by a coincidence met a local councillor, Billy McAnany, who was also on the board of Harton Workhouse. He had heard that she was looking for a job and, although he didn't tell her at the time, Father Bradley had mentioned Catherine's name to him in connection with a position as a checker in the workhouse laundry. Unknown to Catherine, who felt Father Bradley to be unfriendly towards her, the priest had been quietly watching Catherine's progress for some time and felt that something should be done for her. The position of laundry checker was a responsible one, requiring a degree of literacy and mathematical accuracy. Catherine had been taking sixpenny lessons in book-keeping while

[85]

she was pen-painting and was certainly proficient in maths. The job was quite a step up from the girls who actually did the washing and ironing – many of whom were also inmates of the workhouse. It was the female equivalent of a foreman's position.

Catherine was interviewed by the formidable Matron Hill and almost wrecked her chances of the job by telling her that she hated 'being a servant, and being worked to death'. Perhaps the matron was impressed by her frankness and temerity. Catherine had inherited her mother's ingenuousness and ability to endure, but she had also inherited a considerable fighting spirit. Combative and feisty were words that would always be applied to her. With considerable satisfaction Catherine gave her employer a week's notice, laughing inwardly when she was told, 'You're much too intelligent for a laundry.'

7

Talk about an upstart bastard. And her being in
service an' all. Can you imagine where she gets
it from?

Workhouses were not pleasant places. They were intended to be
daunting and austere, in order to discourage people from wanting
to live at the expense of the community. Life within them was deliberately uncomfortable, and charity was handed out as if ill health and
destitution were punishable offences. Harton Workhouse still exists,
but it is now part of South Tyneside Hospital Trust. Like many
workhouses, it continued to function as a hospital after the social
structures created by the poor law were dismantled and the welfare
state was introduced. The Victorian buildings of Harton have
remained much as they were, including the laundry and the tall brick
chimney, all set apart from the modern hospital and surrounded by
green lawns. You can still stand outside the imposing gates and see
the entrance where people once queued for admission. Inside, the
tall brick frontage has a forbidding, institutional aspect, and it is
possible to imagine why the workhouse was so greatly feared.

Catherine described it in *Colour Blind*. 'All around, weeping
women and grim-faced men had watched their last sticks of furniture
being carried out by the bums before wending their heart-breaking
way down the Jarrow Road to East Jarrow, through Tyne Dock and
down Stanhope Road to where Talbert Road showed the grim gates
at the far end.' Once inside, 'a family was no longer a family but
merely segregated individuals, with numbers on each of their gar-
ments'.[1] Many of the women and girls, among them unmarried
mothers, the mentally handicapped and those classed as 'morally

defective' – often young girls convicted of minor misdemeanours, or prostitutes recovering from venereal disease – worked in the laundry. They were distinguished from the employees by the colour of their dresses and the type of cap they wore on their heads. Shown a photograph of the laundry later, Catherine explained that you could tell which were the inmates because they were the only ones not smiling when it was taken.

As a checker, Catherine was a junior officer, supervised by the assistant laundress and the head laundress, who in turn worked under the matron. She wore a uniform similar to that worn by the nurses; a pale-blue, long-sleeved dress, a voluminous, white, starched apron, broad, white cuffs and a frilled cap. The officers had their own dining and sitting room, referred to as 'the Mess', and they had separate meals cooked for them. This was fortunate, since the workhouse residents' food, prepared by a woman who had been an inmate before she was employed as their cook, was virtually inedible – even the smell of it was enough to make Catherine nauseous and there were cockroaches in the porridge, which had been left to soak overnight in the kitchen. In contrast the officers had cooked breakfasts of bacon and egg, unlimited supplies of fresh bread and milk, and for dinner, plenty of meat and vegetables.

Catherine worked long hours, but the time off was more generous than it would have been had she been in service, and the work was not as physically arduous. If only she had known, she wrote later, the time at Harton was one of the happiest and most carefree of her life. She worked from 8 a.m. to 5 p.m. on weekdays and on Saturday mornings, sitting behind a glass partition booking in the dirty linen from the hospital and the workhouse wards item by item and then booking out the clean. The laundresses sorted and counted the linen for the wash and Catherine was very grateful for this, because some of the sheets and underclothing that came down from the infirm wards were stinking with filth. Catherine had two helpers, both inmates called Mary. One was an elderly lady who was in the work-house because she was homeless, and the other a deaf girl who had been brought up there and become so institutionalised she couldn't settle to a job outside.

It was Catherine's responsibility to see that the ledgers for the week were balanced and in the master's office by nine every Monday morning. Between six and eight every other night she worked as an infirm attendant on the wards, and on Saturday afternoons there were other duties. Once a month she had the job of taking the unmarried mothers to visit their children in the cottage orphanage at Cleadon. This always made her think what might have happened to her and to Kate if her grandparents hadn't taken her in. She hated witnessing the mothers' distress. On the way back, many of them would joke about jumping off the bus and escaping, but they never did because then they would have forfeited all contact with their children.

On other Saturdays Catherine would be asked to do afternoon visiting duty in the workhouse hall. Like the inmates of a prison, the residents were not allowed to have private visitors – they were always supervised. Catherine loathed doing it. She had to witness the grief of married couples who now lived in separate wards, sitting in bleak silence, unable to touch each other; or a girl put into the workhouse by the court for a minor offence begging her parents to take her home. After doing hall duty she always went back to her room and wept.

Catherine earned two pounds ten shillings a month for this and had her food, her room and uniform included. This was a fortune for Catherine and she was determined not to squander it. She put money away each month in the South Shields Building Society to make sure that John McMullen didn't have the same pauper's funeral that had been given to Rose. She insured Kate's life for a penny a week with the Prudential and there was plenty left to spend on clothes and an occasional luxury such as the small pot of Ponds Vanishing Cream she had to hide from Kate, who didn't approve of cosmetics. She also felt obliged to 'tip up' some money at home, despite the fact that John McMullen had his war pension and Kate was getting her husband's wages – and Davie was well paid. But at the end of every month Catherine would always be touched for something. In *Our Kate* it is Kate who asks for money, but in Catherine's earlier, unpublished writings it was usually John McMullen who asked for the loan of a pound – almost half her wages. He always assured Catherine that it would be returned: 'I'll pay you back, lass.' Catherine always gave, knowing that the money was really for Kate, that it would be spent on drink and that it would never be returned.[2]

Catherine spent very little on herself; she was used to self-denial, practising it almost deliberately as a kind of penance. And there was also a money-wise, commercial streak in her, rather like her character Maggie Rowan in the novel of the same name. Maggie, like

Catherine, has been brought up in the pinching poverty of a north-eastern community. She too works in a laundry and is determined to better herself, to get out. Maggie puts away something every week out of her meagre wages until she has enough to invest in a business, prepared to deny herself every pleasure in order to further her ambition – a trait which does not make Maggie popular with her contemporaries. Like Catherine, she even conceals how much she is earning from her family. Catherine's thriftiness had begun in early childhood when she went to get the beer and saved the halfpenny Kate gave her for the tram fare – preferring to stagger back under the painful weight of the grey hen so that she could add the coin to her hoard in the rafters of the privy. Unlike Maggie Rowan, the other side of Catherine's character, the generous side, meant that she often gave away what she saved.

Catherine made a bad start at Harton. Fired up by the fantasy of herself as a gentleman's daughter, she nurtured the ambition to turn herself into a lady, both inwardly and outwardly. She gave the impression to other people that she considered herself too good for her surroundings. An 'upstart'; 'Lady Muck of Muck Hall'. She was also at the height of her Catholic zeal. 'I was at that time bigoted about my religion . . . It sustained me and comforted me, I neither questioned nor probed but accepted it, and therefore was happy in it.' Catherine's bigotry extended to the use of bad language and what Kate had always called 'midden chatter' – particularly in women: 'some women have only to say bloody to set my teeth on edge'. These were the days when a respectable man would not swear in front of a woman or a child, and when any woman who wished to be thought of as a lady was 'clean-spoken'. Certain swearwords were tolerated in extreme circumstances, but the only obscenities Catherine heard as a child were from the men of the household when they were in drink, or from a character called Prop Annie – an itinerant woman who went from door to door selling props for the washing lines and whose vocabulary was comprehensive. Catherine grew up to regard such language as a sign of moral decadence. There was within her a deeply Puritan streak – masochistic, self-critical, but also judgemental and intolerant towards others, demanding the same impossibly high standards from them as she did from herself. When she was a very young woman, this did not make her popular with her peers.

It was this 'holier than thou' eighteen-year-old who stood at the end of the dining table in the Mess, where as the newest recruit she was doing bread duty, and heard one of the senior officers tell a smutty story. Without thinking she turned round, brandishing the bread knife, and threatened to complain to the matron if there was any repetition of this kind of dirty talk in her hearing. Although one of the women tried to defuse the atmosphere by making a joke out of Catherine's outburst, christening her 'Bloody St Catherine', many of those at the table took offence. To her great distress, Catherine was sent to Coventry for almost a year. 'Time and again I would feel like death when, coming back from my night out, I would go to the mess room ... and would open the door on to laughter and chatter which would fade away on my entering, as would also the people in the room.' For someone who wanted to be liked as much as Catherine did, her colleagues' rejection was agonising.

She also had trouble with her room-mate at Harton. For the first two years she shared a small room with another officer, who took it upon herself to contribute to Catherine's campaign of self-improvement by pointing out the aspects of her physique or personality that needed attention. Her hair was too coarse, her bust too big, her legs too thin, eyes too small and the clothes she wore were unflattering. Her constant negative comments had a devastating effect on Catherine's self-esteem, which was already low. Catherine privately considered the girl a bitch, but bit her tongue because she had to live in the same room with her. The rooms were small – space only for two iron bedsteads with a chest of drawers between, two single wardrobes and a washstand. There was a tiny maid's fireplace where a fire could be lit once a week so that the occupants could dry their hair in front of it. It was not a room you could share easily with someone you didn't get on with. The climax came when the girl made yet another unflattering personal remark at the dining table in front of the other officers. It was the streetwise Katie McMullen who 'sprung on her' and had to be restrained. 'Boy, did she get a surprise!' Catherine wrote later.[3] She suspected her room-mate of stealing some soap from a box given to her by Davie McDermott when he returned from one of his trips. When accused, the girl insinuated maliciously that the chocolates and flowers which Catherine's boyfriend Kit Gannon sent to the workhouse for her when he had a winning bet had not been innocently earned. Catherine told the girl that as long as they were under the same roof she would never speak to her again. She found herself in Matron Hill's office the following day, but her campaign of silence continued – she had learned how effective it was as a weapon. After several months her room-mate could stand it no longer and Catherine was given a room of her own.

Through her militant and tactless conduct in the Mess hall and her quarrel with her room-mate, Catherine had made important enemies. One of the women she alienated was also a Catholic who lived in the same area of Jarrow and knew Kate's circumstances. She was quick to inform the others of the details of Catherine's birth, her home life and her previous employment as a domestic servant. Catherine believed it was this woman who tried to blacken her character in a much more serious way to the matron. The first hint she had that someone was trying to besmirch her reputation was a complaint that Catherine had 'indecent pictures' in her room. Catherine had been cutting images of handsome, muscular men out of a magazine called *Health and Strength*. Fortunately she was forewarned about the complaint and when Matron came to inspect she found Catherine's altar set up on the mantelpiece with only a Renaissance reproduction of the lovers Paolo and Francesca (in Dante's *Inferno*) on one side and a print of Hiawatha's Minnehaha on the other.

The second incident was more serious. At the time Catherine was enjoying a lively social life with a young miner (who was also a bookie on the side) called Kit Gannon and his friends. Kit was one of Catherine's huge tribe of cousins – actually the stepson of John McMullen's nephew – all of whom went to the Catholic youth club. The relationship was quite innocent; in fact, Catherine was secretly in love with someone else at the time. Sometimes Kit would take her to parties. One Christmas party at his aunt's house had gone on until two o'clock in the morning, but Catherine thought nothing of this as Christmas and New Year festivities often went on all night in Jarrow. She also felt that her conduct when she was at home on her Saturday nights off should not have been anyone's business but hers and her family's. However, someone told the matron that Catherine was regularly staying out until the early hours of the morning and was associating freely with men. Catherine was hauled up before Matron Hill and questioned about her behaviour in a manner that left her in no doubt that she was considered to be in moral danger. She was given a warning, and it was another humiliation in a growing list.

Catherine knew if she was ever going to get a better job, she would have to be able to speak properly. She had to know about grammar and pronunciation. When she said 'if only there was someone to learn me' it was corrected at the Mess table by one of the officers, who said 'Only you can learn, others teach,' and Catherine felt like spitting in her face. So deeply was this incident ingrained in her memory that, fifty years later, she gave the exact words to Miss Brigmore in *The Mallens*, the governess whose gentle breeding is a civilising influence on the wild Mallen tribe. Catherine secretly began to study grammar and consciously edit her speech. She took elocution lessons and tried to learn French, a necessary accomplishment for a lady, but the accent defeated her. She then bought a violin in a junk shop and paid for lessons. She persevered for months against the disapproval of the matron's dog, and the ribaldry her practice sessions generated among the workhouse staff and inmates. The only person who encouraged her was John McMullen, who liked a jig or two on the violin and was optimistic enough to hope she would improve with practice. Catherine blamed the instrument for her lack of progress and it was discarded.

She then discovered the public library in South Shields and began borrowing books. It seems incredible now that someone who loved reading so much should not have been introduced to the free reading room earlier. But no one from her family ever went there – books were not part of their daily lives. Catherine's forays to the library were not always successful. She didn't know what books to choose in order to educate herself. 'If only', she wrote later, 'if only I'd had someone to guide my reading!' Still with nursing in mind, an ambition now informed by her relief duty on the workhouse wards, she began to study books on anatomy and physiology and to copy out the anatomical drawings. She even wrote a letter of application to the general hospital in Newcastle asking to be considered for training. She was told initially that her name would be put on a list for consideration, but she never heard from them again.

Many of the workhouse officers read and books were often discussed round the Mess table. The slightly risky, romantic novels of Elinor Glyn were very popular at the time and there were jokes round the table about women lying on tiger skins (referring to a famous scene from her novel *Three Weeks* about an illicit affair in Venice), or someone would repeat the phrase 'I did but kiss your little feet' and the Mess would collapse into laughter. Catherine was

[93]

curious to know what it was all about, but Elinor Glyn was one of the authors prohibited by the Catholic church. Being a good Catholic, she was not allowed to read any of Glyn's books. But someone subversively left a copy of *The Career of Catherine Bush* in Catherine's room, perhaps knowing that she would be unable to resist taking a peep, if only to see why the book was banned. Their strategy worked. Catherine read it avidly. The heroine, her namesake, also comes from a working-class background and serves in a pork butcher's shop, but she manages to better herself and become secretary to a duchess. Mingling in high society, she catches the eye of an elderly duke who wants to marry her. Catherine's employer, the duchess, recommends that she embarks on a programme of self-education, beginning with *Lord Chesterfield's Letters to His Son*.

For Catherine McMullen it was the equivalent of being struck down by the blinding light of revelation on the road to Damascus. 'When I read this story ... my desires, my craving to be different were compressed into a simple fact. I, too, wanted to be a lady.' At the earliest opportunity she went down to South Shields library and borrowed the letters of Lord Chesterfield. It was a simple act that was to change her life. Lord Chesterfield spoke directly to her. 'If you improve and grow learned everyone will be fond of you, and desirous of your company.' He was a father writing to his illegitimate child about self-improvement and education and the letters became the basis of Catherine's own education – 'I would fall asleep reading the letters and awake round three o'clock in the morning my mind deep in the fascination of this new world, where people conversed, not just talked. Where the brilliance of words made your heart beat faster.' She read so much that she was often late for work and her eyes became sore. But the letters answered her deepest desire and throughout her life Lord Chesterfield remained her mentor; the tattered volumes were as often consulted as the Bible. Lord Chesterfield also appears in several of her novels – Katie Mulholland is taught from his book by Theresa Rosier, and Kate Hannigan reads the letters aloud to her employer.

Catherine's own second-hand copy is now in Newcastle University, the pages rubbed brown and turned over at the edges, the covers loose. One volume is held together with an elastic band. Catherine's favourite places in the elegant prose are marked with strips cut from typed drafts of her novels and there are occasional pencil markings on the same pages. They flag her struggle to leave behind the rough working-class culture she'd been brought up with and reinvent herself in a new persona – a young woman who spoke properly, dressed like a lady and was suitably accomplished. From Lord Chesterfield she learned not to flaunt her new education in public; 'avoid . . . learned ostentation. Speak the language of the company you are in; speak it purely and unlarded by any other. Never seem wiser, nor more learned than the people you are with. Wear your learning, like your watch, in a private pocket.'[4] She learned that the basis of good manners is to defer to others in company, and to please. 'Take, rather than give, the tone of the company you are in . . . Avoid speaking of yourself, if it be possible . . . Whatever pleases you most, in others, will infallibly please others in you.' If she wanted to be thought a lady, she must cultivate 'a distinguished politeness, an almost irresistible address; a superior gracefulness in all you say or do. It is this alone can give all your other talents their full lustre and value.'[5]

Lord Chesterfield did little for Catherine's developing snobbery, however – he was not a democrat. The quality of a gentleman or a lady was shown in the way they dealt with equals and inferiors – 'respect, regard, esteem and attention, where they are severally proper'. But always with a certain distance and a degree of conde-scension.[6] Chesterfield's letters took Catherine down the road towards pseudogentility where manners and appearances were every-thing. But he was the only mentor she had.

Catherine's campaign for self-improvement gained extra momen-tum when the man she had been secretly in love with suddenly began to show an interest in her. Jim Dailey was an insurance agent, well dressed and attractive, ten years older than Catherine and what would now be described as 'upwardly mobile'. For years he had sat in front of her during Mass, an object of silent admiration, without noticing the girl behind him. However, by the age of twenty, Cath-erine had grown into a very attractive young woman, tall, with a good figure and a mass of thick auburn hair. She was at the time cultivating a lively, extrovert personality to disguise her insecurities and this too was very attractive to men. One day, to Catherine's surprise, the object of her hopeless affection walked with her to the bottom of the road after Mass and asked her if she would like to go to the cinema with him the following Saturday night. Catherine was ecstatic. This was what she had dreamed of.

Unrequited love is a terrible, painful experience. 'You didn't ask for it or, when it came, welcome it, because such love began with a troublesome feeling; it was based on hopelessness. Yet one couldn't stop it growing, even though in a way despising oneself for the weakness that allowed one to foster such a thought.' Catherine, like Bridget Mordaunt in *The Black Candle*, 'had even tried to kill it with ridicule . . . But it hadn't made any difference.'[7] Catherine knew in a remote part of her consciousness that she was being used by him, but accepted the resulting suffering as her due. She was used to rejection and humiliation and had come to expect this kind of treatment from other people. Jim Dailey would not be seen with her in public places. He accompanied her to the cinema, went with her to Mass and in the evenings would walk up into the country lanes with her before seeing her back to the workhouse gate. But he refused all invitations to take her to the staff dances, to meet her family or be with her in any situation that might have allowed people to think they were a couple. The only inference that Catherine could draw from this was that he was ashamed of her and thought her not good enough.

Much of her unhappiness found its way into the stories and poems she somehow made time to write. One of these was 'Cinders and her Prince', written while she was at Harton:

> If horses could talk
> And pigs could fly
> And dogs could sing a lullaby,
> Then you and I,
> Hand in hand,
> Would dance before the village band,
> And together for ever
> Live in a hut.
> But . . . But . . .
> But . . . But . . .
>
> [. . .] where would you put
> Your butler, footman and your maid?
> As for the canopied bed,
> Oh dear . . . Oh dear . . .
> All has been said
> All has been said
> You and I can never be wed.[8]

Catherine still wanted to be a writer, but had no idea how to go about it – she knew her grammar and spelling were inadequate. Dialogue was different. She had an ear for the idiosyncrasies of speech and a great talent for mimicry. Vigorous dialogue is one of the reasons that her novels adapt so well for television or film. One of the first things Catherine wrote at Harton was a satirical play about the rivalries between the hospital staff and the workhouse officers. Her friends thought it very funny and there was a plan to act it out, which never came to anything. Catherine was encouraged to send the script to a writing correspondence school, hoping that they would take her on as a pupil. After weeks of waiting, the play was sent back with 'strongly advise author not to take up writing as a career' scrawled in red ink across a blank page. Anyone else would have been put off, but Catherine couldn't stop writing. Words flowed naturally from her pen and she filled exercise book after exercise book with stories, sketches and poems, but she was reluctant to show her work to anyone.

With money of her own, Catherine continued to buy good clothes, sometimes second-hand. For years she wore a Henry Heath hat in grey felt that had been given to Kate by one of the ladies she cleaned for. It suited Catherine and she kept it in good condition by rubbing it with flour and salt every time she wore it. For best she wore it with a brown linen costume in the new, fashionable twenties style. The straight, elegant lines looked good on Catherine. Her one great extravagance was a coat she saw in the window of an expensive clothes shop in South Shields. The price was seven pounds fifteen shillings, nearly four months' wages, but Catherine was determined to have it. The shop was persuaded to put it aside and let her pay something off every month. It was almost a year before she was able to walk out of the shop wearing it. Her enemies at the workhouse spread gossip that it had actually been bought by the man she was going out with.

Catherine had discovered that people liked her better if she made them laugh. She took lessons in juggling Indian clubs and found that she was good at it. The child who had enjoyed entertaining at school concerts and in front of the fire at home, now had a wider audience. She entered the Shields street carnival dressed up as a 'woman of the night' in imitation of a contemporary music-hall character, with a placard that read 'Sailors Beware!', and was awarded first prize 'for causing most amusement on route'. It was an odd choice for someone with Catherine's moral principles. Colleagues at the work-house were astounded. The matron asked her to dress up in her costume and tour the wards to cheer people up.

Catherine was also learning to live with the undercover war of attrition being waged against her at the workhouse. When someone spiked her ginger wine at the Christmas party, she resolutely went to work the next day, disguising an appalling hangover. When her room was trashed when she was out on a late-night pass, she laughed it off. Once she returned to find the room stripped bare, a dress-maker's dummy clothed in her uniform, the violin and the Indian clubs tied to it and a French book on a music stand. A face had been painted on her pillow with her pen paints and a piece of card pinned up in the window saying 'Queen of the Arts'. Although Catherine loathed practical jokes, she took it in good part, putting a notice on the board downstairs saying 'The Queen thanks her subjects' and signing it 'Catherine McMullen'. It was the right thing to do. The more Catherine laughed and clowned, the less opposition she encoun-tered. She knew the battle had been almost won when she was awarded a nickname. She was known as 'Mac' or 'Miss Mac' from then on.

Catherine was learning other forms of disguise too. She found that she could protect her valuable privacy if she could convince people that she was being totally open with them. In her unpublished auto-biography she admits that she became 'quite cute'. She would talk freely about herself and what she was doing to other people 'as much as I wanted them to know' but at the same time using this openness and honesty as 'a barricade'. It was a clever technique which Cath-erine used effectively for the rest of her life. Her apparently ruthless honesty concealed all the terrible things she didn't want anyone to know. 'I had something to hide, so I appeared to have nothing to hide.'[9]

Away from home and the shadow of Kate, she gradually allowed the extrovert side of her personality to grow. But the feeling of being two people – she called them her Siamese twins – was growing stronger. The most visible personality was a clowning extrovert, 'Kitty McMullen, good for a laugh', while inside was the lost, fear-filled child from the New Buildings. Catherine quoted an old proverb to illustrate it: 'the man who's always laughing is a very lonely man'.[10]

Although Catherine was unpopular with many of her fellow officers and regarded as something of an upstart for her attempts at self-education, she was always respected as a good worker. The ledgers she presented to the master every Monday morning were neat and accurate. She learned new tasks easily and worked fast. One of the laundry workers later remembered that 'she was so quick on her feet, running here and there, it made you tired just watching her'. Soon Catherine was promoted to assistant laundress, even though she was not yet twenty-one. The money was considerably better and Catherine was able to put more aside towards her future. The promotion had made her even more ambitious for herself.

When a young woman called Annie Joyce joined the laundry to work as a presser, operating one of the heavy steam-driven irons, she recalled that Catherine's reputation gave her a few qualms. Annie said her 'heart was in her mouth' on the first day because she'd been told that Catherine drove the people under her very hard and that she had a sharp tongue. Catherine's particular enemy at the workhouse – one of Annie's relatives – had also told her that Catherine was 'big-headed' and 'thought too much of herself'. But Annie, who was two years older than Catherine, got on well with her from the beginning, and found her lively, good-humoured and easy to work for, 'quick on her feet and quick to laugh'. Catherine, Annie remembered, had something about her that made her stand out from the rest of the staff, a 'finer streak', so that Annie wasn't surprised to find that she got on in life and made something of herself.

Catherine was making other friends too. Her job at Harton allowed the employees two weeks' holiday a year – an almost unheard-of luxury. In those days, the cooperative movement (which was very strong in the north) organised holidays for single working people with little money. You could pay in so much a week to a fund that paid for travel and accommodation. The latter was often communal. This enabled many young men and women to get out into the country and see a different way of life. Catherine's boyfriend Jim Dailey made it possible for her to leave Jarrow for the first time and see something of the world outside. He paid for her to go on holiday with him to Gilsland, a small, picturesque village in Cumbria, built near the Roman ruins of Hadrian's Wall. To preserve appearances, they were to be together but separate. Catherine arrived there a day before he did and had already struck up a number of friendships by the time he arrived, which apparently unsettled him. Catherine met an elderly couple called Mr and Mrs Chisholm and their niece Elsie, a hairdresser from North Shields. When Catherine returned to

Jarrow, she kept up the relationship and often went across to North Shields on the ferry for her days off. There were also two elderly gentlemen who took a fancy to Catherine and invited her to come to Edinburgh for the day in their car. Jim Dailey went with them and, although Catherine had a good time, he does not appear to have enjoyed it. He was not pleased when Catherine was subsequently offered a job by one of the men.[11] Jim's attitude to Catherine during the holiday was possessive, but back at Harton he reverted to his cool and distant behaviour.

Catherine worked hard during the day and spent long hours reading and studying at night, so she was not surprised to find herself constantly tired. But then she began to have occasional nosebleeds which were unpleasant and antisocial – particularly inconvenient when working in a laundry. Although she did not know it at the time, this was the first manifestation of a rare genetic condition she had inherited from her father, a blood disorder called haemorrhagic telangiectasia, which causes internal bleeding from the mucous membranes. Shortly after this, Catherine developed unpleasant spots on her stomach and upper legs and these were noticed by one of the other girls. Catherine had no idea what they were – she thought that perhaps she'd been eating too much fried food – but it provided another, much more dangerous, opportunity for her enemies.

Someone maliciously informed the matron about the rash and to Catherine's consternation she was suddenly whisked away from the laundry and put in an isolation ward without visitors. The attitude of the nurses looking after her was insolent and unfriendly. Catherine couldn't understand why she was being treated like a criminal. Matron, when she came to see her, was also severe and brought a doctor to examine her. The intimate nature of the examination shocked Catherine. But it was only when she heard the doctor say 'You're mistaken, she's never been touched', and saw Matron's face relax, that she realised what they had suspected. Catherine believed that her boyfriends, her habit of staying out late, the fact that she was the illegitimate daughter of a woman whose reputation was not particularly respectable, had led them to think that her rash was a symptom of venereal disease. Catherine, who scarcely dared allow men to kiss her, was scorched by the injustice. It made her even more determined to get away from everyone who knew her or her mother.

Her love affair was also something she needed to escape from. Most nights she cried herself to sleep. Jim had now told her that for the past year he had still been in love with someone else. He hurt and dismayed Catherine by telling her that he had been going to marry another woman, but had discovered just before the wedding that she had epileptic fits. Catherine was so deeply in love with him that his callous behaviour towards the other woman, as well as towards herself, was instantly forgiven. Jim assured Catherine that he had got over it and was now truly free.

Catherine expected him to begin taking her out properly, and was sure that his behaviour towards her would change. She must remain loving and understanding and he would grow to love her. She knew she wasn't good enough for him but was committed to changing herself into the ladylike person she knew he wanted for a wife. Kate was very sympathetic to Catherine through this period. She understood what her daughter was going through and tried to support and encourage her. Sometimes it would simply be a word that showed she knew of Catherine's heartache. At other times it was advice. 'I'm not going to interfere with your life, lass, but you'll never be happy with him . . .' But for a long time Catherine didn't have the willpower to break free. She was repeatedly stood up on dates and humiliated in front of her friends. Several times she was offered a way out. The matron at Harton offered Catherine a job in a laundry in London through one of her contacts; she even recommended Catherine for midwifery training at a London hospital, but Catherine refused to leave Jim, even though he was actively encouraging her to go by offering to lend her the money.

A turning point was reached when Aunt Mary gave a party for Catherine's twenty-first birthday. She invited her closest friends and their boyfriends and, of course, her own, who promised to come and meet her family for the first time. Mary had prepared a lavish meal, but although they waited for some time Catherine's boyfriend never came and they had to sit down to eat without him. Catherine put on a brave public face and tried to enjoy the party, but she felt utterly humiliated in front of her family.

Later Jim sent a note saying that he couldn't come because he had lost some money – a claim he was supposed to pay that afternoon – and had spent the time looking for it. Catherine didn't believe him. She was tired of the excuses and evasions, the gossip, the snide remarks at the laundry; tired of being on her own at the staff dances when all her friends had partners. She wrote him a letter that she hoped 'would scorch his fingers as he read it'. To make a stand required all her strength and resolution: 'it was like performing an operation on myself without an anaesthetic'.

Fortunately Catherine was due her annual holiday and Davie McDermott came to her rescue. She could go to Belfast to stay with his blind sister. Catherine accepted the idea wholeheartedly. She had spent her childhood listening to songs and stories about the land 'across the watter' from John McMullen – now she would be able to see it for herself. Whilst she was there, Kate forwarded a letter from Jim telling her an extraordinary story. He said that he had gone to a priest and confessed how much he had hurt her and been told that he had done Catherine 'a great wrong' in allowing her to become so involved with him when he had so little intention of forming a lasting relationship. He had been told by the priest to write and ask for her forgiveness.

It was not forthcoming. Catherine wrote 'GO TO HELL' in large letters across the paper and sent it back.

The holiday in Ireland should have been therapeutic, but afterwards it stood out in Catherine's memory as a bizarre episode. On Newcastle station she was asked if she would look after a young woman who was going to Belfast for the first time, to meet her soldier husband. Catherine acquiesced because the woman was related to one of the officers at Harton. This request in itself was unusual, in that Catherine, a single woman, was being asked to look after a married woman older than herself. On the boat-train, Catherine met a man she found very attractive and spent the journey in his company, but something happened and Catherine became frightened. When she and the other woman had boarded the boat, Catherine vanished downstairs, leaving her luggage, her handbag and all her possessions on deck. When the boat docked at Belfast she found the gentleman sitting on her luggage at the dock, having missed his connection in order to look after it for her. Later she regretted her precipitous flight and hoped that he might make contact with her again, but he never did.

Davie's sister lived in a run-down area of Belfast off the Falls Road and this was a great disappointment to Catherine. She spent as much time as she could walking in the park, or sitting on one of the benches writing. She became afraid when she was approached by a strange man who sat down on the seat next to her, engaged her in conversation and then asked if she'd 'like to have a bunker' – an invitation Catherine knew instinctively to be sexual. She fled. When she was invited to go to a circus in one of the villages by her travelling companion's family, she was delighted at the chance to get out into the country. On the way back into town on a crowded bus, Catherine, her married companion and her sister were offered knees to sit on by three young men they obviously knew, amid much laughter and fooling around. It was the kind of thing Catherine hated, but she didn't like to be thought of as a 'bad sport', particularly in front of someone connected with Harton. Catherine sat on a young man's knee at the back of the bus and he began to molest her in the dark, with his hand on her breast and up her skirt, twisting her arm behind her so that she couldn't move. He refused to stop and told Catherine that if she cried out he would tell everyone she had asked for it. She was in Ireland now and no one would believe her. When Catherine got out of the bus she was violently sick in the ditch.[12] 'It was Kate's Irish boyfriend all over again.'[13]

Catherine's absence in Ireland and the cooling of her affections towards her devious lover had had the opposite effect on Jim Dailey. One night some time after her return she found him waiting for her at the tram stop as she came out of the cinema to catch the last tram home. He pleaded with her to let him have another chance. Catherine wavered, and while they argued the tram came and went, but in the end she held on to the last shreds of her pride and stood firm. He had hurt her too deeply. She now had to catch the night tram, packed with drunken men coming off the North Shields ferry, and had the strange experience of her former lover still pleading with her even as the tram moved off and the men calling out to her to take pity on him, making a joke out of what was for her a tragedy. Her relationship with this man left her bitter and pessimistic about her future chances of marriage.

The end of this relationship was one more event in the chain that led to her decision to leave Jarrow. One compelling motive was the postwar slump which was paralysing the Tyne. Catherine remembered the atmosphere, the permanently grey skies that seemed to be sitting on the ships' masts, all idle. 'Everything was dark . . . the streets, the people.' Another spur was the situation at the laundry. When the head laundress left, Catherine hoped to be promoted into her position. But she was turned down – not once, but twice, despite the fact that they had great difficulty finding anyone to fill the position. Finally they employed a young woman who had run a small private laundry and who had no experience at all of the kind of large, complex operation at Harton. It was very galling for Catherine, who knew that the job was well within her capabilities. She was actually doing the work already, but the other woman was getting the money and Catherine was quick to let her know how she felt. When the woman gave in her notice, it was Catherine who got the blame and she was informed by Matron that under no circumstances would she be employed as head laundress. Catherine believed she was being passed over because of her illegitimacy and was sickened by the experience. She was determined not to be defeated, and began to look at advertisements and apply for jobs in other areas. There was a vacancy for a head laundress at a workhouse in Essex. Catherine applied, took the train to Clacton-on-Sea for an interview and was offered the job. She accepted straight away.

Before Catherine left Jarrow in April 1929, she went to Sun Life and, using the knowledge she had gained from her former boyfriend, took out a big insurance for herself – an endowment policy with annual bonuses. This was an unusual thing for a young single woman to do and there were many questions to be answered. The insurance agent, half joking, asked whether she intended to commit suicide. She was also asked to provide her birth certificate. Catherine did not know what to do about this. She says in her autobiography that she had a vague idea that because she was illegitimate she might not be entitled to a birth certificate, or, if she was, that it might state clearly that she was a 'bastard child'. It was common for illegitimate children to be described like this. Occasionally, and more sympathetically, the birth would have been registered as 'Catherine, child of Kate Fawcett, single woman'.

But even if Catherine had had the courage to go to the register office to ask about her birth certificate, she would have drawn a blank. There was no certificate there for a Catherine Fawcett or even McMullen born on 20 June. Kate's forgery meant that Catherine was denied what she most needed. Catherine found it impossible to ask Kate about her birth certificate, and simply could not face admitting the stigma of illegitimacy, so in the end she told the agent that she didn't have one. He probably guessed the truth. A lien was added to the policy which meant that, because her parentage was unproven, if Catherine died from an inherited condition, the insurance was invalid. This was ironic in view of the fact that Catherine did indeed, unknown to anyone, have an inherited illness.

This incident once more brought the question of Catherine's father into the forefront of her mind. During her years at Harton, and especially while she read Lord Chesterfield, Catherine had become obsessed by the idea of finding her father. 'I felt I had only to see him and he would take me into his world – which of course was the upper class world.' She had once asked Kit Gannon to find out about him – had even joked that she would marry Kit if he could find out who her father was. Now she decided that, before she left the north, she would go to Lamesley herself in one last attempt to discover his identity. She had the name given to her by Mary, and she talked to people in the village, hoping to find someone who could remember events twenty-two years earlier. She talked in particular to the black-smith's wife who had known Kate when she worked at the Ravens-worth Arms.

Catherine never made public what she was told. People who knew her say that she was told who her father was, but Catherine refused to confirm this. One theory is that she was told he was an employee of Lord Ravensworth who had been dismissed in 1906 and returned south. But if this was true, she did not accept it, and there is no Alexander Davies on the list of servants employed at Ravensworth Castle in 1904. Catherine's own subsequent writings suggest that she still believed he was a member of the minor gentry, something along the lines of the dissolute Lionel in *The Black Candle*: 'From what I understand, he hunts and shoots, plays cards and also plays at being a farmer ... He works on the estate, too ... goes to an office in Newcastle. I think they used to be in shipping. He mentioned his father has had a number of losses at sea recently, the latest on the London run from the Tyne, you know, with coal.'[14]

This may only have been wishful thinking on Catherine's part. She very much wanted to believe that her father was not only a gentleman in manners, but also by birth. She believed that all her sensitivity, her artistic talent, her creativity, her desire for knowledge, her longing for beautiful things, came from him. If someone had told her at twenty-two that her father was a servant, she would not have believed them – the myth she had created, and her need for it, was too strong. So she may have continued the fiction of the unknown father simply to obscure unwelcome knowledge. Kate did tell Catherine about her father in the years just before she died – Catherine admitted it. But she was still reluctant to reveal his identity in her many autobiographical memoirs, even though Kate had told her he was dead. After 1956 Kate too was dead and there was no one left to protect. When a journalist published a group photograph in the *Sunday Sun* of the servants from Ravensworth Castle and suggested that her father might be among them, Catherine telephoned him and was adamant that he did not appear in that photograph. But she was still unwilling to divulge his name or any clue to his identity.

There has been considerable speculation that his name was not Alexander Davies, and that Kate gave a fictional name on the birth certificate. However, this argument doesn't stand up to close analysis. When Kate gave the information to the registrar, she had only recently seen Catherine's father, and he had promised to come back and marry her. In the terrible aftermath of Catherine's birth, it seems likely that the reason Kate delayed registering her daughter was that she was still waiting for him to return and legitimise her child, as he had promised. It would also explain why she committed perjury on the birth certificate. To Kate it was not a lie, simply an anticipation of what she hoped would soon happen. In Kate's disordered mind, she really believed that in a short time she would actually be Mrs Alexander Davies, and Catherine would have a legitimate father.

This is a much more likely scenario, and much more in keeping with Kate's character, than the theory that she plucked a name out of the air on the way to the register office and committed a criminal offence simply to make sure her child had a legitimate birth certificate. If this had been Kate's intention, why didn't she tell Catherine of its existence while she was growing up? Catherine suffered agonies every time she was asked to produce her birth certificate, making excuses for its absence, because she didn't want to be known as a bastard. If Kate's motives had been to protect her from this, why didn't she make it known to Catherine and save her so much grief? It is much more likely that having registered her daughter as Catherine Davies, hoping that this would soon become a reality, Kate was later too ashamed and embarrassed to produce the fraudulent certificate and admit what she had done until pressed to do so when Catherine had grown up and left home.

If Alexander Davies was the real name of Catherine's father (and Kate later confirmed to Catherine that it was), there are two or three candidates for his identity. Davies was an unusual name at that period in the northeast, and the name Alexander even more so. It rarely appears in the registers or censuses. There were two families of miners in Lamesley called Davies, both of whom had men employed in the Ravensworth pits (though none called Alexander).

However, a visiting miner's relative would definitely not have been compatible with Catherine's dream father. There was a Davies family – lawyers and businessmen – who were living in Barnard Castle, County Durham, at this time and had occasional business with Lord Ravensworth and his agent. There was also a family in Gateshead called Davies, who owned the Redheugh Ironworks and had dealings with the Ravensworth coal business. Neither family was particularly wealthy, but both were of a social status that would have made it impossible for a son to have married a barmaid from the back streets of Jarrow. However, Kate was quite emphatic that Catherine's father came from the south, which, if it was true, would rule out any of the local families. There are other intriguing possibilities.

It is possible that the man who seduced Kate did not give her his full name. In Catherine's novel *Fenwick Houses* her character Christine Winter is based almost entirely on Kate, or, as Catherine put it, 'how Kate might have been'. Christine is seduced as a young girl by a gentleman who is staying at one of the nearby 'big' houses, who takes her for walks by the river. When Christine discovers she is pregnant, her mother goes to the address Christine has been given, but the family deny knowing anyone of that name, though Christine recognises her lover from a photograph in the drawing room. Later Christine finds out that he had given her only part of his name, Martin Fonyere – his full name was Fonyere-Belling – which had made it possible for his family to deny her. Perhaps Alexander too gave Kate only part of his name. One of Countess Ravensworth's lawyers, based in Devon, had the surname Davies-Bewes. Whatever the truth was, and for whatever reason, Catherine decided that the secrets of her father's identity should go to the grave with herself and Kate.

8

I have learned that you cannot blot out an etching
that has been burnt into the metal by wishing or by
words.

'Rejection,' Catherine said later, 'was the spur' that drove her south
towards a different future.[1] She left the northeast without regret.
'There is a spot between Tyne dock and Jarrow where from the
train window you have a clear view of the New Buildings. I
had the carriage to myself, and standing up I looked for the last
time on those few streets that had been the centre of my life for
as far back as I could remember.'[2] She vowed never to go back. This
was going to be the new beginning she had longed for. But on the
train, Catherine once again experienced another of the unpleasant
sexual encounters that plagued her. She was sitting opposite an
elderly lady and gentleman and chatted to them in a friendly way.
When she went to the toilet, she found the gentleman waiting in the
corridor when she came out, looking through the window. 'And
what did he do? He started to paw me!'[3] Catherine was too polite
to move her seat, and had to sit opposite the couple for the rest of
the journey.

Catherine arrived in Tendring 'a stilted, status-conscious person'
on her own admission, determined to leave her roots behind and
turn herself into a lady. She took with her some copied passages
from Lord Chesterfield's letters and a poem torn from the *Happy
Mag*. It was called 'Believe This' and had been written by Minnie
Aumonier, who wrote didactic, sentimental verse. Catherine learned
it by heart, particularly the last stanza:

The word 'impossible' is black.
'I can' is like a flame of gold:
No whining heart; eyes look not back;
Be strong, oh Will, and bold;
You're winning though the journey's slow,
You're gaining steadily each day.
Oh Courage, what a warmth and glow
You shed along the way!

Catherine had been interviewed for the job in Clacton-on-Sea and had taken away the impression that the workhouse was on the outskirts of the town. But when she arrived she was very disappointed to find that it was ten miles outside and there were very few buses. Tendring is in the centre of a triangle bounded by Harwich, Clacton and Colchester, on the edge of the Essex marshes. Catherine was used to an urban environment, to crowded rooms and constant company. The solitude of an isolated rural location did not appeal to her at all. She later referred to her time at Tendring as the loneliest eight months of her life. They were certainly some of the unhappiest. She rarely spoke about it and deleted the account of what happened there from her published autobiography. Although this was her first major job and her first attempt at totally independent living – a momentous period in anyone's life – Catherine devotes only two sentences to it in *Our Kate*. What happened at Tendring represented a damaging failure for Catherine in both her job and her personal life.

From the beginning Catherine had difficulty with the people who worked in the laundry. These were southerners, unused to the directness, the wry, almost black Geordie sense of humour, or the work ethics of the north. The staff were, almost without exception, older than Catherine and did not take kindly to being told what to do by a very young girl. Catherine had a suit made in a severe style, 'darkish tweed, the plainest cut you could imagine', buttoned up to the neck in order to make herself look older, but she didn't have the experience to know how to handle her workforce and quickly crossed swords with some of the women – making enemies as she had done at Harton.

Before she left Jarrow, Catherine had impulsively asked Annie Joyce if she would be willing to come down to Essex with her, if a job became vacant. Annie said yes automatically, not believing that she would have to keep her promise. After all, she and Catherine had never been particular friends. But when a vacancy arose at Tendring for a relief worker and the matron asked jokingly if there were any more girls like Catherine in the northeast, Catherine remembered and wrote to Annie offering her the job. In a passage deleted from *Our Kate*, Catherine confessed that she had done so 'with the idea of retaliation' rather than any wish to help Annie. Because Annie was the relative of her hated room-mate at Harton, she had a vague notion that employing Annie would 'show everyone' at Harton what a superior position she now occupied. Annie, innocently ignorant of Catherine's motives, had no particular desire to leave the northeast, but said she felt obliged to go, because Catherine had mentioned in the letter that she was lonely and needed a friend.

Almost as soon as Annie arrived it was obvious it wasn't going to work. Catherine confessed that she knew instantly it was a mistake – she had been wrong to bring Annie to Essex and she could never, ever be friends with her. Catherine was deeply ashamed of her conduct. Despite the fact that she knew Annie to be 'desperate with loneliness', Catherine kept her distance. Part of Annie's misery was caused by the fact that the workhouse was seething with emotional politics she was not sophisticated enough to deal with. One woman in particular, a Mrs Atkinson, had begun to make Catherine's life difficult and she soon targeted Annie in an attempt to undermine Catherine.

Somehow Mrs Atkinson had become aware that Catherine was concealing something about her background. This would not have been difficult to surmise – Catherine was terribly defensive when anyone enquired about her home life and her family. When Annie arrived, Mrs Atkinson questioned her relentlessly. Annie tried to avoid her, sensing what she wanted to know, and aware how much Catherine hated the stigma of illegitimacy. 'She'd been humiliated a lot,' Annie said later, 'so she didn't want anyone to know. But it came out everywhere she went.'[4]

Annie began to dread being assigned to the mending room, where Mrs Atkinson worked, because she knew she would immediately become the target of persistent enquiries about Catherine's family. Did Annie know her parents? Had Catherine any brothers and sisters? What did her father do? Annie hardly knew what to say. One particular day, working in the sewing room, Mrs Atkinson asked Annie point-blank whether Catherine was illegitimate. Annie wanted to protect her friend, but was flustered and confused by the questions.

In trying to avoid giving direct answers, she felt that she must somehow have given Catherine away.

The woman went straight to the matron and told her that Miss McMullen was illegitimate. Catherine, summoned to the office, had no choice but to tell the truth. As far as the matron was concerned, it mattered a great deal. Catherine was made to feel that if they had known this at the beginning, she would not have got the job. All Catherine's newly found respectability and ladylike veneer were suddenly ripped away, and her bid to shed the past she was ashamed of was thwarted. The matron was furious with Catherine, and there was a terrible row between Catherine and Mrs Atkinson.

It might only have been her own paranoia, but Catherine felt that the people who worked for her treated her with less respect afterwards. This may not have been just because everyone now knew she was illegitimate, but because she had given herself such airs and graces when she arrived, and was suddenly diminished by the truth about her birth and background. The incident also affected her relationship with Annie Joyce, who believed that Catherine blamed her for the leakage of information. Catherine's manner towards Annie cooled even further.

Then another incident occurred, which made Catherine's position at Tendring intolerable. She had become involved in a strange triangular relationship. Her own account of it is difficult to disentangle. Feeling lonely and isolated at the workhouse, Catherine had taken to making long walks into the countryside during her time off. On one of these she passed a house where a child was playing in the garden with his mother. She stopped to talk and was invited in to tea by a young woman she gauged to be as lonely as herself. Later the husband arrived and Catherine was surprised to find that he was an educated gentleman, from a very different class to the woman, who was, Catherine observed, of 'inferior intelligence'. Catherine got on well with the husband and was invited back again, becoming a regular visitor on her days off. On each occasion the husband drove Catherine back to the workhouse because she was afraid to walk down the dark country lane that led to the gates. Often when he took her home, they would sit for some time in the car and talk. This was noticed by various people at Tendring and gave rise to a great deal of gossip. Catherine flatly denied that she was involved in any wrongdoing, but continued to see the couple and develop a friendship with the husband. On the rebound from Jim Dailey's rejection, lonely and needing to be loved, Catherine was vulnerable and seems to have become involved in something that contravened her own high moral standards.

In her unpublished autobiography she describes the climax of this situation – a bizarre, emotionally charged visit to the cinema, where the woman and the child sat in the front seats, leaving Catherine and the husband to sit alone at the back, at the husband's express request. Afterwards in the car there was a terrible row between the man and the woman, which Catherine professed not to understand. Was she really so naive? Or was Catherine seriously in love with this man, whom she saw as living in an unhappy, mismatched relationship? If she was, then it would certainly explain her subsequent pains to avoid the various married men who became interested in her. To have fallen in love with a married man was a serious lapse of morality for the good Catholic girl Catherine wanted to be.

Annie Joyce, believing Catherine to be in moral danger, wrote back to her relatives in Jarrow telling them that Catherine was having an affair with a married man. Something of this was relayed back to Catherine, who was utterly furious. Annie came to her one evening 'looking white and ill' and confessed that she had been the source of the information, and that she was afraid that she had also unwittingly given Mrs Atkinson the details she needed to confirm Catherine's illegitimacy to the matron. Annie was sure that Catherine would never speak to her again.[5]

Catherine knew she had to leave Tendring – it was now impossible for her to stay. The only solution was to go somewhere else, where her personal history was unknown. She began to look for another job, and was soon asked to interview for a post as laundry manageress at the workhouse in Hastings, Sussex. To give herself confidence she wore her smart coat and the Henry Heath hat.

The interview panel consisted of the master and matron – Mr and Mrs Silverlock – and the guardians of the workhouse. Catherine and the other interviewees had been conducted round the laundry earlier in the day and one of the panel, a local councillor, asked Catherine what she thought of it. Always frank to a fault, Catherine blurted out the truth: the laundry was dirty by northern standards. There were three applicants for the position, and the other two women were much older and more experienced than Catherine. One of them even held a management qualification. But the guardians offered the job to Catherine, much against the matron's advice. Mrs Silverlock later told Catherine that 'it was that coat that got them!' The concept of 'power dressing' had not been invented yet, but Catherine knew how to use it.

Unlike South Shields, Hastings makes no claim on its former resident. Despite the fact that one of the world's most famous authors lived there for forty-six years, the town has little available information on her. The library has a slim folder of newspaper cuttings, mainly obituaries, and the two houses where she wrote some of her most important novels are unmarked. Yet Hastings is where her remarkable literary ability flourished. Hastings, like South Shields, is a seaside town with all the brash attractions of the seaside – the pier, the amusement arcades, ice-cream parlours and fish-and-chip shops. Beyond the modern shopping complex there are Regency crescents and elegant squares dating from the days when it was a fashionable resort almost as popular as Brighton; and clustered at the foot of the cliffs below the ruined medieval castle there is a network of narrow streets, the Old Town, where no two houses are the same.

When Catherine first arrived, she took lodgings above a grocer's shop in Clifton Road, on the fringes of Ore village up on the heights above Hasting with a clear view of the sea. The workhouse gates were at the bottom of the road. The workhouse became St Helen's Hospital after the Second World War, but has now been demolished. Only the imposing gates – a listed structure – have been left standing. The workhouse laundry, also now demolished, was ten minutes' walk from Catherine's lodging, along the ridge, at the bottom of Hoads Wood Road. In 1930 this road was lined with big Victorian houses set in large gardens protected by hedges of laurel, holly and yew. Now only a few of the big houses remain and the gardens have been sold off to build thirties-style bungalows and semidetached houses. A cluster of modern houses has been built on the site of the laundry.

When Catherine took up her post at the beginning of February 1930, she said it was 'like entering a war'.[6] She found herself responsible for an assistant laundress, twelve other staff and about twenty-five mentally handicapped inmates from the workhouse, one of whom attacked her with an iron bar. The really heavy work was done by men sent down on a daily basis from the casual ward, which took in passing vagrants. Although she was earning amazingly good money for such a young woman – three pounds a week – Catherine was secretly ashamed of what she did. Being a laundress – even a laundry manageress – was menial work and it always linked her with the hated workhouse. She felt it was beneath her. Catherine said later that she knew she had the brains and the determination to go further and that she was wasting her talents in the laundry. Yet when people asked her what she did, she would tell them defiantly that she was employed in the workhouse laundry. It was a kind of reverse snobbery.

The run-down laundry needed all Catherine's energy to reform. Sloppy work practices, poor hygiene and low standards had all to be dealt with. Catherine went through the laundry with ruthless efficiency. The staff were not used to being driven so hard. 'I was known among my staff as a nigger-driver and among some as a bugger.' Always a perfectionist, Catherine drove herself equally hard and regularly worked herself into a state of exhaustion. She was also denying herself food and comfort in order to save obsessively. Instead of eating her meals at the workhouse, as she was entitled to do, she took six shillings a week and endeavoured to live on this amount of money. Although she was only twenty-four, she confessed that she 'looked every hour of thirty'. The stress that Catherine was under began to affect her health and for the first six months she was desperately miserable. The staff made it apparent that they resented having someone so young and inexperienced placed over them. Catherine felt more isolated and lonely than she had done at Tendring – there at least she had had Annie Joyce. Making friends among the people who worked for her was impossible – she had learned that this made it more difficult to manage people; they couldn't be subordinates during the day and friends by night. She was also beginning to realise that her programme of self-education was isolating her from the people around her. At times she asked herself why she went on; 'knowledge, I was finding, didn't bring happiness, not even contentment'.[7] It was a dilemma that Willy Russell described perfectly in the play *Educating Rita*. Catherine, like Rita, had abandoned her working-class roots and could no longer go back, but she did not belong anywhere else either.

She spent her evenings walking along the seafront, a two-mile stretch from the fish market right to the bathing pool in St Leonards, and then two miles back. Sometimes she would stop and listen to the band playing on the pier. Although the sea air refreshed her after a day spent in the foetid, steamy atmosphere of the laundry, what she saw only increased her own inner longings. Her most fundamental need was for human companionship, a mate. 'The beach was strewn with people lying about trying to keep cool. The couples canoodling under the promenade wall added to my feeling of loneliness.' But her other self, her Siamese twin, had desires that were less easily identified. When she stood looking out to sea, watching the moon 'bury itself in deep water', she was aware of a whole section of her personality that was not being satisfied by anything in her daily life. 'There is a feeling of what I call aloneness in most of us. There are parts of us that are empty and need to be filled.'[8]

Catherine's problems with men continued and she despaired of ever finding someone to share her life with her. She longed to be able to talk to someone about the questions that were churning around in her brain, or discuss the books she borrowed from the library. She had only recently discovered *Books and the Man* by Sidney Dark, and this had opened up new avenues of literary exploration with an influence almost as powerful as Lord Chesterfield. But none of the men she met shared her interest in literature. The Silverlocks organised fortnightly dances in the basement of the workhouse, which Catherine attended, but although she was a good dancer, she rarely attracted men of her own age. Most of them were put off by her air of confidence and independence. She was her own woman, earning good money in a managerial position. It's a problem familiar to successful career women in the nineties – it takes a very secure male ego to handle sexual equality. This was even more true of men in the 1930s. Married men, on the other hand, were attracted by her self-reliance and lack of family ties. Several times she met men who appeared to be single, only to find out later that they were married.

One of these men danced with her and then quaintly asked Mr and Mrs Silverlock whether he had their permission to take their daughter out. Catherine was very impressed by such old-fashioned courtesy and amused that he should think the Silverlocks were her parents. He took her to classical concerts at the Hastings Pavilion – something she valued for their educational value rather than a love of classical music. They shared other interests. He was also a writer and had had a short story published. Catherine grew to like him very much. But when he took her for a walk along the cliffs and told Catherine that he was married, although separated for almost ten years, and that he had asked his wife to give him a divorce so that he could marry Catherine, she was appalled. She would never have gone out with him if she had known he was married, and, still being a good Catholic, she could not marry a divorced man. She was so angry that she wanted to push him off the cliff. The experience contributed to Catherine's growing wariness. 'I was beginning to be afraid of men. [They] were becoming people you had to guard against.'[9] She became aloof and defensive, and this in turn contributed to her isolation – 'one alone and out of it'.[10]

Although she portrayed herself as friendless and solitary, Catherine was not entirely alone. She became friends with the Silverlocks' daughter Beryl, who was of a similar age, and an older woman called Margaret whom she met in a café, 'one of those places where you sit four to a table'.[11] Margaret seems to have been similarly lonely. She worked in London and came down to Hastings for the weekends to stay with an uncle and aunt. Catherine was convinced they were really her parents. It was, Catherine said, a strange situation. She was invited to tea in their basement flat and given 'ten winkles on a plate to eat with a pin', which Catherine thought was rather quaint. She and Margaret soon became close friends.

Catherine's new independent life was suddenly threatened by the – now inevitable – experience of having to reveal her illegitimacy to the matron. Mrs Silverlock, as Catherine's employer, routinely asked for her birth certificate. Catherine had always got on well with the matron, but now, almost sick with fear, she confessed that she couldn't produce her birth certificate because she hadn't got one. Mrs Silverlock knew why – had suspected already from the details Catherine had given her about her mother – and she was very sympathetic. She told Catherine that, as an illegitimate child, she would indeed have a certificate and that she ought to write to Kate.

For the first time, Catherine wrote to Kate asking for the details of her birth. She got a long, angry letter back. Unfortunately the letter has not survived. According to Catherine, Kate assured her that, yes, she did have a birth certificate and, far from revealing her illegitimacy, it had her father's name on it. Why had Catherine given herself away? There was no need. Kate also told her that Alexander Davies was dead, so it was useless to go in search of him. The letter gave Catherine some temporary consolation, although in the depths of her mind the subject of her father 'was continuously active, forever churning itself in a morass of shame'. She was also bitter that Kate had never told her and had allowed her to suffer at the hands of other people when it was totally unnecessary.

John McMullen died on Easter Thursday 1930. Catherine's grief was compounded with guilt when she decided not to go home for the funeral. She found it hard to explain her decision even to herself. She loved old John, in spite of his faults, the violence, the drink and his sexual advances to Kate. She admitted that he was 'a torment to himself and everyone else', but he had loved her. 'As he once said to me he had never wished me to be born, but then he had made the best of a bad job and we had shaken hands on it.' Catherine told herself that it would be better if she sent the train fare to Kate with the twenty pounds she had saved in the building society for the funeral expenses. Yet Catherine knew that much of the money would be spent on drink, and that part of her reluctance to go home was because she didn't want to witness Kate's behaviour. Catherine sent the money, but a letter from Aunt Mary confirmed her fears. Kate had been hopelessly drunk at the funeral – 'rotten with it' – and only half the undertaker's bill had been paid. The rest of the money had been spent on whisky. Later, Catherine questioned why she had sent the money to Kate, knowing how it would be spent. Why hadn't she paid the undertaker's bill directly? Or sent the money to Aunt Mary? It was as though Catherine couldn't resist challenging Kate to behave in an acceptable way. And every time she gave Kate the opportunity to show that she was capable of redeeming herself, Kate let her down. Catherine and her mother had become locked into a destructive cycle of expectation and failure. Catherine blamed Kate for everything, even for her deteriorating eyesight.

She had been having trouble with her eyes even before she left Harton. The years spent painting cushions in dark rooms, often by the light of a flickering gas mantle, and then doing all the detailed ledger work had taken their toll on her eyesight. In those days children's eyes were not tested at school as they are now; if this had been routine, Catherine's short-sightedness would have been picked up much earlier. At Hastings Catherine found that the ledger figures swam in front of her eyes and she had difficulty keeping them in focus. Reading too was an effort. When she couldn't see the small print at all, she became afraid that she was going blind. She was referred to an eye specialist at the hospital who scolded her for letting things go so long – she should have had glasses as a small child. Catherine was indignant. Where would Kate have found the money for oculists and spectacles? At the same time she was also angry with Kate. As her mother, she should have noticed her bad eyes. If Kate had really cared for her ... It was one more thing to blame Kate for.

Wearing glasses was a revelation. For the first time in years Catherine saw everything clearly, although it took time to get used to the slight distortion of distances caused by the strong lenses: 'the pavement moved, and steps disappeared from under my feet'. Catherine's fear of going blind was temporarily appeased, but very soon she began to experience another defect in her vision – she saw moving spots in front of her eyes. The more she worried about them, the larger they became. She went back to the specialist and he reassured her that there was nothing wrong with her eyes, the spots were probably a temporary phenomenon and would go away as she got used to the glasses. But Catherine's eyes began to hurt and the spots became worse. Catherine could hardly see past them. They were there at night, even when she closed her eyes. She went back to the eye specialist's clinic. Although annoyed by her persistence, he gave her eyes another thorough examination and then sat her down in his office and told her plainly that the spots were psychosomatic – there was nothing wrong with her eyes at all. 'You're the kind of woman who, if you want to see spots, you'll see spots.' The diagnosis made Catherine feel very depressed and she cried on the way home. It was not comfortable to be told that she had a 'hysterical' condition – Catherine knew that that was what the doctor had meant, even though he had wrapped it up in kind words. 'He showed me a side of my character of which I hadn't been consciously aware.' But when Catherine thought about it afterwards she said that she realised that this trait had a positive aspect too. It meant that she was strong enough to do whatever she set her mind to.

Catherine's general health, like her eyesight, suffered from her punishing schedule. She had been experiencing occasional nosebleeds for the past five or six years. In Hastings their frequency increased. Almost every day her right nostril bled and she began to feel tired and anaemic. On one particular evening, nearly a year after her arrival in Hastings, she came back from her nocturnal walk along the seafront in a state of deep depression. She had once again been jilted by a man she had grown to care for. Like other men, he had pressed her and pressed her to allow him to make love to her. Of course he was going to marry her; if only she would show him how much she loved him. Catherine was resolute. Whatever the temptations, she was never going to risk having an illegitimate child.

Furious, the man accused Catherine of being a tease, of being frigid, and wrote her a letter 'in which he said that women like me should be hanged'. Utterly devastated, Catherine walked until she was exhausted before returning to her lodgings. 'All the loneliness in the world was wedged inside me, it had to come out. It swelled, and swelled, threatening to choke me. I began to cry as I'd never cried before; the tears seemed to gush out of every pore in my body and the blood flowed from both my nostrils.' When she woke in the morning, the bed was drenched with blood. Frightened by the extent of the haemorrhage, she went to see a doctor, who told her that she was suffering from epistaxis – the medical term for nosebleeds. Catherine didn't know what it was. The specialist warned her not to pick her nose (something that deeply offended her fastidiousness) and told that she would have to go into hospital to have it cauterised.

When the appointment came through, for 23 December, Catherine didn't keep it. She had arranged to spend her first Christmas with her friend Elsie at the home of Elsie's cousin in Hull. Catherine had been living with her bleeding nose since she was eighteen; what she needed desperately at the time was friendship and the kind of comfort that she could draw from Elsie and the Chisholm family. When she had been working at Harton it had been easy to take the ferry across to North Shields. Years later Catherine recalled sitting at the kitchen table pouring out her troubles in front of Elsie and her aunt, who offered her a cup of tea saying, 'Look! try this yeasty-cake; it's just out of the oven. It'll likely give you indigestion, but you'll enjoy it . . . And move that jar of flowers out of your way; the bairns tramped into the country to get them for me . . . Hasn't it been a grand day? The sun's been shining on the backyard wall for hours; it makes you glad you're alive . . .' and Catherine felt herself imperceptibly soothed by the simplicity of it, like a fractious child calmed by the warmth of her mother's lap. The Chisholms and Elsie 'offered the barren waste that really was myself at that moment three things; food, flowers, and the sunshine'.[12] After moving south she hadn't seen any of her northern friends at all.

Catherine's loneliness made her vulnerable and, despite her resolution never to make friends with any of her employees, in 1931 she became involved with an Irishwoman called Nan Smith. Nan was thirty-five, eleven years older than Catherine, and had a husband and a mentally handicapped child she had left behind in Ireland. She seems to have been a lively extrovert, used to living on her wits and extremely worldly-wise. According to Catherine, whose prejudiced view is the only one we have, Nan was also dominant, manipulative, indolent, deceitful and used to getting her own way. Nan had a colourful history. She had been a nursing auxiliary and noncomissioned officer in the First World War and had had an affair with a female officer. After the war she had set up in business in Ireland with a market stall, helped by her brother-in-law. She had apparently made an impulsive marriage to a man while they were both drunk and woke up the next morning believing herself to be 'clean mad' – according to Catherine. The marriage did not work out and when Nan's brother-in-law was killed on the road as he pushed the barrow from one market to another, Nan sold up, bought a pension for her sister, who was also looking after her child, and came to England. She told Catherine that things had got so bad she couldn't stand it any more. She lived at first with a girl she had met in Ireland, though this relationship seems to have foundered – perhaps under pressure from the girl's family

Catherine met Nan when she was working as a cleaner at the hospital and was sent down to help out in the laundry during a flu epidemic. Catherine knew her already by reputation and her first impressions were not favourable. When she talked about it later on tape, she said that she was wary of Nan because she had been sexually assaulted by Irishmen once as a child and then again as a young woman, and this had left her with a natural distrust of the Irish. It is an odd statement, since it seems to put Nan straight away into a sexual context. Whatever the reasons for Catherine's instinctive dislike, within days of Nan's arrival at the laundry Catherine had made up her mind to sack her. Catherine described her as lazy and disruptive. Whichever part of the laundry Nan worked in, whenever Catherine was out of the room, 'Nan would have the place in an uproar'. She got away with it by making people laugh – what Catherine called her 'blarneying'. Everyone liked her. On one occasion when Catherine came back into the laundry, everyone had stopped work to watch Nan doing a sword dance with two broom handles. Catherine made her opinion of Nan very obvious, but staff were in such short supply during the epidemic that it would not have been possible to let her go.

Catherine herself was doing three jobs – laundry manageress, assistant matron and porteress – and had to move into the assistant matron's flat in the workhouse in order to cope with the workload.

As porteress Catherine was responsible for supervising the admission of the female 'casuals' – homeless vagrants, often accompanied by children, who came in off the streets each night for a warm bed and a free meal. Not only did Catherine find the business of bathing them and dealing with head lice and other vermin utterly repugnant, but the chore clashed with her responsibilities on the wards as assistant matron. However, none of the other staff could offer to help out, despite the attraction of paid overtime, since they all had families to look after. Nan offered, but was refused. Later that day, Nan came to Catherine's office after the others had gone home and said in her broad Irish accent, 'Look, I know that you don't like me, but I'm on my own and I've got nothing to do. I could do the nights.'[13] She told Catherine that she was ready to start work there and then if she would only give her a chance. Catherine told Nan that if she wouldn't work properly during the day, how did she expect Catherine to believe that she would work at night? Nan promised that if she was given the job she would work for Catherine like no one else. Desperate for the help, Catherine gave Nan a week's trial.

In spite of her misgivings, Catherine was drawn to Nan's 'low masculine voice and deep, attractive brown eyes', her 'mannish' looks and her warm, extrovert personality – so unlike Catherine's own.[14] Nan worked for Catherine 'like ten men'. She washed the casuals as they came in, combed the lice out of their hair, entertained them with jokes, and they all loved her. Catherine became convinced that she had been wrong about Nan. Her final misgivings left her when she went back to her flat late at night, utterly exhausted, and discovered that it had been tidied for her and 'made beautiful' by Nan, who had also left a warm supper waiting for her in the kitchen. Catherine was touched. Nan did this every night. Sometimes she left presents for Catherine – flowers, cream cakes, particularly meringues, which Nan knew were Catherine's weakness. Nan made Catherine feel cared for and special. Catherine admitted that she was so lonely and disillusioned with men that instead of sacking Nan as soon as the staff shortage was over, she 'clung to her like a drowning man to a raft'.[15] Catherine felt she really understood Nan when Nan explained that she only laughed and clowned to cover the tragedies of her life, because this was exactly what Catherine had tried to do at Harton. 'It was strange,' Catherine recalled, that a month after she had first employed Nan, 'I had hated this woman and now I thought the world of her'.[16]

Since coming to Hastings, Catherine had had a succession of furnished rooms and penny-pinching landladies that left her with a temporary, rootless feeling that only aggravated her homesickness. She could have continued to live in the workhouse, deputising for the assistant matron, but Harton had sickened her of 'living in'. Nan advised Catherine to find a flat of her own. After thinking it over, Catherine decided to spend the money and leased a flat in West Hill, a lovely area of Hastings just above the castle, on the ground floor of one of the big period properties. Today it would be described as a studio flat – one large living room and a kitchen that had a bath in the corner with a wooden lid over it. Furnishing and decorating the flat gave Catherine the opportunity to create a context for herself more in keeping with her own ambitions. The furniture was bought by instalments – she was determined to have new, not second-hand. The walls were decorated with a dark-blue wallpaper, an idea taken from a book, and the woodwork was glossed in black. The single, long Georgian window had coral-coloured satin curtains draped back on either side, and in front of them Catherine placed two antique chests, supporting a pair of white porcelain figurines. She bought a Chinese carpet in grey and black. The finishing touch was a Victorian print above the mantelpiece called *The First Piano Lesson*. It cost her almost a year's wages but the effect was spectacular.

At this point Nan wrote Catherine a letter asking if they could be 'friends'. When Catherine talked about this episode later, she said that she had been 'as pure in mind as a nun who'd never been out of a convent', the inference being that she was unaware of what was actually being asked of her. Catherine wrote back addressing Nan as 'My dearest Nan', assuring her that, of course, she would be her friend. 'There was nothing to stop us, and nobody had been as kind to me as she had.' Catherine went on in the letter to confess that she had no ties, was completely disillusioned with men and did not intend to marry. She also told Nan that she had taken the place of Catherine's mother in her life and she had found that Nan 'was a comfort' to her. Nan seems to have regarded the letter as a declaration of commitment. She kept it all her life and later used it against Catherine.[17]

Nan came to the flat almost every night. At first, Catherine had to keep the relationship secret, because she didn't want it known that she had begun to associate with one of her employees. For three months they carried on seeing each other in this clandestine fashion until Nan suggested that it was ridiculous to be paying two lots of rent. There was also the question of furniture. Catherine 'had a carpet, sideboard, table and chairs, curtains' but no sofa or armchairs. Nan, on the other hand, owned a three-piece suite and was in the process of looking for new lodgings. According to Catherine, Nan said, 'Can I come in with you and bring the suite?' Catherine agreed, 'and so I realised that we were friends'. Nan moved in and they slept together on the Put-U-Up bed. 'We lived together; we slept together.'[1]

They had now been together for five months and Catherine felt that, whatever anyone thought about Nan, it was time to bring their relationship out into the open. Catherine argued to herself that Nan was a good woman. 'She's done more for me than anybody in my life. She's worked for me, she's given me things. She thinks of nobody but me. I'm not going to keep her hidden any longer.'[19] Catherine went to the matron and told her that she had 'taken Nan as her friend' and was sharing a flat with her. Mrs Silverlock 'nearly went through the roof'. Catherine put the matron's reaction down to female jealousy, but even the master, George Silverlock, took Catherine to one side and told her that what she was doing was inadvisable. Catherine's relationship with Nan also upset one of the other officers – a Frenchwoman whom Catherine accused of having made sexual advances to her when she went into her room. Apparently this woman was so jealous of Catherine that she tried to make Nan '*her* friend' in order to separate them. Catherine found herself mixed up in what she described as 'a kind of awful, intricate, emotional scene'. Her friend Margaret was also somehow involved – 'it became so intense that life became hell there, life just became hell'.[20]

'I entered the world where there was nothing but women,' Catherine said later. She always protested that she had been extremely naive. 'I didn't even know what the word lesbian meant.' When talking on tape she repeats over and over again that she herself was not a lesbian; Nan was not a lesbian, though she admitted that Nan had 'a love as strong as any man' for her. She was also very defensive about the fact that she shared a bed with Nan over a period of several years. It was normal for Catherine to share a bed with women; she had done it all her life; 'I shared a bed with my mother'.[21] Catherine insisted that sharing a bed with Nan was no different to sleeping with her mother. She said that Nan gave her comfort and the mothering that she had never known from Kate. 'Although I was in every way the stronger, I got from her a feeling of protection. I had never known a father, or a mother as such and although Nan Smith was the outward antithesis of anything relating to a mother, this, as I see it now, was primarily the function that she performed for me.'[22] But sharing a bed with someone who is deeply and obsessively in love with you is very different to sharing a bed with your mother – unless you have a rather odd relationship with your mother. It is clear from subsequent events that Nan's feelings for Catherine were far from motherly and grew into a possessive passion that almost wrecked Catherine's life.

9

She gazed about the hall. She should be happy, very
happy, for now she was mistress of this house, this
beautiful, beautiful house . . .[1]

After the initial euphoria of having Nan's daily care and companionship had worn off, Catherine sometimes found her exasperating.
Nan, like Kate, had a dominant personality and could be very
manipulative. As the older woman, she wanted to take control of
Catherine's life. One incident stuck in Catherine's mind for years –
infuriating at the time, but later something to laugh at. Catherine
lacked a kitchen table for her flat and Nan refused to let her pay
good money for a new one when a second-hand table could be
bought in the auction rooms for almost nothing. Catherine reluctantly agreed. When she came home from work, 'I thought I had
come into the wrong flat'. Nan had bought a seven-foot-long kitchen
table, standing end-up in the middle of their living room, as part of
a job lot from a hotel kitchen. From the door to the window the
floor was piled high with gas stoves, washing baskets of old kitchen
equipment, several aspidistras in large jardinieres, and a box holding
forty corkscrews. She later discovered that Nan had paid eighteen
shillings for all this – more than the price of a new table! Catherine
was furious.

Nan was also responsible for the reappearance of Kate in Catherine's life. It was Nan's friendship and her gentle persuasion that
finally gave Catherine the courage to go home for a holiday. In
August 1931, more than two years after she had left, Catherine went
back to Jarrow. The economic depression was at its worst. Half of
Jarrow was out of work, ships lay idle and Davie McDermott was

on the dole. It affected rich and poor alike – shipyard owners were reduced to the same straits as their former employees. Fewer people could now afford domestic help and even Kate – who would turn her hand to anything for ridiculously low wages – found it impossible to get work. The scenes Catherine witnessed eventually found their way into her novels, particularly *Katie Mulholland*, whose great-grandson comes from America to find her and is appalled by the extent of the suffering.

> The town looked dead, it even smelt dead to him. The district around the station had appeared dreary enough, but these dejected grey streets with groups of men leaning against the end walls, all attired in similar uniform, cap, muffler, and greasy-looking oddments of suits, were depressing to say the least. Men who smiled thinly, and chatted, and said at intervals, 'Watcher there,' yet who looked bewildered and numb and at the same time aggressive.[2]

Catherine's horror at what she saw on the streets also spilled out into poetry – not good poetry, but with some arresting lines. 'Jarrow 1930' recalls men 'standing in the sockets of doors', their idle hands and feet 'like long dead flesh'. Jarrow's 'steel heart' that had once 'pumped out ships' had ceased to beat and the arc furnaces that had lit the night sky above William Black Street were extinguished. Men, prematurely old, went 'clumping through bone-chilling dawns' to pick cinders from the tips as Catherine herself had done as a child.

Since the death of old John, Davie McDermott and Kate had the house in William Black Street to themselves and Catherine thought they seemed very happy in spite of the lack of money. Kate was in one of her sober phases – there was no money to spare for drink. They were poor enough to go through the means test to get welfare assistance. Davie too seemed content. After eight years of marriage he still adored Kate. Catherine felt much happier about her own decision to leave the north and her mother. It had all worked out very well. Everything seemed so hopeful that when Kate said how much she would love to see Catherine's new flat and meet her new friend Nan, Catherine unthinkingly offered her a holiday in Hastings, an act that she regretted as soon as she returned home.

Catherine need not have worried; Kate's holiday in Hastings was a great success. She, Nan and Catherine shared the small flat in

Westhill House amicably and Kate managed to stay off the drink the whole time she was there. She even refused the beer that Catherine brought in for her. Kate said, 'I don't need it any more', and Catherine believed her. She took her mother into the laundry, although afraid that Kate would let her down by revealing her 'common' origins. 'Everyone thought I came from a very good background,' Catherine said.[3] But the staff all liked her instantly, except the matron. Mrs Silverlock was shrewd enough to see through Kate's façade and told Catherine that she should be thankful that she didn't take after her mother.

Kate charmed Nan and they immediately formed an alliance. At some time during the visit, Kate must have communicated to Nan that she was no longer happy living with Davie. She wanted to get out. The details of what happened next are not very clear. Catherine records Nan saying, 'Fancy having a mother like that and living apart. She has no ties in the North, why on earth don't you have her to live with you?' A husband in the north was certainly a tie. The statement seems to suggest that from Kate's point of view the marriage to Davie had broken down, as Nan's own marriage had done, and Kate was looking for a means of escape. Did Kate put Nan up to what she said next? Apparently she turned to Kate in front of Catherine and asked, 'Why don't you come and live here, mam?' Catherine remembered Kate turning to her 'beseeching as she said quietly, "It's up to Katie." ' Catherine was not strong enough to refuse.

Her mother's return meant that the process of growing away from Kate and everything she represented, of becoming a fully independent adult, was interrupted. Three years after leaving Jarrow, and Kate's influence, Catherine was thrust back into the complex emotional politics of childhood. But the most immediate result of her rash offer was that Catherine and Nan had to take a larger flat. It was impossible for three of them to live in one room. So Catherine's beautiful room was given up and she took a three-year lease on five rooms – actually two flats on adjacent floors further up in the same building, costing a massive twenty-five shillings a week. Kate and Nan had mooted the idea that Catherine should take in lodgers and summer holidaymakers and that Kate would run the house as a business while Catherine and Nan carried on working at the laundry. It all sounded very practicable.

On the day Kate arrived, Catherine was late picking her up from the station and it was obvious that Kate had been on a binge while she waited. She was drunk and aggressive. When Catherine saw her sitting on her suitcase outside the station, she suddenly realised what she had done, but it was too late. Catherine quickly found that, between Kate and Nan, she had trapped herself in a kind of waking nightmare. Catherine later looked back on her first ten years in Hastings as 'a hell of jealousy with women'.

But, as Catherine herself realised, much of her torment was self-inflicted. 'When did I first start to be a victim?' she once asked. Catherine's adolescent experience had led her to expect persecution; for being illegitimate, for being a Catholic, or simply because she had different ambitions and interests from the people around her. On a more personal level, Catherine's feelings of guilt and aggression towards Kate made her easy prey for her mother's needy behaviour, and her own need to be loved and to be approved left Catherine vulnerable to people like Nan. Catherine admitted that her emotions were 'as strings for certain people to play on, and once they discovered this weakness in me they twanged them all the harder'.

The latter part of 1932 saw Catherine swinging wildly between optimism and despair. At times everything seemed to be going well. Kate behaved like the affectionate, good-humoured mother figure Catherine wanted her to be. Kate, Nan and Catherine had a wonderful Christmas together; 'we laughed and we ate', and Kate stayed sober for three days. However, with a public house at the bottom of the street, Kate was unable to stay on the wagon for very long. Soon she was there every night, staggering home afterwards, loud-mouthed and hostile. All Catherine's misgivings had become realities and she was once again looking for a way to escape from her mother. But it was more difficult now that she had committed herself to a three-year lease, and there was Nan to be taken into account. Nan missed her mentally handicapped daughter, left behind in Ireland, and had recently begun to lament that she couldn't bring Maisie over to England. Catherine began to think about taking another property, something further away from the pubs of the town to keep Kate sober, and where she would be able to give a more permanent home to Nan and her handicapped child.

Catherine had been walking to the laundry along Hoads Wood Road for over two years, past a big, empty Victorian house. The house matched her childhood fantasies. 'Here was the picture come down from the wall . . . Here was the place I had bragged about in the school yard at Simonside.' Every day she looked through the overgrown hedge as she passed and let her imagination carry her inside. When she saw the house advertised as a 'Gentleman's Residence for Sale', she couldn't resist contacting the agent and asking if she could look round.

The Hurst is a big neo-Gothic house with a tower, stained glass and the mock-Tudor decorative features characteristic of this style of architecture. It is built close to the road, separated from the pavement by a tarmac drive sweep. From the gateway it doesn't look particularly large, but this is deceptive, for the longest aspect fronts the garden and is extensive. There are several roof levels, innumerable chimney stacks, two towers – one with a viewing gallery – and on the ground floor a conservatory and terrace leading to lawns that used to be a tennis court. To buy such a large, rambling building would be quite an undertaking for a young single woman today, but in the 1930s when women rarely owned property in their own right, it was even more extraordinary.

Catherine used the house as a setting in *The Obsession*, which centres on a young woman's increasingly unhealthy preoccupation with a house, an obsession which leads her to manipulate everyone around her and ruthlessly sacrifice everything, including herself, in order to keep it.

> It was called Pine Hurst . . . In front of the main building was a balcony from which shallow steps led down to a gravelled area which in turn gave way to a large lawn. It was a most attractive-looking house from its long front up to its ornamental chimneys, of which . . . there were several, suggesting the house was even larger than it appeared to be from the outside.[4]

Like her character Beatrice, Catherine had a love affair with the Hurst which drained her resources and made her ill with the physical effort of trying to maintain it.

The Hurst is now a residential home, which – ironically – is what Catherine intended it to be when she bought it. She had a notion that she would like to take in 'mental defectives', as they were then called, whose plight she had pitied in the workhouse, and epileptics – perhaps stirred with sympathy towards them by her former boy-friend's callous attitude towards the woman he had been going to marry. Like many people who have a deep need to be loved and valued, Catherine wanted to be a carer. Caring for people, doing things for them, gave her a sense of worth. But it would be simplistic to say that her kindness, generosity and compulsive giving sprang only from this. She grew up with a strong sense of the social injustices she saw around her, stung into pity by the cruelty and neglect she witnessed. Even as a child she had had a penny to spare for those she considered less fortunate than herself. While she worked at Harton the docker Billy Potts, whom she had once frightened with a firework, was often given sixpence to buy himself a drink when Catherine passed him standing in the dole queue. When she was eleven she once gave two shillings to a little boy she saw begging in the street.

Like Arabella Lagrange, born in a brothel but brought up as a gentleman's daughter in *The Glass Virgin*, Catherine was always bothered by the assumption of moral superiority that seemed to come with the possession of money. How a gentleman could beat the butler who had served him faithfully for years, 'yet could still be considered a good man'; while children who were so hungry they 'rammed the strawberries into their mouths with the stalks on, and were so poor that their clothes were in rags,' were considered to be 'nothing but scum'.[5] The ability to dispense charity gave Catherine a taste of both the moral and the social superiority of the gentleman's daughter she would have liked to have been, but it was something she never openly confronted.

Catherine fell in love with the Hurst the instant she stepped over the threshold; 'I knew it was for me'. The dining hall was twenty feet long, with wood panelling up to the dado rail, and a huge stained-glass window. There was a drawing room with ornate mouldings on the ceilings and windows that looked out over the lawns to mature trees. At one end, glass-panelled doors opened into a domed conservatory. There were fitted bedrooms, a wine cellar and a butler's pantry. Catherine was no match for the estate agent. 'That man knew that a Katie McMullen from William Black Street could not resist a house that had a butler's pantry and a wine cellar.' She was too inexperienced to recognise the signs of extensive woodworm or the pungent smell of dry rot, which she thought was only the musty odour of a house that has been empty for two years. It was pouring with rain outside and there were damp patches where the roof leaked – but these seemed minor things that could soon be fixed.

The house was going cheap, partly because it had been empty for so long and was so run down, and partly because during the thirties slump, big houses that needed servants to run them were difficult to sell. The idea of buying it was utter madness, but Catherine was determined to have it. The snobbery of her childhood vision was only one part of her desire to possess the Hurst. She was also driven by a deeper need. 'I never wanted to walk in public parks or through someone else's wood. I wanted a square of ground . . . leasehold from God. Outside my square, nations could rage, governments could fall, but nothing would be able to touch me . . . It was a sort of faith with me that once I had acquired a piece of ground for myself I'd know happiness.' She knew already that life-assurance policies could be mortgaged. When she had first arrived in Hastings, Catherine had raised her insurance to £750 and then to £1,000, paying the extra premiums by cashing the annual bonuses instead of allowing them to accumulate. She went to the building society and mortgaged her policy for £950 to buy the Hurst.

In 1933 Catherine was still only twenty-seven. It was four years since she had been a laundry checker in Harton Workhouse; four years since she had left behind the poverty of Jarrow and the limitations of the New Buildings. Now she was the owner of a fifteen-bedroom mansion with a tennis court. She also held the lease on a double flat in Westhill House, which she subsequently found impossible to sublet and had to continue to pay twenty-five shillings a week for. Despite Nan's contribution to the household and the fact that Kate was now receiving five pounds a month (nearly half as much as Catherine was earning) from Davie, who was back at sea again, Catherine was once again starving herself in order to afford it all.

But in spite of the financial limitations, initially the plan worked well. Catherine continued to work at the laundry and while she was out, Kate worked tirelessly to clean the house and get it ready for the lodgers and summer visitors they soon hoped to have. Kate boasted of her ability to do ten hours a day and 'then come up for more'. As soon as Catherine came home from work, she too put in several hours on the house and garden until she was ready to drop from exhaustion. Whenever she complained of being tired or depressed, Kate would say, 'Work it off, lass. You'll cope.' It was Kate's creed.

Nan helped whenever she could. She sent to Ireland for her daughter Maisie. The first Christmas they were all together was happy and serene. Kate knew that Catherine wanted a brass coal scuttle shaped like a helmet and on Christmas Day she and Nan presented the scuttle to Catherine, with a black-and-white fox-terrier puppy inside it. She had never had a dog – or any kind of pet – before and she was enchanted. Catherine called the puppy Terry and soon the mischievous little terrier was digging for rats in the garden and getting stuck up drainpipes. Terry was the first of Catherine's much-loved canine companions.

Once Christmas was over, disillusion began to tinge the initial euphoria. During the first violent storm of the winter, the roof leaked like a sieve – almost every pan and bowl in the house had to be used to catch the water pouring through. Some of the gullies between the different roof levels were blocked by leaves and moss and rain gushed through to the landing and down the stairs. A man was brought in to clear the gullies and patch some of the worst leaks. Then Catherine discovered the dry rot. The drawing-room floor had been replaced by the previous owners, but not the two-foot-high skirting boards that ran round the edge. Shortly after Catherine moved in, the Hoover went straight through the wood, revealing the ominous white shrouds of the fungus.

There was also trouble of a different kind. Kate found it difficult to cope with Maisie. Although Catherine described the child as 'an innocent, clinging thing wanting love', Kate did not like children and found living with mental illness or any kind of congenital defect unsettling. Plans to take in more people needing residential care were temporarily abandoned. Then Kate became jealous of Nan and her influence over Catherine. The affection and gratitude Catherine offered her friend could not be tolerated. Kate wanted all Catherine's affection for herself. Did Kate also suspect that Nan's relationship with Catherine crossed the boundaries of ordinary female friendship? Whatever it was, Kate tried very hard to separate Catherine from Nan. As both Kate and Nan were dominant, forceful women, the atmosphere in the house soon became unbearable. Nan and Maisie were forced to leave and go back into lodgings.

Throughout the summer of 1934 there was a steady stream of visitors, though no one stayed very long. Kate had begun to drink again, the obstacle of the long distance to the nearest bar having been overcome by getting the bottles delivered. And she began to practise what she called 'practical jokes' on the guests. Catherine believed that these were malicious and vindictive acts directed against herself. Others saw them as a kind of dementia brought on by drink.

The mildest acts involved the smearing of jam on doorhandles, which had Kate whooping with laughter at the victim's embarrassment. The more serious episodes caused Catherine considerable pain as well as inconvenience. On one occasion a scouring pad was put into the plate of scrambled egg served up for breakfast. Then, when Catherine had a French couple staying whom she particularly wanted to impress, Kate brought in one of her enormous and justly famous meat pies. When the crust was cut, Catherine found that she had inserted a scrubbing brush instead of a pie funnel. On another occasion, a mousetrap was spooned on to someone's plate. This was clearly beyond the normal range of the practical joke. The food was totally wasted. If, as Catherine believed, Kate was deliberately getting at her daughter, either consciously or subconsciously externalising a lifetime of anger because Catherine's birth had ruined her life, it is significant that Kate used the medium of food. But Kate did not just feel angry towards Catherine, she was also jealous – jealous of the independent life her daughter enjoyed (which had been denied to Kate), and jealous of everyone Catherine gave her affection to.

Catherine got on particularly well with the Frenchwoman, Mme X, and the closeness of their relationship seems, as with Nan, to have attracted Kate's jealousy and suspicion. Apparently unknown to Catherine, Mme X had fallen in love with her. She introduced Catherine to French literature – *The Pasquier Chronicles* by Duhamel, the short stories of Guy de Maupassant and Voltaire's *Candide* – here at last was someone Catherine could talk to about books and she was ecstatic. Kate felt excluded. Kate's hostile actions may also have been motivated by her awareness of the woman's real feelings towards Catherine.

But the pie did nothing to damage their friendship. Mme X invited Catherine over to France for a holiday, all expenses paid. Catherine had rarely needed a break so much. The visit was such a success that Catherine was invited again. But on the second occasion, what she discovered when she reached France was that the woman whose friendship she valued so much was interested in more than just her mind. As Catherine crossed the landing to go to bed for the night, Mme X embraced her and kissed her in a way that terrified Catherine. She left immediately. Catherine later told her agent John Smith that she had several times been the recipient of lesbian advances. It was, she recorded in her unpublished autobiography, something that had 'pursued' her since she was a teenager. This was one of the most upsetting episodes, because she genuinely cared for the woman and it made Catherine question her own sexuality and the way she appeared to others. What was it in herself that attracted married men and what she called 'unnatural women'? 'I became terribly afraid of what I had in me that attracted both men and women.'[6] There was also Catherine's involvement with Nan to be taken into account. Other women certainly saw Catherine and Nan as a couple and Mme X may well have made assumptions about Catherine's sexuality based on what she knew of this relationship, as did some of Catherine's other friends.

Her experience in France left Catherine shaken and drained. She returned almost as stressed as before. At the Hurst, although both Nan and Mme X had gone, Kate's manic behaviour continued. This was a period so painful that Catherine never liked to talk about it afterwards. It was something 'better left undisturbed'. She desperately wanted to be rid of Kate. On one occasion Kate began to scream at the dining table and then got up and ran up the stairs that went round the hall, screaming 'like a Bedlamite' from the banisters to the astonishment of the guests. There was also a money problem. Behind Catherine's back Kate was taking money off the guests as payment in advance and then spending it on drink. Davie, home on shore leave and staying at the Hurst, begged Catherine to give Kate another chance. Kate blackmailed Catherine emotionally – Catherine owed it to her mother to care for her in her old age and anyway, how would she manage the guesthouse without her help? Catherine tried to get Kate to promise to stop drinking. There were 'fights, reconciliations, promises . . . over and over'. Catherine told a friend that she had attempted suicide, and she began to have dreams about killing her mother.[7]

At Christmas things reached a climax. Nan was there with Catherine and there was a quarrel. Kate lined up four bottles of spirit on the sideboard, filled a half-pint glass with a mixture from all four and swallowed it. Then her aggression vented itself on Catherine. She picked up Davie's heavy, steel-capped stoker's boots from the hearth and threw them with all her force at Catherine's face. They missed by only a fraction of an inch. Further violence was averted by the presence of Nan, 'but for [her] intervention she would have had a corpse on her hands'.

The only possible solution was for Kate to move back into the flats, which were still under lease and vacant. Catherine furnished them from the Hurst so that Kate could take in lodgers and pay her own way. Nan and Maisie moved back into the house and Catherine employed a deaf cook, Mrs Webster, partly because she felt sorry for her and partly because she was cheap. But Catherine soon learned the truth of the saying 'you get what you pay for'. Mrs Webster was so incompetent 'she could burn water'.

Although Catherine now had Nan back under the same roof, 'life', she wrote later, 'was not only nerve-racking and hard but frightening'. The years from 1937 to 1940 were 'a time when I rarely smiled; a bitter period'. Catherine portrays herself, in *Our Kate*, as being frightened of Kate and what Kate might do. But in reality it was Nan she struggled with. Nan seems to have seen the Hurst as 'their' house, and Catherine as her partner, someone who was under an emotional obligation to her. Catherine was depressed at the situation she found herself in. She was also broke. Replacing the furniture at the Hurst and paying Mrs Webster's meagre wages left Catherine in difficult financial straits and, despite her talent for squirrelling money away for emergencies, she discovered that there was no money to pay the rates when they fell due. That evening, Catherine saw an advertisement in the *Hastings Observer*, seeking accommodation for twenty poor children from the Midlands who needed a fortnight's holiday. Catherine had two weeks' leave due from the laundry and with help from Nan and a friend who ran a bakery, she felt she could cope. She applied for the contract and was accepted. The agreement Catherine had to sign before the children arrived stipulated that any breakages and other damage would be Catherine's responsibility. Catherine was so desperate for the money, she didn't read the small print too closely. Within hours of the children's arrival most of Catherine's garden ornaments had been smashed as well as windows, and some of the antiques she was beginning to accumulate from the small shops in the old town were also damaged. By the time the children left, Catherine was thin to the point of emaciation and utterly exhausted; 'I'd had so much mental worry I was ready for jumping off somewhere'.[8] But she had the money to pay the rates and, apart from Nan and her daughter, she had the Hurst all to herself.

After the first happy months of their relationship, Catherine had begun to realise that Nan held her in an emotional noose. Catherine now needed her help to run the house and Nan and her daughter had become dependants. Catherine felt responsible for them and she complained that Nan played on this for all she was worth. Catherine gave Nan the security she craved for herself and Maisie, and Nan set out to make herself indispensable. It is a pity that we only have Catherine's side of the story, for Nan seems to have genuinely loved Catherine and to have devoted almost a decade of her life to trying to make Catherine happy. Without Nan or Kate, Catherine would never have managed to run the Hurst as a business as well as holding down a full-time job. Gradually, Catherine was attracting holidaymakers and paying guests. There were a number of semi-permanent lodgers; among them, an epileptic girl, Pansy, who often had fits during the night and a young anorexic called Muriel, who may have been the victim of sexual abuse. She was afraid of everyone and had a particular horror of men. Muriel's wealthy parents paid Catherine to look after her, since they couldn't cope with her at home, and Catherine was scathing about the way they beat her down to the last penny for it. There was also a retired Indian army officer, Captain David Evans, who lived on a small pension and sometimes couldn't pay his board, and a tuberculosis patient who was slowly wasting away and should really have been in a sanatorium.

Catherine rarely visited her mother and Kate never came to the Hurst because of Nan's presence there. When the lease on the flats came to an end, Kate took a larger terraced house and ran that as a boarding house. Catherine divided her time between the workhouse laundry, which she managed now as a matter of routine, and the Hurst – running the few hundred yards between the two. She was also finding time to write again. In her meal breaks and late at night in her room, she filled book after book with sketches of workhouse life, vignettes of the people who passed through the guesthouse, as well as poetry – writing generally in rhymed verse, which was the only kind of poetry she knew. She hid the exercise books in the airing cupboard. Catherine had little time for a social life – her one relaxation was a fencing class she attended one evening a week. This seemed a strange hobby for Catherine, whose work already physically exhausted her, but it provided an outlet for her destructive energies: 'with a foil in my hand I struck out at life'.

One evening Catherine made a duty call on Kate as she passed the house. Kate was relatively sober and insisted that her daughter meet her new lodger. Catherine demurred, as she was in a hurry, but Kate threw open the sitting-room door to reveal a slight figure, conscientiously marking exercise books. This was Catherine's first sight of Tom Cookson. Her first impression was of a small, timid man with 'beautiful hair and a kind face and a quiet voice'.

For Tom, the moment Catherine appeared in the doorway behind her mother was revelatory. He remembered her first words, prompted by nerves: 'Do you fence?' Fifty years later Tom wrote, 'I can still hear those words being spoken. The voice was strong; it was vibrant with life. I had heard nothing like it before. No, I hadn't overlooked that this girl, this woman, was beautiful; but it was the personality through the voice that was affecting me.' Catherine had by this time lost the strong Jarrow accent and the dialect phrases that characterised Kate's speech. Her voice 'sounded cultured; she articulated correctly, there was no deliberate effort whatsoever about her pronunciation'.[9] But it also had a fascinating lilt to it, a musical inflection that some people identified as Irish, but that was unmistakably 'Geordie'.

Tom was twenty-four and had recently graduated from Oxford University where he had studied mathematics – appropriately at St Catherine's College. Tom, like Catherine, had had a difficult life. He never talked about his early life at all. If asked, he would say, 'My life only began when I met Catherine.' Although he had been born in South Woodford, his family lived in Grays, a small, bleak town on the Essex coast between the Dartford tunnel and Tilbury. His parents were working class; his father had been employed as a verger (a kind of church caretaker), but had died in 1915 when Tom was three. His mother had remarried and Tom had a stepfather who treated him very well, but Tom was always aware of being the odd one out in a family of half-brothers and sisters. His home was happy on the surface of things and he was his mother's favourite child but, like Catherine, he was plagued by feelings of difference and isolation. His shyness and inhibition had been exacerbated by a feeling that his real father had somehow rejected him at birth, something his mother unconsciously encouraged by telling and retelling a story about how 'when he had been born his father had looked at him and exclaimed, "My God! isn't he ugly. Did you ever see a mouth like that?"'[10] Allegedly the family dog had also looked at the baby and run out of the house, never to be seen again. Because of this, Tom was afraid to laugh, keeping his lips closed or putting his hand over his mouth. The scars from Tom's childhood meant that he too, like Catherine, suffered from bouts of depression.

For Tom, education was the passport out of his environment. He won a scholarship to grammar school, where his brilliant mind was coached to pass the scholarship exams for Oxford. He went up on a bursary of £150 a year. At Oxford he distinguished himself both academically and on the sports field. But he found his financial circumstances and social background isolating – he had an accent usually identified as cockney. His stepfather was out of work at the time and the family could not afford to give him anything but moral support, so he worked as a crammer in the holidays to earn extra. His shyness and the endemic snobbery of the university meant that he made few friends there. When he met Catherine he had recently been appointed (out of several hundred applicants) maths teacher at Hastings Grammar School.

On the Friday after their first meeting, Tom called at the Hurst with the evening paper, having learned from Kate that Catherine's housekeeper usually did the football pools. The paper was only a pretext and Catherine was not surprised when Tom asked her if she would like to go to the cinema with him. Catherine accepted. Despite the age difference and the fact that they were poles apart in terms of education and religious belief, it was obvious from the first night that they had an empathy and understanding neither had ever felt for anyone else.

> In temperament and character, at least outwardly, Thomas Henry
> Cookson and I were at opposite poles, yet beneath the surface of
> flesh and bone, in the channels where the intangible but real life
> runs, we were one and we recognised this. I had what he needed
> – strength of purpose. He had what I needed, kindliness, a loving
> nature, a high sense of moral values, and above all he had what
> I needed most – a mind.

That first evening every moment that was not occupied by watching the screen was spent talking. Catherine was bursting to talk about Voltaire and to her great delight found that Tom had also read *Candide*. When Tom kissed her gently at the end of the evening, Catherine said that she knew that this was something very special.

It was soon obvious to everyone around them that they were involved in a serious love affair. Kate and Nan were appalled as they began to think about how this relationship would affect their own situations. Their jealousy of each other was put aside in view of a joint enemy. They agreed that Tom was totally unsuitable. He was a grammar school teacher, an Oxford graduate, a Protestant, six years younger than Catherine and two inches shorter. All these things were true, but their real motives were fear for their own future security. If Catherine were to marry Tom, Nan and her child would have to find a new home and Kate would no longer be able to count on Catherine to pay her debts. Catherine's loyalties would lie in a different direction.

With total selfishness Kate and Nan set about separating Catherine and Tom. Letters from one to the other were intercepted, lies and malicious stories were told. 'Devious wasn't the word for these two women.' Kate and Nan had no hesitation in blackening Catherine's reputation not only to Tom, but to others too. They tried to destroy 'the only thing I really valued, my good character'. There was plenty of material for them to twist for their purpose. Catherine had had a number of boyfriends – some of them married, so there were those who found the stories believable. Kate knew all about the Frenchwoman too and she had a good ally in Nan, who was always 'full of blarney' and willing to spread a good tale.

Eventually Kate and Nan succeeded in their objective. Catherine's relationship with Tom was broken off. She was too old for him. The priest and the nuns told her she couldn't marry a Protestant unless he was received into the Catholic church, and Tom, at that time, was not prepared to do something so contrary to his own beliefs. Tom was moreover a timid and diffident young man, easy for two ruthless older women to discourage with ridicule. Both Tom and Catherine accepted that their love affair was impossible. The breach between them was, on the face of it, an amicable one. For Catherine there was a sense of relief that she had escaped commitment and the risk of being badly hurt again. Catherine's early experiences with men had made her afraid to give herself to anyone either physically or emotionally. The teenage wish to be a nun may have been denied by Father Bradley, but the fears that had prompted it were still there. A close friend who knew her for more than forty years said that 'despite her extraordinary generosity she never perhaps gave herself – she was never, I felt, truly emotionally warm towards anyone, not perhaps even to Tom'.[11] If this is true, it was very sad for both Nan and Tom, who loved Catherine deeply.

Once the possibility of a relationship with Tom Cookson had been extinguished, Kate and Nan were prepared to leave Catherine in peace. Kate had other troubles. She was drinking heavily almost every day, neglecting her lodgers, and had accumulated sizable debts.

She turned to Catherine for help, but Catherine had reached breaking point. When Davie McDermott wrote to say that he had a new job on a weekly boat out of Shields and wanted his wife back home to look after him, Catherine more or less forced Kate to return – an act which took great resolve. She paid Kate's extensive debts, took over the remainder of the lease on the empty house and put her on the train north. At the station, Catherine almost gave way again. Kate 'was crying so much she couldn't see me. She was sober and sad. She was the Kate I loved . . . She was my mother. I had a duty to her because she was ill. What did it matter what she had done to me, perhaps God meant that I should suffer in this way . . .' Catherine's mind was tortured by guilt and grief. She was almost ready to put her arms around Kate and tell her she could stay when she heard a voice inside her head shouting 'Don't be such a bloody fool'. She watched Kate board the train, almost fainting with the relief. 'Thank God it was over. I was free again. And I must never, never, never, let her live with, or be near me ever again in my life.'

Catherine held firm. When Davie died the following year in a mysterious accident, Catherine refused to have Kate back.

When Tom returned from his summer holiday in 1937, he found his landlady gone. Catherine had promised Kate that she would look after her remaining lodgers and so she gave Tom the option of coming to the Hurst or finding new lodgings. He chose the Hurst. Once they were under the same roof, it was a very short time before both realised the depth of their feelings for each other. Catherine entered into an understanding with Tom, though they were never officially engaged. For the next three years they lived under the same roof but, because of Nan, 'for three years we daren't even look at each other'.[12] Never once did Catherine allow Tom into her bedroom – which she still seems to have been sharing either with Nan or with the young epileptic girl she looked after. Those who didn't know about Nan speculated that Catherine and Tom were either lovers or secretly married already. Even today, most people who read Catherine's published account of this period, which doesn't mention Nan, find it puzzling that Catherine, who declared herself passionately in love and a 'reluctant virgin', took so long to get round to marrying Tom. His commitment was not in question, but over the next few years he began to doubt that she would ever marry him. Catherine procrastinated. There was always some obstacle to be overcome; some reason why the time was not right.

Apart from Catherine's reluctance to commit herself, the main problem was her relationship with Nan, who was now in her forties. She and Catherine had made a home together, had been living together almost continuously since 1931, and Catherine was the centre of Nan's life. When Catherine proposed making a life with Tom instead, it tore Nan apart. Once more there were terrible scenes – what Catherine described as 'open warfare'. Nan's passion for Catherine led her to extremes of behaviour. On one occasion Catherine was going to the Saturday-evening dance at St Helen's with Tom and Captain Evans. Just as she finished getting dressed and was ready to go out, Nan came into the room and told her that she mustn't go. If Catherine went to the dance with Tom, Nan said, she would hang herself while Catherine was out. 'You won't find me alive when you come back.'[13] Nan told Catherine that she would have her death on her conscience for the rest of her life and it would ruin her chance of happiness with Tom. Catherine went downstairs to the hallway where the men were waiting for her and told them that they would have to go without her – she couldn't be responsible for what Nan might do if she went with them. The Captain, older and a more experienced judge of character, told Catherine not to be a fool. Nan was emotionally blackmailing her. Nothing would happen. But Catherine was too afraid of what Nan might do to believe him. She told him that if Nan did do 'something silly' she wouldn't be able to live with herself afterwards. What Tom's feelings were can only be guessed at. He said nothing to Catherine, but she was aware of his eyes on her; 'Tom just stood looking at me'. The men went out to the dance and Catherine went back upstairs to an emotional scene that lasted until the early hours of the morning, 'Nan screaming and carrying on'. Nan threatened Catherine that if she ever tried to marry Tom, she 'would do something to stop it'. Catherine was terrified of what Nan might do to Tom. 'When women are jealous they are stark, staring mad. I never imagined jealousy to this extent.'[14] According to Catherine, incidents like this took place all the time.

Catherine often asked herself, later, why she had put up with it. 'Why didn't I throw the lot of them out? Incompetent cooks, possessive friends, sponging lodgers?' Publicly, Catherine answered the question by saying that 'anyone who does me a good turn has me for life ... [Nan] had been good to me when I was lonely.' But when she wrote that charitable paragraph in Our Kate, Catherine was trying to conceal the truth about their relationship. There was another story which concerned certain letters that Nan had kept whose content was potentially damaging. Catherine never wrote about it, but she often told friends that Nan had done her

> a great evil ... If you have been kind and good to somebody and it's returned by evil, that's another long, long story. It's a terrible story ... That a person can want to ruin another person that they are supposed to love ... The result of it was that I learned how to hate, to hate with such intensity that I knew that if I let it have the upper hand, my future life would be ruined.[15]

The letters that Nan had in her possession gave her a powerful hold over Catherine. If she had shown them to Tom it would probably have ended their relationship. Nan also had public opinion on her side. She told everyone that Catherine was throwing her out, and Catherine was very upset because people liked Nan and believed Nan's side of the story rather than hers. In the end Catherine had to buy Nan off, like a divorced husband, in order to get rid of her. She bought another property and set Nan up in her own guesthouse. Catherine paid for it by selling off the garden as building land, which paid for half of it, and by taking out another mortgage, which almost bankrupted her.

Catherine should now have been free to marry Tom. Once Kate's house had been leased out again, there was adequate money. Her financial situation was secure. She owned two large properties, had money coming in from paying guests, and there was Tom's salary as well. The lodging house was profitable enough by August 1939 for Catherine to give up her job at the laundry. She had been there for ten years and the strain of having two jobs had been affecting her health for a long time. There was also friction with other members of the staff – particularly the matron, Mrs Silverlock. Catherine accused her of trying to run her life: 'she, too, wanted to dominate my life, and pick my friends'. Catherine was never an easy person to employ and always had problems relating to other women. But even though Catherine had settled her 'private wars', as she called them, given up her job and was now at home all day at the Hurst, she still would not agree a date for her marriage to Tom. At the last hurdle she was afraid. Her hope of happiness with Tom was undermined by threats from Nan, the years of attrition with Kate, money worries and the conflict of faith. Twice in all her troubles with Kate and Nan she had stopped going to church, though it filled her with fear. Each time she was persuaded back into her religion. The priest and the nuns from the convent were frequent visitors at the Hurst and they were not prepared to let her go.

How much influence the relationship with Nan had had on Catherine's growing religious unrest is difficult to assess. During these years Catherine's view of her religion certainly changed. She no longer felt compelled to confess every impure thought to the priests and was more aware of the essential humanity – sometimes flawed – of those who wore a priest's robes. Catherine had been shocked as a teenager when Lily MacGuire told her she'd seen a priest kissing a woman. Nan, much more worldly than Catherine, had been able to open her eyes to many other things. Since she left the northeast, Catherine had not always been a regular church-goer, but when she was depressed or unhappy, she still turned to the Catholic church for comfort and guidance, though she was increasingly at odds with its dogma.

In Hastings Catherine attended St Mary Star of the Sea, a small nineteenth-century church in the Old Town, at the top end of the High Street almost opposite Charles Dickens's cottage. Catherine's supplications were never made directly to God, always through intermediaries such as the Holy Family, the saints – particularly her patron St Catherine – and the martyrs. Even Jesus was too remote and had to be approached through his mother.

Jesus was more frightening than the rest, for he was dead, dead and aweful, so dead that no resurrection could ever bring him to life again. Every Sunday, in church, I sat opposite to him, a life-size Jesus, just taken down from the cross, his limp body trailing to the ground from his mother's arms, his blood realistically red and dripping from his wounds. He was naked but for a loincloth, and all his body had that sickly pallor of death. He was quite dead, and Easter Sunday could do nothing to bring him to life again.[16]

Catherine also had problems with Communion. Since she was a small child taking her first Communion, Catherine had found it difficult to swallow the Host. The idea that the wafer actually turned into the flesh of Jesus Christ in her mouth was totally repugnant. 'This conception of flesh and blood was rejected by both my stomach and my mind.' But Catherine continued to go to Mass, because the spiritual side of her personality was always attracted by its beauty – the music and the words and the setting – and she continued to struggle with the rationalisation of her faith.

Catherine's relationship with Tom only increased her doubts. Tom had been brought up in the Church of England. He was a Christian, but he was not a Catholic. They had many ardent discussions on the subject. Catherine simply could not believe that Tom was doomed to Hell simply because he belonged to a different branch of the Christian faith. She was deeply troubled and the forces that would precipitate her serious breakdown a few years later were already warring inside her head: her hatred of Kate, the shame of her illegitimacy, her need for love and physical intimacy, her fear of sex, and the demands of her religion – 'this great dominating, fear-filled religion, a religion that has kept people bound to it by terror of the hereafter'.[17] There were still two Catherines – the Siamese twins – one, a laughing, vivacious extrovert who played tennis, organised evening singsongs for her lodgers and fancy-dress parties for her friends in the garden; and the other twin, the fear-filled, phobic girl who had once given up the chance to go to Italy simply because she wouldn't have been able to attend Mass every Sunday.

Once she had given up her job at the laundry, Catherine had more time to write. She had accumulated quite a few manuscripts in the airing cupboard and one day she showed them to Tom. 'I was with her on the landing . . . and she opened the door of the linen cupboard and took out a number of notebooks and a stack of sheets of paper all covered with pencilled writing, and handed them to me.'[18] Tom was a mathematician, not a literary critic, and he was astounded by what he read. The spelling and grammar were atrocious, but the talent for storytelling and character creation was self-evident. He recalled later that these early stories were in the style she used later for her lightest and most humorous novels, such as *Hamilton* and *Bill Bailey*.

Tom couldn't give Catherine the type of feedback she badly needed if she was to become a writer. One of her other lodgers, the man who was dying of TB, had had a considerable education and liked to be thought of as an intellectual. Catherine gathered enough courage from Tom's response to her work to ask this man to read some of her stories. Tom remembered how Catherine had had 'a great longing for a few words of praise', and how devastated she had been when the man returned her work with the comment that it was utterly worthless. He was a scholar, and not equipped in either personality or education to see in Catherine's early efforts any spark worth encouraging. Catherine made a bonfire in the garden and burned every scrap of paper in the cupboard. Forty years later Tom still cringed when he thought of 'all the humour and pathos that went up in flames'.[19] This stoic ruthlessness directed against herself was characteristic of Catherine. The process was, in this case, cathartic, allowing her to move on. She stopped writing 'for about a fortnight' before beginning again.

War broke out in the autumn of 1939, but even that did not change Catherine's mind about marriage. She still put it off, saying she felt that they should wait until her personal situation was 'more settled'. During the first months of the war Nan joined the army (Catherine does not record what happened to the unfortunate Maisie), Mrs Webster went to take charge of Nan's lodging house under Catherine's supervision, and a new – and much superior – cook was employed, called Gladys. The Hurst was relatively empty at the outbreak of war. Catherine had only her two female residents, Tom and the Captain. She was told that unless she accepted a quota of either children or blind evacuees, her house would be requisitioned. After her experiences with the children from the Midlands, Catherine opted for the blind.

She had expected a dozen women, but when the coach drew up at the front door, twelve dejected men evacuated from the East End of London were helped out of it. The eldest of them was ninety, bedridden and senile; the youngest a nineteen-year-old boy who was totally blind. Few of the men were clean, and some of them looked, Catherine remarked, as if they had been sleeping in their clothes for years. One of them was accompanied by his wife, which meant that there were actually thirteen people to accommodate.

The months that followed were some of the most physically taxing of Catherine's life. Tom was filled with wonder and astonishment at Catherine's abilities: 'the work and responsibility this young woman took on was mind boggling'.[20] For twelve pounds a week she had to feed, clothe, wash and nurse a dozen men, plus an extra wife and the two anorexic and epileptic girls, with help only from Gladys during the day and Tom after school in the evenings. Some of the men were incontinent and their filthy underwear and bedlinen could not be sent to the laundry. Catherine could not bear to touch the soiled items with her hands, and used to put them in the bath and tread them clean with her feet. She was also bleeding every day from her nose or mouth – sometimes internally as well, having attacks of vomiting and suffering from deep depression. It took her a long time to acknowledge that she needed help and when she did finally go to the doctor he diagnosed 'nervous debility' and prescribed rest. Catherine had to repress hysterical laughter.

Talk of a German invasion provided a new source of fear for Catherine. Within a few weeks Hastings was considered too unsafe for evacuees and she was told that her blind men were to be moved on. Pansy, the epileptic girl, had to go to hospital, and Muriel was sent back to her reluctant parents. There was now talk of Tom's school being evacuated, and it seemed only a matter of time before he was called up. With Nan safely out of the way in the army, there was no obvious reason why Catherine and Tom should not get married. When Tom was told that the school was going to St Albans at the end of June, Catherine went to a shop in Hastings and was measured for a wedding dress, but she was still vacillating and would not set a date.

In the third week of May a letter arrived at the Hurst from Nan. She told Catherine that a friend of hers, another army officer, was coming to Hastings on Saturday for a fortnight and she asked if Catherine could provide her with accommodation. Catherine said she knew immediately that the woman was being sent 'to spy on me' and that this was another bid by Nan to separate her from Tom. Catherine was convinced that if this other woman came, 'there would be another cleavage' between Tom and herself, though she never explains why.[21] But Catherine was afraid that this time she might lose him for good. Tom had just left for school. Catherine made a sudden decision. She ran to the gate and called after Tom as he walked up the street, 'We'll be married on Saturday.' Tom was absolutely elated, although he didn't at this point know what had prompted Catherine's change of mind. He had given up all hope of ever persuading her. 'I was so happy,' Tom said, 'I ran all the way to school.'

PART THREE

❖

The Thinking Years
1940–1950

I will seek beauty all my days.

Within the dark chaos of a troubled world I
will seek and find some Beauteous Thing.

I will seek beauty all my days, and in my quest
I shall not be dismayed.

Minnie Aumonier

10

Katie McMullen is dead . . . Long live
Catherine Cookson! Mrs Catherine Cookson.

The ceremony was arranged for two o'clock on Saturday 1 June
1940, just a couple of weeks before Catherine's thirty-fourth birthday. As soon as Catherine had made the decision to marry Tom, she
dealt swiftly with the obstacles that had previously seemed insur-
mountable. She went first to the priest and told him that she wanted
to get married at the end of the week. Father Treacy refused. It
wasn't possible, he told her. He reiterated his original arguments.
Tom wasn't a Catholic and would have to be received into the church
before a wedding could take place. But Catherine knew that this
wasn't strictly true. There were such things as dispensations. She
could be married to Tom if he signed an agreement that their children
would be brought up in the Catholic church. Tom was willing to do
this. Catherine told the priest that if he wouldn't marry them it
would have to be a civil wedding, the Catholic equivalent of living
in sin. She was amazed at her own temerity – she had never stood
up to a priest before. Eventually Father Treacy agreed and Catherine
went to the register office to purchase the necessary licence. Marriages in a Catholic church had to have an attendant registrar.

Catherine didn't buy a new dress to wear for her wedding. She
wore a favourite blue dress she had bought second-hand from a
mail-order catalogue. This was something she had begun to do a
couple of years earlier. The dresses were good quality, sometimes
model gowns, worn only a few times and 'as new'. They provided
Catherine with clothes suitable for the lady she felt she had become,
at a price that did not offend her compulsive need to save every

possible penny. Ordering clothes by mail also meant that Catherine did not have to go shopping. She felt nauseous and anxious every time she entered a shop. This irrational but uncontrollable fear had grown from her childhood terror of the shameful weekly visits to Bob Gompertz's pawnshop; her memories of vomiting with fear after Kate stole the bolt of cloth from the draper's in Jarrow, or guiltily throwing up into the gutter when she herself stole comics from the corner shop. Catherine's fear of shops was to last for the rest of her life.

Tom bought Catherine a small fur cape as a wedding present. He knew she longed for such luxuries, but would never buy them for herself. Tom didn't feel it was possible to buy her a bouquet to carry – 'I never bought Kitty flowers . . . it wouldn't have gone down very well . . . I think that's because of the first years I knew her, she kept a book in which she wrote down every half penny.' But there was another reason why Catherine didn't like flowers. They made her sneeze, and sneezing often brought on a bad nosebleed – something she didn't want on her wedding day. However, she did consent to wear a small corsage.

Although Catherine wrote to Kate, telling her what she was going to do, and Tom wrote to his mother, neither family was invited to the wedding. It was to be a completely private ceremony – ostensibly to prevent Nan from arriving to disrupt the proceedings. The Silverlocks were invited, but no one else was told until Friday evening, when Catherine told one of the staff at the grammar school. However, even though she claimed to be terrified that 'Nan would do something' to prevent her marrying Tom, Catherine wrote to Nan telling her that she was getting married; 'I felt I had to.'[2] It was a curious thing to do. Either Catherine was subconsciously hoping that Nan would step in to rescue her at the last moment, or felt that, after a nine-year relationship, she owed it to Nan to be honest with her. Catherine said that she always forgave Nan her behaviour because, however outrageous she was, 'she did it out of love'.

On Saturday morning Nan telephoned the Hurst to say that she had been loading ammunition on a lorry at Dover and would be passing through Hastings about twelve o'clock. Nan insisted that Catherine must meet her at her house. Catherine was already dressed for the wedding, her hair and make-up done, but she felt she had to go, otherwise Nan would come to the Hurst and 'create a scene'.

When she got to Nan's house, the lorry was parked outside and three soldiers were in the kitchen being plied with tea by Mrs Webster. Catherine and Nan talked in another room; Catherine never revealed any details of their conversation. Afterwards Nan walked her to the door and said 'So you're going to do it?', as though she could hardly believe that Catherine was finally going to abandon her. Catherine didn't reply. She went down the steps and out of the gate, feeling Nan's eyes on her and expecting at any moment to have a bullet in her back before she reached the corner. Apparently Nan had threatened to shoot Catherine if she went through with it. Catherine believed her because she knew that Nan had her service pistol with her and a lorry full of guns and ammunition parked outside. Catherine was terrified the whole length of the street. 'I was walking, and then I realised that I was round that bend and I was alive. I was alive! And I couldn't believe it. I just fell onto the railings and just hung onto the railings. I thought I was going to pass out, because I was alive! I was alive!'[3]

Tom taught until twelve thirty on Saturday mornings. He hurried back to the Hurst, only to be told by Gladys that Catherine had gone to meet Nan. He was beside himself, believing that Catherine would not come back. When she returned she found him in 'a dreadful state'. There was only just time for him to change and take a taxi with Catherine to St Mary Star of the Sea. No one else was aware of the drama that had preceded their arrival at the church. The master of the workhouse, George Silverlock, gave Catherine away, although he had broken his arm the day before and had it in a sling so that Catherine had to walk up the aisle on the other side of him. Mrs Silverlock, who had always tried to be a second mother to Catherine – something Catherine didn't always appreciate – acted as the other witness. Although Tom and Catherine had tried to keep the ceremony secret, there were a number of well-wishers in the church, including some of Tom's pupils.

The priest went through the ceremony swiftly, as if it was something unpleasant he wanted to get over as quickly as possible. Catherine remembered that the service was 'short, even ugly', but as with Kate's wedding, this may simply have been Catherine colouring it with her own negative emotions. She and Tom were shaking with nerves, still afraid that Nan might arrive to create an unpleasant scene in the church. In the vestry, signing the register, Catherine and Tom gave the same address and Catherine gave her occupation as 'guesthouse proprietress'. For the first and last time in her life she had to put her real name on the register alongside that of her father. To describe herself as Catherine Ann Davies, child of Alexander Davies, deceased, added a further sense of unreality to the occasion. In the middle of all the happiness and laughter, the kissing and congratulations, she felt only 'this great sadness inside me'. This feeling of loneliness and grief was a symptom of the underlying clinical depression that Catherine was suffering from – exacerbated by the guilt and fear she felt at having dealt such a terrible blow to Nan.

But to others she seemed radiantly happy as she left the church on Tom's arm, Catherine, in her high heels and big-brimmed hat, a good six inches taller than Tom. They were snapped by one of Tom's pupils with a Box Brownie and it is the only photograph of their marriage that exists. Tom treasured it. Catherine described her wedding later as the act that legitimised her – 'He made an illegitimate legitimate by giving me his name'.[4] Now she had a name that fully belonged to her and to which she had a proper legal entitlement. Katie McMullen was a creature of the past. Catherine Cookson, or Kitty as Tom always called her, was going to be the self-possessed, secure and socially acceptable person that Katie McMullen had always aspired to be. The wife of a grammar-school teacher, owner of a large house. Catherine really believed that she could now leave her old identity behind. It was yet another new start, another part to act out.

Catherine's delight in burying her past concealed the fact that she was in such poor health. She had been suffering regular haemorrhages and attacks of nervous vomiting, overworking and undereating for far too long. The fur cape in her wedding photograph hides just how thin she had become. But a photograph taken with the blind evacuees outside the Hurst a few months earlier shows how emaciated she was, compared to photographs taken in 1936. She was also in a very precarious mental state and had been treated by a doctor for several months for depression.

Back at the Hurst there was a small celebration with wine and cake. Kate sent a telegram wishing them well, but to Catherine's great relief her mother didn't come. Instead Kate had organised her own celebration in Jarrow, which Catherine heard about later from Mary. Kate had been very drunk, excusing herself by saying, 'Whoever heard of a dry wedding?'

Afterwards, Catherine and Tom took the train to London for a brief honeymoon and were unwittingly caught up in the evacuation of Dunkirk. Until then, Catherine's only experience of war had been a few false alarms and the occasional uncomfortable night on air-raid alert. But at Tonbridge station the platform was crowded with exhausted and filthy French and British troops, some of them wounded. Catherine was told that France had fallen. Thinking of her French friends now in German-occupied territory, and confronted with the realities of human suffering caused by war – 'the men looked so bitter, so angry, so full of despair' – Catherine cried all the way to London.

They booked into the Charing Cross Hotel, shocked at the extent of wartime restrictions on the life of the city and the very real fear of invasion present in everyone's minds. People were saying, 'France has gone . . . We're next.' They went to the Comedy Theatre to see Ibsen's *Ghosts* and found almost all the seats empty for what was to be the production's last performance. The play represented the culture Catherine longed for, but it was an interesting choice, given its theme of tainted heredity. Tom kept the tickets. He had no qualms about admitting that he was a sentimental man – 'men who say they're not are missing something from their lives'.[5]

The following morning Catherine and Tom went out to Grays, Essex, to meet his family. Although Tom's mother must have felt some misgivings about her son marrying a woman so much older than himself who was also a Catholic (marriages across religious boundaries were viewed much more seriously then than now), the family welcomed Catherine warmly. In the evening, Tom and Catherine travelled back to Hastings, both feeling a reaction to the elation of the previous day. Tom was developing a cold that would turn into flu and Catherine's nose started bleeding and wouldn't stop. Though neither said much, there was also apprehension on Catherine's part about the physical side of their marriage, what Catherine called 'that first unsatisfactory business'. Like many women, she expected the loss of her virginity to be a momentous event. Afterwards her only thought was 'is that what all the fuss is about?'[6] They were both sexually innocent – something very difficult to imagine today for a woman of almost thirty-four and a man of twenty-seven. Sexual compatibility can sometimes take months to achieve even now, with all the available handbooks and information about sex. But before the 'enlightenment' of the sixties, many women knew only the stark biological facts of the sexual act; most were completely ignorant of the existence of orgasms or methods of contraception. This information was often deliberately withheld on the grounds that if women know that sexual pleasure could be obtained without consequences, mass immorality would result and society would break down!

This was the principle on which Catherine had been brought up – girls were kept chaste by fear and ignorance. Catherine certainly seems to have been afraid of her own sexuality. On her own admission, she and Tom didn't 'come together again' for many weeks after their wedding night.[7] Catherine made the excuse that over the next month or so first Tom had flu, then she had a succession of nosebleeds and then there was all the upheaval of packing up the house for evacuation – none of which seems particularly convincing. Tom was too timid and considerate to push Catherine into something she didn't want to do.

By the end of June Catherine had packed up her more precious possessions to store in the attic, emptied the Hurst of its remaining lodgers and put her personal belongings into suitcases ready for evacuation. She had resigned herself to the fact that the Hurst would probably now be requisitioned, and that there might even be an invasion. When Catherine closed the front door in July 1940 she didn't know whether she would ever see her home again. Nor did she have any idea where she and Tom were going to live.

Like many evacuees, she found herself sitting on her suitcases in a hall that had been commandeered for the purpose, clutching a small, lively fox terrier, waiting to be given temporary lodgings in St Albans. She and Tom eventually found a small flat for themselves above a shop in Victoria Street, opposite the police station. It had only two main rooms, a bedroom and a sitting room, but the kitchen was big enough to contain a dining table and there was a separate bathroom. The Cooksons were together for the first time on equal ground and Catherine felt very happy. This was not an emotion that had featured greatly in her childhood and there had been few moments of it in the preceding years of emotional warfare. For the first time in her life, Catherine was in a secure relationship with someone who adored her, who had stubbornly served a four-year apprenticeship in order to marry her, who had held firm against the worst assaults of her mother and Nan, and who believed in her as a person of worth. Their friendship grew daily.

For the first time Catherine also had unlimited leisure. Cleaning the small flat, shopping and cooking for herself and Tom took no time at all for someone who had previously managed the Hurst and an entire platoon of lodgers. Free time was something Catherine couldn't cope with. When asked in an interview how she relaxed when she wasn't working, she replied brusquely, 'I don't.' As Tom put it, 'To her, work is the essence of being; not the type of work . . . it is work itself.' Work was the means of blocking out all her fears, of silencing the negative voice of her Siamese twin.

Catherine decided to use the time to address her lack of education. As Tom's wife she felt she should try to be worthy of her position; she didn't want him to be ashamed of her. She had been mortified when introduced to one of Tom's colleagues who had also been evacuated with the school and found herself being asked advice on how to get his shirts clean. In the eyes of Tom's colleagues, Catherine felt she was still an upstart from the workhouse laundry. So she set out to make herself into a wife Tom could be proud of.

The public library was quite close to their flat and Catherine drew up a reading list of about a hundred books, based on Lord Chesterfield's recommendations to his son, and began to put herself through a rigorous course of English literature. Catherine could hardly wait to get home from the library and experience what she described as the 'golden moment . . . when the pages of a book open to reveal a light, like a candle in the night, so bright it illuminates the mind'.[8] She aimed to borrow a new book every day, starting with Chaucer. She progressed through Shakespeare, Milton and Donne, through the eighteenth-century rationalism of Dryden and Pope, to nineteenth-century romanticism (much more to her taste), and even attempted twentieth-century experimental fiction such as *Finnegans Wake*. She read the classics of history, including Gibbon's *Decline and Fall of the Roman Empire*, and ventured into philosophy, reading Erasmus, Descartes, Plato and Socrates. Much of it she found incomprehensible and there was no one to enlighten her, but certain passages leaped out at her and were copied down so that she could return to them again and again. One of these was the Apologia from Plato's *Last Days of Socrates*. Not only did Socrates' words echo her own feeling that the more she learned, the more aware she became of how ignorant she actually was, but it also showed her a new kind of ethic, based on the morality of truth and love, which she would use in the future to replace the troublesome ethics of her Catholic faith.

I knew that here were all the ingredients for a good life. I could never hope to follow them implicitly, but should I try and fail I would have no fear of his censure, whereas when I aimed to follow Christ's teachings and failed I was consumed with guilt and had to run to a priest and tell him of my sins, and ask him to ask Christ to forgive me.[9]

Catherine's literary tastes were always towards the didactic: 'Good plain writing, no hyperbole.' Most fiction bored her. Though she did enjoy the Brontës, Jane Austen, J. D. Salinger and the religious novels of Lloyd C. Douglas, years later she could still say emphatically, 'I never read for pleasure, only for instruction.' When a friend lent her Patrick White's celebrated novel *Riders in the Chariot*, Catherine returned it with the words, 'Well, he's got a good story, but he doesn't know how to write it!'[10] This blind spot towards other novelists was to have a big influence on her own writing, which she was also using her leisure time to develop. Catherine longed to talk to someone about the things she was learning. Tom's field of expertise was in mathematics and logic, and attempts to discuss literature with his colleagues at the grammar school ended in humiliation. One of her favourite poets was Ella Wheeler Wilcox, and she found her choice ridiculed by the men she talked to. She had no intellectual armoury with which to respond. Catherine didn't know how to pronounce unfamiliar words, or marshal an argument. Time and again she was put down. Neither her delight in knowledge nor her 'urgent groping' to acquire it were acknowledged by any of the educated men she met.

The poor state of Catherine's physical health was in complete contrast to her emotional happiness. She was still far too thin. War-time rations did not provide the kind of diet Catherine needed to build up her strength. She was also very anaemic from the frequent nosebleeds that plagued her. Meat and other iron-rich foods were hard to obtain and she was not in good shape to cope with the extra demands of pregnancy. Within a couple of weeks of her arrival in St Albans, Catherine had begun to feel ill and was aware that she had missed a period. When she was late for another, aware of her ignorance in matters of human biology, Catherine went to see a local GP, a woman, who told her that she was pregnant. There was no reason to doubt it. She was a married woman, had missed her periods and was being sick in the mornings. Of course she was pregnant.

Catherine reacted with disbelief. She told the doctor quite emphatically that she couldn't possibly be pregnant. 'No, I'm not. I just know I'm not.' Was her husband impotent? the doctor asked. Catherine felt too embarrassed to explain that she had not allowed Tom to make love to her since their wedding night. She refused to accept that a single sexual encounter with Tom could have made her pregnant. This obstinacy ran completely counter to Catherine's belief in Kate's statement that she had conceived Catherine from one moment of weakness and Catherine's own insistence that she had held on to her virginity because she was convinced that she would 'fall' the first time, just like her mother. Now she could not accept the idea that she might be having a child. The doctor told Catherine to come back in a month's time 'and we'll see which one of us is right'. Catherine went home and told Tom, 'I'm not going back to her again – she says I'm pregnant.' Tom looked at her and said, 'Well, you could be.' But Catherine refused to listen to him either. 'We didn't talk about things like that, or discuss anything.'[11]

Unwilling to wait for another month, Catherine sought a second opinion. The next doctor she saw had been brought out of retirement to fill the position of someone called up for war work. Not only was his knowledge of medicine almost half a century out of date, he had been a naval doctor whose working experience had been confined to men. By now Catherine had not had a period for three months and was suffering from morning sickness so severe she spent most of her time in bed. The doctor felt Catherine's stomach and told her what she wanted to hear. She wasn't pregnant. He focused on one of the most troublesome symptoms of her pregnancy and talked about 'a stopped bowel'. Catherine had suffered from constipation ever since she was a child. Rose's cure had been to insert a piece of washing soap into Catherine's rectum and hold her over a steaming chamber pot of boiling water. The St Albans doctor's solution was almost as horrific. 'If anything can scoot it out of you this will,' he told Catherine. Twice a week over a month he prescribed a French emetic no longer obtainable in England since the fall of France – something one suspects was used to procure abortions (strong purgatives were a frequently used back-street method). The emetic caused diarrhoea and sickness so severe that Catherine was confined to bed. Then she remembered the doctor coming to see her, examining her internally, then sitting on the edge of the mattress to tell her, almost apologetically, that they had both been wrong – she was indeed pregnant, about four months by now. The emetics he had used were powerful enough to have induced a miscarriage – the miracle was that it hadn't happened. Catherine wondered for the rest of her life whether they had in fact harmed her baby. It was another source of guilt. If she had only believed the first doctor she had consulted . . .

The incident raises a number of questions. If Catherine believed that her mother had become pregnant from a single sexual encounter, then why could she not accept that she herself was pregnant? Was her naval doctor really so ignorant and naive? Or did he interpret her denial of her pregnancy as a desire to terminate it and act accordingly? In the days of private medicine the euphemistic prescription of emetics and other cathartic substances was much more common than is possible today when medical practitioners and pharmacists are tightly regulated. Catherine used this back-street knowledge in her novel *The Obsession*, where the young doctor refuses to prescribe a laxative he knows is being asked for to bring on a miscarriage. In *Colour Blind*, the corrupt midwife sells a potion that will guarantee the baby is stillborn. The complex morality of abortion is discussed more fully in *Fenwick Houses*, where the worldly Mollie offers help when Christine Winter becomes pregnant for the second time. Although Christine will not consent to go to a professional abortionist because this would be a sin meriting eternal damnation, she is prepared to swallow emetics, because then it would not be a deliberate act. 'If I took the stuff and it worked, the child would come away in a sort of miscarriage.'

In October Catherine received a letter from a family friend in Jarrow telling her that Kate was ill. All Catherine's feelings of guilt and anxiety about her mother were immediately reactivated. Catherine was herself still in very poor health, confined to bed in the aftermath of the doctor's maltreatment, suffering daily nosebleeds and exhausted by anaemia. For the good of the child she was carrying, she knew she should have stayed there. But she became consumed with fear that Kate might die before she had seen her again – if not from this illness, then from a bomb or through drink. The spectre of Davie McDermott's death was constantly on her mind. Catherine had travelled north a year earlier to help Kate to sort out the problems this had caused. While on the way to board his ship, on his sixty-second birthday, Davie had been found floating in the docks late at night with his pockets weighed down by beer bottles. The coroner brought in a verdict of accidental death and so Catherine had been able to help Kate claim a sum of money in compensation from his employers. Knowing Kate's weakness, she had arranged for the £200 to be paid to Kate in weekly instalments like a pension. But as soon as Catherine returned to Hastings, Kate persuaded the company that she needed the money in a lump sum to set herself up in the guesthouse business again. By the time Catherine received the letter, Kate had managed to drink most of the money and was once again in debt.

Wartime travel was difficult. Catherine and Tom arrived in London in the middle of a huge air raid and had to take refuge in one of the underground shelters. When they finally managed to board the sleeper for Newcastle, they had the eerie experience of travelling northwards overnight in complete darkness, in order to avoid becoming the target of enemy planes. To underline the danger, there was an air-raid warning in South Shields almost as soon as they had left the train.

Kate was no longer living in William Black Street, but in rooms over the very shop where Catherine had had to queue for beer as a child. When she arrived, she found her mother looking better than she had at the time of her last visit. Kate told Catherine that she'd had a cold, but that she was over it now. There was nothing wrong with her.

The long winter trek north and the stress of the air raids in Newcastle and London took their toll on Catherine's already fragile health. She was never well after they came back and spent most of her time in bed. When she wasn't reading, she occupied herself by writing a book of poems for her unborn child. They were to be humorous and simple, in the nursery-rhyme genre.

> He said the clock wanted taking to bits
> And when I did it he nearly had fits.
> Fancy making such an e . . . nor . . . mous scene!
> Why do people never say what they mean?

At the end of November Catherine went into premature labour. She was barely six months pregnant and knew that her baby was not going to survive. Yet she refused to go into hospital, where there was just a chance that the full onset of labour might have been postponed. Talking about it on tape, she said regretfully, 'If I'd gone into the hospital . . . it was a very good baby hospital . . .' and leaves the sentence unfinished. Instead she insisted on staying at home with Tom, attended by the local midwife. The nurse was convinced at one point that the baby was dead and tried to hasten the process by pushing down very hard to try to expel it manually. Catherine said it felt as though she was being jumped on and she screamed so loudly she could be heard in the shop next door. Catherine knew the baby was alive because she could feel it moving until a few hours before the birth.

Nine days later, on 5 December, in the early hours of the morning, Tom delivered their stillborn son, David. The midwife was asleep with exhaustion. At six months David was a perfectly formed baby, something Catherine had not expected. She says poignantly, 'I thought it would come out as a lump of mush. And there was this replica of Tom. His big head . . . his hands, his perfect feet . . . every little thing.'[12] Their grief was terrible. So, too, was Catherine's guilt. Neither was helped by the attitude of the authorities, for whom neonatal and prenatal deaths were routine occurrences.

Until quite recently, official treatment of the bereaved parents of stillborn or miscarried children was unbelievably callous. They were often not allowed to hold the child or to say goodbye to them, and a proper funeral service was denied to the small being who had never officially existed. Catherine was devastated when the priest told her that her child could not be christened because it had never lived. And then she learned that because the baby had not been christened, he could not be buried in his own grave, but would have to be placed anonymously in someone else's. When she recovered from the birth and was able to get out of bed, the first thing Catherine did was to go to the cemetery to try to find her son's grave. An elderly workman told her that her baby had been buried with an old lady who had died in the workhouse, and this information gave Catherine an obscure sense of comfort. She could imagine David being held in the arms of a surrogate grandparent.

Catherine blamed many people for the loss of her baby – the doctor for mismanaging her pregnancy, Kate for the fatal journey north, God for punishing her for her sins, but most of all herself for the mistakes she had made and for not being good enough to deserve a healthy child. Later Catherine was to realise that there were many factors conspiring against her, though her hereditary blood disease was, ironically, not one of them. At thirty-four she was quite old for a first-time mother and not in good health. She also had a rhesus-negative blood group. The discovery of the rhesus factor in blood was relatively new and its implications for pregnant women unknown at that time. Most rhesus-negative women manage to have one healthy child before antibodies are created that cause problems in subsequent pregnancies, resulting in death shortly after birth or, as in Catherine's case, stillbirth in late pregnancy. It was Catherine's tragedy that her first foetus was given so few chances of survival.

The loss of the baby also deepened Catherine's crisis of faith. One of Catherine's first actions when she came to St Albans had been to find the nearest Catholic church. After a great effort, she managed to persuade Tom to come with her to Mass. Once there, she was embarrassed and ashamed to find another young missionary priest, in the mode of Father Bradley, declaiming from the pulpit. The gist of his sermon was that everyone who was not a true Catholic was bound for eternal damnation and the fires of Hell. Catherine's awareness of the bigotry and irrationality of the message was heightened by the presence of Tom beside her. 'How I kept my seat and kept Tom there I don't know,' Catherine said afterwards. 'He was a man recently down from Oxford, and I had brought him to listen to this ignorant pig of a priest.'[13] It dashed any hopes she might have had of bringing Tom into the church. Tom's religious beliefs were always subjected to rigorous intellectual examination. His church was like a college, with God as the 'Headmaster of Men' and its members his eternal students.

After the death of her child, Catherine was tempted to go back to the Catholic church for comfort, though she was racked by doubts she scarcely dared acknowledge. 'Every time I questioned the existence of God I vomited with fear.' Catherine saw God as 'a screen against fear or a prop to help you through this mystery called life'. The alternative was to be 'thrust into the wilderness where all is night and there is no hand to guide you'.[14] She was still secretly praying that Tom would change his mind and convert to Catholicism, because once in the church, he would be 'a stave to which I could tie myself' and blot out all her doubts. She began to have nightmares again, this time the sinister figure 'of a black-robed priest' who could appear anywhere, in otherwise benign dreams, but whom she saw mostly 'on the altar with his back towards me'.

While she lay in bed recovering from the birth, Catherine began to experiment with one of her other talents. She began to make little illustrations to go with the children's poems she had written.

Dissatisfied with her efforts, as soon as she was out of bed, she went to St Albans art college to ask whether it was a project any of the students would want to undertake. She was already thinking of possible publication. Someone suggested that Catherine might like to come to some of the open life-drawing classes and improve her own skills. She went eagerly, but didn't complete the course, feeling out of place among the young students. She said afterwards that she was made to feel that her efforts were useless. Catherine's inferiority complex was against her, as were her postnatal depression and grief. She had wanted to be able to draw a child, but found that she could not. In her first radio broadcast, 'Learning to Draw at Thirty', Catherine described how she had gone to the life classes to learn to draw a little boy called David 'to illustrate a story I had just written'.[15] But the child refused to come to life on the page. Catherine could depict him lying down or standing up, but as soon as she wanted to draw him doing anything, it was a total failure.

But the urge to draw wouldn't go away. One day, walking past St Alban's Abbey, she was suddenly seized with a strong desire to draw the façade. 'I remember standing open-mouthed, while the poetry of stone and brick was revealed to me for the first time.' A voice inside her head said, 'You could draw that.'[16] If she couldn't draw the human form, perhaps she could draw buildings. There was an art-supplies shop next to the art college in Victoria Street and Catherine went in to ask the assistant's advice. She came out equipped with a sketch pad, some drawing pencils, charcoal and 'academy chalk'. Without any lessons, other than the years of practice painting designs on cushions, Catherine sat on a seat outside the abbey, day after day, sketching the façade, trying to capture the texture of the stone and the way the light fell across the carving. Having drawn something she was pleased with, she went inside to make sketches of the interior. Her main difficulties were with perspective, and she didn't know how to use the charcoal or the chalk properly, but the surviving pencil drawings are remarkable for their detail and texture and the artistic ability they reveal. Tom always regretted that Catherine had never had the opportunity to have a formal education as a child when all her talents might have been fostered. Had she been born twenty years later, Tom said, or in better circumstances, she could have won a scholarship to high school (as he had himself) and received 'guidance from the educated people around her'.[17] Catherine had to fight to release her own natural creativity without any guidance as to the direction it should take, and with little confidence in her own abilities.

Her slow recovery after the loss of her baby was hindered by what could have been a fatal accident. Doing the washing by hand in the bathroom sink on a cold February morning, Catherine decided to bring the electric fire in from the kitchen. As she grasped the metal handle with her wet, soapy hands, she experienced a strong electric shock. The fire was stuck to her hand, but her screams attracted the dog, Terry, which began to jump up at her and may have been instrumental in releasing her grip from the handle. Afterwards, she didn't remember running down the stairs or opening the front door, but the policeman standing on guard outside the station saw her fall down the steps and collapse on the pavement. He rushed over and, with the help of passers-by, carried an unconscious Catherine upstairs and laid her on the bed. The kitchen carpet was in flames where she had dropped the electric fire, and had to be put out. A message was sent asking Tom to come home from school and a local doctor came and gave Catherine a large dose of sedative for the shock. The next thing Catherine remembered 'was waking up in bed with the screams tearing through my head. My mouth was opening and shutting but no sound was emerging, but the screaming inside had not abated.'[18] The screaming inside her head didn't stop for over a month, and even after that she was prone to wake up in the night screaming from a nightmare she couldn't remember, but which was merged somehow with the image of the black priest. It didn't help her deteriorating mental state. The endless scream she had begun to hear as the electric current coursed through her body seemed to Catherine very close to her childhood visions of Hell.

With the onset of spring and warmer weather, Catherine made up her mind to get out into the country at weekends and walk to build up her strength. Tom was interested in bird watching and one of his friends at the school suggested a route that would not be too taxing for Catherine, and where they would be able to observe a particular type of bird. It should have been a short evening stroll. They left St Albans at about six o'clock and walked down the pleasant country lane Tom's friend had described. Quite soon they came to a picturesque old village with an inn and a quarry behind it. Puzzled, since the directions they'd been given didn't mention a village, they stopped a man and asked where the bus stop was so that they could catch the bus back to St Albans. The man didn't appear to understand what they were asking. They then stopped a woman and she pointed to an alleyway between one of the houses which led into a cart track and told them that if they walked in that direction they would come to the road.

Catherine was already exhausted and felt that the track went on for miles. In the end they came to a farmhouse, which appeared to be empty, and then to another large house, where they were given more directions over the fields to the main road. It was private land, the man said, but in the circumstances they could walk across it. It was getting dark by the time they reached the road, having had to climb through hedges and over fences, and Catherine's nose had begun to bleed profusely. They flagged down a bus and Tom had virtually to carry Catherine on to it and then home to bed, where she spent several days afterwards, resting.

When they talked about the incident to other people, they were told that there was no village up that road. They must have imagined it. That particular lane led straight up to the main road and there were no houses. The whole walk from one end to the other shouldn't have taken more than about fifteen minutes. Weeks later, when Catherine had recovered, she and Tom went back to what they believed to be the same road and, as they'd been told, found only a country lane that led to the main road and a bus stop.

Catherine became convinced that she had experienced the paranormal. In her case it might just have been written off as hysteria, she joked, but Tom was too much of a realist to have shared a hallucination. 'What happened to us?' Catherine asked. 'Why were we taken into that village? Did we enter a time warp?' But far from being a manifestation of the paranormal, it is much more likely that they took the wrong lane on the first occasion and simply got lost. There were no signposts during wartime and it was very easy to get lost without a map. To people brought up in the town, one narrow country lane with hedges on either side looks exactly like another, so it would have been quite credible for Tom and Catherine to have believed on the second occasion that they were walking down the same lane again. However, Tom and Catherine were shaken and Catherine believed to the end of her life that she was gifted with psychic perception.

11

We make our own hells with our thinking. And
there's no hell to equal a self-made hell . . . A
breakdown is like the eruption of a volcano. Your
mind is boiling with the most terrifying thoughts, all
negative, and . . . the absolute loss of self-confidence
and faith and hope.[1]

In the summer of 1941, Tom received his call-up papers for the
Royal Air Force. But to Catherine's relief he failed the medical and
was therefore unlikely to be assigned to flight duties. Tom was sent
to training camps, first in Leicestershire and then Lincolnshire. Catherine did not want to be parted from him for a single day. She needed
his constant presence and support. When he wasn't there, she was
sometimes disabled by terror at the thought that she might never see
him again. Without Tom, Catherine confessed that her 'life became a
void I couldn't fill'.[2] She opted to travel with him, living in temporary
lodgings. Travelling with Tom meant that Catherine had to part
company with the fox terrier which had been given to her by Kate
and Nan. Keeping a dog in lodgings, particularly a bitch, had proved
very difficult. Fortunately Terry had taken a liking to a dispatch
rider and spent many happy hours riding pillion on his motorcycle.
Catherine and Tom were relieved when he offered to adopt the dog.

For Tom, living in lodgings rather than at the RAF base often
meant a long journey every day to and from the camp – but fortunately he was not the type of man who enjoyed the all-male culture
of the forces and he was content to live out. However, looking after
Catherine must have put a great strain on him. For most of this
period she was either mentally or physically ill and sometimes both.
When she was well she was vivacious and wonderful company, but

when her spirit was overwhelmed by exhaustion it was a different matter. Tom never knew whether he was going to come home to the happy extrovert or her depressed twin. At one point Catherine took a voluntary job in the local maternity hospital. 'I thought I might learn here how I'd come to lose my baby.'[3] She also had vague thoughts of fulfilling one of her original ambitions to become a nurse or a midwife, but she found watching births a nauseating experience. When the doctor snipped the cord she had to put her head out of the window to stop herself fainting, and the job had to be given up. This was a very difficult period for both the Cooksons and by the end of the war the strength of their feelings for each other must have been tested to the limit.

Living in lodgings during the war gave Catherine a wealth of material for stories. In Leicester Tom brought one of the other RAF students home one evening to give him extra coaching in maths. Catherine said she was outraged when the landlady banged on the door and insinuated that the three of them might be up to no good, though she and Tom laughed about it afterwards. Catherine was always very sensitive to double entendres. She details so many of them in her life that it is almost impossible to resist wondering whether some of them were imagined. Her persecution complex, the constant feeling of shame about her illegitimacy, worries about 'going the same way as Kate' if she acknowledged her own sexuality, and memories of the slanders she had endured at Harton, made her see slights that were never intended. When a doctor had visited the Hurst to see one of her blind evacuees and had asked, quite innocently, how, as a young single girl, she had managed to afford such a beautiful house, she imagined that he must suspect her of immoral earnings. So, instead of telling him the truth, she told him provocatively that she made select trips to France and London. Later, when she attended his surgery to be checked for internal bleeding, she had drawn great satisfaction from imagining his discomfort when he discovered the evidence of her virginity.

In Sleaford, Lincolnshire, Catherine could only find a small bed-sitting room with a thoroughly uncongenial family. There was little privacy and she suspected the landlady of regularly going through her belongings. The family spent their time in the large kitchen which acted as a living room, and it embarrassed Catherine, who was always fastidious, that she had to pass through it to go to the lavatory. She had become pregnant again before leaving St Albans, and it was a trip she had to make fairly often. She was also horrified by the family's meanness. The landlady was always pleading poverty. She boasted that they had only one change of clothes, and their underwear, displayed on the line on wash day, was in rags. But Catherine noted that they could afford to run a car and go away for holidays.

On the same day that Tom was told he was to be posted as an instructor at Madley Camp near Hereford, Catherine began to bleed again. She went to bed and was attended by the local doctor, who anticipated that by the following day she should have lost the foetus. On the Friday morning Tom had to leave for Madley before the doctor arrived to tell Catherine that she had had an incomplete abortion. On Saturday her landlady was going on holiday and Catherine was taken by ambulance to Grantham hospital, where, late that evening, she was given a D and C (dilation and curettage) under general anaesthetic. Tom had not been informed, owing to the erratic nature of wartime communications, and Catherine felt very alone. She discharged herself from hospital three days later against medical advice in order to join him in Hereford.

After this tragic repetition, Catherine's need for spiritual comfort and support sent her back to the church. She attended Mass and confession for the first time in over a year. Coming out of the church, she was outraged to see a notice in the porch concerning mixed marriages, which, Catherine thought, seemed to place the Protestant partner 'on an animal level' in the marriage. This offended all her rational sensibilities. She was further upset when the priest, in answer to the desperate question why her babies had been taken from her, told her that she was being punished for abandoning her faith. She must learn to be a better Catholic. Again, her logical twin recognised that she was being coerced by fear, even while her other self was driven to obey.

In Hereford, Catherine attended Mass regularly and had long discussions with another priest, who was a convert and therefore more aware of the Protestant point of view, put forward by Tom. Catherine was also a regular visitor to the convent, where she talked to the nuns. She was trying to find some kind of accommodation so that she could retain her faith. She could simply have allowed it to lapse, as so many Catholics do, and become a 'wooden' Catholic like her mother, going to confession once a year 'for a good rake out'. But such hypocrisy would not do for Catherine.

Her reasons for wanting to break free from the church were complex. She hated the idea of a religion that relied on fear to keep believers in line. Intellectually there was a great deal of the doctrine she didn't believe, such as transubstantiation, the infallibility of the pope – 'only another man' – and what she saw as the tyranny of the priests over ordinary people's lives. But it was no longer just a question of whether she stayed in the Catholic church or became a Protestant Christian. She felt she could no longer believe in a just God. All her life she had witnessed the cruel injustices meted out to Kate, which had turned a loving, warm-hearted girl into an embittered, violent alcoholic. Now Catherine was being told that her babies had been killed to punish her. Any god who could do that was not a god she wanted to believe in.

Catherine needed a faith that allowed her the intellectual freedom to work through her doubts. The Catholic church offered her every other kind of freedom; 'I could lie, drink, bash out, hate or whore if I were so inclined, knowing that I would be forgiven after confessing my sins. But what I found I wasn't allowed to do was to let my mind jump the boundary and wander among new thoughts.'[4] Rationally, Catherine could no longer remain in the Catholic church; emotionally she could not do without it. Tom could do little to help her. In fact he felt guilty that perhaps it was his influence that had caused many of her doubts to flourish. Quietly he decided to put his principles to one side and take instruction from the priest. When Catherine discovered what he was doing, she was horrified. 'I could now see Tom inside the Church and me out.' When he told her why he was doing it, she persuaded him not to continue.

Catherine's early novels are full of dialogue about Catholicism. In her first novel, *Kate Hannigan*, there is a 'damned priest' who fills the children's heads with 'fear of Hell and Purgatory'. Kate's friend Dr Prince despairs of being able to reason with their parents. 'It's no use trying to explain even the weakest psychology to adults who are eaten up with fear and superstition, which they call faith.' Kate Hannigan, whose education has taken her away from the church, is still 'attracted by the mass and . . . always will be. There is a lot of beauty in the religion, if one were allowed to look at it without its coating of Hell and sin.' Soon, like Kate, Catherine could no longer believe, but she still loved the beauty of the Mass and she had found nothing to replace her religion with. It left a spiritual void inside her. Catherine said that it was like being mentally blind, wandering in a vast, frightening wilderness – 'the mind can't cope with it; it breaks down'.

Hereford is a particularly lovely market town with dignified old buildings, set in the beautiful landscape of the Welsh borderlands. Catherine spent almost three years there, living in lodgings, but afterwards could not think of it 'without a shudder'. Yet it was there that she achieved one of her most remarkable feats. Without any formal training, she became a commercial artist. Catherine had continued to practise her drawing techniques while in Leicester and Sleaford and now had a series of cathedral sketches. She had almost mastered the use of charcoal and academy chalk. In Hereford she made a drawing of the cathedral, partly on the spot and partly from a postcard, and was really pleased with the result. She went into a printer's shop to ask how much it would cost to have it printed for use as a personal Christmas card.

The man Catherine talked to was very impressed with her drawing. He suggested printing it commercially and selling copies in town. During the war, Christmas cards were scarce. He admired her technique, particularly the difficult trick of showing the texture of different materials, and enquired whether she was a student at the art school. When he heard that she wasn't and that the drawing had been made without any tutoring, he told her that she should go and show her work to Mr Milligan, the head of the art school.

Catherine had the cards printed and they were accepted by many of the shops in town, including the bigger stores, such as Woolworth's. She even made a profit. She also took her small portfolio of work to the art school. Mr Milligan not only suggested that she join the school as a student and study to go to the Slade (which Catherine had never heard of), he arranged to have her work exhibited in the town. It was a prestigious exhibition – not just the work of students. Catherine found her cathedral drawings hung alongside a painting by Dame Laura Knight.

Someone suggested to her that her skills could be used to do illustrations, and Catherine sent off a copy of a magazine cover she had done to the printer J. Arthur Dixon. They promptly sent a cheque for five pounds and asked if she would do more work for them. Catherine, with characteristic honesty, sent the money back, explaining that the drawing was a copy, but accepting their offer of work. She was asked to copy photographs from Arthur Mee's *King's England* series. This meant scaling up illustrations as small as an inch square, which Catherine didn't know how to do. Tom showed her how to divide the original up with a grid and then, using a magnifying glass, copy the detail into larger squares. Catherine filled her days with drawing between the time Tom left for his job at Madley Camp at six thirty in the morning and his return at six in the evening. The close pencil work almost ruined her eyesight, but it filled the long, solitary hours. She began to study perspective from textbooks and to copy Dutch interiors; 'the parquet floors were a marvellous exercise'.

The printer put her in touch with an elderly Dutch painter called Andre van der Meersh who was living in Hereford and doing a temporary job as maths teacher at the cathedral school. Catherine took to van der Meersh and his wife immediately. The painter told her that he would not teach her – 'either you can paint or you can't' – but she could come and watch him work. On Saturday afternoons, as often as she could, she went to sit in his attic studio. Under his guidance she did a pencil drawing of her landlady's elderly father, and another of Tom, which she converted into an oil painting.

Catherine's landlady had a piano and, when there were no draw-ings to be copied, she started to play again, often practising two or three hours a day. She found a piano teacher and began to study for exams. Exams meant a great deal to Catherine. They proved to herself and, she believed, to others that she had a measurable value. Through open classes at the art college she also studied for art exams. Music and drawing filled Catherine's days and kept her fears tempor-arily at bay. The idea of going to art college or to the Slade was something she dreamed of, although she realised that it was not practicable. Catherine was a married woman, whose life was dictated by her husband's career and the anticipated demands of the family life she still hoped for.

When van der Meersh died quite suddenly, Catherine felt bereft. His studio had been a haven of peace where she had spent tranquil afternoons watching him lay paint on canvas. She bought his easel and brushes in the hope that she could capture something of his spirit in her own work.

Catherine was now pregnant again and hoped that this time she would be able to carry the baby to term. She was obeying the priests, in spite of her doubts. Surely this time God would allow her to have a child?

Catherine's devastation can hardly be imagined when, in 1943, she lost her third baby, with massive haemorrhaging. She was already anaemic from the almost daily nosebleeds she suffered, and her own life was in danger. The doctors told her that she must not have another pregnancy. Apart from the grief caused by this pronouncement, there was also a moral dilemma. Contraception was forbidden to a Catholic. This would mean disobeying the priest and committing a cardinal sin. When she discussed it with her priest, he offered a cynical solution. Catherine's husband was a Protestant; 'Let him do the sinning,' she was told. This hypocritical pronouncement removed the last remnants of the faith Catherine had been clinging to. She was now even more afraid of sex, partly because it might result in another pregnancy with tragic results, and she was also afraid of allowing Tom to make love to her using any form of contraception, because this was a sin equivalent to murder.

Although Catherine had been told to rest, any kind of leisure was fatal for her peace of mind, allowing her fears to flood in and overwhelm her. As soon as she had recovered sufficiently from the miscarriage, she decided to undertake some kind of war work. Married women without children were by now being conscripted into the services alongside the men and Catherine too had been called up, only to be declared medically unfit. She became obsessed with guilt that she wasn't doing enough for the war effort and volunteered for work in a munitions factory – a particularly wearing, repetitive type of work that turned the skins of the people who packed the shells bright yellow. Catherine was appalled by conditions in the factory and wrote a letter to the management making a number of suggestions to improve training and efficiency. As a result, she was offered a junior management position, but shortly afterwards she became ill with cordite poisoning and had to be discharged. Once again she was at home all day with too much time on her hands.

Catherine was now very depressed and her marriage was suffering. Catherine blamed herself for failing to give Tom the children she knew he wanted. She also blamed Kate. Kate had never wanted children, had never liked children, and Catherine admitted to a close friend that she too had not really wanted children except for Tom's sake. This magnified her feelings of guilt because she believed in some obscure way that she had lost the babies 'because of Kate and because of the way I was born'.[5] Tom had to suppress his own grief because it only increased Catherine's guilt. He was also unhappy in his job as an instructor. It was 'a cushy job he hated and loathed'. He longed to be posted to something more exciting, even active service, but it was increasingly impossible to leave Catherine. She was convinced every day when Tom left the house that he would never return. 'Every moment of every day and every second of every moment' was filled with fear for his safety.[6] If Tom had been in a more vulnerable position, he knew Catherine would not be able to cope alone.

After the third miscarriage, Catherine's mental health had begun to deteriorate with alarming rapidity. Her whole life was now ruled by fear – so much so that she made a list of everything she was afraid of.

Fear of drink . . . of Kate in drink.
Fear of God.
Fear of not living a good life.
Fear of dying an unhappy death.
Fear of the priest and of his admonition from behind the grid in the confessional.
Fear of loving in case I slipped the way of my mother.
Fear of loving, even when it was legalised by marriage, because I might have a baby.
Fear of preventing this fear with a pessary.
Fear of being different.
Fear of being alone even during the day.
Fear of the night.
Fear of people and what they might say about me having no 'da'.
Fear of losing Tom in the war – a great consuming, agonising fear.
Fear of doctors.
Fear of operations, of blood spattered floors and blinding arc lights.
Fear of swear words . . .
Fear of going mad.[7]

She was increasingly paranoid about her illegitimacy and Tom's safety. As Catherine herself put it, she 'turned into a solid block of fear'. This she tried to hide by putting on a gay façade. Sometimes she was manic with laughter that bordered on hysteria in her attempt to conceal her misery; sometimes she was so depressed she couldn't even smile. She became unable to sleep and the aggressive impulses she had had as a child began to return. 'Indiscriminately it was turned against all mankind, but in particular, and powerfully, it settled on Kate.' She began once again to dream about killing her mother. According to the psychiatrist Anthony Storr, Catherine was suffering from the 'intensely hostile feelings' left by the 'scars of infantile deprivation'. These feelings, well recognised by therapists, are often the residue of unsatisfactory mother–child relationships. A sense of rejection can cause an individual to 'hate those whom they love since they cannot get from them what they really need' – in Catherine's case the evidence of her mother's love for her – and because the hatred cannot be openly displayed and has to be suppressed, the individual turns these hostile feelings 'inwards against themselves in self-torment and despair'.[8] These feelings in an extreme form are often the result of child abuse – either emotional or physical. Catherine's hatred of Kate was so extreme it was almost palpable. She blamed her for everything bad that had happened to her in her life, and went over and over in her mind every episode of neglect and ill-treatment. But, as in childhood, her hostility and aggression were turned in other directions as well. Catherine was filled with terrible urges every time she saw a baby in a pram. Sometimes she wanted to seize the baby and carry it off; at other times she felt like dashing it to the ground. She said she wanted to 'wreak retribution on someone' for the loss of her children.[9]

Catherine tried to sublimate her impulses with work. She threw herself back into her drawing commissions, working compulsively until she was exhausted and almost blind with the effort. Her undiagnosed blood disorder was always present; her frequent attacks of bleeding and chronic tiredness tended to be put down to neurosis by the doctors she consulted. This often meant that real illnesses were overlooked. When Catherine's leg became inflamed and painful she was seen by two doctors, one of whom was convinced that it was 'all in her mind'. The other more accurately diagnosed phlebitis and sent her home to rest in bed. But it was the worst thing she could have been told. Lying in bed all day alone in her lodgings, she had nothing to do but look at the blank wall of the factory outside the window and think. Her thoughts became confused and more and more unbearable. The doctors grew impatient with her. One of them told her that all she had to do was to make up her mind to be well.

After six weeks Catherine had a full-blown panic attack. She had experienced anxiety before, but never this. As she lay in bed, her heart jerked and then pounded as though it was going to burst through her chest, she trembled uncontrollably all over and felt nauseous and giddy. Like Prudence Dudley in *The Iron Facade*, she thought she was going to die, fearing and desiring it at the same time: 'wasn't that what I wanted – to die?'[10] When she tried to get out of bed, her legs crumpled under her and remained paralysed.

Catherine was admitted to hospital under observation. It was hoped that the change of location and contact with other people would help, but she did not improve. She took a strong dislike to one of the women in the ward, who she was convinced was conducting a whispering campaign against her. Back at home, Catherine still fought the idea that there was anything wrong with her mind, but lying in bed she discovered that her fears began to materialise from the patterns on the wallpaper, just as her childhood demons had come out of the walls during her pubescent breakdown in William Black Street. She also found that her head was full of obscene language which threatened to burst out of her mouth whenever she opened it. When her doctor suggested that she should see a psychiatrist, she finally gave up the struggle. She was afraid that if she didn't accept help, she would become insane. It was also increasingly difficult to control her aggressive impulses. Catherine was afraid that she would harm someone. She had even turned against Tom and told him that she no longer loved him. On the advice of the psychiatrist she was admitted as a voluntary patient to St Mary's Hospital, just outside Hereford, where she helped the matron in the storeroom, 'made gloves and wove cloth and suffered the torments of hell'.[11]

Catherine doesn't deal with mental illness very often in her novels; she told an interviewer that she didn't write about certain subjects because 'in doing so I know I should have to show a side of me that I want to forget'. In *The Obsession*, Beatrice experiences dizzy, dissociated episodes before her attacks of mania, and these tired and muzzy feelings were among Catherine's symptoms. But Beatrice's madness, which makes her crawl round the house like a creature possessed, is more like something from a horror film than a realistic portrayal of insanity, though her violent, destructive impulses towards the people she is supposed to love were certainly experienced by Catherine. *The Year of the Virgins*, set in the 1960s but published in 1993, also has a Gothic account of madness that manifests itself in religious mania, sexual abhorrence and 'twisted mother-love', resulting in a final bloodbath that would do justice to a seventeenth-century revenge tragedy. The asylum where Winifred receives shock treatment for her condition is only lightly sketched – the 'haunting sights and sounds', the damaging mixture of severely psychotic patients with those having temporary breakdowns, are reported at second hand.

In *The Garment*, the descent into madness is more graphically described. Grace is driven insane by her husband, who is a male personification of Catherine's mother. Everyone else sees him as a kindly, humorous man who makes people laugh, whereas towards his wife his manner, motivated by self-protection, is destructive. He is impotent, but cannot admit it, condoning his wife's adultery and accepting her children as his in order to conceal his own weaknesses. However, he will not set her free to marry the man she loves. That he is also a clergyman, reiterating his own hypocrisies from the pulpit, only serves to increase Grace's torment. The impossibility of being able to admit the truth is the chief factor that precipitates Grace's breakdown. Gradually her confidence and self-control are eroded until she lapses into the violence and abuse of madness. As she does so, she screams the name of Kate – a minor character in the novel – as if to underline the autobiographical parallel that is undoubtedly there.

The most convincing account of breakdown is to be found in *Maggie Rowan*, where the childless Ann collapses after discovering that her husband has made another woman pregnant. After five months of paralysing terror, Ann is promoted to the recovery wing. In the surreal setting of Hope Block, Ann picks up books and magazines in order to escape prying questions from the other women.

> Sometimes she even tried to read, but she would read no more than a sentence or two before her thoughts would be on the page staring up at her, forcing her to go over and over them until the repetition became wheels that would gather momentum and whirl round in her head; and, in their turn, they would fill her with fear, and the fear would make her sick.[12]

At St Mary's, Catherine found herself in a ward with about twenty other women suffering various degrees of mental illness. Some of them had been there for a long time. There was an elderly woman in deep depression after the death of her husband, a woman who believed that her husband was poisoning her, a young girl who kept trying to run away, and a middle-aged Catholic who spent much of her time in bed crying and screaming 'in mental agony'. Although Catherine portrays her treatment in the ward as relatively humane, the atmosphere did little for her own sanity, and the treatment by modern standards was barbaric. Catherine had long-term psychological problems dating from her childhood. She felt rejected, first by her unknown father and then by her mother. She saw herself as having been emotionally and physically abused by Kate and there was also the possibility that she had, as she asserted, been sexually abused. Apart from the incident with the Irish lodger and the sleazy behaviour of the old man in the shop, Catherine gives no clues to the identity of the perpetrator. It would be natural to look towards the men in the family, particularly as they were already abusing her mother. However, Catherine never seems to have regarded either of them with anything other than affection. All her hatred and fear is directed against Kate.

Most people react angrily to the idea that women can be the perpetrators of sexual abuse. The picture of a mother as a nurturing being is so strong that society is inclined to view mothers who abuse their children as monsters rather than women who are ill and who have often been abused themselves – as Kate had been. Yet clinical studies have shown that it is a great deal more common than we are prepared to acknowledge and victims, even in the closet-opening nineties, still find it harder to admit to being abused by a woman than by a man. A radio phone-in with Philip Hodgson which touched on the idea that women might be abusers as well as men was inundated with more calls than it could deal with and many of those talking on air were in tears with the relief of being able to talk about it. The letters that were subsequently received led to a television *This Morning* programme which flooded the switchboard with over a thousand calls.

If Catherine was being abused by her mother in more extensive ways than those she has already publicly accused Kate of, it would have exaggerated the devastating effect of discovering that the woman she thought of as a sister was actually her mother, and increased Catherine's feelings of rejection and betrayal. To be ill-treated by your mother, who is supposed to be a loving, nurturing figure, is one of the most damaging things that can happen to a child. One woman who was abused by her mother described it as 'soul murder'. It is a psychological commonplace that if an infant's earliest experience of his mother is such that he has not acquired the conviction of her essential 'goodness', he will then find it impossible to achieve any conviction of his own essential 'goodness' or lovability, and will possess no inner sense of self-esteem upon which to rely. However successful he may be in later life, he will remain intensely vulnerable to failure, rejection or disappointment, which will seem to him the end of the world, and throw him into profound depression.[13]

Sexual abuse of any kind is 'an attack on all levels: psychological, emotional, physical, sexual and spiritual'.[14] But results of recent studies show that female abuse seems to be more emotionally damaging than other forms. Survivors often experience 'lasting feelings of guilt, self-blame, and worthlessness and to have disturbed interpersonal relationships and to have elevated rates of mental illnesses . . . post-traumatic stress disorder and panic and anxiety disorders'.[15] These include phobias – particularly agoraphobia – and aggressive behaviour, gender-identity problems, eating disorders and bowel problems. They are often also tempted to be sexually promiscuous, even though they fear sex and suffer from persistent feelings of bodily shame. Women who have been abused by their mothers sometimes find that it alters the dynamics of their adult relationships with women and some may even feel driven 'to act out' their feelings with women.

If Catherine was abused by her mother as a child, it would also answer another enigma. She constantly asserted that she had not told the whole truth about Kate. The list of wrongs that Catherine cites to justify her fear and hatred of her mother is incomplete by her own testimony. She talks about Kate's harsh treatment, her drinking, her rejection of Catherine as a baby, the fact of Catherine's illegitimacy. These instances, though horrifying, are hardly substantial enough to justify the intensity of Catherine's feelings. Although she promised one day to tell 'the whole truth' and made several attempts to write frankly about Kate's behaviour towards her when she was a child, all were abandoned. Fuelled by anger, the last attempt to write a 'warts and all' account of her mother was burned by Catherine a few years before she died. Reading the various drafts of her autobiography and listening to tapes of Catherine talking about her childhood, the biographer is forced to acknowledge that something has been left unsaid, and to ask what was so unspeakable in Kate's behaviour that Catherine – whose books are packed with lurid accounts of the worst things that human beings can do to each other – found herself unable to write about it? Catherine describes Kate's unkindness towards her as a child with apparent candour in both published and unpublished sources, yet says repeatedly that there are episodes that have been withheld. One day, she promises in her unpublished autobiography, she will tell the whole truth about Kate. So what were the 'tragic secrets' and 'things so terrible' Catherine pledged herself to tell before she died,[16] yet could never bring herself to write? Often when Catherine touches on the subject of her mother's behaviour, it is the context of what she says and the way in which it is said that disturbs – one illuminating instance of this is where she talks on tape, in a considerably heightened emotional state, about sharing a bed with her mother while she is defending her relationship with Nan. There was undoubtedly something that Kate had done to Catherine that, although she came to understand, she could not forgive, though she tried several times to do so, realising that she would never achieve peace of mind until she could.

As well as the conviction that she was worthless, guilty and sinful – a 'bad person' – Catherine was also suffering from deep depression following the three miscarriages. What she needed was good-quality psychotherapy and appropriate temporary medication. Unfortunately sophisticated antidepressants were still in the future. All that could be prescribed in 1945 was crude and addictive tranquillisers. And the standard treatment for women suffering chronic depression was the administration of electro-convulsive therapy, popularly know as electric shock treatment.

This is vividly described in *Maggie Rowan*, where Ann is taken each week

down the grand staircase, with its great balustrade and its thick red pile carpet, and along the hall of mirrors to a door at the end, which seemed the dividing line between two worlds, the world of the grand mansion, full of strange and terrifying people, and a world of bare stone steps, leading in a spiral down to a tiled passage, then into a room with wooden benches and a lavatory that stank from over use. When your turn came you were led through a green baize door into a room in which the familiar nurses and doctors were different – the trusted Doctor Dickinson was no longer in nice smelling tweeds, but in a white coat, sitting

The Hurst as it was just after Catherine bought it.

A tennis party at the Hurst. Kate is sitting in the middle with
Catherine on the left of the photograph. The woman sitting
on the right may well be Nan Smith.

Catherine looking thin and unhappy, taken between 1937 and 1940, at the height of the conflict with Nan.

(*Below*) St Helens Hospital, the workhouse in Hastings where Catherine met Nan Smith and experienced 'a hell of jealousy with women'. The picture was taken in 1911, but it still looked the same when Catherine was there.

(*Above*) The sea front at Hastings in the 1930s, where Catherine, lonely and unhappy, often walked at night.

Catherine and Tom Cookson were married on June 1st 1940. George Silverlock is standing in the doorway behind them with his arm in a sling.

Catherine's drawing of Lichfield Cathedral. During the war years, she became an accomplished commercial artist.

(*Below*) An engraving of St Mary's Psychiatric Hospital, Hereford, where Catherine was admitted as a voluntary patient after her breakdown and 'suffered the torments of hell'.

Catherine at the beginning of the 1950s
after the publication of her first novels.

Loreto, the house in Hastings where Catherine wrote
some of her most successful novels between 1954 and 1973.

The swimming pool Catherine built with the proceeds from *Katie Mulholland*.

Catherine in the garden
with her labrador Simon.

Catherine in a relaxed and happy mood on the beach in Northumberland.

Catherine picnicking beside the car on a research trip
to Northumberland for one of her novels.

Taken the same day. Catherine sitting in a graveyard
in the hills above Allendale where she set many of her books.

at the head of a high couch. He placed something on your head; it pressed against the temples ... then bang. You were shot into nothingness.[17]

Catherine was subjected to this many times during her stay at St Mary's. She was repeatedly sedated and led down stone stairs to the basement where patients queued on wooden forms outside a lavatory. Catherine's most vivid memory of the hospital afterwards was of the smell of urine – a smell connected in her mind with the degradation of the workhouse infirm wards, and feelings of disgust and shame from a childhood memory: 'I was crossing the road from the last arch, near the dock gates, and in my line of vision was the men's urinal, and out of it came two women accompanied by two men, and they were hanging on each other and laughing.' In Catherine's mind, 'the depravity of that moment' became synonymous with the smell of the basement room and the physical humiliation of ECT.

When her name was called, Catherine was led into the room, strapped to the table and then 'shocked into unconsciousness'. Afterwards, patients were led back to the wards, 'walking as if in a dream' on feet almost too heavy to lift. On one occasion, the machine was set incorrectly and Catherine's whole body lifted off the table with the shock. Repeated episodes of ECT left Catherine with permanent brain damage. Although she could remember everything clearly up to the point of her admission to hospital, afterwards there would be huge gaps in her short term memory. Tom came every day to see Catherine. After he had cycled a fourteen-mile round-trip to the camp, he then cycled the seven miles out to the hospital and back, often to be told that Catherine didn't want to see him. But he still came.

After four or five weeks of ECT, Catherine was allowed to go into Hereford for the day on a supervised outing. She had another panic attack and realised that she was not ready to be discharged. But after another three weeks she began to be afraid that if she didn't get out soon she would be unable to do so. She had seen the dangers of institutionalisation in the workhouse. Her thoughts focused more and more on the Hurst. She became convinced that if she could only get back to the Hurst, everything would be all right.

The war was coming to an end and the Hurst, which had been briefly let, was empty again. Catherine discharged herself from the hospital, against the doctor's advice, Tom took two weeks' leave, and together they travelled back to Hastings. The first thing to hit Catherine's nostrils as she went through the front door was the stench of stale urine. For one panicky moment she thought it was a manifestation of her breakdown, but when she went upstairs she discovered overflowing chamber pots in every room – even some in the airing cupboard – a legacy of their last tenant, an officer's wife who had sublet the rooms to soldiers.

The Hurst had come through the war relatively unscathed. Incendiary bombs had grazed the building in two places and one of the towers was so damaged it had to be removed, but otherwise, apart from dirt and neglect, the house was almost intact. Catherine threw herself into the cleaning of it with every ounce of energy she had. When it was time for Tom to go back to Hereford, it was agreed that Catherine should stay in Hastings – she simply couldn't bear to go back even if it meant being parted from him. Tom's mother came to stay and helped Catherine with some of the heavy cleaning, but when she left Catherine was on her own and still in a dangerous state of depression. The worst of the pain was kept at bay by tranquillisers and sleeping pills. But this too was a source of shame, something else to be concealed. Catherine quickly found that she was dealing with an additional stigma: that of mental illness. Word spread among her friends (was this Nan's doing?) that she had been in an asylum. Catherine was indignant and quick to correct anyone who mentioned the word. Her instinct for denial and concealment took over – she told anyone who asked that she had been treated for 'nerves' in a private hospital.

Once more she took Kate's creed as her own: 'Work it off girl – you'll cope' and made out a rota of duties for every hour of the day. There must be no time to think. She also kept a chart of her mental wellbeing, marking down how she felt each day, and the number of times she vomited with fear. It was over a year before she could leave this space blank. Sometimes Catherine's depression was merely a blue haze that pervaded everything and the dots on the chart in the kitchen would rise optimistically; at other times it opened up like a black pit beneath her feet and she felt that she stared directly at insanity. 'I know that the only hell comparable with that of losing God, is the hell of conscious madness.'[18] Kate wrote twice a week, but Catherine ignored her letters. She could not bear to have anything to do with her mother, whom she blamed for precipitating her breakdown.

In *Our Kate*, Catherine tells readers that she was alone at the Hurst for seven months – 'that was how I wanted it'. But this was not the case. In the early, unpublished version of her autobiography she described how she was afraid to be alone at night – fear of the dark was one of the manifestations of her breakdown. The people who lived across the road 'kindly allowed me to sleep there'. Catherine became very close to the grandmother. 'She liked me and I was fond of her, as fond as I could be of anyone in those days, but she hurt me one day when she said to me "You are not happy, and you won't be because you don't know joy, and knowing joy is going to be difficult for you." She knew joy, it was shining in her face.'[19] Catherine's jealousy in the end destroyed the relationship. Peace of mind and joy were the two things that Catherine craved more than anything else.

The consequences of Catherine's brief but loving reunion with Tom after her discharge from hospital were soon apparent – she was pregnant again. She was now thirty-nine and her biological clock was running down. If she was unable to keep this baby, she knew that her chances of conceiving again would be diminished. When Catherine miscarried she reached the absolute bottom of her endurance. There seemed to be no point in carrying on. The pain of living from day to day was overwhelming and she felt that she was ruining Tom's life as well. In the middle of the night she collected three bottles of pills from the bathroom cabinet and decided to swallow them all.

Catherine never knew afterwards what had stopped her, but after a long internal struggle she made a supreme effort of will, emptied the pills down the toilet and pulled the chain. Looking at herself in the mirror, haggard with lack of sleep and mental anguish, she knew she had to devise her own way of coping with her illness. As she had educated herself, so she would cure herself.

12

Like the Scot, I must go me ain gait,
Be it on mud, gravel, stone, or mossy hill.[1]

When Catherine looked back on this time, she recalled being in a dark underworld: 'I lived hourly in depression and anxiety, added to which was a deep feeling of aggression . . . It was the black night of life and my rope ladder of will power had swung far out of reach . . . My heart had definitely forgotten how to sing.'[2] She had violent impulses, urging her to strike out at the world for everything she had suffered, and was often afraid that she would 'do something desperate'. Her condition was not helped by the knowledge that one of her male friends from before the war had committed suicide.

Without the sleeping pills, there was nothing to alleviate Catherine's insomnia. But as she lay awake in the dark, words began to form themselves in her mind, rearranging themselves sometimes into stories, sometimes into poems. The latter were a direct expression of her feelings as she lay rigidly awake watching for the first glimmers of daylight.

Dawn breaking:
Light like steel grey paint
Slithers down the window
And drags back the curtain on day,
Day that I've longed for
Through each black hour
When wide-eyed I've stared
At fear and watched
It grow . . .[3]

Catherine's fingers itched for a pencil to write them down. She hadn't been able to touch a drawing pencil since her breakdown – even the sight of one made her nauseous. Nor could she play the piano. These things were too closely connected with the long, painful period after her third miscarriage before she was admitted to hospital. However, one day she picked up a pencil and began to write down the thoughts in her head, and was immediately aware of a difference in the way she felt. 'It was like being washed up after a shipwreck and finding that you had brought ashore with you a locked shelter, in which, once you got the door open, you could live.'

She was later to admit that although she had scribbled throughout her teens and twenties, 'I didn't *write* until I was forty'. She also acknowledged the part that illness had played in her writing, though her position wasn't always consistent. When she was interviewed by Professor Honigmann at Newcastle University, she was upset when he assumed her writing had only begun at the time of her breakdown, the inference being (she thought) that it was merely therapy. 'I was writing from eleven,' she protested. She was born to be a writer – even as a child she was aware of seeing people differently. It was simply that 'the breakdown held up a mirror to me and showed me myself ... I was living quite a false life.'4 Writing helped her to retrieve the lost self. But she insisted to Professor Honigmann that it wasn't therapy: it didn't help her, because when she wrote fiction she was using her talent, not 'writing it out' as she tried to do in her autobiography *Our Kate*. Yet in other articles and interviews she describes how the voice in her head had instructed her to 'write it out' in her fiction and how she had realised that it was the only way to understand and come to terms with the ill-treated child she felt so sorry for.

During the day at the Hurst, remembering her success at Harton, she tried her hand at plays – three of them, in which 'cardboard characters worked out a nice ordered existence'. She dreamed of having them produced in London at one of the West End theatres. Then she wrote poetry, this time attempting contemporary rather than rhyming verse. Catherine could never get to grips with modern poetry at all; metaphor and allusion were foreign to her and she couldn't grasp a principle of structure and rhythm dictated only by the language itself rather than a system of external rules. She called it 'prose on short lines' since she couldn't see what made it poetry rather than prose. Her own 'poems' were simple thoughts or expressions of emotion, and they remained obstinately wooden no matter how hard she worked at them, because she had not grasped the idea that the statement had to go through a process of transformation, what the poet Anne Sexton described as the trick of transforming *rats* into *star*, whereby the juxtaposition of words can send complex layers of meaning rippling outwards from the page, often creating new meanings far beyond the conscious intention of the poet. Prose on short lines is not poetry.

But poetry was an important emotional safety valve for Catherine, where she could express her own feelings without having to dress them in the masks of characters in a story. One of her better poems, which she puts into the mouth of the posing poetess in *Kate Hannigan*, is a lyric called 'Solace', and Catherine also set it to music, working out the tune and harmonies on the piano while she waited with increasing impatience for Tom to be demobbed. The sentiments of the lyric are trite and the words clichéd, but every one of them was deeply felt. Natural beauty, peace of mind and the joys of human companionship were the life rafts she craved. If she could only hold on to these things, spiritual healing would be possible.

Let the beauty linger in my soul
Of a rose just bursting into bloom
Of a bird in flight,
Of the moon, new born into the night,
Reflecting on a sea of gentle ripples . . .

Let the beauty linger in my soul
Of firelight in a darkened room,
Of kindly words
Of lovers' laughter coming through the night,
Until, at last, I know no greater peace or ease
Than to remember these

In order to cure herself, Catherine read every book she could find on the subject of 'nerves', including some that stressed the power of positive thinking and the use of autosuggestion. She told herself at frequent intervals throughout the day that she was feeling perfectly well – convinced at first that it was useless, but willing to try anything. She wanted to believe that her mental condition had a physical cause;

she still hadn't totally accepted that there was anything seriously wrong with her mind.

Catherine devised a system whereby she stood in front of a mirror and gave herself a lecture – one twin talking to the other. 'Pull yourself together,' she would tell herself. 'You're B. well not going to get the better of me this time.' Often the person standing in the mirror turned out to be Kate: 'It's very odd ... I never see my reflection ... the person standing in that mirror is Kate.'[5] And Kate would use the words that she had used to Catherine as a child when she came in with her socks round her ankles, her shoulders drooping and a miserable face: 'Pull your stockings up; get Charlie off your back. You're just like Delia Norton!' Delia was a spectre from her childhood – a girl who had been 'not quite right in the head'.

Soon Catherine had to admit to an improvement. 'I was forced to face the fact that my type of nerves was caused not so much by my physical health as by my mental attitude.' She used the same technique to try to resolve some of the problems she had in relating to other people. Most people found Catherine pleasant, cheerful and inordinately kind, but occasionally she would develop inexplicable feelings of paranoia towards another person, convinced that they were hostile towards her, and the relationship would go spectacularly downhill. One of her closest friends described this paradox; Catherine, although she appeared to be straightforward, was in reality 'not so uncomplicated. The strongest affections of her life were matched by a counterbalance of hostility and disillusionment.'[6]

Catherine's attitude to her neighbour at the Hurst was a good example of what could happen. Catherine was convinced that the woman either disliked her or was jealous of her and said things behind her back, 'cutting my throat with her bitchiness'. Every morning when the woman went to work, Catherine would go into the lavatory where she could see the neighbour's back door from the upper part of the window, and she would peer unseen from behind the casement to watch her leave the house. On good days Catherine would force herself to recite, 'Good morning ... I hope you'll be happy and at peace today ... And when we meet you won't say anything nasty to me. God bless you.' On bad days, Catherine would have to suppress her feelings of hatred and force any expression of good will through her teeth.[7]

Seven months after Catherine went back to Hastings, Tom was demobbed and came home for good. The grammar school had reassembled and he was given his old job back. He and Catherine settled down to establish a routine of married life for the first time in their own home. For five years they had lived in one temporary lodging after another; now they occupied a fifteen-bedroom house with a large garden, both needing a considerable amount of attention. During the bad winter of 1947 the ramshackle plumbing system sprung what Catherine described as '26 leaks all over the house at once'. Water poured through ceilings and cascaded down the stairs. The garden, similarly neglected during the war years, was heavily overgrown. Catherine cleaned the house wrapped in two woollen dressing gowns on top of her clothes, a headscarf and fur-lined boots, in order to save their meagre ration of coal. In the garden she sawed tree branches and dug out ponds, while Tom taught himself plumbing, electrical wiring and carpentry in order to renovate the house without employing expensive builders. As a teacher, Tom was only earning thirty-two pounds a month. There was a mortgage to pay, not only on the Hurst, but also on the other property that Catherine had bought for Nan. Catherine seems to have remained in contact with Nan throughout the war. Shortly after Tom's return, there were bitter exchanges between Nan and the Cooksons. Catherine eventually made the property over to her by deed of gift for only £250. Nan sold it a few weeks later for £4,000, none of which was given back to Catherine. Catherine felt very bitter towards her.

The Cooksons were also having to come to terms with the knowledge that Catherine had miscarried four times, was now over forty and it was unlikely that they would ever have a child of their own. Tom, still only thirty-two at the end of the war, had a wife who was virtually an invalid from a combination of depression and the repeated haemorrhages which sometimes put her to bed for days at a time. Catherine suffered bleeding from her tongue and beneath her fingernails as well as frequent nosebleeds. She had no idea what caused them and neither did the doctors, to whom she made frequent visits. Her list of complaints also included backache, which she blamed on her childhood hip injury, neuralgia, and extreme lethargy, which she attributed to anaemia or lead poisoning from her cushion-painting activities.

Tom loved children – in the words of a close friend, he was 'devoted . . . gentle and generous in his way with them' – and would have been quite happy to adopt a baby. In fact, he often acted as a surrogate father to the boys in his care. In some of her autobiographical fragments Catherine makes the excuse that it was a question of faith. The Catholic adoption agency would not allow a baby to go to a household where one partner was a Protestant and the other a lapsed Catholic, and it was not possible for her to pretend to be a good Catholic simply in order to adopt a child. However, in the forties and fifties before the advent of the contraceptive pill and the Abortion Act, there were many, many adoption agencies, both public and private, who would have welcomed parents like Tom and Catherine with a secure income and a home of their own to offer. Age and religious belief were immaterial. The true reason is likely to lie in Catherine's state of mind. The symptoms of her depression included feelings of violent aggression towards babies. She constantly feared that she might harm an infant and it was fifteen years before she could trust herself to hold a baby in her arms. Catherine later said that although she regretted not having a child, she and Tom were closer than they would have been if they'd had children. She also thought that if she'd had a family, she might not have published anything, though she was quick to add that books could never be a substitute for a child.

Tom threw himself into his work. He often brought boys home for extra coaching and he ran a Scout troop at the school. Out of school hours he devoted his life to looking after his wife, who became, in a sense, his child. Caring for Catherine fulfilled a need deep inside Tom. Like Virginia Woolf's husband Leonard, he protected her, nursed her, and often gave up his own interests to make a secure and peaceful life possible for her. Catherine was fully aware of everything he had sacrificed and enormously grateful. She was well aware that few men would have set aside their own egos for their wives. But it was not accomplished without a struggle. Tom Cookson was a strong character under the mild exterior and he and Catherine had innumerable battles during their early years. When thwarted, Catherine could be irrational and intransigent. Tom was long-suffering, but he had an 'Irish' temper and when he lost it, the result could be surprising. In the end, Catherine said, she and Tom decided that since neither could be captain of the ship, they'd both be 'second mates'. But in reality it was Catherine who was the dominant partner. Friends observed that she often put Tom down in company. Once when he was sitting playing 'Für Elise' on the piano, Catherine came in and said, 'Oh, Tom, you can't play it, let me show you.' On another occasion, when he had baked some cakes for guests, she tasted one and said, 'They're quite nice, but he doesn't really know how to make them like I do, do you, dear?'[8] To which Tom could only say no. These were just two small but revealing instances. Tom told a friend that in marrying Catherine he had replicated his own mother's relationship both with himself and with his stepfather. He was used to dominant women.

Like many childless couples, Tom and Catherine became the dedicated owners of a succession of pets. The first was Bill, who appears in a number of Catherine's novels, particularly *Mary Ann and Bill* – the last book in the series featuring her character Mary Ann Shaughnessy. Both the real and the fictional Bill were bull terriers, the runts of their particular litters. Catherine fell in love with Bill on sight and, although she had other dogs, he always held first place in her memory; apart from Tom 'there is no one in my life I have missed as I did Bill'. For Catherine he was not an animal but 'a special being who loved me'.[9] The dog was a gift from a friend who was looking after the puppy for someone else who, apparently, wanted to get rid of it. However, a few days after Catherine took possession of the dog, a woman who claimed to be the owner turned up and told her that it had all been a mistake and if Catherine wanted Bill she would have to pay ten pounds for him. Catherine didn't have ten pounds to spare at the time, nor was she prepared to allow the owner to take some of her cherished pieces of antique brass in lieu of payment. So Bill was carried off to the car, leaving Catherine in floods of tears. Then, at Tom's instigation, she dashed out into the road and agreed to let the woman have the brasses in exchange for Bill. The story eventually found its way to the ears of the woman's husband and the items were returned with a letter of apology.

Bill caused Catherine and Tom endless trouble. As a puppy he left a trail of devastation all round the house. The scene described so humorously in *Mary Ann and Bill* was written directly from Catherine's own experience:

Bill was in the middle of disembowelling the armchair; he was covered all over with kapok . . . Inside the fender was the remains of a cushion; on the hearth rug was what had once been a tea towel; the woollen hand-knitted tea-cosy that she had bought from the bazaar just a few weeks ago had almost returned to its original state of unknitted wool . . . And pervading this chaos was a peculiar smell . . .[10]

Bill proved difficult to train and on several occasions had Catherine flying down the High Street grimly hanging on to the end of his lead. He also caught the mange and gave it to Catherine, who spent several days indoors stinking of what she described as 'sheep dip'. But his worst problem was aggression towards other dogs. After an altercation with the neighbour's Labrador, he took every opportunity to escape from the garden and inflict damage on other unsuspecting beasts – though he never went for their owners. Catherine was afraid that eventually someone, perhaps a child, would get hurt and reluctantly arranged for Bill to be put down. However, when the day came, she was unable to go through with it and instead, with the agreement of the vet, decided to try neutering. It didn't make a great deal of difference to Bill's homicidal instincts, but having reprieved him from the death sentence once, Catherine couldn't bear to go through the process again. He was her child, 'a tearaway, a bad lad but a loving bad lad'.[11]

Although superficially Catherine could sublimate her mothering instincts in the care and affection she showered on Bill, at a deeper level she had found nothing to fill the spiritual void inside her, left by the abandonment of her Catholic faith. A close friend tried very hard to persuade Catherine to come to faith-healing and spiritualist sessions at the 'House of Healing' in Hastings. Although Catherine was sceptical, her mystic experience in St Albans had led her to think much more deeply about psychic phenomena. There had also been an incident with a woman on a train who had once touched Catherine and told her that she was probably herself a healer. Catherine decided to give it a try.

The first thing Catherine attended was a seance. In an extreme state of nerves, she sat at the back listening to messages being relayed to various other people in the room. She was shocked when the medium pointed her finger at Catherine and delivered a message that she felt could only be for her. It was from her male friend who had committed suicide a couple of years earlier, at the height of her own breakdown. The medium also claimed to see an elderly man standing behind Catherine's shoulder and he, too, had a very important message. Catherine was to return to her own way of working, 'to how your heart dictates'.[12] This mysterious message validated something Catherine had wanted to believe for some time.

Catherine was determined to become a published writer and was acutely aware of the gulf between her own scribblings and the books she borrowed from the library. She knew she had the imagination but lacked the intellectual tools to enable her to express it. After the war, when Tom returned, she had shown him the stories and plays she had written while she was alone at the Hurst and, although she had asked for an honest, critical opinion, had been deeply hurt by his reaction. Tom told her the truth, as gently as he could. If she wanted to be a writer, her knowledge of the English language simply wasn't good enough. She had asked him to help her to write in a more grammatical and literate way. She wanted to be able to spell correctly and understand the rules of grammar. Tom was very willing to help and shortly afterwards he began to teach Catherine 'King's English', Oxbridge style.

But as soon as Catherine began to study under Tom, she found herself unable to write fluently. The people she wrote about turned into one-dimensional puppets and the story refused to flow. Catherine went into writer's block and was terrified by it. Tom told friends that he felt that she had only to persevere a little longer and the linguistic effects she was learning would come quite naturally. It was like learning a new way of wielding the racquet in tennis – once she had these new skills at her disposal, Catherine would be off again. Catherine didn't believe him and it was, for a time, a major source of friction between them.

So when the medium gave Catherine the message, purporting to come from her grandfather – whom Catherine identified as being the first person to recognise her talent for storytelling – she felt vindicated. She went straight to the school, where Tom was leading a Scout troop, and told him that she wasn't going to study any more – she was going back to her own instinctive way of writing. Tom was extremely disappointed – 'she was so nearly there,' he told friends – but not surprised by Catherine's decision. He regretfully accepted that she could write only in her own authentic voice.

At the end of the week Catherine went for her first session of 'spirit' healing with the same medium. She had been suffering from a painfully inflamed face for some time and the doctor had told her that she must go into hospital for an operation on her sinuses. Catherine talked to someone who had had the same operation and was very alarmed by what she heard. She decided to try alternative medicine. On the couch at the House of Healing, her face was gently massaged while the medium, in communication with a 'spirit doctor', murmured healing words over her. Three days later the pain in her face had gone and Catherine cancelled her hospital appointment.

A spiritual healer features in her novel *The Fifteen Streets*, where he saves the life of a woman in childbirth. Catherine describes the experience of lying above the bed 'on a sort of soft platform . . . with queer sensations passing through her body . . . It was odd, but rather nice, lying here thinking untroubled thoughts.'[13] For a northeastern Catholic, spiritualists, usually referred to as 'Spooks' in Jarrow, were even less acceptable than Protestants. 'Looking hard at John, [the doctor] asked, "Do you believe in spiritual healing?" John answered simply, "I'm a Catholic." "So am I," said the doctor. "And I'm dead against it professionally and otherwise . . . yet . . ."'[14] Although Catherine always declared herself an agnostic towards spiritualism, she became a convert to the idea of psychic healing.

Around this time, Catherine was introduced to the work of Harry Edwards, regarded by some as a charlatan, and by others as one of the great mystics of the twentieth century. He had started out as a soldier during the First World War, serving in India and the Middle East, where he quickly gained a reputation as a healer, although he had no medical training and his only equipment was an army first-aid kit. He brought his reputation back to Europe with him and in the thirties and forties he had a huge following, including members of the royal family, politicians and film stars, as well as millions of ordinary people. His mass rallies, where people were invited to come to the front and be healed by the touch of his hands, attracted thousands, their format closely resembling some of the evangelical services of healing broadcast on American TV channels today.

Harry Edwards came to Hastings, where he held a rally in the pier theatre. Catherine went to see him and was very moved as she watched people throwing away their walking sticks, apparently healed by his touch. Carried away by the highly charged emotional atmosphere, she too went to the front. 'I stood in an apparently endless line and waited my turn to state my need, and to feel the touch of his hand.'[15] Although for her there was no miracle, she remained convinced that he was a channel of power direct from some kind of divine source, 'God, if you like'. What Harry Edwards did for Catherine was to provide a spiritual support system to replace her lost faith: 'with this man I had only to lift the phone and help or advice was immediately forthcoming'.[16] If she had a problem she wrote to him at the Healing Sanctuary and would receive a reassuring answer. She was being prayed for; she would be healed; she would not be called upon to endure more than her strength was equal to; everything was going to be all right. It was the kind of positive reinforcement she needed. Friends say that Tom was very sceptical about all this, but felt that if it helped Catherine, then there must be something in it. He had already learned that Catherine would go her own way, whatever anyone else said.

The priests at St Mary Star of the Sea and the nuns from the convent, who had all known Catherine before the war, were horrified at her loss of faith. Catherine's fragile equilibrium was often disturbed by their attempts to win her back to the church. Someone sent her, anonymously, a copy of the tract 'A Letter to a Lapsed Catholic'. Catherine's revulsion at the crude arguments and threats it contained answered the often repeated question why she no longer wanted to be a Catholic. 'To a trained, logical and educated mind' its statements were ridiculous. 'God does not want to have to damn you . . . If you do go to hell – which God forbid – it will be through your own deliberate fault . . . possibly through refusing the appeal of this letter.' The alternative was to come back to the faith where the believer would be exempt from eternal punishment and invited to view him or herself as 'a little child being carried through life like a tiny baby being loved in its mother's lap or upon her knee'. Years earlier that would have been a powerfully attractive image for Catherine, but now she found it infantile. What level of mentality was it supposed to appeal to? she asked. One of the subsequent paragraphs made her even more angry. It was addressed to those who married out of the church.

I have met many people who have done what you have done. Very, very few of them were not, deep down in their hearts, worried and anxious to come back home. Probably your marriage can be put right; do please see a priest about it as soon as you can. You will be the first to agree with me that it is foolish to go on living in sin. Sin never pays. Why delay?

Although Catherine could now rationalise her departure from the Catholic church, she was still troubled about the existence and nature of God. Emotionally she could not do without the idea of God, if only 'as a screen against fear' and a spiritual prop. But if God did exist, in what form, and how could she talk to him? As a Catholic she had been brought up to address him only through intermediaries, such as the priests, the saints and the Virgin. The notion of talking directly to him was unfamiliar. 'Then came the day I revolted and actually spoke to God ... here I was, this day, facing Him and actually swearing at Him; I told Him I was fearing Him no more ... from now on, I said, I was going it alone.'

It happened on a Friday afternoon – Friday the thirteenth – in 1948 and was triggered by a reaction against superstition. Kate had always been very superstitious and Catherine had been brought up navigating a minefield of prohibitions. The word 'pig' must never be uttered in the house, the sound of a cricket singing in the grate or a picture falling from a wall presaged a death, crossed knives on the table signalled bad luck – the list was endless. One of the things she was not supposed to do was to use a knife to sharpen a pencil or scissors to cut her nails on a Friday, actions which were somehow linked to Christ's agony on the cross. On this particular Friday Catherine unthinkingly picked up a pair of scissors and began to trim her nails. Realising what she had done she was at first overwhelmed by a spasm of fear so great that it drove her to vomit and then by an even greater surge of anger. Was her whole life to be dominated by fear and superstition? And what was religion if not another kind of superstitious fear?

> Going to the window and looking upwards over the top of the trees and into the sky, I sent tearing heavenwards words that made me tremble with fear even as I forced them out ... To blazes and bloody damnation with it all! ... God, dogma, the Catholic Church, the Devil, Hell, people, opinions, laws, illegitimacy ... and fear. Bugger them all ... I'll fear no more ... I'm vomiting for the last time.

As she shouted back at God, Catherine experienced a brief feeling of ecstatic freedom and catharsis.

Catherine's attempts to learn Oxford English had highlighted broader aspects of her psychology which were also now becoming clear to her. She began to recognise that part of her problem was her denial of her real self. She said later that she believed that her breakdown was God's way of saying to her that she had to face up to the person she really was – 'a self-educated illegitimate [she rarely used the word bastard] with no real knowledge of the world', rather than the pseudo-lady she tried so hard to become. 'I was very good at façades.' Being able to act had helped her to create a new persona for herself and she sometimes wished she'd been sent to drama school. 'If I'd had training I might have been an actress.'

Catherine was still performing a double act. To other people she was Tom's wife, friendly, humorous, talkative, a good hostess who gave wonderful dinner parties. But behind the protective gates of the Hurst, her mental state was precarious. 'Outwardly I'd laugh . . . But underneath I was writhing in fear . . . The shadows never leave you.' Even as she began to recover from the breakdown and have long periods of remission, she still had attacks of what she sometimes labelled 'neurasthenia' or, later, 'ME', which paralysed her legs and put her to bed. There were also terrifying, unpredictable recurrences of aggression.

One of the incidents she remembered most distinctly was the occasion when she was on her way to watch a school cricket match. On her way she passed a Timothy White's chemist's shop with a big plate-glass window. There was a baby in a pram outside it. Catherine was overcome with a wave of terrible aggression and felt a compulsion to snatch the baby from the pram and dash it to the pavement. Opposite the shop some builders were at work and the street was littered with debris, including some loose bricks in the gutter. Catherine focused on the bricks. Perhaps if she could pick up a brick and throw it through the window, it would release the violent feelings she struggled with. She stood on the pavement for a long time looking first at the brick and then at the shop, trying to resist the urge to smash the window or harm the child. Eventually one of the builders came over and jokingly asked if she'd like to take the brick home. Catherine said later that it must have looked very funny – a middle-aged lady in a smart suit and hat, hovering outside the shop with a brick. The builder's question helped Catherine to come to her senses. In order to get her feelings under control she went into one of the shops, a small bric-a-brac shop, to look around. Still trembling with emotion she felt she should buy something to justify her presence and picked up a small ginger jar. 'The beautiful thing in my hand soothed me,' Catherine said later. She bought it and it remained in her cabinet until the day she died, as a reminder of what might have happened. Afterwards she was able to continue up the street to the school, where she sat with Tom's colleagues making polite conversation with only one half of her mind, the other half occupied with imagining the appalling consequences that would have ensued if she had not been able to divert her aggression.

Very little of what was going on in her mind was evident to other people. In 1949 Catherine met Margaret Charrot, who became a lifelong friend. Margaret and her husband John had just moved into one of the houses in Hoads Wood Road. John was a teacher at the secondary school and Margaret was pregnant with her second child. Margaret remembers that she and Catherine took to each other straight away, as did their husbands: 'From our first meeting we felt that Tom and Kitty were very special people.' Catherine, in particular, had 'a radiance about her', noted by many people who knew her then, a spiritual quality that shone out of her and was enormously attractive.

One of her most striking features was her speaking voice – a resonant, musical alto. One day, goaded by the next-door neighbour whom she believed to be putting her down by commenting on the carrying quality of her voice, Catherine decided to try writing something for radio. This was a happy conjunction. Catherine's conversational, colloquial style suited the medium of sound. She listened to the radio quite a lot and was therefore familiar with the format. After many drafts she finally had something she was happy with, a script called 'From the Laundry to the Arts' which was later renamed 'Learning to Draw at Thirty'. She practised reading it for weeks until she almost had it by heart. Catherine was very surprised when the BBC accepted her script straight away and even more pleased when she was asked to read it on air. Her second broadcast was more personal still. She called it 'Putting Nerves in Their Place'. By going public about her breakdown, she hoped to cure herself of the fear that people would find out that she had been treated for mental health problems. She also hoped that her own experience would help others. Catherine was not prepared for the avalanche of letters that followed the broadcast, from people who were suffering as Catherine had suffered and were too ashamed to talk about it. It helped her considerably to know that she was not alone in her struggle for sanity and peace of mind.

The acceptance of her radio broadcasts was an important boost for Catherine's confidence. In them she had written and spoken as herself, not some invented character in a drama. Just as the denial of her real self had been a factor in her breakdown, so it had hampered Catherine in her writing. She realised now that she had to ditch the 'stilted, status conscious' person she had become before she could 'write a word that anyone would want to read'. In moving south and trying to get on in the world, she had alienated herself from her roots and her class and in doing so had lost her own real identity.

The big breakthrough came one day as she stood in front of the mirror, berating herself for lack of 'gumption'. In one of her short autobiographical fragments Catherine describes how she suddenly became aware of a small child who stepped out from behind the mirror and looked at her. There was something very familiar about the young girl's appearance, the 'long nut-brown ringlets, a heart-shaped face, round blinking eyes, a pert mouth and an uptilted nose with a little cut on the left side'. Catherine's description of Mary Ann Shaughnessy is exactly that of the young Katie McMullen. Catherine even had a similar cut on her nose that had been done with a broken bottle. Mary Ann was about eight years old, the age at which Catherine most clearly identified herself as a child. It was the time when she had been told she was illegitimate – and consequently 'orphaned' by the children in the alley. When she thought of herself as a child, it was always around the age of eight. When she talked about the death of her grandmother, she recalled that Rose died when Catherine was 'about eight', although Rose actually died some years later, when Catherine was an adolescent. Mary Ann Shaughnessy was the irrepressible eight-year-old from the New Buildings that Mrs Catherine Cookson had been trying for years to conceal behind a middle-class façade. Catherine later admitted that 'Mary Ann was me as a child'. The appearance of Mary Ann was an important step, not only in showing Catherine the direction her writing should take, but also in revealing a way out of the breakdown. Catherine left the mirror, sat down at the kitchen table with her pad and pencil, and wrote a story called 'She Had No Da'. It was her own story. In writing about her experiences she could begin to reconnect the two fragmented halves of her personality and begin to deal with the legacy of mental anguish left by her childhood.

She joined the Hastings Writers' Circle and maintained her connection with it even after she became a well-published author, eventually becoming the secretary. There are still several members who remember her. In the beginning she was very nervous. Though everyone was supposed to stand to read their work, Catherine had to sit. She made the excuse that she had rheumatism, but in reality nerves made her legs unreliable under stress. She was also very sensitive to criticism and when people analysed her work honestly she was inclined to burst into tears. But it was there that she read the first of her Mary Ann stories.

The story was so well received that everyone clapped and clapped. Catherine knew that she had something worth keeping. She could also now see a clear way out of her breakdown. She cried all the way home. 'I knew then that the way to get rid of the pity I felt for the child was to write her out of my system.' But it wasn't until several years later that she expanded the Mary Ann stories into a novel. Catherine's first book was written even more directly out of her own autobiographical experience and that of her mother. It was about a woman called Kate who lived in Jarrow and had an illegitimate daughter whose name was Annie – a variation of Catherine's own middle name. It was generously dedicated to 'My Mother, who has found her expression through me'.

Years later she wrote an article in *The Author* about the creation of her first novel. After her success with the Mary Ann story at the writers' workshop, she sat down at the kitchen table and told herself, 'Forget about Chesterfield and Lords and Ladies and their big houses. Get rid of them. Face up to the fact of your early beginnings; think of the people you knew in the New Buildings ... weave a story round them. Bring in Kate as you know she could have been and that will sublimate this terrible feeling that you have against her. Go on, get down to it!' The result was *Kate Hannigan*.

PART FOUR

— ❖ —

The Regional Novelist
1948–1968

Like a great sponge I'd taken it all in: the
character of the people; the fact that work was
their life's blood; their patience in the face of
poverty; their perseverance, their kindness, and
their open-handedness; their narrowness and
their bigotry . . . I couldn't write with any
strength about any other place.

Catherine Cookson

13

Write about what you know.[1]

Even when she could see what to write about, Catherine's first novel did not take shape overnight. There were no miracles; just a great deal of time spent carefully working and reworking the story. Her initial idea was to make each chapter independent, rather like short stories, each episode taking place on a particular Christmas Eve and ending on a cliff-hanger. It was a technique that Dickens had used very successfully when his novels were being sold in separate instalments. When she got further into the book, Catherine found that the structure began to dictate the story and some chapters had to be adapted to a different time scale, but the novel still has a tightly structured feel and the episodic nature of the chapters gives it tremendous narrative drive. The novel begins at a dramatic moment of action as Annie Hannigan is about to be born, and the first paragraphs have a gripping pace to them, consisting almost entirely of dialogue or internal monologue. The reader is pitched into the heart of the story straight away.

Although her method was initially instinctive, gradually, over the years Catherine began to formulate her approach to writing and talk about it in order to encourage others. She admitted that she sometimes spent two years thinking about a book and its characters before it came to fruition. There would be several storylines in her head at any one time at various stages of development. The early novels were written in pencil on the infamous kitchen table bought by Nan when Catherine first came to Hastings. Her friend Josephine Austin remembers that her forefinger was bent back with the pressure of 'long-handing' so many hundreds of thousands of words.

In the middle of the night, when sleep eluded her, Catherine composed the story in her head. 'There I am in the black dark at 2 o'clock in the morning, grappling with characters . . . The characters come first – never the plot.' For Catherine character and environment were the two most important things. 'It's environment that sets character . . . environment that gives one education or no education.'[2] The story came into being on the interface between the two. Catherine's novels are about relationships, not ideas; visceral rather than cerebral, coming from the guts and the heart rather than from the head, and this is why some critics find them intellectually lacking. But the directly comparable novels of Mary Wesley and Joanna Trollope scarcely stretch the intellect either, though they have more literary claims made for them than Catherine's. Her novels are also sometimes criticised for being 'linguistically impoverished' and this is also unfair, particularly with regard to her early work. She doesn't use complex or poetic language, but the words she does use have the rich muscularity of colloquial speech, its colour and rhythms. They are also very tightly constructed. Catherine said that the secret for her was in 'simple writing' – the hardest thing to do – and it was also vital to cut out the padding. She would sometimes cut a manuscript down by as much as two thirds.

Catherine's hints to budding authors were born from all the discouragement that she had suffered through the long years of her apprenticeship. According to Catherine, a determined writer should 'turn deaf ears' to all those who tell them that 'the market's swamped already and that there isn't a hope in hell for newcomers'. They should also ignore those who tell them they will never earn any money for it; ignore the 'frustrated writer', an expert in the field, who has had forty rejection slips for the same book in one year though it is 'really first class stuff' – all his family and friends say it's wonderful. 'Finally,' Catherine advised drily, 'steel yourself to look that other dear friend straight in the eye when he casually remarks that without a suitable education, by which he means university, your chance of landing on the literary planet is on a par with that of you being selected to orbit the moon.'[3] Catherine's use of the male pronoun throughout is instructive.

Catherine still had a chip on her shoulder about her lack of education, which was never completely remedied by all those years of reading. The cultural poverty of her early years left a deep mark that could never be eradicated. An old lady on Tyneside explained the dilemma very clearly: 'How do you get on, how do you learn any-thing where there's no books, no discussion of ideas with anyone who has an educated mind, and where every attempt to better yourself is laughed at? Ee, you're gettin' above yourself, lass!' Even if you did get the opportunity sometimes to talk to people who knew anything about literature or art, 'you'd condemn yourself as working-class ignorant every time you opened your mouth'.[4] It left Catherine with a lifelong inferiority complex.

The legacy of this early deprivation was felt most in the area of poetry. When Josephine Austin, one of Catherine's friends from the Hastings Writers' Circle, decided to set up a separate poetry group, Catherine joined that too. Josephine recalls how desperately Cath-erine wanted to write poetry but seemed to have no awareness of just how short of the mark her work fell. Where her novels were concerned, she had total control of her craft; with poetry she failed utterly, although she cherished the poems and longed to have them published. She wanted to be a poet more than anything. It was here that her lack of education and early reading became important: poems from the *Happy Mag* were not the best training for the ear. However, educated writers too have had a similar problem. The short-fiction writer Katherine Mansfield, one of the great prose writers of the twentieth century, had a critical blind spot towards her own poetry, which is inferior to everything else she wrote, though the language of her stories and her notebook entries is as close to poetry as anything in English.

The autobiographical nature of *Kate Hannigan* made it both easy and also very difficult to write. Though Catherine had all the back-ground, the characters and the plot to hand, she had to trawl through the painful childhood she had tried so hard to leave behind and relive it in her imagination before she could put it down on the page. She sat at the kitchen table in the Hurst and thought herself back into the kitchen at number 10 William Black Street, where Katie McMullen, alias Annie Hannigan, sat on the fender and there was 'pan-hacklety sizzling in the big black frying pan on the hob, and the wind would be whirling down the chimney and the gas mantle making little plop-plopping noises'.[5] The kitchen of Catherine's child-hood was 'the hub of my life; it was the centre of the universe from which all pain and pleasure sprang'. Much of the action in *Kate Hannigan* takes place in one kitchen or another.

The effort it cost Catherine to write the book was reflected in another nightmare that began to appear night after night, in which she was struggling to climb a cliff, 'clawing my way up, hand over hand'. There was always an overhang to be negotiated and the terrible fear of falling, but Catherine usually made it to the top, only to wake exhausted and sweating. She comforted herself with the thought that 'writing it out' would rid her 'of all the fear, the night terrors, the dreadful aggressiveness that lay behind the façade'.[6] The climbing nightmare vanished shortly after the publication of her early novels, but the dreams of a black-robed priest, and another in which she found herself in public half naked, would not go away.

Nor did the dreams about Kate which had invaded Catherine's sleep ever since her breakdown. They 'all followed the same pattern. She was in a state of drink and I was beating her with my fists, or choking the life out of her. Always I was struggling with her.' Catherine's dreams seemed to underline the split she felt in her personality between the 'staid and sober' writer whose pen was 'poised probingly' and the other twin who could 'act so mad and foolishly'. Which side of her was the real Catherine, she asked in her poetry?

> My dreams are rarely happy.
> Which is me?
> Am I who write, the phantasy
> And she in dreams, reality?[7]

Despite the dreams, by 1947 Catherine felt that she was strong enough to renew contact with her mother. 'She wanted to see me, and in a way I wanted to see her. I wanted to see what effect she would have on me.' So Kate came to the Hurst for a visit. The result was a terrible setback for Catherine's recovery. Even though Kate didn't touch drink at all during the two weeks of her holiday, just having her in the house brought back all Catherine's unresolved feelings of hate and fear. So afraid was Catherine that she might get up during the night, cross the landing and murder Kate in her sleep, that she discussed the possibility of getting Tom to tie her to the bed. These extreme instances of aggression towards her mother go far beyond a reaction to childhood rejection and lend some credence to the suggestion that Catherine may have been abused by her mother while under the influence of drink.

During the winter of 1948, Hastings library organised a talk by a visiting writer – Charles Bush, who wrote thrillers under the name of Major Christopher Bush. Catherine, along with several other members of the Writers' Circle, went to hear him speak. It was a particularly wild night, so windy and wet that only about a dozen people turned up for the event. Undaunted, Major Bush began his standard talk for would-be authors, designed to encourage and stimulate. One of his main points was that 'anyone who could write a laundry list could write a novel'. This incensed Catherine so much that she sprang to her feet at the end and challenged him. What he said was untrue, she told him; 'I . . . had written thousands of laundry lists, but they hadn't helped me to write a novel'. Outside in the street, Catherine's anger subsided and she began to feel guilty. Fearing that she had been rude to the major, she went back into the library and apologised. Major Bush was charming to Catherine and asked about her novel and whether she had an agent. If she wanted to get pub-lished, it would be a good idea to have one, he told her. Catherine had no idea how to go about finding an agent. She had been given the impression by members of the Writers' Circle that 'they were a species who should be avoided'. Major Bush recommended that Catherine send the first three chapters of *Kate Hannigan* to his own agents, Christy & Moore.

A friend of Catherine's typed up the first chapters at a shilling per thousand words and Catherine posted them to Christy & Moore. There they were given to John Smith, who had not been with the firm long and was looking for new clients to build up his list. John was 'instantly gripped by the vigour and directness of the writing . . . I felt she had a real voice coming directly from her and not from a background of literature.'[8] The head of the firm wasn't so impressed but agreed to back John's instinct. John wrote back to Catherine quite quickly, telling her that in his opinion it was very promising, and he urged her to finish it and send him the completed manuscript.

This was exactly the encouragement that Catherine needed. 'I worked on that story every minute I could.'[9] But it still took her a year to finish. The parts of the book that dealt with Catholicism were the most troublesome. Catherine wanted to hit back at the church, but she also wanted to be fair. She opted in the end to have two priests, as there had been in Jarrow – one of them an orthodox, inflexible man who goads people into the church by fear, and the other a kindly man who hands out penances with a twinkle in his eye. These priests represented what Catherine saw as the negative and the more progressive sides of the Catholic religion. She was careful to ground her arguments in the characters of the priests and their interaction with the hero and heroine, using the age-old maxim of the novelist – 'never express ideas except in terms of character'. The conflict gives the book considerable dramatic tension.

Catherine was a natural, intuitive, gifted storyteller. She had been brought up in an oral culture, without books or radio or television, where people told stories around the fire in the evening – family stories, tales of things that happened to them when they were young, stories about their relatives in Ireland. The memory stores of older people such as John McMullen went back a long way. He had been born in the 1850s and could tell stories about the lives of his parents and grandparents stretching back to the beginning of the nineteenth century. The natural shaping of a narrative for retelling, knowing what to emphasise and what to leave out, how to create suspense and hold the listener's attention, were all things that Catherine had learned as a small child sitting on the fender hearing the adults talking.

Her friend Margaret Charrot still remembers the first time she heard Catherine tell a story. Catherine had come to the Charrots' house on Christmas Eve bringing a present – what she still referred to by the northern term 'Christmas box'.

> Our daughter, then two years old, came to the door in her night-gown and Kitty said, 'Not in bed? Do you know what night it is? Come here.' And she sat herself on the bottom stair with her arm round the child and spoke of Father Christmas and his reindeer – the old story. Marion was entranced. Her eyes never left Kitty's face. There was something in the telling that was magical.

John Smith was 'elated' to find that the completed manuscript of *Kate Hannigan* lived up to its initial promise: 'after ploughing through countless MSS by struggling writers ... it seemed to be the real thing'. He gave Catherine lunch at the Café Royal and was delighted to find her 'as straightforward as her book'.[10] However, first novels, even well-written ones, do not sell easily and John expected to have to send *Kate Hannigan* round several publishers before it found a home. He decided to send it initially to Macdonald, where, but for the intervention of a secretary, it would have been rejected. Murray Thompson, then the head of the firm, looked briefly at the first pages, thought it much 'too grim' to fit into their romantic fiction list and gave it to his secretary to return. Out of curiosity she also glanced at the first pages, became hooked and took the manuscript home, where she sat up far into the night in order to finish it. When she brought it in the following morning, she asked Murray to have another look at it and as a result, the book was sent out to a reader, Malcolm Elwin. His report was encouraging: 'I don't know how old this writer is, but if she is young she will go somewhere.' He took exception to the last chapter, where Catherine had gone overboard in a tirade about the Catholic church, and recommended that the book be accepted if the last chapter could be rewritten. At this point Catherine had too much of an inferiority complex to be precious where her work was concerned. If the publishers thought the piece had to come out, then she would rewrite it. She sent the revised manuscript off and received the first, glorious letter of acceptance.

Catherine's first action was to run down the road to Margaret Charrot in a state of great excitement. She gave Margaret some money to buy herself a treat, 'something I really wanted – not something useful. I bought two flower prints and a jar of face cream!' Catherine was ecstatic. She dreamed of what she was going to do with the money. She would be able to repair the roof on the Hurst, employ a gardener, buy a car for Tom and, for herself, a fur coat. But the dreams vanished when the publisher offered her £100 for the book. After Catherine had paid the typist, her agent's commission and other expenses, there would be very little left for more than a year's work.

Later she was often asked, 'What is it like to have your first novel published?' And she would describe the mixture of 'joy, ecstasy, slight delirium and that understandably superior feeling that comes with the publication of a first novel . . . Only those who have undergone this ego-inflation can hope to understand. You have written a book; it is going to be published. You are an author. AN AUTHOR. You are on top of the world; it is there kneeling at your feet.'[11] But after the sobering reality of the publisher's advance, a further element of realism was injected by the bread-delivery man. Tom, immensely proud of Catherine's achievement, was showing off the book to everyone who came. The baker looked at it and then at Tom and then turned to Catherine and asked, 'White or brown?' Tom's sister was staying at the Hurst when the first copies arrived and she too, although interested, wasn't as impressed as either Catherine or Tom would have liked.

Catherine was also disappointed that her friends virtually ignored the event. She had a great need for public approval and was longing to be congratulated. But at an early-evening working party for a charity bazaar the talk was on other things – 'an absent friend whom they all agreed made herself sick only to get her husband's attention, through the six o'clock news, to the dizzy heights of finance when they debated the price one could put on a hand-made cosy'.[12] Catherine cried all the way home. Later she discovered why they had been silent. Several of these women were shocked at the 'earthy' realism of the novel and thought that it should not have been published. Violence, sexual abuse and illegitimacy were not subjects for respectable middle-class women to read and certainly not to write about.

There was another disappointment when Catherine went up to London to have lunch with Murray Thompson. This first meeting is a big event for any author and Catherine was concerned to make a good impression. She borrowed money from the various kitties she kept in the kitchen for rates, electricity and coal and bought herself a cream linen suit from a dress agency in St Leonards that sold 'nearly new', good-quality clothes. She altered a black straw hat to go with the suit. All the way to London, on buses and trains, Catherine had to repress the desire to tell everyone she met that she was a novelist, on the way to lunch with her publisher – 'I discovered that morning that you can always be charming when you feel successful'. So preoccupied was she that she stepped off the kerb in front of a taxi, causing him to brake sharply and the vehicles behind to swerve into each other. Catherine 'acquired a lot of new words' as the drivers of the taxi, a bus, a lorry and two other cars involved, all told her what they thought. Always disturbed by bad language, Catherine was so shaken that she had to stand quietly in a side street until her legs stopped trembling and she could carry on.

When she reached Macdonald she was surprised at the smallness and shabbiness of the premises. Directed up the steep, dark stairs to Murray Thompson's office, she found that he was otherwise engaged. Catherine had come on the wrong day. The mistake she blamed on her agent, John Smith. So Catherine found herself having lunch with Murray Thompson's secretary, the woman who had rescued her book from the slush pile. She was 'a charming person', Catherine said, 'but the glory of the day had vanished'.

Back at the Hurst, Catherine threw herself into her next book, which was to be a sequel to the first and would tell the story of Kate's daughter, Annie Hannigan. In effect, this was to be Catherine's own story rather than that of her mother. Annie is the illegitimate child brought up by her grandmother and step-grandfather, who is told by her friends in the street that she 'has no da' and who fantasises about the doctor as her father. At the end of *Kate Hannigan*, Kate does actually marry the doctor. But although she had been able to write about Annie as a small child, when Catherine came to the sequel, she had to write about her own growth into adulthood and found that she wasn't yet ready to do so. There was too much deep water between mother and child that would have to be charted before Catherine could complete her own story. It was a shock when the publishers wrote back saying that they thought it not quite as good as her first novel, though they were willing to publish it with alterations. The reasons were complex. John Smith remembers that 'it posed the problem of so many second novels. I felt it lacked the directness of *Kate Hannigan*; it was also more romantic and contrived.'[13] In addition, it was even more hostile to the Catholic church than *Kate Hannigan* had been and there was too much of Catherine's own bitterness in the book. John Foster White, her editor at Macdonald, also felt that the character of the hero and the way in which his sexuality was portrayed had not been successfully resolved. There were other reasons too. The 'Catherine Cookson' genre had not been established and her work did not fit easily into the romantic fiction list published by Macdonald – *Annie Hannigan* even less so than her first novel.

Catherine later said that she 'could not bear the condescension of that letter' from Macdonald.[14] Typically, she reacted decisively. Unlike the reader's comments on the last chapter of *Kate Hannigan*, which Catherine had willingly complied with, something in the second reader's report struck a raw nerve with her. She had always found criticism difficult to deal with, and in this case, criticism of the book was criticism of Catherine herself. This novel *was* Catherine. With the ruthless resolve that had led her to burn all her early work, instead of sitting down to rewrite the novel, she immediately telephoned Murray Thompson to say that she would like him to send the manuscript back and that she didn't want it to be published. As she herself said, this was a very courageous act given the amount of work that had gone into the book and the difficulty – for a new author – of getting a novel published at all. She didn't even ask her agent to submit it to another publisher for a second opinion. Although Catherine did eventually revise the manuscript, *Annie Hannigan* was never published in her lifetime. Transworld plan to publish it as her hundredth novel to coincide with the millennium.

At the time, although she tried not to admit it, the failure of *Annie Hannigan* lacerated Catherine's pride. After speaking to Murray Thompson, she came out of the alcove under the stairs where the telephone was kept, feeling utterly devastated. Catherine later told editor Piers Dudgeon that she had no idea what she was going to do. 'There was me, who was never without an idea, never without a story to tell to someone, yet my mind was utterly blank. I thought I was finished.'[15] In this state of bleak despair, Catherine went into the drawing room and sat on the sofa. She told friends that, without knowing why, since she no longer consciously believed in God, she looked upwards and uttered a silent, desperate prayer: 'If there is anyone or anything there, please give me a story.' She continued to sit in the unheated room until she was shivering with cold in an almost trancelike state; 'never before that, and definitely never since, has my mind known such a void'.[16]

Suddenly, in a way that she couldn't explain, a complete story began to form in her head – characters, incidents, background, the opening lines, the last scenes and then the title. Catherine went straight into the dining room, picked up a pencil and wrote *The Fifteen Streets* at the top of a new page. It was a miracle, she said later, a gift that came 'from some spirit deep within me, that is below the subconscious'.[17] The novel was to become one of Catherine's most popular books, eventually made into a stage play and then a television film.

The O'Briens are a fighting family, like the McMullens, but their son John longs to better himself through education and get out of his environment. His favourite sister, Katie, is another version of Katie McMullen – an imaginative, sensitive child being brutalised by life in the fifteen streets. The ten-year-old child has to go to the pawnshop and it fills her with shame. 'To walk up the dock bank, under the knowledgeable stares of the men idling there against the railings caused her throat to move in and out; and to meet any of her schoolmates on the journey made her want to die.'[18] There are continual parallels – some of them related in almost identical words – with incidents in Catherine's own life, later revealed in *Our Kate*. It is Katie O'Brien/McMullen who steals the *Rainbow* comic from the shop and vomits with fear, Katie whose soul is harrowed by the strict Catholic priest, Katie who witnesses her mother in a deathlike coma from which, unlike Rose McMullen, she is revived.

As in *Kate Hannigan* and its flawed sequel, the religious conflicts in Catherine's own life are played out on the pages of *The Fifteen Streets*. There are warnings about the dangers of intellectual bigotry. 'The minds of people are moving. They are searching for the truth – they are reading. And what are they reading first? – the very books that are forbidden by your Church, for the first question the groping mind asks is: Why have these books been forbidden?'[19] When John O'Brien falls in love with Katie's Protestant teacher, Mary Llewellyn, the conflicting viewpoints of the religious divide are argued out, alongside the difficulties of marriage across the class barrier, both of which Catherine had personally experienced.

> God knew there was no happiness came out of a mixed marriage … And yet, as awful as that possibility seemed, he would have had a little show of happiness in a way, whereas now there was none for him that she could see. For what was the obstacle of religion compared with the obstacle of class? Had he gone mad? … Her da was a boatbuilder; and a docker, even a gaffer, would be so much midden muck to him.[20]

When Mary Llewellyn finally does move to the fifteen streets to be with John, the smashing of the porcelain nude figure she had treasured (like one that had graced Catherine's room in Hastings) represents all that Mary will have to give up in order to live there.

> The statue had been a symbol of truth to her; a figure indeed of her emancipation from cant and hypocrisy; a symbol of her growing freedom. But now it was gone. Never until this moment had she fully realised what coming to the fifteen streets would mean … her life would not only have to be altered from the outside, but from within. Not only her actions, but her thoughts must be restricted.[21]

At the time she wrote *The Fifteen Streets* and the subsequent novel *Colour Blind*, the Cooksons' marriage was again under considerable strain. As well as the severe depression left by her breakdown, Catherine was also going through a bad menopause aggravated by her blood disorder. She had very heavy bleeds that kept her in bed and underwent several operations on her womb between 1948 and 1952. When Catherine was ill, the burden of running the household fell on Tom, and during 1948 he had begun to suffer crippling attacks of migraine. Tom was a very sensitive man, who often experienced periods of depression and despair that had their roots in his own upbringing – what Catherine identified as 'the struggle to make a compromise between a working-class background and a pre-war university education', as well as 'the little things, stupid little things that happened in childhood to us both and which, buried deep, grow with the years almost into phobias'.[22] He was a giver, who sublimated his own needs in order to care for the needs of others, particularly those of his wife, and this put a great strain on his emotional resources. A close friend who knew the Cooksons for more than forty years said that although 'it seems they were an ideal couple deeply in love throughout their lives ... love does not necessarily embrace every aspect of one's life and I think Tom gave her love and absolute devotion but at a considerable cost. Most of his activities soon had to be abandoned because they did not fit in with her life.' In the words of another friend, 'there was a great deal swept under the carpet where Tom was concerned'.[23]

Apart from the emotional politics of their relationship, an additional source of stress for the Cooksons was the unresolved problem of Kate, living alone in Jarrow and getting progressively older and less capable. One night Catherine dreamed as usual that she was struggling to climb the cliff face, but on this occasion she didn't succeed. Instead of finding herself at the top, she found herself in a deep valley surrounded by sheer, high rock faces she couldn't climb.

> There was no way out, the only thing was to go back the way I had come. I stood still looking upwards to the unreachable summits, and in this position I woke up, and I said to myself, 'What now? I've got to face something, or go back. What is it?' The answer was, Kate, I had to conquer my feeling towards her or retreat into myself by way of the dark road I had come.

14

We are murdered by our ancestors. Their dead hands
stretch forth from the tomb and drag us down.[1]

From 1947 onwards, Kate spent her annual holiday at the Hurst.
For Catherine, having Kate to stay was a duty she had to undertake,
though she dreaded the visits and the bouts of depression they precipitated. There was, additionally, the strain of having to keep Kate
away from alcohol. Tom too found it difficult to welcome Kate
wholeheartedly. Not only did he have memories of her determined
efforts to dislodge him from Catherine's life, he was also horrified
by the effect Kate's drinking and the resulting behaviour had had
on Catherine. He blamed Kate for the breakdown. Tom found her
presence irksome in other ways too. While she was at the Hurst,
Kate insisted on doing the cooking and neither Tom nor Catherine
liked the kind of food she prepared – they were currently following
the healthy-eating plan ('Live longer – feel younger') of Gayelord
Hauser. Kate, used to cooking for manual workers, produced large
meals of meat and two veg swimming in thick, greasy gravy. But she
really enjoyed the weeks she stayed there, despite the battles for
dominance in the kitchen and having her drinking habits policed by
Catherine. She gradually extended her holidays. After she contracted
a chest infection, she stayed for six weeks to convalesce and returned
for a similar period the following year. Soon she was staying for
three months.

Although most of the Cooksons' friends loved Kate and found
her convivial, these were difficult periods for Catherine and Tom.
Margaret Charrot, who was sometimes charged with keeping an eye
on Kate if Catherine had to go away, thought her great fun. Another

friend, who also liked Kate, admitted that she could understand why Catherine found her mother's visits so difficult. She recalled how Kate would occasionally escape Catherine's vigilance and have to be retrieved, blind drunk, from a local pub. For a couple in the Cooksons' position, this was extremely embarrassing, though it was merely an amusing anecdote to their friends.

It was hard for Catherine to be honest about her feelings for Kate when she was constantly being made to feel guilty in the face of Kate's popularity with other people. If they found her warm, lovable and entertaining, why couldn't she? Catherine was once humiliated by one of her cousin's children. On a family visit to Jarrow, Catherine had said something critical about Kate and one of the boys had leaped up and said, 'Don't you dare say a word about Aunt Kate – you're not fit to wipe her shoes!'[2] The words cut Catherine to the quick, but the incident underlined the fact that the problems originated in the relationship between mother and daughter. Catherine was unable to stand back emotionally and experience Kate as other people did. There were too many failed expectations, too many hurts and rejections to blame Kate for. Whatever it was that Kate had done, she had damaged Catherine too deeply to be forgiven.

After the publication of Catherine's first novel in 1950, Kate watched her daughter's growing reputation as a novelist with great pride as well as a certain amount of incredulity. Apart from the gap left by the unpublished *Annie Hannigan* in 1951, Catherine was now producing one or two novels a year. Kate would often say, 'Well, lass, I always knew you'd make something of yourself.' She read all Catherine's books and was staying with her when the proofs of her fourth novel, *Colour Blind*, arrived. Kate read this too and it was on this occasion that she talked to Catherine about being sexually persecuted by her half-brother and stepfather. Catherine began to realise how much she had blanked out in her own mind that was now resurfacing in her novels. Like many other children who have been abused, or have witnessed abuse, Catherine seems to have pushed her memories down into what she called 'the dark cupboard of my mind'.[3] Her novels were 'pages from my subconscious'. But the fact that she could retrieve these memories and use them constructively confirmed Catherine's belief that she could, indeed, write herself out of the breakdown, whose symptoms she was still experiencing.

Colour Blind, like Catherine's other early novels, features a child who is different. In this case it is because she is the product of a mixed-race marriage. Rose Angela has a black father – an almost unheard-of thing in Jarrow. Catherine had been fascinated as a child by an African man, 'Black Charlie', who lived in Tyne Dock with his family and earned a living by translating for foreign sailors. He had always been treated with courtesy and respect by the community, but Catherine was aware, even as a child, how this tolerance would have changed if any of his children had wanted to marry into it. To marry someone of a different colour was far worse than marrying across the boundaries of religion or class. This northern intolerance to mixed-race relationships was subsequently explored by Shelagh Delaney in *A Taste of Honey* in 1958. She claimed to have been inspired by Terence Rattigan; but could she possibly have read Catherine Cookson?

Whenever Kate returned to Jarrow, she sent pitiful letters back to Catherine. Kate was lonely in her upstairs flat. She had always been gregarious, had spent her life in an overcrowded house surrounded by people and couldn't cope with her own company. She also missed the comfort of the Hurst and its large garden. Catherine put the letters on one side, but could not ignore the nagging fear that, as Kate got older and physically more frail, she would need to be cared for. The crunch did not come until 1953.

Creatively, 1952 and 1953 were particularly fruitful years for Catherine. Casting around for ideas for a new novel, she picked up the old story 'She Had No Da' and one or two other sketches she had done featuring Mary Ann Shaughnessy and wondered whether they could be turned into a book. In her unpublished autobiography she tells how the irrepressible child from Jarrow, Katie/Mary Ann, stepped out from the mirror again and told Catherine that she'd written four books already without remembering any of the pleasant or funny things that happened. 'It's about time you changed your tune,' she said, and anyway wasn't it time she featured as the heroine of Catherine's story? 'Aw, go on,' she urged, 'aa'd like to be in a book!'[4] The result was *A Grand Man*, the first of her Mary Ann novels. It is lighter than the earlier Jarrow stories, full of humour, pathos and optimism. Mary Ann Shaughnessy is given a father who drinks too much, though his daughter tries to deny it. She recognises, as other people do not, that it is only circumstance that has brought him down. Mary Ann sets out single-handedly to redress the family fortunes by finding her father a job on a farm owned by the rich and reclusive Mr Lord. Many of the people who had lived in the New Buildings make an appearance, deftly caricatured. Catherine rewrote her childhood in these novels and made it humorous and much less tragic. Mrs 'Swanky' Smith, who had once told Katie McMullen to get away from Jarrow, appears as Mrs Flannagan, the mother of Mary Ann's arch-enemy – the beautifully behaved Sarah. Another neighbour is re-created in the character of Fanny McBride, who eventually grew beyond Mary Ann to inhabit a novel of her own. Fanny was one of Catherine's favourite characters – a strange choice since she exhibits many of the characteristics Catherine hated so much in both her mother and Aunt Mary. Fanny is a big, earthy, turbulent woman, quick with her tongue and her hands. She is someone for her children 'to live down', coarse enough to make them cringe. She doesn't love her children either, except for one, and is difficult, bigoted and unforgiving. However, Fanny has humour and a depth of humanity that redeems her.

In the same year, Catherine was goaded into beginning another novel along completely different lines. Walking along the London Road in Hastings, she was accosted by a well-dressed, well-spoken woman who obviously knew who she was. The woman addressed her as 'Mrs Cookson, the regional author' and asked why she always wrote about Tyneside. Why not Hastings? Catherine was ruffled by the remarks. She knew she could write. She could write about anything. In one of her most recent novels, *The Solace of Sin*, her feelings about being thought of as a 'regional writer' are put into the mouth of one of her characters:

> I'm not going to be dubbed a regional writer ... Ten a penny, that's what they are ... That kind of writing is dead. Oh, they make me sick ... glorifying the back streets and the blowsy women – 'earts of gold. Real Geordie characters; taking a pride in using a dialect that nobody else on God's earth, only their own kind, can understand ... The term 'worthy' is even tagged on to them.[5]

So Catherine took up the challenge and began to research the history of Hastings, browsed through the ships' chandlers, talked to fishermen in the old town and wrote a story set among the fishing community at the turn of the century. Catherine had written about 40,000 words before she was forced to acknowledge that it didn't work – 'the only thing in the story that had any guts in it was the fish'.[6] It took a great deal of courage and determination to abandon the manuscript, dumping it in the cupboard alongside *Annie Hannigan*.

But some of the characters were salvaged and made an appearance in a new book (the third in a year), *Maggie Rowan*, a searching novel about driving ambition, bigotry and misdirected love, whose 'environment' had been given to Catherine on a trip to Tyneside in 1952. While on a visit to Jarrow to see Kate, Catherine made contact with her Lavelle cousins in Birtley – the first time she had seen them in more than twenty years. Aunt Sarah had had four sons who had all gone into the mines like their father Mick. Catherine had been brought up with all John McMullen's prejudices about miners, and something of this attitude became apparent in the conversation. Catherine was complaining about the price of coal and the men, particularly Peter and Michael, became angry and challenged her to come down the pits and see for herself. Peter, who was a deputy at the Betty Pit, took her down in the cage and then along one of the 'roads' to the coal face. It was a revelation. 'From that moment, [I] wanted, sincerely and genuinely to pin medals on every pitman.'[7] When Peter Lavelle put out the lamps at the bottom of the pit, Catherine experienced the total panic she describes in *Maggie Rowan*. 'They were standing in darkness, the like of which she had never imagined possible – thick, heavy, clinging darkness, that hurt the eyeballs, that became alive and pressed on you.' There was also an eerie absence of sound. It was 'the darkness and silence of the eternity of the damned ... here there was nothing, yet everything, everything that was needed to bring the dark terrors of the soul to the surface.'

It was the setting Catherine needed for her next novel. She came back to Hastings, ditched the fishing manuscript, and began the history of illegitimate, ugly Maggie Rowan who starts work in a laundry and works her way up to achieve the status of a successful businesswoman living in a gentleman's residence.

While she wrote so prolifically, Catherine was continuing her search for a spiritual home. She had come across a book called *The Christian Agnostic* by a Methodist minister and writer, Dr Leslie Weatherhead. The book stated her own position exactly and she was grateful to discover someone who shared her doubts, particularly a minister, someone who had followed the same quest. She wrote to

Leslie Weatherhead telling him how much he had helped her, and received a warm letter in return. It was only later that she learned that he too suffered from depression. Like Harry Edwards, Leslie Weatherhead became one of Catherine's spiritual support team.

Despite her progress, there were still terrible moments. In 1952, Catherine had to go into St Helen's Hospital for yet another operation on her womb. She had been haemorrhaging for weeks beforehand and was quite weak. When Tom admitted her (husbands in those days had to sign consent forms for their wives' operations), he disobeyed her instructions and wrote 'Roman Catholic' in the space for religious denomination on the admission form. Catherine usually left this blank. When she came round from the anaesthetic, Catherine found two nuns at her bedside. She was stricken by fear and immediately told them that she was no longer a Catholic. But they wouldn't leave. Catherine was prayed over and subjected to a barrage of emotional blackmail. They told her that she had come through this operation by the grace of God and been saved so that she might have the chance of redemption. If she ignored this opportunity she might die and go down to the eternal flames of Hell. By the time they left, Catherine was in tears, retching with fear, 'back, almost, to the breakdown'. So great was her terror that the nuns would come back, perhaps with a priest, that when Tom arrived at visiting time Catherine insisted on discharging herself. Tom called a taxi and she was carried out to it and then back to her own bed at the Hurst.

In 1953 Aunt Mary wrote to Catherine telling her that her mother had cancer of the stomach and was in a very bad way. Catherine also heard from Dr Carstairs, Kate's doctor and former employer, that Kate might only have a few weeks to live.

This was the moment Catherine had been dreading. She herself was still very low, worn down by frequent nosebleeds and heavy menstrual haemorrhage, and she didn't know where she was going to get the strength to bring Kate back to Hastings, let alone nurse her. Catherine and Tom discussed the possibilities and Tom was insistent that Catherine should bring Kate to live with them. If not, Tom argued, she would have the guilt of it on her conscience for the rest of her life. In deep depression, Catherine wrote to Harry Edwards at the Healing Sanctuary. A reply came back, reassuring her that she would be helped and would be given the strength she needed.

Reluctantly, Catherine dug deep into her resources of willpower and travelled north. She found Kate extremely ill. Besides the stomach cancer, she had a long-standing heart condition that caused her body to swell with fluid retention. Kate's kidneys and liver were also damaged by years of drinking. It was obvious that she couldn't be left alone and needed constant nursing care. Hospital was not an option. Despite the fact that Harton Workhouse was now an NHS hospital, Kate was terrified by the prospect of ending her days there. Catherine had no choice but to take her back to Hastings.

Moving the bedridden Kate three hundred miles on public transport was not easy. Catherine booked a sleeper to London and a series of ambulances provided by the St John Ambulance organisation. With the help of station porters and a luggage hoist, she was able to get Kate aboard the train. They were taken across London by ambulance and the same procedure repeated for the journey from Waterloo to Hastings and then to the Hurst. Catherine consoled herself with the thought that it was only for a few weeks.

For years Catherine had wanted Kate dead, had dreamed of killing her almost every night during her breakdown – realising instinctively that she would never be free to be herself until she was free from Kate. But at the Hurst Catherine 'stared pityingly down at the great balloon of water that her body had become, at the faded blue of her eyes, and the colour of her nose, bulbous now. There was no beauty left, not even the beauty of age.' Catherine suddenly realised that she could not let her mother die without at least one attempt to get to know and understand her. She felt that she was being given one last chance to overcome her hatred and fear of Kate.

By 1954, Catherine was a well-established author with five novels either published or awaiting publication, and she was working on another. But the financial rewards she had fantasised about had still not materialised. For each of her first five books she was offered only £100 – not much for a year's work, and though they were selling consistently in the shops, they never made enough to buy the luxuries Catherine anticipated, or even to replace the leaking roof of the Hurst. Catherine's agent and publisher also failed to get a paperback deal for her; Catherine would have to write a lot more books before she entered the mass market.

However, after the publication of *A Grand Man*, the J. Arthur Rank organisation made an offer for the film rights. Catherine was ecstatic, and even Kate, not given to displays of affection, hugged her spontaneously. Tom, beginning to be awed by his wife's success, was enormously proud. Catherine still discussed her novels with Tom. She would tell him the story as it came to her 'to fix it in my mind', listen to his comments and then begin to write it down. She discussed it with him at all stages of development and then the finished manuscript would be given to him to correct – not the story-line, she insisted, or the dialogue, just the grammar and the prose style. This was true for all the early books. Even when she was successful enough to disregard criticism, however constructive, from every other quarter, the drafts of her manuscripts were always discussed with Tom.

A Grand Man was to be filmed in Ireland and the title altered to *Jacqueline*. Although not happy with this transposition, Catherine was not important enough an author to have her reservations about it taken seriously. Once an author has sold the film rights to a book, it is very difficult to make stipulations about the treatment. Catherine was asked to go to Belfast to work on the script. Although she had been scheduled to go into hospital for a hysterectomy, Catherine postponed the operation until after her return. She said she would have gone even if she'd had to get up from her coffin. Arrangements were made to care for Kate, and Catherine travelled to Belfast full of anticipation. The film company gave her fifty pounds to cover her expenses and Catherine, typically, kept an account of every halfpenny spent, cutting costs wherever she could. She even suggested staying in a cheaper hotel, and when she went back to England she sent the film company the change from the fifty pounds. Later she was incensed to discover that one of the other scriptwriters had run up a bill of several hundred.

Catherine worked on a 'treatment' of her book, spent a lot of time looking at locations and even found a young girl she felt would make an ideal Mary Ann. Not every author can write a script. It is a very special kind of craft, but one that Catherine was willing to learn. Her flair for dialogue and dramatic situations, all those years of writing the plays she subsequently burned, were now put to good use. She was working with Patrick Campbell and Liam O'Flaherty, who wrote the screenplay, and Catherine felt that she learned a great deal from them. But she was very disappointed that so little of her own work survived. She was only credited with 'additional dialogue' and all her suggestions for location and casting were ignored. The extrovert in Catherine liked the social side of filming, she got on well with members of the cast and she enjoyed the feeling of celebrity.

However, although the film should have established her reputation, it was never a great success. The story was maimed by the shift of location. The embattled politics of an expatriate Irish community and the strong, gutsy Tyneside dialect were lost and although the basic plot was there, the characters became 'screen Irishmen' – jaunty, fey caricatures.

The doctors' insistence that Catherine needed a hysterectomy preyed on her mind the whole time she worked on the script. She no longer trusted the medical profession and she had been told old wives' tales about the operation ending her sex life and turning her into an old woman overnight. She and Tom were still very much in love and she feared the effect it might have on their relationship. She felt she had already failed him by not giving him children. The prospective removal of her womb underlined her childlessness and brought home to her the fact that she would now never have a child. While she still had her womb, it had seemed as though there was a chance. For Catherine, it was the end of her life as a woman. On her return from Ireland she went straight to hospital for another D & C and an appointment was made for her to be admitted for the hysterectomy.

Catherine wrote once more to Harry Edwards. The hospital appointment arrived in the post on a Friday morning, advising her that she should report to St Helen's on the following Wednesday. The finality of it terrified Catherine almost as much as the thought of another visit to the operating theatre. But as she lay on the sofa in her nightdress, she suddenly heard a voice in her head telling her to go out into the garden and put her hands into the soil. Catherine went outside, knelt down on the concrete path and thrust her hands into the flowerbed. Both Tom and Kate thought that it was a recurrence of her breakdown, but they humoured her and Tom brought a cushion for her to kneel on. Every day Catherine did the same thing for an hour at a time. On the Tuesday she received a letter from Harry Edwards telling her that she was being prayed for, she was already being helped and she must simply believe. This was enough for Catherine. She cancelled the operation, though it was another two years before her menopausal problems were over.

Catherine was still recovering when *Jacqueline* was premiered in London with the Cooksons as guests of honour. Catherine was particularly proud that the Queen had asked for a private screening. The film was the realisation of her greatest ambitions and Catherine hoped that it marked a new phase in her literary career. But despite the increased earnings generated by the film, the Cooksons were still struggling financially. The Hurst drained all their resources of money, time and energy. With Catherine's health so poor and the dying Kate to care for, Tom began to feel that they should move to a property that was easier to maintain. They had no prospect of children now, and it was ridiculous to have a fifteen-bedroomed house for only two – increasingly middle-aged – people. With the sum of money they could realise from the sale of the Hurst, Tom argued that they could buy something smaller and easier to manage, but equally beautiful – perhaps even have something specially built. Although she saw the sense in Tom's arguments, Catherine did not want to move. She was emotionally attached to the Hurst, which represented everything she had achieved; it was the symbol of how far she had come – something that was entirely hers. But perhaps this too was one of the reasons that Tom wanted to move, to a new house with no other associations or memories – particularly of Nan – a house that could belong to them both. In the end Tom's view prevailed – he could be very forceful when necessary – and they began to look for another home.

Catherine describes Loreto in *Our Kate* as 'a charming house in a wood'. Only fifteen minutes' walk from the Hurst, it sits in a dell below the level of the road, sheltered by a thick barrier of maturing yew, oak and laurel planted by the Cooksons. Loreto had been built in 1938 by the single and rather eccentric daughter of a millionaire, who had become estranged from her father when she became a Catholic convert. She and her sister both built houses in St Helen's Avenue on plots of land that had belonged to their father. Miss Harrison was something of a recluse – an invalid with a skin condition that meant she never ventured outside the house without being coated in white ointment. She had been cared for by a succession of resident nurses and when she died, the last of their number persuaded her to leave the house and its contents to her.

Loreto is a substantial house by any standards, white, half-timbered, with large latticed windows. Climbing rose and clematis cling to the walls. It is the perfect home for a writer, offering privacy and peace, but it is a wealthy executive's residence rather than the 'gentleman's dwelling' that Catherine always envisaged as her natural setting. When Catherine first glimpsed the house, it had been up for sale for quite a while. The nurse, almost as eccentric as her employer, was not only holding out for a good price, but wanted it to go to 'the right people'. Catherine and Tom made an appointment to view and within minutes of entering the house were convinced that this was the place they were looking for. The secluded woodland setting would give them privacy, and they could see the potential of the large, neglected garden. There was no central heating, but a big Aga in the kitchen, and though the rooms were dark, Catherine could see that when the walls and the woodwork were painted in light pastel colours rather than old-fashioned browns and greens, they would seem airy and bright. There was also a downstairs room that could be made into a bed-sitting room for Kate, who was beyond tackling the stairs.

The Cooksons made an offer on the spot, which Miss Harrison's former nurse seemed willing to accept. But when she rang the agent, he told her not to agree anything straight away as there was someone else interested. Shortly afterwards, Catherine was told, a wealthy businessman came to look at it and seemed prepared to make an offer. While he was on a chair changing a light bulb at the owner's request, the agent rang to tell her that she should accept the Cooksons' offer. The businessman was far from pleased. But Catherine felt that it was 'meant'.

They moved in on 5 November 1954 in pouring rain. It was a difficult move from a large house with almost unlimited storage space to one that was much smaller and more modern. There was a large quantity of furniture that had to be sorted and either put to one side for Loreto or discarded. Catherine had begun to go to auctions and comb the little antique shops in the Old Town, hunting out bargains. From the time she moved into Loreto, one third of every royalty cheque that came in was earmarked for this hobby. Catherine had a remarkable eye for good-quality furniture and bric-a-brac. Most of the cheap junk that she had bought to furnish the Hurst for lodgers in the early days was left behind.

Leaving the Hurst was a wrench. Catherine said it was like 'leaving someone beloved to die alone'.[8] She was unsettled for over a year after the removal and homesick for the house she still regarded as home. She wondered at times whether they had made a terrible mistake. Then, two days before Christmas, she had another of what she thought of as her paranormal experiences. The Cooksons were using the school holidays to decorate some of the most pressing rooms in the house. They were in the bedroom, Tom perched on a plank hanging wallpaper while Catherine pasted another length, when they both heard their bull terrier, Bill, begin to growl and then to make 'the most weird sound like a long, painful, drawn-out whimper'. Catherine ran out on the landing and saw the dog sitting on the half-landing below, staring at the hallway with his hair standing up on end all the way down his back. Attempts by Catherine and Tom to make the dog go downstairs were resisted, until suddenly Bill relaxed, walked down as though going to greet someone and sat at the foot of the stairs looking up as though being stroked by an invisible person. Tom, always sceptical and convinced that there was a scientific explanation for everything, had to admit that the dog was certainly seeing something that they could not.

Catherine believed that the house was haunted. On New Year's Eve, cold and tired, she left Tom upstairs and went down to check on Kate, who was in bed unwell, and then went into the sitting room to warm herself in front of the electric fire. As Catherine sat there, she was suddenly aware of a presence behind her and, as she turned her head, became convinced that it was the previous owner of the house – 'her presence was as strong as if I were seeing her'. Catherine told friends that she didn't feel afraid, it was actually rather comforting. Aloud she said, 'It's all right, Miss Harrison. Don't worry, we'll look after your house. I'll make it beautiful for you ... Go in peace.'

Moving house, ill health and nursing Kate took their toll on Catherine's creative output. There are no published novels between *Maggie Rowan* in 1954 and *The Lord and Mary Ann* in 1956. Although Kate had been given only weeks to live when Catherine brought her to Hastings in 1953, with care and abstinence from drink – particularly whisky – Kate rallied. Nursing her mother brought out the best in Catherine, who had once believed that nursing was her vocation. This new relationship altered the balance of power between them, giving Catherine the upper hand. 'When her dominant character was low ... she became Our Kate to me, the nice Our Kate.' It also gave them an opportunity to talk about subjects that had previously been avoided. 'We came to know one another. We talked openly about the past for the first time in our lives.' Catherine came to a better understanding of the forces that had ruined her mother's life. And Kate told Catherine that she had never understood her and admitted, in an oblique fashion, that she had rejected Catherine because she had sensed that her daughter was different from the day she was born. 'You were like him, you didn't belong to the North or anything in it.'

Kate talked about Alexander Davies for the first time since the letter she had written to Catherine when she first went to Hastings, but there was little more that Catherine could learn. Either the information Kate gave was too vague – there was a distance now of fifty years – or she herself had known few details of his family or background in the south of England, to make his identity any clearer. Whatever the reason, Kate doesn't seem to have told Catherine enough to dispel the fantasy image that she had cherished in her mind as she grew up – although after Kate told her how he had treated her, Catherine always put the word 'gentleman' in inverted commas when she wrote about him. In her unpublished autobiography she let her bitterness flow. 'Gentleman? He was a skunk wasn't he?' She didn't blame him for not wanting to marry into the McMullen family, but 'the years of longing to see his face, to hear his voice had turned sour on me'. She blamed him for abandoning 'the seed he had set and left to grow up in an environment of fear and shame, of drink and poverty'. He was 'a weakling . . . a weakling with which I am stuck, for I am he in part as much as I am Kate'.[9] Afterwards Catherine told friends that she knew little more about him than she had done before. She sometimes regretted not having pressed her mother harder on the subject.

On good days Kate got up and pottered around the house, doing a little cleaning and cooking, often getting under Catherine's feet. Kate needed to feel useful, and she was pitifully grateful and eager to please. But by the early afternoon her limited resources of energy had been used up and she went to bed in the downstairs room with its view of the garden. Catherine thought afterwards how painful her craving for alcohol must have been. It was only after Kate's death that she realised that her mother had been an alcoholic and discovered what the word actually meant. She had previously thought that, because Kate could go without a drink for quite long periods, this meant that she was not an alcoholic, just a heavy drinker who could have controlled her habit if she had tried. On one occasion Kate asked to go out and, as they passed the door of a pub, she stopped and said, 'I won't be a few minutes, I just want a half, just a half.' The desperation in her voice made Catherine aware of what Kate was suffering. With death so imminent, she reasoned, why should she deny her mother the anaesthetic she craved so badly?

From then on she bought in a bottle of beer for Kate every day and occasionally gave her a small bottle of whisky, which had to be hidden from Tom. 'The look on her face when I would give her the bottle . . . She would be happy, and laughing, and gay for days.' It was undoubtedly the restriction of her alcohol intake that prolonged Kate's life. But when Catherine and Tom went away on holiday, Kate's cravings were not so easily controlled.

Tom was keen on boats and the Cooksons tried to get away once a year to rent a boat on the Fens. These holidays were always a trial to Catherine. She suffered from agoraphobia and was constantly afraid that the boat would sink and they would both drown. But she endured it because Tom loved it and she was aware of how many other things he had given up for her. Eventually, when her earnings increased, she bought Tom a boat and would make her friends laugh at dinner parties with stories about her own cowardice and comic details of the terrible discomforts she had endured on board. When they asked her why she went on the boat when it was so difficult, her reply was always, 'Well, I bought the thing, so I have to use it!' Catherine often took her work with her on these holidays and, as Tom sailed the boat up the East Anglian waterways, she sat in the galley and corrected the drafts of the current book.

In 1955 the Cooksons rented a boat on the river Cam and arranged for friends to stay with Kate while they were away. This time Catherine was quite glad to go. She was desperately in need of a holiday. Tom too was exhausted with the strain of having her mother living in the house. There was no privacy and they were rarely able to go out together – even entertaining friends had become difficult. Kate had been spending more and more time in bed and became agitated whenever Catherine was away from her bedside for any length of time. Catherine left her only for essential shopping or trips to the library. She had little time to herself that wasn't constantly interrupted by having to see to Kate's needs. It was impossible to write. Some evenings Catherine would go into the sitting room and fall asleep in front of the television from pure exhaustion. When this happened, she knew that when she went in to tuck Kate up before going to bed, Kate would inevitably ask where she had been; 'she would make a joke of it, but I always took it as a reprimand'.

While Catherine was away in Cambridgeshire, Kate's condition deteriorated. One of the first things she had done after Catherine left was to telephone the nearest off-licence and ask to have some whisky delivered. Its consumption was the final blow to her cancer-riddled digestive tract. Four days after Catherine's return, Kate began to vomit blood and was confined to bed. One of her last requests was for whisky. She knew she was dying and the doctor, she told Catherine, had said she could have what she liked. For two more days Kate vomited continually, being kept alive by ice and brandy. Either Catherine or Tom was constantly beside her bed and Tom's mother also arrived to help. By Friday evening, Kate was struggling to remain conscious and was obviously in great pain. She held Catherine's hand and said, 'I've been a wicked woman to you, lass.' Pity enabled Catherine to reassure her that it was not true, 'You have never done a bad thing in your life.' Kate refused to see a priest. She tried to tell Catherine that she would take her chance with God, who knew all the 'whys and wherefores' of her life, better than any priest. Catherine, still struggling with her own lack of belief, was awed by her mother's simple faith. It was the kind of unquestioning belief that she herself had sought.

The doctor arrived at twelve o'clock on Sunday and found Kate sinking fast. Realising how near to death she was, he took Catherine into another room, leaving Tom and his mother to sit with her. The doctor talked seriously to Catherine about how her mother's death would affect her. He warned her that she must expect to feel guilty and worry about whether she had done enough, or loved her enough. In spite of the doctor's kindness, in the days following Kate's death Catherine's mind 'became a battleground for conflicting emotions'. Initially the most prominent was relief. She had been given her life back; she was free – almost as if she had been released from a prison sentence. After the funeral Tom took Catherine out for the first time in many months and she confessed that she felt 'like a young girl being let out of school'. It was only later that the negative emotions that had always been part of Catherine's relationship with her mother began to have a corrosive effect on her new equilibrium. Self-condemnation and guilt once more began to erode her happiness. She was being reminded again, very forcefully, that it was impossible to be completely free from the past. There is a recurring theme of fatalism in many of her novels, where heredity and family trauma reach into the future to destroy people's lives, with the inevitability of classical tragedy. Phrases and chapter headings such as 'The path is mapped out' and 'The course is set; no wind can alter it' pulse through the books like a refrain.[10]

In 1956 Catherine found that it was not just her mother's legacy she had to contend with, but also her unknown father's. Towards the end of the war, Catherine had noticed a small reddish mark on her left cheek. At first she thought it was just a spot, but it didn't go away and gradually developed a ring around it – the characteristic halo of telangiectasia. She covered it up with make-up, but over the next two or three years several more appeared on her face, neck, lips and tongue. Catherine went to see the doctor and was reassured that they were simply the result of the ageing process and nothing to worry about. Catherine's doctor was tired of her constant anxiety about her health and Catherine had begun to feel that she wasn't getting the close attention that she should. So when the marks became more noticeable, despite concealing make-up, Catherine went to a different doctor – a woman, recently qualified – who immediately suspected that they were a symptom of something more serious than middle age. She sent Catherine to see a consultant physician in the local teaching hospital.

The consultant recognised the marks on Catherine's face straight away. He asked her a number of questions about her nosebleeds and the bleeding she sometimes suffered from the tongue. Then, rather callously, without explaining anything to Catherine first, he announced to the reverent group of medical students he had called in to examine her that she was suffering from a rare blood disease, hereditary haemorrhagic telangiectasia. To the stunned Catherine, it sounded like a life sentence. She felt ill and afraid. 'I was back on the table having an electric shock. I could smell urine. My heart had leapt up into my throat and was checking my breath.' There was also a surge of anger that, after everything she had already suffered, now she had to bear this burden as well.

A further trial was to come. The consultant explained the hereditary nature of haemorrhagic telangiectasia and asked whether any members of her mother's family had suffered from nosebleeds. Catherine told him that they did not. Then, inevitably, he asked about her father and his family. Suddenly Catherine was sweating with fear. The specialist and his attendant students became 'the man who had turned me down . . . the children in the back lane saying, "You haven't no da" . . . the girl who wouldn't let me into her party . . . the people of the New Buildings who pitied little Katie . . . the girls in Harton . . . who would have taken away my good character.' Catherine was tempted to lie, as she had lied about her birth all her life, but she gathered her courage together and for the first time in public said, 'I am illegitimate.'

Catherine waited for a reaction to her statement but the specialist scarcely blinked an eye. She sat rigid in the chair, barely listening, while he went on to tell her that there was no cure or treatment available for her condition. She must eat as much iron-rich food as she could to counteract the anaemia and rest in bed whenever she began to bleed. Within minutes the consultation was over and Catherine was free to leave. She walked down the hospital steps utterly dazed.

15

The past exists only in versions, which differ
according to our motives at the moment of recall.[1]

Between 1950 and 1960 Catherine wrote some of her strongest
novels, a fact she was herself aware of: 'some of my best writing
was accomplished in those years; books that I considered were the
social history of the North-East . . . interwoven into the lives of the
people'.[2] It is a list of hard-hitting eventual best-sellers that includes
Kate Hannigan, *The Fifteen Streets*, *Colour Blind*, *A Grand Man*
and *Maggie Rowan*. Another of Catherine's Mary Ann stories, *The
Lord and Mary Ann*, was published in 1956 – the same year that
Kate died. For the next ten years new episodes of Mary Ann's life
would be interspersed between the heavier, more serious novels.
Perhaps needing light relief after Kate's death, Catherine also
embarked on the story of *Rooney*, the romantic escapades of a Tyneside dustman. This proved to be one of her most popular books and
the film rights were immediately bought up by J. Arthur Rank.

Like *Jacqueline*, the story was ruined by its translation to Ireland.
Rooney became, not a rip-roaring Tyneside 'Jack the lad', but just
another unexceptional screen Irishman, and the Rank Organisation
made him, not a dustman, which had a certain amount of humour,
but a champion hurler. As one of Catherine's friends remarked,
'What's the point in buying the rights of a book if you're going to
do that? You might as well just invent the whole thing.'[3] But the
film brought Catherine her first paperback deal. Corgi offered her
£150 for *Rooney* – not a great deal of money even then for an author
with seven novels and two films to her credit. But when the film
flopped and the paperback did not sell as well as Corgi had hoped,

they let their option on her subsequent novels lapse and it would be another ten years before Catherine's novels were available in paperback.

Between 1956 and 1967 she wrote at least one novel a year, sometimes two or three. This prolixity caused her publishers some problems, since they felt that two titles a year was all that they could handle. In 1962 Catherine had three novels published, one of them under the pseudonym Catherine Marchant. In the following year there were two by Catherine Marchant and one by Catherine Cookson. And there were other, unpublished novels. In 1957, the year that *Rooney* was published, Catherine began another novel, *The Bonny Dawn*. This was to be a new departure for her – a contemporary narrative with the action taking place during a single day. Seventeen-year-old Brid Stevens gets up at four to watch the dawn rise over the sea with the young Joe Lloyd, whom she had met at a dance the night before. It is all quite innocent, but their meeting sparks off a series of incidents that reveal terrible secrets festering beneath a veneer of respectability, including child abuse, illegitimacy and homosexuality. It nearly ends in tragedy as Joe is tortured by crucifixion and then almost drowned by Brid's sadistic half-brother – saved at the last moment by a schoolteacher and his wife.

If the novel had been published when it was written in the late 1950s it would have caused something of a stir, dealing as it did with difficult and rarely talked-about contemporary social problems. It might also have encouraged Catherine to develop in new directions, towards the mainstream fiction market. However, the book did not fit either into Macdonald's popular fiction list or into Catherine's established work. On the recommendation of her editor at Macdonald, the novel was held back, since it was 'not the kind of book that her readers had come to expect from her'. *The Bonny Dawn* was eventually published almost forty years later, in 1996, when its content, controversial in 1958, had become dated and unremarkable.

During this period Catherine was also working on her own life story. The foreword to the published version of *Our Kate* is aptly headed 'Why does one write an autobiography?' In Catherine's case the question needed an answer, because when she began the book she had already been 'writing out' her life for eleven years in fiction. Why did she suddenly feel the need to write her life story and that of her mother (for it is much more Kate's story than Catherine's) as a factual exercise? In Catherine's unpublished first draft she asks,

'What urges one to write the story of their life? Great deeds done, impressions left by travel, tragedy, the sacrifice of love? If it were any of these I would have no excuse for writing.'[4] Catherine answers the question by explaining that although she had hoped to work her way out of breakdown by writing about herself and her early life, she had discovered that however many novels she wrote, the fears and the depression were still there. She would never be cured, she told herself in 1956, until she had exorcised her feelings towards Kate and publicly admitted the truth about her own birth. The book was intended to 'open the door on tragic secrets and sweep clean the mental torment' that had been festering in her mind for so many years.[5]

Catherine began *Our Kate* in the emotional aftermath of Kate's death and the diagnosis of her hereditary, incurable blood disorder. She wrote it sitting in the room where Kate had died, which she now used as an office. Kate's imagined presence peered over her shoulders as she wrote and she often imagined that she heard Kate's voice. Catherine said later that writing the first draft was one of the most painful things she had ever attempted. When asked in an interview whether she had found autobiography at all similar to writing fiction, Catherine replied emphatically, 'No book that I have ever written, has taken so much out of me as *Our Kate* . . . It wasn't a pleasure to write . . . It was an operation on myself.'[6] She admitted that at the time she wrote the first drafts 'there was much wrong with my mind. First it was bent on retaliation; secondly, there wasn't one happy memory in it. As for telling it to forget and forgive . . . never!'

Catherine found herself having to work through her worst feelings towards Kate, particularly the periods when she hated her and wanted her dead. She made a list of the instances of Kate's cruelty towards her:

Behaviour in drink.
Making her go to the pawn shop and the pub when Kate was too ashamed to go herself.
Depriving Catherine of precious schooling in order to do so.
Causing her to be a bastard.
Not telling her about her father.
Dominating her.

Catherine said that Kate had 'humiliated and hurt' her as a child. She could never forget this. Although she now understood the reasons why, the hurt still remained. Catherine felt that Kate had been neither kind nor caring towards her. When she looked back at her childhood she could never see anyone giving her anything, especially her mother. 'It was always me doing the giving, someone expecting something from me.'[7] Catherine had hoped, when she brought Kate to live with her before she died, that getting to know each other properly would heal the breach between them. But this hadn't happened. 'I thought that all the bitterness had gone with living with her [Kate] for those three years, but it hadn't. There was, behind that, deep in my consciousness and subconsciousness, this hate and this bitterness, at what life had dealt me through her.'[8]

Dr Louise Kaplan, an eminent psychologist who has written a number of excellent books on parents and children, is particularly illuminating on the failure of mother–daughter relationships. When things go badly wrong, as between Kate and Catherine, mother and daughter become locked into a 'tormented dialogue' from which others are excluded. They 'possess each other like demon lovers, alternately clinging together as one and then separating in furious mutual rejection. They encircle one another in a bond of steel . . .'[9]

Catherine's novels are littered with tormented mother–child relationships. At the extreme end of the spectrum are monsters such as the embittered and violent Alice in *Pure as the Lily*. Alice is a woman driven by frustrated ambition who dominates her entire family. As her children begin to develop lives of their own and go in directions she doesn't approve, she tries to thwart their progress. When her daughter Mary marries a man she herself has been in love with, Alice encourages her husband to attack him, which leaves the man scarred for life and Mary's father in jail. Her violent hatred is then turned on Mary, who is forced to break off all contact with her mother. When Mary's brother leaves his wife to live with a woman Alice hates, she burns down the house Mary has bought for them, maiming her son and killing his pregnant girlfriend in the fire. The lengths that Alice is prepared to go to in order to damage the lives of those around her are scarcely credible, unless the reader has previously read Catherine's account of her mother's own behaviour.

Hannah Massey in the novel of the same name, and Maisie's mother in *Hamilton*, are also women who will stop at nothing in order to ruin their children's lives. The warped Winifred Coulson in

The Year of the Virgins actually tries to batter her husband and son to death. Others, like Christine Winter in *Fenwick Houses*, are merely incompetent. Prudence Dudley's mother in *The Iron Facade* is more interested in men and her own selfish pleasures than she is in motherhood. Then there are the mothers who are so difficult to deal with that it is better to cut off all contact. Fiona Nelson's snobbish mother in *Bill Bailey*, Joe's ill-natured termagant in *The Black Candle* and Fanny McBride in the novel of the same name all come into this category.

One of Catherine's difficulties was that she had never developed a proper relationship with her mother as a child and was therefore not able to grow away from her naturally and develop a secure sense of independent selfhood. She could believe in herself as an independent adult only when she was away from Kate. When she was with Kate she feared that her mother would possess and dominate her (as Kate did). Catherine felt that Kate did not allow her to have adult status but always put her straight back into the powerless position of the young, ill-treated child again.

Catherine feared that loss of control more than anything, she feared Kate's dominance because it stripped her of her own precarious selfhood, and she also feared the things in herself that were like Kate. Part of Catherine's problem in her relationship with her mother was the fact that she was very like Kate – something that generated a great deal of self-hatred. In a good mother–daughter relationship this does not happen.

> A girl who comes into possession of her own selfhood will later perceive her mother as she really is – not as a dangerous, withholding, damaging, all-powerful creature. Then the girl will be free to become something like her mother without fearing that she must relinquish her own self to her mother in the process. The girl will admire her mother's actual power and see in it the strength and power she one day will acquire for herself.[10]

Catherine did not want to be like her mother. She always imagined that her strengths had come from her unknown father and attributed the negative things in her personality to Kate, although it was just as likely to be the other way round.

But there are also serious questions to be asked about the nature and depth of Catherine's hatred for her mother and her sometimes extreme desire to kill her. The 'hurts and humiliations' that Catherine puts forward in explanation hardly seem sufficient to justify the lifetime of mental torture and resulting illness that she suffered, which began at the age of thirteen – the date of her first breakdown. Catherine's symptoms of dissociation, vomiting, low self-esteem, night terrors and aggression are characteristic of child-abuse survivors. There is a mystifying gap between the known facts of Catherine and Kate's relationship and the extent of the trauma that resulted, particularly her desire to kill her mother and her compulsive vomiting.

The writer Linda Gray Sexton had a similarly unhappy relationship with her mother, the poet Anne Sexton, which has many parallels to Catherine's with Kate. There was a childhood separation caused by her mother's illness and the complete failure of the bonding process. Linda, like Catherine, felt rejected and unloved. She too grew up to become a high achiever and a writer – her novels are often written directly out of her childhood experience of neglect. But in her thirties Linda had a breakdown and under therapy worked backwards through the pain of her relationship with her mother into something she had suppressed all her life – something that made her vomit repeatedly. Linda had often shared a bed with her mother and, under the influence of drink and extreme sexual frustration, Anne Sexton had occasionally been tempted into 'inappropriate sexual behaviour' with her sleeping daughter. It was, Linda wrote later, something she found almost impossible to admit even in the liberated nineties, but it was the terrible secret that had brought her into breakdown.

The abuse of children by women is something so unthinkable that it is rarely discussed. Yet it occurs and encompasses emotional and physical as well as sexual abuse. This took place much more often in the days when children and adults shared beds in overcrowded houses. It tended to happen under the influence of drink and was often disguised as cuddling or nurturing, sometimes so insidious that the child was unsure what had taken place. Linda Sexton, whose mother had problems with both alcohol and tranquillisers, was forty before she could admit to anyone that her mother, under the guise of cuddling her, had made explicit sexual contact with her. Like many other young children, Linda did not realise that her mother's behaviour could be classed as sexual. Sex was something that happened between men and women. She simply knew that the way her mother touched her body was frightening and that she didn't like it. Did Kate too, under the influence of whisky, needing the comfort of another warm human body, make inappropriate advances to her daughter as she slept beside her in the narrow featherbed they shared until Catherine left home as an adult? If she did, it would explain Catherine's extreme feelings of revulsion towards her mother and why she had a mental breakdown at thirteen and again at thirty-nine.

Linda Sexton spent years in therapy 'shouting my resentment, stoking my anger over the betrayal I still felt ... I hated her for having refused to mother me, for using me sexually and emotionally.' It left Linda with a fear of sexual contact that would plague the adult Catherine too. Linda wrote:

> sometimes at the first embrace, a kiss ... I am flooded with pictures I try to beat back ... No matter how hard I try to change this scenario – through years of psychotherapy or with sheer determination – I sometimes come back to that dark night when my mother's sticky body lay tightly on mine, the stink of her booze breath, the legacy of fear and self-hatred with which she left me. Of all the mistakes Mother made, this one was the hardest to forgive.[11]

The words could have been written by Catherine, so close are they to her own feelings for her mother. 'She was bending down to me and the hateful smell of whisky wafted from her as she said, "Give us a kiss." My stomach turned over. I wished she was dead. I pushed her face away with the flat of my hand and hissed at her. "I hate you. I do. I do. I hate you, our Kate."'[12] Like Linda Sexton, Catherine not only hated her mother but also loved her and needed to be loved by her. As for Catherine, for Linda Gray Sexton the only healing path was through the writing of an autobiography charting her painful relationship with her mother – a book full of compassion and understanding.[13]

The first draft of *Our Kate* produced about four hundred pages of typed or handwritten autobiography. Completed in 1958, it is not a narrative and was not intended at that point for publication. Catherine was working through her religious crisis, her relationship with her mother, and trying to understand episodes in the past where she had behaved badly and fallen below the standards she set herself. She pledged herself to tell the truth, but with qualifications. 'Whatever I write will be true as far as the faded eyes of memory and the diluted emotions allow. But there are things I cannot write . . . some truth will not bear translating.'[14] Even so, the first draft is devastatingly frank – at times she writes as if she is talking to herself. Many of the episodes Catherine relates did not appear in the later drafts of the book, and many others were fictionalised to make a better story. The first draft was an exercise in therapy – part of Catherine's search for peace of mind. But she was afraid that, if writing the book did indeed cure her psychological problems, she would be unable to write the novels. At the end of the first draft she asks herself, 'Will I ever let this go to print? Will I ever let it out of my possession? Perhaps the very fact of doing it might be the real symbol of release. I don't know. Perhaps if I were to achieve this release, the urge that is forever driving me . . . to attempt . . . to create, would die . . . What am I to do? I don't know.'[15]

The second draft was begun in 1962. Catherine was incensed to hear the agony aunt Evelyn Home on the radio asserting that 'illegitimacy runs in families'. Her anger fuels the text. She was now also afraid that what she was writing would lay bare 'the tumours in my heart' and destroy what little peace of mind she had managed to achieve. She discovered that she was too afraid to be completely frank about the 'dark secrets and mental torments' she had set out to exorcise.[16] The autobiography now had a title, *From the Seed of All Sorrow*, and was prefaced by a poem which begins:

> From the seed of all sorrow
> All loss, all pain
> All agony from that grain
> All love[17]

Love and pain were always interwoven in Catherine's mind. The second draft was a much more polished exercise and she deleted many of the incidents she was ashamed of. Others were altered to put her own conduct in a better light. It was now 'a true but partial view'.[18] She eventually rewrote *Our Kate* eight times and still wasn't satisfied with it. In 1968 Macdonald, who had been waiting several years to publish it, eventually insisted that it was finished. They had seen only four of the earlier versions.

Feedback was critical. Despite Catherine's excisions, and her desire to be seen as a 'good Catholic girl', she was told that she projected herself in the book 'as an egoist and a snob . . . because of an almost masochistic determination to present myself honestly'. There was a 'pathological consciousness of [her] bastardy' and she came over as 'a snob and a prig'.[19] One of the readers sent back a very negative report questioning the coherence of the narrative and commenting that 'this person cannot write'. The reader also identified the fact that the book was neither biography nor autobiography. She was right – defying categorisation, it is essentially the story of a flawed relationship. Catherine was terribly upset by the criticisms and tried very hard to discover the identity of the reader. When Macdonald refused to tell her anything except that it was a young woman recently graduated from university, Catherine made cutting remarks about 'a girl in her first job'. What did she know!

Ernst Honigmann, a professor of English at Newcastle University, interviewed Catherine in 1986 for the university's archives. He had pioneered a course in autobiography at the university and he was particularly interested in the writing of *Our Kate*. According to Professor Honigmann, autobiography is therapeutic because it is an important means of clarifying the mind, ordering the material and coming to terms with the experience. He asked Catherine searching questions about the number of drafts she had to make. 'Autobiographers who have to rewrite their autobiography because they are not satisfied are often the most interesting.'[20] He makes the parallel with Gibbon, who wrote and rewrote his autobiography because he found great difficulty in facing up to what he was and what he'd suffered. Professor Honigmann thinks that *Our Kate* is probably the best thing Catherine ever wrote because it is the most human. When he mentioned this to Catherine in conversation, she agreed with him.

Autobiography is always a highly subjective view of the truth, *Our Kate* particularly so. Catherine found, as she wrote, that she could not after all tell the whole truth about her childhood. When Professor Honigmann pressed her on this point, she admitted that she had 'used her author's guile' to structure the material to make a good story, and that in order to satisfy the readers she had made Kate 'to be much softer than she really was . . . kinder'.[21] She told Professor Honigmann that she had also omitted to include the largest and most terrible part of Nan's story. 'That would take another book . . . There was evil there and I experienced evil and it nearly ruined me.'[22] There was also the involvement of publishers and agents and their editorial influence on the inclusion of one story or another.

The early drafts of *Our Kate* are now lying in the archives of Boston University Library. There are 800 pages of handwritten notes and typed manuscript, which presumably comprise the two very early versions, and six completed drafts varying in length from 460 pages to 320. The final proof runs to just over 300 pages. After the excisions of the first two drafts, many of the subsequent alterations have to do with the tone and style in which it is written and the ordering of the material. Sometimes Catherine opts for chronological narrative, at other times for a more thematic approach. In places, Catherine's bitterness towards Kate and others spreads across the pages like acid. It took several drafts before Catherine could bring herself to write with pity and compassion about the people who had hurt her so severely in the past, but it was something she had to do. As she herself said, 'hate is ruinous'.

Otherwise, even in its final, expurgated version, the frankness of the narrative is breathtaking. Catherine, who had spent so long creating an educated, middle-class image, was graphically describing the often sordid details of her working-class childhood and even admitting her illegitimacy. How much she was influenced by the newly fashionable 'kitchen sink' realism of playwrights and novelists like Stan Barstow and John Osborne in the late fifties is difficult to tell. This kind of gritty, northern poverty was suddenly an advantage in the literary market. The publishers kept pushing Catherine to finish the book throughout the sixties, realising that by the end of the decade its shock value would be much lower. Something of a backlash was already setting in – there were a number of 'beer and whippet' satires, the best of them undoubtedly the Monty Python sketch in which each character boasts a more deprived childhood than the last, ending in total surrealism.

From the time Catherine wrote the final draft of *Our Kate*, she talked about her life as if she was reading from a script. Writing the book allowed Catherine to formulate the 'definitive version' of her early life. In interviews and articles, the same stories in the same words would be repeated over and over again. She rarely revealed anything new. It was as if she had created both Catherine Cookson and Katie McMullen as characters in one of her novels. She told Professor Honigmann when he interviewed her, 'Catherine Cookson doesn't exist. What I am is from that kitchen and Katie McMullen.' In her novel *Katie Mulholland* she explains in detail how this felt:

She was known as a wealthy woman, and she knew she could carry herself in almost any company . . . But all this was a veneer, for she also knew that just below the surface she was still the product of her early environment. She was still the child who had emptied slops into the wooden buckets . . . still the child who had suffered . . . The rest was a façade, a pleasing façade . . . which protected her with a thin armour.[23]

In Catherine's case, both the child and the adult were her own creations and she was never completely at ease with either of them.

Fenwick Houses, a major novel written when Catherine was writing and rewriting *Our Kate*, was born perhaps from the effort she made to understand her mother's state of mind. One of Catherine's best novels, written in the first person, it is a golden view of her mother as a good woman ruined by circumstances – the consequences of the loss of a good name – and the actions of one cruel and perverted individual. Catherine intended the heroine of *Fenwick Houses*, Christine Winter, to be a picture of 'Kate as she might have been'. Christine is an unmarried mother, sexually harassed and abused, misunderstood and cheated of happiness, but still retaining her warmth of character and her integrity. Christine was one of Catherine's favourite characters – a strong, gutsy woman with a profound sense of beauty and joy, who is betrayed both by women and by men. Heartbreakingly innocent and vulnerable, she is unable to survive like her tough, worldly friend Mollie. Christine is just not practical enough. She has dangerous and unreliable romantic dreams. Like Kate, Christine drowns the tragedies of her life in drink, which produces violent mood swings. Some of the strongest writing in the novel is a scene in a pub, an excellent vernacular comic sketch informed by episodes Catherine must often have witnessed as a child, where Christine becomes talkative, then aggressive, creates a scene and is finally taken away to spend the night in a police cell.

Catherine was by now regularly employing a secretary. Being unable to type, Catherine had needed assistance from the beginning and initially her novels had been typed by a friend for so much a page. But her prolific output soon demanded a more professional arrangement. Tom did buy Catherine a typewriter, but she never learned to use it – two-finger typing was fine for letters, but not quick enough for writing. She wrote in longhand first, very fast, believing that the thoughts travelled from her brain to her fingers.

When she had a reasonably neat draft, it was given to someone to type. Her secretaries were nearly always friends, if not before they worked for her, invariably afterwards; and one of them, she admitted to the editor Piers Dudgeon, inconveniently fell in love with her. This was not surprising. Catherine was still a beautiful woman; even as she declined physically, she retained a radiant, inner spirituality and strength of personality that people found irresistible.

Catherine didn't employ a full-time secretary. She needed someone who could come when she had something to type. But the continual revision of the manuscripts of two or three books a year, plus letters, provided three or four hours of work every week. She rarely needed to advertise and help often came from unexpected quarters. When one of Catherine's secretaries left to get married, she received a phone call from an extremely well-spoken young woman who had heard about the vacancy through a friend. Catherine was glad to give her the job. The woman had been a court stenographer and was very efficient – too well qualified, Catherine thought, for the copy typing she gave her. She also had the most marvellous mink coat – something Catherine had long coveted for herself as part of the visible trappings of success. Catherine was curious about the circumstances that had brought such an obviously educated woman from a wealthy background to such a low point that she was prepared to accept a few hours of badly paid work. Eventually the young woman explained that she had brought her children back to England after a marriage breakdown and was endeavouring to bring them up alone on very little money. Her husband was in Australia, living with a Chinese mistress.

When the woman needed money to go back to Australia to sort out her marital situation, she tried to sell the mink coat, first to friends in London and then to Catherine. But no one could afford to pay her what it was worth. In the end Catherine, with characteristic generosity, lent her the money she needed, telling her that it didn't matter when it was repaid. The woman insisted that Catherine take the coat as a gift, but Catherine refused. However, when Catherine and Tom came back from a few days' holiday on the Fens, a brown paper parcel was waiting for them. Catherine sent the coat back, but it was returned with a note telling her that she must keep it. At this point, Catherine gave up and accepted it gratefully, on the understanding that if its former owner ever needed the coat, she could have it back.

A few months later, the loan was repaid by cheque, leaving Catherine, a compulsive giver, in the uncomfortable position of being the recipient of a very striking and valuable present. She loved the coat and the stir it created whenever she wore it – 'it was so posh that I could wear it only on occasions, but wear it I did!'[24]

The occasions when she could wear it were multiplying rapidly. Catherine's increasing popularity as an author meant that she now got invited to library festivals, book promotions, weekend writing courses and was also asked, as a celebrity, to open local events such as the Hastings Flower Show. Although she enjoyed the public acclaim, she still found public speaking an ordeal and could often only do it sitting down. She pleaded rheumatism as an excuse. But Catherine need not have been nervous. She was a natural communicator – those who heard her found it magical.

One of the reasons that Catherine feared public speaking was her fear that, as soon as she opened her mouth, the mask of the educated, literary lady would fall away to reveal the uneducated, badly spoken little girl from the New Buildings. 'In the workshop of my mind, not only do I know big words, but also I can pronounce them . . . it is only the transport section that is at fault . . . for in transport invariably two syllables will have got mixed up and Mrs Malaprop appears. How I want to slay that woman!'[25] But invariably, once on a platform, the latent actress inside Catherine would take over and the part would be superbly played out to the audience.

Nancy Martin heard Catherine give a talk to a writers' group in Croydon and was so enthralled that she asked if Catherine would come to a writers' weekend that her daughter was organising. Catherine did, and as a result of her performance there was invited to Swanwick for the twenty-first anniversary of its prestigious summer school. Catherine was very apprehensive. It was a much bigger event than any she had addressed before and there would be three hundred and fifty people in the audience. The organiser, Bill Smith, had previously heard Catherine speak at the Writers' and Journalists' Club in London and was very enthusiastic at the prospect of having her. He knew how nervous Catherine was and every effort was made to make her feel comfortable.

The Swanwick summer school lasts for a week and Catherine and Tom stayed for the whole event among a group of writers that included the TV dramatist N. J. Crisp, the children's author Edward Blishen and the novelist Elizabeth Jenkins. Catherine was delighted to find that she was a celebrity, sought out by people who told her how much they enjoyed her novels – 'any writer who says he gets bored with this is a liar'.[26] There were also a number of would-be writers from Newcastle who told her how proud they were that she set her novels in the northeast.

The Friday-night speech that Catherine made as a kind of finale to the summer school was one of her best ever. She was at ease among people she had grown to know during the previous six days, and aware that she was also among appreciative fans. For Catherine it was a landmark experience which she recorded in her journal: 'Something happened that night on that platform; I entered into all of them, and they welcomed me with open arms . . . How good it is, how wonderful it is, to make an audience laugh, really laugh.' On that evening she also made them cry. Catherine Cookson the novelist, aided and abetted by Katie McMullen the natural storyteller, held the audience spellbound, as she was to do many times again before she withdrew from public life. She once said, 'It is Catherine Cookson who writes, but only Katie McMullen can talk.'[27] Standing in front of an audience was an ordeal for her, but she was a good public speaker, witty and human and very articulate. Although she feared the experience, she actually craved the adulation that she received. The approval of her public was a validation, a compensation for the love and approval she felt she had not received as a child.

16

Why me? Who planned my destiny anyway? Who
cut its pattern? Why was I sent to such a hard school,
full of battle and strife to learn the lesson of life?
Why?[1]

Freed from the burden of nursing Kate, and with the menopause
behind her, Catherine entered a new phase of life. She and Tom
spent a lot of time and money making Loreto into their dream home.
Catherine's royalty cheques were always strictly divided into three:
one part into a savings account, one into their joint account to cover
the expenses of authorship, and the third into Catherine's antiques
fund. She bought some wonderful things at the beginning of the
sixties when large pieces of Victorian and Edwardian furniture were
unfashionable. One of her finds was a huge mahogany breakfront
bookcase, which features as a backdrop in many of her publicity
photos. Purchased for only a few pounds, it was eventually valued
at more than £10,000. Catherine also bought Chinese carpets, silver-
plated tea and coffee services, oddments of porcelain that appealed
to her, quantities of questionable bric-a-brac, nineteenth-century
prints and a reproduction Louis XV writing desk. Catherine always
had an eye for a bargain, but she occasionally got carried away with
her purchases. For Loreto she bought a reproduction dining table
for sixteen people which almost filled the room and two large crystal
chandeliers to hang above it. Among friends who were present at
the first dinner on the new table was a friend who said that the effect
was absolutely blinding. 'Good God, you've really done it this time,
Kitty!' he remembers saying, before he realised that Catherine was
right behind him. But she only laughed and said jokingly, 'I know I
can always rely on an honest opinion from you, Brian!'[2]

Unexpected windfalls such as film, paperback and serialisation rights paid for other luxuries. Loreto initially had no garage, although the garage belonging to the adjoining house had been for sale when they bought the house. Catherine always regretted that she had allowed Tom to talk her out of spending the extra £200. He had argued that they didn't have a car and Loreto had already stretched their resources to the limit. But by the time the garage came up for sale again and Catherine was able to buy it, the price had increased to £8,000 and it hurt her frugal soul to have to pay it.

Catherine bought both a boat and a car for Tom, made one of the rooms in the house into a billiard room, purchased extra land to extend the garden and eventually built an indoor swimming pool as an extension to the house. Catherine had always wanted to learn to swim in order to overcome her fear of water. As a child she had almost drowned when she fell into the river while 'playing the piano' – jumping from plank to plank across the floating wood in the Jarrow slake. Her life had been saved by a passing workman who hauled her out of the filthy water by the hair. Previous attempts to learn to swim at public pools had not been successful, but Catherine was convinced that in the privacy of her own pool it would be possible. Swimming would also keep her body healthy and alleviate the back and shoulder problems that were beginning to trouble her. On one occasion, the simple act of digging up a clump of polyanthus in the garden put her in bed with sciatica for six weeks.

Gardening took up much of the Cooksons' time. The garden of Loreto had been considerably neglected when they arrived and the woodland around it had been a dumping ground for refuse – the new plots they acquired were littered with bedsteads, old gas cookers and broken bottles. Catherine and Tom between them cleared the land, cut down old, diseased trees and undergrowth, replacing the old woodland with new saplings and an underplanting of rhododendrons and azaleas. They also put in more than twenty thousand spring bulbs. It was hard physical work and Catherine often suffered for it, something she blamed on her childhood hip injury. *The Gambling Man* was written while she lay in bed for months with backache.

The Cooksons' relationship was stronger now than it had ever been. Catherine and Tom had the almost telepathic understanding that develops in couples who have been together for a long time. Their relationship worked, Catherine argued, because they were friends. They actually liked each other. They were also, under the observable differences between Tom the mathematician and sportsman and Catherine the writer and artist, strangely alike. Unable to sleep one night, Catherine joined Tom in the kitchen where he was recovering from migraine and feeling depressed. Catherine confessed that she too had woken up having 'a fit of the blues'. They made a cup of tea and talked, asking the question why they should both be haunted by so much depression and guilt, when both of them had so much – a beautiful house and garden, a way of life they both loved, as well as each other. The answers were also the key to why they suited each other so well. For Tom, it was the 'sensitivity of the idealist coupled with a rapier-sharp critical mind, a thoughtful gentle creature who gives the impression to the world that he is of a quiet, placid, self-effacing nature, when incongruously he is more often than not burnt up inside about causes, injustice and people'. On Catherine's side, 'the sensitivity of the artist, the agonising sensitivity of awareness; the awareness of the pain of life, the awareness of the fears on which happiness is built, the sensitivity that gives sharp outlines to life and strips off layers of skin and makes one vulnerable to the sting of the unkind word, even to the lowering of the supercilious eyelid'.[3] Their apparent ability to talk to each other with complete frankness was something their friends marvelled at.

Catherine and Tom were fiercely loyal to each other. Whatever her health problems, Catherine always accompanied Tom when he took the Scouts away to summer camp, though often she spent her time propped up against a tree, forced into immobility by nosebleeds. She was trying to save enough money to make it possible for Tom to retire from teaching. He was having increasingly severe and prolonged attacks of migraine and Catherine was convinced that they were caused by the stress of the job. When he had migraine he would have to sit quietly in a darkened room until the headache dispersed, which could take days. Catherine, powerless to alleviate the pain, would sit and watch him with tears rolling down her face.

Tom was equally protective towards Catherine. Although a quiet, mild man, he could become quite ferocious when roused. Once on a train journey, a drunken man made insulting remarks about Catherine which Tom overheard. When the man came and deliberately sat in a nearby seat, Tom, who had been a good amateur boxer at university, had to be physically restrained from hitting him. He was also apt to become angry if he felt that Catherine was being exploited and he was sometimes, understandably, jealous of the new life Catherine was enjoying. Catherine had a coterie of editors and agents to accompany her to functions and take her out to dinner when Tom's teaching responsibilities prevented him from coming with her. Catherine once joked in front of Tom that she would have liked to have had a lover. But Tom need not have worried. She was always glad to see him waiting for her at the station when she came back and she once said that Tom was 'a bigger man than any of them'.

Friends of the Cooksons say that Tom was in the beginning occasionally jealous of Catherine's relationship with her first agent, John Smith, whose poise and erudition she admired tremendously. Catherine was always grateful for John's initial help and wouldn't hear a word said against him. In the fifties and sixties, at the time he was handling Catherine's affairs, John Smith was in his thirties, a handsome, intelligent and charming man. Tom may well have been jealous of John, not just because of Catherine's affection for him, but also because of his influence. However, John had few illusions about their relationship. Although he held Catherine in great affection

and I knew that she felt strongly toward me as a friend ... she was not, I think on reflection, someone who inspired or gave friendship in that sense of absolute ordinariness. In this she was very different from Tom, whose emotional responses were much simpler, so that with Tom I felt he was concerned with *me*, but Catherine, I felt she was concerned for herself *through* me.[4]

John was one of the few people who spoke his mind to Catherine and she respected that even when it upset her. John, a connoisseur and art lover, always gave Catherine a frank opinion, but even when she disagreed she didn't hold it against John for long – he had sold her first books for her and she trusted his professional judgement and remained loyal to him over more than forty years. Once she became really famous and a best-seller, he was the only person who would dare to tell her the truth about her work. He was one of the few people who told her that he thought her novel *Hamilton* was the weakest she had written. She was far from pleased, but Catherine needed people like that.

Catherine loved to fill Loreto with people. Friends recall lively dinner parties with wonderful food, where Catherine could sometimes be persuaded to entertain them with the Geordie songs she had once hated Kate for performing in public. Catherine had a fine alto voice and loved singing, but she had been discouraged, not just by her mother's drunken recitals, but by the negative response of one of her teachers when she was a child and wanted to sing in the school concert.

There were some unexpected visitors at Loreto too. Annie Joyce, now Annie Robson, her old friend from Harton Workhouse laundry, had returned to South Shields after Catherine left Tendring Workhouse and they had lost contact with each other. Annie, feeling guilty about being instrumental in the revelation of Catherine's illegitimacy and her unhappy love affair, had thought that Catherine would not want to keep in touch with her. However, when the Catholic church organised a holiday on the south coast for the women's group, Annie discovered that they were staying not far from Hastings. After much deliberation and encouragement from other members of the party, Annie looked up Catherine's telephone number in the local directory and rang her up. To Annie's surprise, Catherine not only remembered her, but was also very glad to hear from her. Catherine secretly felt guilty about the way she had treated Annie. Now she insisted that Annie should come over to Hastings for a visit.

Annie and a friend came on the following day, but were rather awed by the size of Loreto when they arrived. Catherine was standing outside the front door talking to two people who were obviously just leaving, and Annie hesitated on the pavement for quite a while before she plucked up courage to approach the house. But she need not have worried. Catherine was absolutely delighted to see her. She gave Annie and her companion lunch and insisted that they stay on in the afternoon in order to meet Tom. Annie was able to give Catherine a great deal of news about people they had both known and they reminisced about the past. She got the impression that Catherine was rather nostalgic about the Tyne. Annie was amazed at the luxurious style in which Catherine now lived, but pleased to find that, although she was now a famous author and had assumed the outward appearance, accent and manners of a 'southern lady', underneath she was still the same Kitty McMullen Annie had shared jokes with in the laundry. When Annie left, Catherine embraced her warmly and made her promise not to lose touch again. They must stay friends. From then on they met occasionally whenever Catherine was in the northeast. They exchanged letters every Christmas and

Catherine usually sent Annie money to buy herself a 'Christmas box'.

At Christmas and New Year, Catherine liked to celebrate in true northern fashion and often Tom's family as well as some of her own cousins from Jarrow would be invited to stay. Like most family occasions, these events were not without incident. When one of Tom's relatives brought a very small baby, the parents were deeply offended when Catherine refused to hold it or give it much attention. She still felt very disturbed and upset by young babies and was unable to explain why she didn't want to cuddle the child. She was pressed to do so in a very insensitive way by Tom's mother and others – who must have known of her tragic history. Did they think that cuddling someone else's baby might comfort her? The misunderstanding ruined the holiday and caused a long rift between the two families. This may have been part of the reason why Tom's sister lost contact with her brother, only to be reunited with him after Catherine's death. Catherine had no problems with older children. 'Tom's boys' were welcome at the house at any time and Catherine became a surrogate mother to more than one of them. One boy, she joked, came to stay 'and it was four years before he left'. She was always invited to the birthday parties of friends' children. Josephine Austin remembers her coming in and sitting on the floor among the children, completely natural and at home with them.

The Cooksons sublimated some of their sorrow at the absence of children in the care they lavished on their dogs. When Bill died at the age of nine, Catherine was devastated. She freely admitted that she loved her dogs more than any human being – other than Tom – and believed that if there was an afterlife, her dogs would be there to share it. Bill was replaced by a golden Labrador called Simon who was their companion for fourteen years until he, too, died in Tom's arms, precipitating another outburst of grief. Catherine's delight in animals found expression in a series of children's books she wrote. The first, *Matty Doolin*, published in 1965, tells the story of a young boy on Tyneside who wants to be a vet. The second, *Joe and the Gladiator*, published in 1968, is about a boy who strikes up a relationship with the rag-and-bone man and his horse Gladiator. When the old man dies, he leaves the horse – and all the problems of finding the money to look after it – to Joe. Later Joe finds that he has been left a great deal of money, the proviso being that he had to keep the horse for two months after its owner's death.

Although Catherine had begun to put on weight in middle age, she was always beautifully groomed. Her nails were filed and polished, and as her natural hair colour faded, it was tinted a complementary light auburn. She never wore perfume. Since the breakdown she had been unable to bear the smell of it. But she loved to wear good clothes – it gave her a feeling of security. One wall of her bedroom was covered by a huge wardrobe hidden behind mirrored doors. Friends who were privileged to see inside were amazed at the racks and racks of dresses, suits, coats and matching accessories. Every beautiful garment she bought helped to eradicate the memory of the embarrassing clothes that Kate had made her wear as a child. With her increasing wealth, Catherine bought exquisite clothes – still sometimes second-hand. After Tom persuaded her to buy herself a new red Jaeger suit in an expensive store, an experience she didn't enjoy, she found an exclusive dress agency in Brighton that sold second-hand model gowns and couture clothes, run from someone's house, so there was never the terror of having to go into a shop.

Earning more money never meant that Catherine worked less. If anything, she worked harder. She had discovered that it was the only thing that kept her depression at bay. Despite the fact that she was sixty in 1966, retirement age, and had twenty-four novels behind her, she still did all her own housework – most of it the hard way. Though she owned a vacuum cleaner, she didn't have either a fridge or a washing machine until the early 1970s. And she said she couldn't sit down to write until the house was absolutely immaculate. As well as helping Tom with the garden, she was still writing at least two books a year. Tom's mother was appalled at the pace at which Catherine drove herself: up at six in the morning and rarely in bed before eleven. Every minute of Catherine's time had to be filled with activity of one kind or another. She had done this all her life and didn't know how to stop. 'I had such a will that I pushed myself . . . making myself do this, forcing myself to do this, telling myself I could do it . . . and this went on for years.' When she was feeling tired and ready to give up, she often heard Kate's voice in her head urging her to go on. 'Work it off,' the voice would say. 'You'll cope.' It was a form of self-punishment. Sometimes Catherine wished that she hadn't been so hard on herself when she was younger.

In a poem 'I Wish', she wondered whether she might have been healthier if she had been kinder to herself during her earlier years.

I wish I were young again;
I wish my body were as young as my mind.
If I were young again,
I would be kind to it:
I would not starve it
In order to save for material things;
I would not urge it to work
Until it dropped with the pain that strain brings;
I would not, for fourteen years,
Tramp laundry floors;
I would not rob my body of rest
In order to improve my mind,
When it begged sleep . . .

I would not pump into it chemists' drugs
To keep it going, the while
Knowing that there'd be a price . . .

Success always leaves
An expensive bill to pay.

But Catherine continued to push her body to the limit. She confessed that 'the aim was to fill every minute so that I should not have time to think'.[5] When she was immobilised by haemorrhage she worked in bed. Friends remember being entertained in her bedroom while Catherine lay on the bed in a pink, fluffy dressing gown and vivid pink woollen bedsocks, making everyone laugh. When she was ill Tom ran the house and did the cooking. He even taught himself to ice cakes, something he often did for friends at Christmas or other special occasions. He said that if you were intelligent and could read a book there was nothing you couldn't learn.

Haemorrhagic Telangiectasia becomes more troublesome as the sufferer ages. Throughout the sixties Catherine had more frequent nosebleeds and was bleeding from the tongue, which she found even more unpleasant because it entailed constantly swallowing her own blood. She had also begun to bleed from her fingerends and from her stomach and bladder. It was not only physically debilitating but also socially inconvenient. Many sufferers are unable to hold down jobs. They are at risk of bleeding to death if the haemorrhage is not staunched. Catherine always carried a handkerchief up her sleeve to catch the first signs of haemorrhage. She found it acutely embarrassing to begin to bleed, particularly if it was what she called 'a gusher', at public functions. Tom accompanied her everywhere she went. When she gave a talk to a roomful of university students on one occasion, Tom declined to take a seat among the audience, but he sat on a chair outside the door during the seminar – an alert, protective figure.

The doctors in Hastings were not always as attentive as Catherine would have liked, and she believed that she had often been neglected. Catherine was, in fact, the average GP's nightmare patient – one who is a frequent visitor to the surgery with a very thick medical file covering a multiplicity of complaints, some of which may be psychosomatic in origin. Catherine felt that the fact that she had had a nervous breakdown coloured their thinking towards her. Everything was put down to her 'temperament'. Although she now had recovered from her gynaecological problems, she still believed herself to be suffering from lead poisoning, and her life was blighted by the chronic afflictions of haemorrhagic telangiectasia, a bad back, anaemia, psoriasis and periods of severe depression. She had also become allergic to a number of drugs and foods. She was supposed to eat as much meat, liver and black pudding as she could in order to counteract her anaemia, but the mere smell of meat began to make her feel nauseous. At one point wheat products also disagreed with her, at another time it was dairy foods. Meals became a problem. In the winter she was prone to chest infections if she caught a cold. So it was not perhaps surprising – though not good professional practice – that when Tom rang the doctor's surgery on a Saturday afternoon, the doctor was reluctant to come out to see Catherine.

On this particular occasion Catherine had been in bed on and off for two months, bleeding and coughing and growing weaker and more depressed, until Tom began to fear that she would die. The doctor, when he came, was brusque and made Catherine feel that she was a nuisance. He examined her carefully, told her that she wasn't going to die, she was simply anaemic and must take iron and eat the right food in order to regain her strength. As for the bleeding, there was no cure for it except rest. Perhaps less tactfully than other doctors in the past, he also implied that what she actually needed was the will to get better and get out of bed. He knew of patients much older and sicker than she was. What Catherine heard, as she lay there, was yet another man telling her that she had no 'gumption', and she was absolutely enraged. It was the combative Katie McMullen who reared from the bed to defend herself.

> What but gumption had brought me from William Black Street to where I was at this moment, an established writer? What but gumption had lifted Katie McMullen from service at fourteen, from a laundry checker at eighteen to manageress at twenty-two, then, at the age of twenty-seven into the gentleman's residence in Hoadswood Road . . . What had given her the education necessary to transfer her racing imagination to paper? . . . and this accomplished without any *man* behind her?

After the young doctor who had looked after the dying Kate with such care, Catherine did not find another sympathetic doctor until she met Dr Gabb in St Leonards in 1969. Although he himself was dying of cancer, he took a great interest in her hereditary blood condition and went out of his way to help, referring Catherine to a surgeon at the Middlesex Hospital in London. This consultant grafted a length of skin from Catherine's hip into her nostril and cut a piece out of her tongue in order to stop the bleeding. In haemorrhagic telangiectasia abnormal blood vessels grow in certain areas of the body, particularly the nose, mouth and gastrointestinal tract, and it is these vessels that haemorrhage. The usual treatment is cauterisation, which works briefly, but the scarring it produces eventually makes the condition worse. The abnormal blood vessels are constantly growing and, as some are dealt with, new ones appear, causing new episodes of bleeding. The consultant asked Catherine if she would consent to be part of a research project at one of the London teaching hospitals. Her disease was so rare, he told her, that it had not been studied enough and until more was known about it there could be no cure. Catherine was happy to help. She hoped that something would be discovered that would make a difference to her own health, although it was a remote possibility. The surgical removal of the telangiectases that Catherine was given at the Middlesex was entirely experimental, but it did stop the bleeding for quite a while. Catherine was always grateful for the respite that Dr Gabb's recommendation gave her, since it came at a time when her career was really taking off.

Despite the fact that neither Macdonald Publishers nor her agent gave Catherine much in the way of hype, by 1960 her novels had begun to sell themselves. Readers recommended them to other readers and they began to walk out of shops and libraries in steadily increasing numbers. Although her books sold as 'romantic' fiction, the classic formula of romantic fiction can rarely be applied to Catherine's work, with the exception of her *Bill Bailey* and *Hamilton* novels and the Catherine Marchants. The central character is just as likely to be male as female. Her heroes and heroines are rarely allowed to have their preferred partner – there is usually some twist of fate to prevent their happiness and make them suffer. In *The Gambling Man*, neither Janie nor Charlotte is allowed to have Rory, the man they love and bigamously marry – he dies after being badly burned in a fire. Mary Walton in *Pure as the Lily* has her married happiness spoiled when husband and child are killed by a wartime bomb. In *Colour Blind* Bridget McQueen is separated from her black husband by a family tragedy, trapped in sexual and emotional limbo by his absence. After the failure of romantic love, Catherine's central characters often have to settle for another kind of happiness. Whenever Catherine was asked by an interviewer if she saw herself as a romantic novelist, she bridled. 'What nonsense that is! My books are social histories of the north, full of the bitterness of reality and no fancy frills.' They are not bodice rippers either, though occasionally described as such, since the violence is not erotic, and the truly historical novels did not begin until *Katie Mulholland* in 1967.

Catherine has been described by reviewers as 'the voice of the North as Dickens was the literary presenter of London' and sometimes as a champion of the working class, 'the people's writer of this generation'. More often her novels are described as 'popular histories of the northeast', and they certainly give a complete and graphic picture not only of the lives of working-class people in nineteenth- and early twentieth-century England, but also of the rise and fall of the industrial classes – the factory owners and shipbuilders whose family fortunes were made and often lost within two or three generations. Catherine's main output during the fifties and sixties could be divided into two main categories. There were the light and humorous books such as *Rooney, Slinky Jane*, the eight Mary Ann novels and their companion piece *Fanny McBride*. Then there were fourteen more serious novels set either in Jarrow or in the Northumbrian countryside just outside Newcastle. She would continue this pattern of alternating lightweight and more complex books throughout her life.

In the early sixties Catherine also ventured into the formula romance market. She occasionally wrote women's magazine stories and in 1961, *Women's Realm* asked whether she would write something suitable for serialisation and offered a substantial sum. Catherine was seriously tempted – could she write a romantic 'Mills and Boon' story as a commercial enterprise? She decided to take on the challenge with a story set in a Northumbrian farming community. Catherine's agent John Smith suggested that she publish it under a pseudonym and chose Catherine Marchant – a name that Catherine never quite felt at ease with, though she eventually wrote five novels in this genre, beginning with *The Heritage of Folly* in 1962 and ending with *The Iron Facade* in 1976. By the mid-1970s Catherine Cookson was selling so well, there was little point in putting any other name on the cover, whatever was inside. Two of these novels are set outside the northeast. *The Fen Tiger* is placed in Cambridgeshire, in the fen country where Catherine and Tom spent their holidays, and *The Iron Facade* is set in the Lake District – another holiday location. The latter is probably the best of the five, in both the quality of the writing and the psychological complexity of the characters. It is a first-person narrative about a young novelist recovering from a nervous breakdown who is healed by the peace and beauty of the landscape and the appearance of a sensitive and caring man.

She was soon earning enough money for Tom to retire from teaching and he did so in 1969, taking over the running of the house and looking after Catherine so that she could devote more time to writing. Inevitably, the increased income generated by international sales began to cause tax problems. In the beginning Catherine, who was quite an astute businesswoman, had handled her own tax affairs. As she began to earn more royalties she employed an accountant, on the recommendation of a friendly tax inspector. But, as most writers discover, the tax system is not always sympathetic to the creative way of life. Catherine was summoned to the tax office to explain why she was trying to claim a £500 deductible expense for an edition of *Encyclopaedia Britannica*. Catherine tried to explain that her physical disabilities prevented her from travelling for research and that she needed the books for information. She sensed from the beginning of the interview that the tax inspector was hostile towards her and, being Catherine, she believed that this hostility had a personal basis. The young civil servant told Catherine that he considered her expenses far too large against her earnings and also insinuated that perhaps she was not declaring all her earnings. How else could she afford to wear such an opulent mink coat? This was more than Catherine's temper could take. She rose out of her seat indignantly and went straight to see her accountant, who took her accounts to a tribunal, where her case was upheld. Catherine learned afterwards that the young tax inspector had been one of Tom's pupils at the grammar school and that his father was the van driver who delivered the Cooksons' groceries. This was enough to convince her that his pedantic attitude had been personally motivated.

By 1969, Catherine was in the supertax bracket and paying income tax at 83 pence in the pound on her earnings above a certain level and 98 pence in the pound on the interest on her savings. This meant that she got a total of only 19 pence for every pound she earned. Her agent and accountant suggested that she should buy a house in Jersey to minimise her tax bill and become a tax exile. So, accompanied by her accountant and his wife, she flew to Jersey to look at houses. Within a few hours of arrival, Catherine was introduced to the team of financial advisers who were going to run her affairs. She was instantly on the defensive: 'the idea of being taken over by any one, let alone by gentlemen who were going to control my earnings . . . didn't appeal to me'.[6] She was told that her income could be tripled, but that she would have to sack her current agent, John Smith, and leave England. The advisers assured Catherine that she could now afford to live anywhere she pleased, 'Switzerland, Barbados, or the Costa Brava', and she would be able to go back to England for a few months every year, providing that her permanent domicile was elsewhere.

Catherine hadn't been in Jersey more than twelve hours when she realised that she couldn't live there. She didn't like the place and she didn't like the people. Coming back on the plane she had an unfortunate experience with a drunken man who played at being a hijacker. He stood at the front of the plane pretending to wave a gun and made an announcement over the address system ordering all the ladies to 'take their knickers off'. Everyone laughed at him. Catherine didn't find it funny and was amazed that the cabin crew not only allowed it to happen, but seemed to be as amused as everyone else. To make matters worse, when the plane landed, the man stood at the foot of the steps kissing the women as they got off the aircraft. Most of them, whatever they actually felt about his offensive behaviour, put a polite face on it and humoured him. Catherine was much too honest to dissemble. She refused to allow him to touch her and told him he was disgusting. These things still upset her. But it was this episode that tipped the balance. She told Tom that she would rather pay 99 pence in the pound tax rather than live in Jersey. Catherine never left England again.

Catherine found the liberal sexual morality of the sixties very alien. While she did not want girls to be brought up as she had been in fear and ignorance, she did not approve of sexual experimentation before marriage. As one reviewer pointed out, most of Catherine's books have their genesis in 'contraceptive failure' and its consequences. Her heroines are usually punished for stepping outside conventional morality, whatever the mitigating circumstances. Men and women who remain 'pure' are rewarded for their patience. In *The Year of the Virgins*, the brother who anticipates his marriage and leads his pregnant wife to the altar is punished by being paralysed in a car crash as they leave on their honeymoon. The bride is doubly punished by losing her husband and then being rejected by her own family. It is the virgin Joe who marries the woman he has always loved and is allowed to live happily – if not ever after, at least as far as the last page of the book.

Catherine was very much a child of both her time and her Catholic upbringing in this respect, and she was always much more at home among the rigid moral standards of an earlier century. When she sets her books in contemporary society, her own attitudes and prejudices become apparent. In *Pure as the Lily* – the title taken from a song Catherine's grandfather used to sing to her – Catherine has the young Patricia Ridley release a tirade of invective against her fellow university students for sleeping around in a manner that recalls how Catherine once stood up at the table in Harton Workhouse and berated her fellow officers for loose talk. 'What are you anyway, but a lot of mediocre-brained animals ... half of your so-called band shouldn't be in the University because you're making it into a cross between a whore shop and an abortion clinic.'[7] This priggish attitude makes Pat a very unsympathetic character, though this is clearly not the intention of the author, who apparently approves of Pat's puritanical attitude and of her decision to abandon her degree and marry the nice man who has been secretly in love with her for years.

In *Bill Bailey*, published in 1986 when a relaxed sexual climate was already well established, the young, widowed heroine will not allow herself to be carried off to bed by the triumphant Bill after she has agreed to marry him, even though they are sharing a house, but retreats to the sanctuary of her separate bedroom where she remains until her wedding day – just as Catherine and Tom had done in 1937. This adherence to old-fashioned morality within novels that explore violence, sadism, cruelty and every kind of sexual perversion is something of a paradox, but it gave her novels a firm moral foundation approved by her mature readers, who also felt they could safely recommend them to a younger generation.

Between 1967 and 1969 Catherine published three major books – *Katie Mulholland, Our Kate* and *The Round Tower*. The last-named won her the Winifred Holtby Award for the best regional novel, a prize endowed by Vera Brittain in memory of her friend, the novelist Winifred Holtby, and administered by the Royal Society of Literature. While it categorised Catherine as a regional novelist, it also gave her a great deal of publicity and literary credibility. She was stunned when the book was given an award by such a prestigious organisation: 'Literature – that was the word.' She felt that she had at last been offered membership of an exclusive club. She was ill when the gilt-edged invitation came from the Royal Society of Literature, and remembered sitting up in bed to open the envelope, saying 'Tom, Tom, look at that. What hat am I going to wear?' before bursting into tears. But in spite of her excitement, Catherine didn't enjoy the reception, which she attended with John Smith and two of her editors. It was too stiff and formal and she felt that people were looking down on her, an attitude she described as 'holier than thou'.

The Round Tower is one of her most successful novels. It contrasts the decadent, declining world of the factory-owning Brett and Ratcliffe families, living in their big houses on the hill, and the earthy fecundity of the Cottons, who live at the bottom of the hill and of the social heap but are determined to fight their way up. When Vanessa Ratcliffe marries Angus Cotton, the two worlds collide. The façade of respectability erected by the houses on the hill is demolished to reveal a deep moral sickness that threatens to infect all who are connected with them. But in the end it is the Cottons who survive because their values are based in pragmatism and their personalities, bred on strife, are strong and vibrant.

Thanks to the award, *Katie Mulholland* was the first of her books to be marketed in America and this was a tremendous breakthrough. Catherine remarked ironically that 'the previous eighteen years and the seventeen books I had written might never have been . . . I was, so some people said, discovered.'[8] *Katie Mulholland*, which must rank high among the ten best novels she ever wrote, was also her first historical novel – in the sense that it is set outside the author's lifetime – and represented what was to be a change of direction. As the seam of her Jarrow childhood was mined out, she moved back into an earlier period based on stories her grandparents had told her. Such novels as *The Glass Virgin*, *The Gambling Man*, the Mallen saga, *The Black Velvet Gown*, *A Dinner of Herbs*, the *Tilly Trotter* trilogy, *The Black Candle* and *The Girl* were to be among her most popular books. The earliest of them, referred to by Catherine as 'this big story', was burning to be written for quite a while, but Catherine, for the first time, had trouble with its environment. She had thought of setting *Katie Mulholland* further back in the period of the Roman occupation, during the time when Hadrian was building the Roman wall across Northumberland. She had discussed it with John Smith and her editor John Foster White over lunch at Brown's Hotel and they were both dubious. But when Catherine went home, Tom, who was putting the kettle on while he took a break from the garden, suggested that she should bring it forward to the nineteenth century and centre it around Palmer's shipyard in Jarrow. It was a casual remark, but Catherine knew instantly that he was right. 'YES. YES. Of course. Palmer's shipyard, the life's blood of Jarrow for so long, and although it was now dead I could recall it vividly when it was alive.' And so Katie Mulholland was born in front of the Aga in the Loreto kitchen.

Catherine did intensive research on the shipyard. She went back to Jarrow to refresh her memory of the area. Palmer's yard had gone out of business and been demolished in the 1930s slump. The cranes that had dominated her childhood skyline were gone, but there were still men there who had worked in the yard and Catherine contacted the grandson of Palmer's original owner to find out more about the history of the company. She read Ellen Wilkinson's *Politics* to get the correct background for her suffragist character Theresa Rosier and even taught herself the theory of ironworking. Then, like all good novelists, she used her detailed research to colour the background of the story as unobtrusively as possible.

This skill was applauded by the reviewers. The *New York Times* was particularly complimentary. There were, the reviewer wrote, two ways in which historical novels frequently fail. In one, the writer spends most of his efforts and attention on historical research, so that his characters are merely symbols of an era who witness its important events. In another kind of novel gone wrong, the characters actually say and think and even desire the same things as 20th-century people – and the historical details surrounding them are only accessories for what amounts to an elaborate costume ball.

Catherine managed to avoid both these pitfalls. She was also able to resist 'sentimentality and write plainly, without avoiding unpleasant fictional truths'.[9]

Katie Mulholland is about cruelty – the worst things that human beings can do to each other. Katie suffers them all. She is raped at fifteen by her employer's son, Bernard Rosier. Discovering that she is carrying his child, she feels obliged to marry a brutal, loveless man who offers for her (and who, unknown to her, is being paid to do it by Bernard) in order to save her family from shame. She is then beaten to a pulp by her husband, who is subsequently found dead, and her father is, perhaps wrongly, hanged for his murder. Katie's much-loved daughter is taken from her by two rich spinsters and brought up to reject her. With her brother out of work and a Downs-syndrome sister to care for, Katie is driven by hunger and desperation to offer herself to a sea captain in return for food. Her brother abandons her in disgust, a female friend is seen to be motivated by 'unnatural attraction' and Katie is framed by Bernard Rosier – motivated by revenge – and wrongly jailed for running a brothel. When she is hauled off by the police, her handicapped sister is abandoned wailing in the empty room and subsequently taken to the workhouse, where she dies.

Katie emerges from prison, believing that she has lost everything, including what little reputation she had left. Although Katie manages eventually to rise above her situation and find a loving man, her old age is marred by bitterness, a brutal stepson who tries to rape her, and the knowledge that her daughter has unknowingly been allowed to make an incestuous marriage to her half-brother – the legitimate son of Bernard Rosier.

It is a very dark novel that raises the question, often asked, why she wrote again and again about such sadism and cruelty. The answer is not so easy to find. Perhaps she wrote about these things because of the hurt she herself had suffered and was unable to leave behind, and to exorcise all the dreadful things that she had witnessed, if not directly experienced, as a child. The books certainly come from the darkest places of her own mind, and illustrate her belief that every human being was capable of the best as well as the most terrible of actions. Many women find the books disturbing to read because they're so full of violence and cruelty. They are bearable only because it all happens in the distant past and never threatens the reader's comfort zone directly. Her novels are fatalistic, stoic, raw. The philosophy she was brought up with is reflected in them. 'The pattern once cut cannot be changed.' Predestination for her characters is rarely benign. Their fates hang over them like Greek Furies. The hopeless, impotent feeling of being merely a pawn in a gigantic game was one that assailed Catherine all the time and she had to fight it constantly, as her characters must battle against what seems to be inevitable. Yet, as Catherine proved, it is possible to change, to escape, to rise above the quagmire of poverty and shame, though there will always be a price to pay for this.

In Catherine's case the price had been paid for by the loss of her mental health. She had several recurrences of depression – the worst in 1960 when she was writing *The Garment*. Realising that not even the writing of *Our Kate* was going to heal the wounds inflicted during her childhood, Catherine was having to come to terms with this and with the reality of her hereditary blood disorder. She knew she was going to have to live with mental and physical illness for the rest of her life. Like most people afflicted with chronic, incurable diseases, she often asked 'Why me?' and went through periods of extreme anger and feelings of futility. But her courage in the face of such formidable adversaries was immense. She even brought herself to admit that it was her difficult childhood and her illnesses that 'in a strange way nurtured my writing', and she threw herself into her work with renewed energy whenever she felt the onset of self-pity. Her career was gathering momentum. In addition to writing the books, she had fan letters to answer and all the business side of authorship to deal with – a formidable amount of book-keeping, research, proofreading, negotiations with agents and publishers, publicity exercises, public appearances and interviews.

Such was the pressure of work by the end of the sixties that Catherine began to be troubled by writer's cramp and a frozen shoulder. Tom suggested that she should dictate her novels on to tape, but at first she was afraid that she wouldn't be able to do it – not everyone can. She feared it was the end of her writing career, and it sparked off another episode of depression. This was before the age of portable machines and the sheer size of reel-to-reel tape recorders was also quite daunting. But Catherine soon found that dictation opened up an entirely new way of working. She was a natural, oral storyteller whose books had always been strong on dialogue. When she dictated she walked around the room acting out the parts, running the story like a play in her head and speaking the characters' voices. The only parts that she found difficult, she confessed, were the lovemaking scenes, and she found it impossible to work with someone else in the room – even Tom. One of the main benefits was that she didn't have to worry any more about spelling words correctly, or about grammar. This was now the responsibility of whoever transcribed the tape. When Catherine was finished, the tapes were given to her secretary to type up and Catherine edited the drafts by hand. When her secretary moved away, the tapes were sent down to Devon to be transcribed and there were some hilarious misunderstandings. On one occasion, Catherine dictated 'I suppose you spent all the war hoeing taties' and it came back as 'I suppose you spent all the war whoring Katies'. The success of this new method of working was reflected in *Katie Mulholland*, one of the first books to be written by dictation.

After the publication of *Our Kate*, Catherine's fan mail increased dramatically. The book was immediately popular and had to be reprinted twice in hardback during the first year. The story struck a chord with many people who had struggled with alcoholism, infertility or depression, the shame of illegitimacy, and difficult family relationships. One woman was so distressed by the episode where Catherine had only vegetables in her Christmas stocking that she sent her one every year, stuffed with seventeen different sorts of sweet as well as small presents. Catherine was surprised and troubled that so many people wrote saying how much they loved Kate – one man even said he wished she was still alive so he could have married her. There were also a number of people who wrote claiming that they were related to Catherine. On several occasions it seemed that the mystery of her father's identity could be resolved. Catherine wrote back to each of them and on one occasion really believed that she had found her father's family, until she checked the dates of birth and realised that this particular Alexander Davies would have been a young child at the time. It was a great disappointment. Catherine was rich enough now to have employed a professional researcher to trace her father if she had wished to do so. But she didn't. Like many adopted children who grow up longing to know the identity of their real parents, she found that she now preferred living with the fantasy to risking the discovery of an uncomfortable truth. In many of Catherine's novels – *The Bonny Dawn*, *The Glass Virgin*, *The Black Candle* and *A Dinner of Herbs* to name only four – it is the revelation of true parentage that unleashes tragic consequences.

The late sixties also brought Nan back into Catherine's life. The money Nan had made from the sale of the house Catherine bought for her had gradually evaporated and Nan had migrated through a series of increasingly run-down houses and apartments to a basement flat on the sea front. Catherine and Tom decided to put the past, with all its drama and bitterness, behind them and Nan once more became a frequent visitor to Catherine's home. Nan's love for Catherine seems to have been undiminished and she lavished gifts on her. Some of these gifts, Catherine later discovered, had been given to Nan by other people as presents, or had been taken from their houses without permission. Catherine forgave her as she always did because she knew that Nan did it out of love: 'I must have been the most important thing in her life.'[10]

By 1969 Nan had lung cancer, which the doctors told Catherine was inoperable. Tom and Catherine tried to help Nan to sort out her affairs, even paying some of her debts and assuring her that they would make sure there was sufficient money for her funeral. Nan was admitted to hospital in St Leonards, where she occupied a two-bedded side ward for the last three months of her life. Catherine had forgiven Nan everything and believed that Nan no longer had any power to hurt her. She and Tom visited the hospital every day and at first Nan was cheerful and loving. But as she grew weaker and was often on oxygen, her attitude to Catherine began to change. On one occasion she accused Catherine of having hit her over the fingers with a poker – an incident Catherine couldn't remember ever happening. On several other occasions she threatened Catherine, saying repeatedly, 'Don't think you'll get rid of me, when I'm gone.'[11]

It became obvious that Nan had only weeks or even days to live. She fretted to go back to her flat in order to sort out her belongings. Catherine and Tom volunteered to take her there for a few hours.

Two of her Irish relatives were there stuffing things into boxes and bags to take back to Ireland, but all Nan was interested in was several suitcases of letters. It quickly became clear that there wouldn't be enough time to go through them all, so Nan extracted one bundle, wrapped in a gentleman's leather pouch, and told the relatives the rest could be burned. That weekend Catherine was due to go to Newcastle for a series of talks, booked months previously. Nan insisted that she should go as arranged and Tom said that he would stay with Nan, so Catherine reluctantly left, knowing instinctively that she would never see Nan again. She left the room in tears as Nan breathed 'Goodbye, Kit,' through her oxygen mask. 'She was dying,' Catherine explained. 'This woman had caused me more trouble than anyone should in ten lifetimes, but she was dying.'[12]

Nan died shortly after Catherine left. Her last act was to ask Tom to open her locker drawer and take the wallet of letters. 'I want you to have them,' she told him. Catherine stayed at her cousin Sarah's in Gateshead and rang Tom on Saturday morning for news of Nan. When he told her that Nan was dead, she wanted to come home straight away. Tom told her that she must not, in uncharacteristically forceful terms. He forbade her to come back even for the funeral. It would have been unusual for Catherine to have obeyed without dissent, but something in their conversation must have carried considerable weight. Nan was buried on the Wednesday and Catherine came home on the Thursday, racked with guilt at having missed the funeral and failed Nan. As she wept, Tom told her to shut up. 'Beside himself with anger, trembling and white with rage,' he produced the letters – one of which Catherine recognised straight away. The others she hadn't seen before. When she read them, Catherine was so shattered, so consumed with hate for Nan, that she said she felt like going into the graveyard and digging up her body in order to 'choke her skeleton'.[13] When she talked about it on tape twenty years later, she became almost hysterical with an anger that had never abated.

The content of the letters rocked the Cookson marriage of twenty-nine years to its foundations. One of them was from a woman officer during the First World War, breaking off her relationship with the nineteen-year-old Nan. Its purpose was presumably to underline Nan's sexuality. Another was from the son of the Frenchwoman who had once wanted to have an affair with Catherine. This woman had obviously remained in touch with Nan and Nan had written to tell her that Catherine was going to marry Tom and was throwing her out. Apparently Nan's letter (returned to Nan by the son?) had included a catalogue of men Catherine was supposed to have had affairs with before she met Tom, as well as details of her relationship with Nan. It was obvious that the Frenchwoman regarded them as a couple. 'Poor Paddy,' the letter began, 'how could she throw you out?' The other letter was one from Catherine herself to Nan – the letter she had written to her at the beginning of their relationship, telling Nan that they could indeed be friends. These explosive letters were Nan's last attempt to separate Tom and Catherine and their content must have been damaging indeed to have affected Tom so badly. Catherine told John Smith that she had kept them in a brown envelope so that after her death people would know the evil that Nan Smith had tried to do to her. 'If that man [Tom] hadn't known me . . . If that man hadn't been the kind of man he was . . .'[14] Without Tom's understanding and intrinsic goodness, Catherine did not believe that her marriage would have survived.

PART FIVE

— ❖ —

Miracles
1969–1998

A best-seller is a miracle.

Catherine Cookson

17

Everything in life has to be paid for, and fame is the
dearest commodity, it's not worth the candle –
believe me.[1]

It would be easy, reading Catherine's autobiography, to claim that
the essential prerequisites for being a best-selling author were childhood deprivation and a Catholic upbringing. But Catherine often
joked that what you really needed were white ankle socks and plim-
solls – remembering a successful author who habitually wore them.
It was a good example of Catherine's sense of humour. She laughed a
lot, and often at herself. Many journalists who interviewed Catherine
found her a delight, 'like an agony aunt; a mother confessor, everyone's grandma or friend, all rolled into one'.[2] However, Catherine
didn't suffer fools, and could be quite tart and combative. Anyone
who suggested she was a romantic novelist was put down severely,
and one journalist who pointed out the irony of making millions by
writing about her poverty was instantly crushed: 'Let me tell you
straight, madam, I've *never* in my life written for money.' And in a
sense it was true. She wrote because she had to. She would have
written the books whatever she had been paid for them. Catherine
told the editor Piers Dudgeon that she had 'the urgent desire to write
and write and write'; it was the only thing that gave her any real
satisfaction.[3] It was an obsession.

Yet, though Catherine would never have admitted it, the money
was important in that it purchased the trappings of success that told
her she had arrived, that she was valued – she was *somebody*. The
house, the swimming pool, the car and the fur coat told the world
that she was no longer Katie McMullen who went every week to

the pawnshop and who was laughed at because she didn't have a father. Every penny she earned took her further from the childhood fear of the workhouse and the debtor's court. The popularity of the best-selling novelist and the financial reward that went with it counterbalanced the inferiority complex she had always suffered from. That she did not become wholly materialistic was remarkable; Catherine herself put it down to the values she had learned in William Black Street. Some of her fortune was dedicated to putting right old injustices and paying off ancient debts. Catherine sent money to her piano teacher in Jarrow to pay for the lessons that Kate still owed. The undertaker was paid, and her uncle Jack's grave was traced in France and a headstone erected. Masses were also bought for Rose and John McMullen.

By the seventies Catherine could look back with much less pain. 'I used to think of my childhood with bitterness, but now I realise that I owe everything to it.' That admission didn't come easily. The realisation that she couldn't leave her childhood behind, even by writing about it, came after a trip to South Shields, where she was to be honoured and given the freedom of the borough. For Catherine it was one of the high points of her life. She stayed with her friends Mannie and Rita Anderson and rehearsed her speech in their sitting room until two o'clock in the morning. She talked about her childhood and how she had dreamed of the future as she walked up the road carrying the beer, but she had never dreamed of anything like this. 'And I cried and the people in the audience cried. It was *something* for this girl who was born in the circumstances that I was.'[4] The freedom of the borough meant more to Catherine than any of the literary prizes she had received, because it was given by her 'ain folk'. She was 'being honoured by the townsfolk – the greatest honour that they could bestow'.[5]

The occasion was a great triumph, but as she came down from the platform in her mink coat, she was greeted by a woman who claimed that she had known Catherine in the New Buildings. This was Belle, who had played with her in the street and even 'picked taties' with her during the summer months at Simonside. She was also the little girl who had told Catherine that she 'had no da'. Catherine claimed that she couldn't remember Belle at all, and this may have been true, because large sections of her childhood had been deliberately blanked out, others blurred by the effects of the electric shock treatment she had been given in Hereford. But from the account that Catherine gave, it seems that when Belle spoke to her, all the pain of her childhood rose up in front of her.

She was also approached by Eddie Richardson, the eldest son of a family she had known in Phillipson Street. He too had managed to get away and was now a practising psychiatrist. With the outspokenness of the northerner, he told Catherine that she was a much nicer person now than she had been when he knew her as a child. His memories of Catherine once again shook her confidence in her own ability to remember the past truthfully. When Catherine protested that she had been jolly and friendly as a teenager, Eddie replied, 'Don't fool yourself. You were so damned stuck-up, so much the lady, so determined to rise above everything and everyone, that you never looked the side I was on, nor anyone else in the New Buildings.'[6]

These incidents disturbed and irritated Catherine for other reasons – 'There I was, dressed up to the eyes, Catherine Cookson the writer ... yet to my ain folk I would ever remain Katie McMullen of the New Buildings.' She was still struggling with Katie in her subconscious mind. All her life, her desire to be a writer had vied for supremacy with something else that she admitted she desired even more and which constricted her creativity. This was her desire 'to be a lady and speak correctly'. Catherine still hadn't succeeded in resolving the conflict, or in 'owning' the little girl who was such an important part of her character. The Siamese twins were still battling it out inside her.

When she thought about it rationally, Catherine knew that it was Katie McMullen's experience that went into the books – Catherine Cookson the author owed her great success to the child from the New Buildings she had tried so hard to stifle.

> I know that inside I am still very much the child, the child that was Katie McMullen of East Jarrow, only the façade is the woman and it hasn't the power to control the child. Somehow I can't ignore the power of the child I once was and still am. I am still hurt as she was hurt. I still laugh as she laughed. I still have the secret insight that she had.[7]

In the eyes of the people of Jarrow, Catherine would always be Katie McMullen and although at first she hated it, eventually she acknowledged that in order to achieve the peace of mind and 'wholeness' she craved, she needed to come back to her roots.

Writing historical novels meant that Catherine had to make longer trips to the northeast in order to do the necessary research in the local archives. In 1968 and '69 she was spending time in the libraries learning about glassmaking. She was delighted to discover that the biggest firm of glassmakers on the Tyne had been called Cookson and she set her new novel *The Glass Virgin* in the glassmaking industry. It is another story of moral sickness at the heart of wealth and respectability, a weakness that will eventually destroy the family. Annabella Lagrange is brought up at Redford Hall on the moors above Jarrow, unaware that she is the daughter of a prostitute and a pimp. The revelation of her true parentage and the exposure of her supposed father's unnatural vices precipitate the family's spectacular collapse. Like a princess in a fairy tale, Annabella learns through her subsequent destitution and her pilgrimage through the Northumbrian countryside that true values are not based on appearances. She is protected and eventually saved by one of her father's workmen who has the moral and physical strength to support her.

The Glass Virgin was published by Macdonald in 1970 and sold to Corgi for the rather low advance of £1,000. Catherine's increasing popularity meant that in the same year they had to reprint *Fenwick Houses* and *The Round Tower* twice. Corgi also bought the rights to *Kate Hannigan* and Catherine's Mary Ann novels – the first of them, *A Grand Man*, had already been reprinted eight times in hardback by the time Corgi issued it in 1971. In the same year, BBC Television decided to film her children's story *Joe and the Gladiator* for serialisation.

Catherine's literary award and her reputation as the north's most prolific novelist brought an invitation to a reception at Syon House, the southern home of the Duke of Northumberland, just outside London. Catherine was one of about fifty northern celebrities invited to meet the new vice chancellor of Newcastle University. When the invitation arrived, Catherine was almost overwhelmed by excitement. She spent weeks planning what she was going to wear, buying new make-up and shoes. James MacGibbon, one of her editors at Macdonald, agreed to be Catherine's escort and invited her out to tea beforehand. He drove her out into the country to a picturesque restaurant where Catherine worried all the time about being punctual for the reception. When he came to pay the bill, James discovered that he had lost it and there was a lengthy negotiation with the waitress. Catherine was all the time on tenterhooks, looking at her watch.

Outside it was pouring with rain. Neither of them had any clear idea where Syon House was and they got lost in the country lanes before finally coming up to a pair of forbidding wrought-iron gates which James got out of the car to open. They arrived at the front door only to be told by one of the gardeners that they had to go round to the service entrance, which Catherine thought was a great insult. They went in, as directed, through the garden centre, picking their way through plants, bricks, implements and wheelbarrows until they found the right door. Inside Catherine said there were about thirty couples standing around looking bored. By now her feet had developed blisters inside her new shoes and she couldn't find anywhere to sit down. She tried to talk to someone but her opening gambit 'Are you from the north too?' met with a frosty rebuff. James didn't fare any better; he discovered that the only person he knew was the outgoing chancellor – someone he wasn't on good terms with. Catherine looked for the Duke whom she had expected to meet, but couldn't see him anywhere.

Eventually James directed her towards a receiving line where a few couples were waiting to say goodbye to an elderly gentleman they were told was the Duke of Northumberland. Catherine and James joined the end of the queue and watched him shake hands and chat with several people who were leaving. But when it was the turn of the couple in front of them, Catherine was horrified to see the Duke look at them and turn his back to talk to someone else before walking off. She was incensed at what she saw as deliberate rudeness. 'It's a good job it was the couple in front and not me,' she said later when her sense of humour had returned, 'or I'd have thought that he'd read my books!'[8] Catherine left the reception absolutely furious. All the way back to Hastings on the train her anger simmered. When Tom met her he knew immediately that something was wrong. 'What's the matter?' he asked. 'Didn't you see the Duke?'

Catherine boiled over and shouted, 'Bugger the Duke!'

All night Catherine seethed because of the insult she felt had been handed out. By morning she had made up her mind to write a letter, but Tom, always the peacemaker, persuaded her not to do so. 'Tom hated rows,' Catherine said. 'He was a bundle of nerves and if I dared to go for someone . . . he would always advise me to let it go. Think twice. You'll see your day with them, he'd say. Keep things quiet. But you can't always, can you?"[9] By lunchtime Catherine had had a stroke of inspiration. If she couldn't write a letter, she would write a book. The result was *The Invitation*, one of Catherine's more light-hearted novels. The central incident in the book is Maggie Gallagher's invitation to the Duke of Moorshire's musical evening. The blister becomes a painful corn on Maggie's heel and she doesn't wait to get home before uttering the fatal phrase. According to Catherine's agent, John Smith, Catherine wanted to call the book *Bugger the Duke* and it took a great deal of persuasion from him and her editors at Macdonald before she would change it. The original also had a preface addressed to dukes, reminding them of their duties, which was deleted.

When Anthony Sheil purchased the Christy & Moore agency at the end of the year, Catherine was one of its greatest assets. He was immediately aware of the undeveloped potential of her work and set out to make sure that it was properly valued. The first change he made was to move Catherine's books from Macdonald to William Heinemann, whose marketing policy was rather more commercial. By 1973 Corgi had to pay £15,000 for *The Dwelling Place*. Change always bothered Catherine and she was, at first, very apprehensive. She insisted that both her former agent John Smith and John Foster White, her editor from Macdonald, should continue to be involved with her books. She was used to dealing with them and trusted them both completely. She felt that they understood her. Catherine hated working with strangers. When John Smith began to spend less time in the office prior to retirement, Gill Coleridge – previously responsible for selling foreign and translation rights – became the person who usually looked after Catherine on a day-to-day basis. Catherine had problems relating to women and Gill was warned beforehand that Catherine didn't like working with them – something that had stayed with Catherine from her days in the laundry. But after a rather formal beginning, Catherine warmed to Gill and they got on very well. Catherine was quite a demanding client and expected a great deal from her agent and publisher. She became upset if telephone calls were not returned straight away and when she sent in a new manuscript she wanted almost immediate feedback. But in return Catherine offered generous hospitality and was very appreciative of everything that was done for her. She inspired loyalty and affection from all those who represented her, whatever their private opinion of the literary merit of her work.

Catherine working in bed at Loreto.

Catherine with her paintings at an exhibition of north eastern women artists.

Catherine in the ruins of William Black Street which was being demolished to make way for a dual carriageway and business park.

Catherine, Tom and their poodle Sandy standing
in the doorway of their home in Northumberland.

An ecstatic Catherine at the opening night
of the stage version of *Katie Mulholland*.

Catherine's 80th birthday party.

Catherine, with Tom behind her, receiving an honorary doctorate
from the University of Sunderland in a marquee in the garden of her home.

Tom Cookson.
'He gave me his life so that I could write.'

Catherine, frail but still smiling, on her last birthday.

At the beginning of the seventies other changes were also being discussed. Since the idea of moving to Jersey had been dropped, Tom and Catherine had continued to talk about the tax advantages of buying property elsewhere. Catherine did not want to move from Loreto, her home for fourteen years and now a showpiece for her own taste. With the money from *The Glass Virgin*, she had just paid for an extension to house a sitting-room-cum-study with views out over the garden, which was just beginning to mature and reward all their hard work. Tom suggested buying a second home in Newcastle, since Catherine was now spending more and more time there to research her books. She disliked hotels and dreaded bleeding in public. Catherine tended to stay with people she knew, and particularly liked staying with a doctor called Mannie Anderson and his wife Rita. Dr and Mrs Anderson had first accommodated her when she came north to address a charity event. They subsequently become good friends and Catherine was a frequent visitor. She was also gradually, through her visits, re-establishing family links. She had become much closer to her cousin Sarah Sables, the youngest daughter of Aunt Sarah, who had visited her from time to time in Hastings.

After much argument, several house-hunting trips and two false beginnings in properties that didn't suit, Tom and Catherine finally bought an elegant townhouse in Jesmond – one of the most exclusive residential areas of Newcastle – and began to commute between Loreto and number 39 Eslington Terrace. Catherine was initially ambivalent about moving back to the northeast, perhaps because it held such difficult memories. And she no longer regarded it as 'home' – after all, Catherine had now lived in Hastings twice as long as she had ever lived in Jarrow. By 1974, the place had changed beyond all recognition, factories and shipyards gone, mines closing down and streets demolished to make way for new developments, including a shopping centre and car park. 'Gone were great sections of the town I once knew; what had been the oldest part was now the newest.'[10] The houses in William Black Street and Leam Lane had been pulled down to make way for a dual carriageway and an industrial estate. Catherine was bewildered and distressed to find that she couldn't recognise the area in which she had grown up.

Catherine had changed too, in the forty years she had been away, and it did not help matters that some of her initial impressions were negative. Apart from the unnerving experience of having to meet people who had known and hurt her as a child, she found that the landscape sometimes triggered feelings of agoraphobia. Catherine had spent her life in the narrow, enclosed streets of an urban environment, and flat expanses of countryside made her feel exposed and vulnerable.

Tom, however, loved the country and he liked to take the car rather than travel north by train, so that he could explore the wilder reaches of Northumberland. On one occasion, when they were on their way to stay with Sarah in Birtley, Tom took the route north up the M6 into Cumbria, across Shap Fell to Appleby and Penrith and then up the steep ascent of Hartside Pass to the Alston Fells. At the top of Hartside, 2,000 feet up, there are spectacular views across the Irish Sea and the Solway Firth on one side and on the other a gradual descent into the wooded upper valleys of the Tyne. From Alston across the roof of the Pennines to Hexham is a particularly wonderful drive on a fine day. But the narrow road with a steep drop on one side, followed by the unending expanse of moor and sky, filled Catherine with fear and she suffered a severe panic attack. 'What I experienced that day went past terror.'[11] Crouched down on the floor of the car so that she couldn't see the view, her heart jerking so much she was afraid it would jump out of her chest, Catherine was hysterical, pleading with Tom to get her out of it as quickly as possible. Used to dealing with Catherine's fears, Tom talked to her calmly and quietly. It was impossible, he told her. There was nowhere to go; she must simply bear with it until the journey was over.

At the top of Staward Pele – a famous viewing spot looking over both the Tyne Valley and Allendale – he stopped the car and begged her to sit up and take a look. Catherine lifted her head up and tried to focus on the view, but the distance 'which seemed to go on for eternity' only renewed her hysteria and forced her to huddle back down on the floor, screaming with fear. When they finally came to a village, Catherine sat on the doorsill of the car and vomited into the gutter. She didn't even have the strength to stand up.[12]

Her first experience should have put her off, but Catherine was always one for facing her fears down. Tom loved the upper reaches of the Tyne with its spectacular hills and wooded valleys as well as the remote beauty of Allendale, and Catherine eventually came to recognise this wild landscape as her own. There was something in it that reflected a part of her personality. 'Up here in the hills I know that I am in my own country, not soft like the downs nor flat like

the fens. This countryside is raw, and it is with me and I feel it.'[13]
She was to use it in several of her most famous novels, until it became
as familiar to her readers as the streets of Jarrow. The top of the
bank where Tom had tried to make her look at the view became the
Tor where Jane takes her crippled brother in *Feathers in the Fire*.
Further on is the cliff where Donald, one of the Mallen bastards, is
killed by his half-brother, and beside the road stands the ruined
cottage where Catherine envisaged Constance Mallen sheltering from
a storm and conceiving an illegitimate child. *The Girl* is set in one
of the villages of Allendale, and *A Dinner of Herbs* among the lead-
mining communities in the fells above Langley.

Travelling backwards and forwards between Newcastle and Hastings between 1969 and 1973, Catherine wrote *The Dwelling Place*,
Feathers in the Fire, *Pure as the Lily* and the three Mallen novels,
as well as two novels under the Catherine Marchant pseudonym.
One of them, *The Iron Facade*, is set in the countryside between
Penrith and Appleby which Tom had driven through on that terrifying journey across the Pennines. Some of the fearful nature of that
journey is in the book and the passenger in the car has to get out
and vomit just as Catherine had done. She was still working through
her experiences by 'writing them out'. When she wasn't writing a
novel or short story she wrote in her journal – more a scrapbook of
occasional pieces, reflections, essays, poems and cathartic paragraphs
than a fully fledged diary or writer's notebook. Some of the pieces
were subsequently worked up into articles for magazines and newspapers, or short radio talks.

Her journal was also a record of her quest for ultimate peace of
mind, a spiritual harbour that would hold her securely and protect
her from the onslaughts of fear and doubt. Although for a long time
she had described herself as an agnostic, she found it impossible to
leave religion behind. When she had a particular success with a book,
friends often heard her say 'the nuns would be pleased with me'.[14]
She was delighted when a Catholic nun wrote to her from a convent
in California to say how much she liked her books and told her
about the Mexican Indian children she taught and cared for. Catherine began to send donations of money to the convent whenever
she could. When the children heard that Catherine was ill, they
inscribed prayers on a long scroll and sent it to her to pin up on the
wall.

Catherine still wrote to Harry Edwards. She saw God now not so much as an omnipotent figure but as a power, rather like electricity, that could be tapped into by particular people. She had experienced this herself, on the occasion when she had prayed for a story and been given *The Fifteen Streets*. There were other occasions too when she had been helped by remote spiritual healers like Harry Edwards, and stranger experiences such as the perfume she occasionally smelled around her. This universal power had other manifestations too. A book by the American author Art Ulene called *Feeling Fine* became one of Catherine's guiding texts. Her great need was for a spiritual mentor who would understand her problems without even having to have them put into words, someone she could talk to inside her head, as she talked to Kate or her Siamese twin. Dr Ulene's book is a self-help manual which sets out twenty-one daily exercises in positive thinking. One of the things that he advocates as helpful is the visualisation of an animal to be the recipient of personal confidences. This struck a note with Catherine, the dog lover. But the animal is not just to be a confidant, there is also a hint of the 'power animal' idea which features in much New Age holistic practice.

After a long day writing in bed, Catherine found that although she was mentally exhausted, her body was not, and she found it difficult to sleep. She developed a technique of visualising a warm tropical beach with the sea gently washing the sand and went through a relaxation ritual, working on each limb in turn until she slipped quietly into unconsciousness. One night as she lay there, Ulene's book fomenting in her subconscious mind, she was suddenly aware of a hippopotamus lying on the sand beside her. This, she realised, was her chosen animal. It seemed an odd choice, but when she reflected on it she felt that perhaps it was because the hippo is an unglamorous animal, ugly and generally neglected by lovers of exotic animals in favour of lions, tigers, monkeys and elephants. The hippo, like herself, was an outsider. She also saw him (he was unquestionably male) as 'the representation of my inner spirit . . . God's messenger'.[15]

Catherine wrote an essay in her journal called 'God Is a Hippo', but didn't dare to publish it, since she was afraid that people would think she was insane. It was finally published in 1995 among a collection of extracts from her journals. He had told her, Catherine wrote, that she must not

shy away from the mystery of the Omnipotent One who could spread Himself, even into the bulk of a mud-coated hippopotamus, in order to have a word with me, but would try to understand and come to believe, that with God, all things were possible, and that there was no channel too dark or too ugly through which He would not travel in order to reach me.[16]

Catherine wanted to be found.

One outcome of Catherine's experience was the creation of *Hamilton*, which many of her fans regard as the strangest of her novels. Maisie, an unhappy child, ill-treated and unloved by her mother, secretly has an imaginary horse, Hamilton, who shares all her troubles and gives her advice. But unlike other childhood imaginary friends, Hamilton stays with Maisie as she matures, even when she gets married and becomes a best-selling author. It is only when she finds a kindly man who really loves her that Hamilton appears with a mare called Begonia and tells her that she doesn't need him any more. Few suspected when they read it that Catherine was writing out of her own experience, substituting a horse for a hippo. Her agent and publisher were less than enthusiastic, but by the time it was published in 1983, Catherine was so well established that almost anything with her name on it would have been a best-seller. She told the journalist who came to interview her for *The Times* that she could dictate her own terms. She was now, she said jokingly, 'the best paid bastard in the business!'[17] *Hamilton* didn't please all her readers, and reviewers didn't always know what to say about the book either. *The Times* stated, 'It was the notion of a young woman having an imaginary horse to talk to that put me off.'[18] The *Yorkshire Post* avoided the issue in a diffuse paragraph that included the comment, 'It is certain that Catherine Cookson has never written better either about animals or about women or about courage.'[19]

Tom, the Essex boy, had fallen in love with the north and soon tired of driving backwards and forwards between one house and the other. He persuaded Catherine that it was time to move back permanently. She was nearly seventy, he was in his sixties, and soon neither of them would be fit enough for such a big upheaval. Catherine joked to friends that he wanted to take her home to die. She still regarded Hastings as home and was very reluctant to leave Loreto. Yet she too felt an urge to return to the source of her inspiration – though not to the city. She still longed 'not for the country exactly but for a different view, something different from the streets, and the river and the ships'.[20]

Tom hoped that the move might break the punishing cycle of work Catherine was locked into. An entry in her journal on 18 January 1975 reveals not only her exhausted state of mind but also the continuing fragility of her mental health.

I felt very ill yesterday. The feeling continued into the night; I couldn't sleep. My siamese twin self-pity, was in charge. This was a real bout of mental exhaustion. For months now it has been a fourteen hour day, seven days a week, up at half-past six in the morning trying to get through my ever growing mail; the day allotted to the phone, visits from agents, editors, photographers, interviewers and, just recently, the BBC Unit. I tell myself it can't go on, but it does.[21]

Catherine felt that she was being driven by an external force.

The Cooksons looked at a number of properties all over Northumberland and even bought a house in Morpeth, but they quickly realised it was a mistake and never lived there. They spent a considerable amount of time exploring the countryside around Hexham to look at settings for the Mallen novels and they grew to love Corbridge, an old border town with a fascinating history not far from Hadrian's Wall, perched on the hill above the river Tyne. It has beautiful old buildings, elegant tearooms catering for a brisk tourist trade, and small upmarket shops reflecting a middle-class professional population, many of whom commute into Newcastle to work. Town Barns, the property Catherine eventually bought, was on the edge of the town, five minutes' walk from the centre, but with views out over the Tyne Valley and the moorland beyond. It was a large house recently built by a local developer in a style described as contemporary Georgian. By 1973, when Catherine saw it, the builder, John Anderson, was living in it himself with his first wife. He had also built a smaller adjacent house, Trinity Barns, which Catherine also bought, and had an option on the field below the houses, with outline planning permission to build three more.

Catherine paid approximately £90,000 for Town Barns, rather less for Trinity Barns, which she planned to use as a guest cottage, and another £27,000 for the field. She thought the price outrageous, but the owner argued that it was building land and wouldn't sell it for less. Catherine needed the field, partly because she didn't want a housing estate next to her home, and partly because there was very little garden with the property. For the money that she spent on Town Barns and the surrounding land, Catherine could have bought a small manor house – the authentic 'gentleman's residence' she had once craved. Instead she opted for what one visitor cruelly referred to as 'working-class posh'.

The house was spacious and light as modern houses are, but not overlarge. Constructed from local stone, outside it has the look of a barn conversion, despite the mock-Georgian windows. It is now owned by Tony and Dorothy Wilson, who take in tourists for bed and breakfast during the summer months, and it is still substantially the same as it was when Catherine lived in it. Inside, the front door opens into a large central hallway with an elegant double staircase on the opposite wall rising up to a gallery which runs right round the hall giving access to the four large bedrooms. Catherine's had an *en suite* bathroom that she joked was 'pure Hollywood', containing a gigantic royal-blue bath with gold fittings.

Downstairs, to the left of the front door, is the dining room and a large kitchen, which in Catherine's day was equipped with all the latest gadgets including an island unit, two built-in ovens, handmade pine cupboards and all-white surfaces. At the back of the hallway is the study and to the right a big drawing room with a door opening into a conservatory and steps down into the swimming pool. This was one of the attractions for Catherine, though within a few years of moving north she found that the chlorine in the water would precipitate nosebleeds and prevent her using it. Other factors that persuaded her to buy Town Barns were that the house was easy to run, close to local shops, Newcastle was only a short drive away, and the moors above Allendale were visible across the river from Catherine's bedroom window. The only drawback was that a public footpath ran right past the gate, only a few yards from the front of the house, though in such a sleepy, out-of-the-way place that didn't seem to matter.

The Cooksons moved to Corbridge in September 1976. Catherine joked that she had come back to die 'like an eel returning from the Sargasso Sea'. On 12 September she wrote a letter to a friend in Hastings saying that she was settled at Town Barns 'with reservations'. Painters were at work inside and out and she had had to resign herself to the fact that it wouldn't be finished until

Christmas. 'Although this is a beautiful house, in a beautiful setting,' Catherine wrote, 'I have to admit that I was very homesick for the first fortnight and still get waves of it hitting me.' She consoled herself with the fact that Tom loved it and was very 'happy and relaxed'.[22]

One of the reasons for this was the advent of Sandy, a white miniature poodle. The Cooksons were both overjoyed to have another dog. After the death of their Labrador Simon they had vowed never to have another – they were too old for pets. But after eighteen months they were lonely; 'the house was empty . . . we were empty'.[23] A friend suggested that they should get small dog, perhaps a poodle, only to be greeted by scorn. Poodles, in Catherine's opinion, were not proper dogs. But shortly afterwards they acquired Sandy, and Catherine was enchanted to discover that poodles weren't dogs at all but 'little men . . . wonderful children that never grew up'. Of all the dogs they had, Sandy was the most fun – 'Sandy was our child'.[24]

Catherine soon had the house immaculate. Downstairs, the drawing room was filled with her collection of antique and reproduction furniture, Chinese carpets and cabinets holding bric-a-brac, Chinese pottery, glass and majolica. Next door Catherine and Tom had an extensive and well-equipped office with adjoining desks. The move made little difference to Catherine's pace of work, though the success of her Mallen trilogy meant that she and Tom were financially secure for the rest of their lives, even if she had never written another word. Catherine quoted a favourite text from Ecclesiastes to one of her interviewers: 'Cast thy bread upon the waters and it shall come back to thee after many days.' She joked that she had done that and got back 'a bakery shop with all the fancies'![25] She told a *Daily Mirror* journalist that her life had been 'just like Cinderella'.

By the time she moved to Corbridge she had published more than forty novels, and most of them were still in print. It was a huge achievement, acknowledged by her publishers. The sales director at Heinemann, Tom Manderson, said enthusiastically in an interview that, from a professional point of view, Catherine was 'a delight. She's clear and concise and knows what she wants, even down to the jacket on the book . . . She's never been influenced by anyone else and she's practised her craft . . . The people walk out of the pages at you . . . There is no one in the same league.'[26] Catherine had become much more confident as an author. She was no longer willing to take outside advice or alter her manuscripts to suit an editor's opinion. It was difficult to persuade her to make changes. When her agent John Smith tactfully suggested that there were several glaring errors in *Hamilton*, such as the heroine arriving at the wrong station in London and going off to the Bahamas without a passport, Catherine was furious, but was in the end persuaded to put them right. On another occasion, when given the printer's proofs, she was convinced that someone had altered a sentence without her permission and insisted on consulting the copy editor's proof so that she could check. The offending sentence was found to be in John Smith's handwriting. However, after a difficult conversation he was able to convince her that she had actually dictated the alteration to him over the phone after the copy editor had picked up the fact that the original didn't make sense.

By 1979, after her Mallen saga had topped the best-seller lists and been filmed for television, Catherine Cookson was a household name, but she had no intention of giving up. She often started to dictate in bed at 6.30 a.m. after Tom had got up to make her a cup of tea. He usually brought her breakfast in bed at about 8.15 and she would get up at ten. The rest of the morning would be taken up with business telephone calls and the mail. Catherine was now receiving more than three thousand letters a year from fans, who also sent her Christmas and birthday presents. Her part-time secretary would come in to type up manuscripts, but the Cooksons dealt with the letters. Each one was read by Catherine and she dictated an answer to Tom, who tapped it out on the portable typewriter. Lunch would be what Catherine called an 'American special' on the lines of Gaye-lord Hauser's healthy-eating plan: a glass of milk, some cheese, fruit and nuts. On most days Catherine would be in bed by 9.30, though not to sleep. She worked in bed, sometimes until after midnight, with the tape recorder on the bedside table and the bed strewn with pages of typescript. Tom begged her to rest, but she couldn't. 'I know that I overwork,' Catherine admitted. 'I know I exhaust myself and am sometimes flat out and speechless . . . but I ENJOY working.' Tom was awed by her creativity. 'I have to shake my head when I watch her . . . The words just come out of her mouth . . . you watch this gift materialise.'[27]

When she moved into Town Barns, Catherine had Andre van der Meersh's easel set up in the conservatory. Although she hadn't touched it for years, she was suddenly overcome by a great desire to paint again. One of the first canvases that she painted was an angry sunset over the sea, with a 'great, curling, wave'. It expressed much of her sadness about leaving the coast – it was the first time that she had lived more than a mile or so from the sea. Catherine painted almost a dozen vivid seascapes one after another. Unlike her drawings and illustrations, which reach a high professional standard, Catherine's paintings are naive and untutored, but vibrant with life and undeveloped talent. Painting, she wrote, brought colour back into her life again. She was particularly pleased with a big canvas of flamboyant red poppies, which hung above the fireplace in each of the Cooksons' subsequent houses. Painting provided a release; it was a welcome relaxation 'when my mind is going dizzy' from working on her books.[28] In April 1979 her work was exhibited as part of the Women Artists of the North East exhibition, featuring twenty-four women, including sculptors, ceramicists, photographers and painters. Several seascapes, pastels and some of Catherine's cathedral drawings were included and attracted a great deal of attention. Very few people, including close friends, had known that Catherine was an artist as well as a writer.

When the Cooksons arrived at Corbridge, they registered as private patients with Dr David Harle on the advice of a friend. He remembers his first visit – Tom opening the door and making a courteous fuss, going off to the kitchen to make coffee while David talked to Catherine in the study. It was the first and last time the relationship conformed to the usual patient–doctor pattern. Thereafter all formality was dropped and David Harle became a family friend. Consultations with Catherine were lively affairs that never went according to plan. He remembers that 'she was used to doctors doing what she wanted, and I was used to patients doing what I told them'.[29] There was a great deal of argument and Catherine usually won. David and his wife were invited to all the family parties: 'there were more doctors there than at a BMA dinner!'[30] Catherine's birthdays were a special treat, when she and Tom would do a comedy routine as the climax of the evening's entertainment. Friends observed that they had perfect timing and usually succeeded in reducing everyone in the room to tears of laughter.

About a year after their move, in 1977 and 1978, Catherine began to suffer from heart trouble and had five heart attacks; three of them were quite minor, though all required hospitalisation. David Harle told her that it was only her will to live that kept her going. She was, he told her jokingly, 'a cantankerous old woman'. This new development on top of her frequent haemorrhages meant that she had to live even more quietly than she already did. She began to spend more time working in bed. Gradually, Catherine ceased to accept invitations and became very reclusive. It was ironic that as she earned the money to live as a member of the jet set and go anywhere and do anything she wanted, she felt less and less able to do so. But the contraction of her horizon was not just caused by her declining physical health. On Catherine's income she could have rested and commandeered first-class medical attention anywhere in the world, even travelled with her own doctors. Mentally she felt less and less able to leave home, and more and more agoraphobic. When Tom gave up work, he did all the shopping. Whenever she did go out, Tom always went with her. One of Catherine's neighbours met them once in the street with a mutual friend and stopped to talk. She described how Tom 'put himself round Catherine', protecting her so effectively that it created a permanent image in her mind of Tom 'surrounding' Catherine, fencing her off as if to protect her from attack. Yet she couldn't think of anything he had actually, physically done to produce that impression. Tom's excessively protective attitude was a reaction, not only to her increasing frailty, but to the unpleasant situation that had arisen after the Cooksons moved to Town Barns.

The Cooksons' purchase of the field and their planning application for change of use in order to create a garden did not please everyone in Corbridge. In 1978 a local paper referred to 'abusive, anonymous letters' received by the Cooksons.[31] Some of the residents, however, were very supportive, preferring a garden to a housing estate, and the debate divided the town. The facts are very difficult to disentangle from gossip and media exaggeration.

The secretary of Corbridge Village Trust remembers that the Trust were in favour of Catherine's plan for a garden rather than a housing estate. But there were one or two areas of concern raised by individual members. On 11 May 1978, the chairman sent Catherine a letter asking that certain points 'following representations by members' be taken into consideration.[32] One of these was that trees should not be planted along the roadside because this would obscure the view of the river Tyne – one of the few unobstructed views in the town. Subsequently a row of Leylandii was planted, which blocked the view and annoyed the neighbours. Another point of concern was that Catherine's garden might 'spoil the natural appearance of a spot which was of historical interest', chiefly the line of the moat marking the medieval boundary of Corbridge.[33]

Catherine also had a battle with the local council, disagreeing with one councillor in particular. Sandy Mearns was a man who held strong views and he was not always an easy person to deal with – several people remembered crossing swords with him on more than one occasion. Catherine did not get on with him and there were frank exchanges of opinion that left Catherine feeling bruised. She claimed that a vendetta was subsequently mounted against her and that local people complained that she was stand-offish because she didn't show herself in the town. She told a local reporter that 'only I and my husband know the extent of the upset that followed. After the initial explosion the niggling continued daily until we were forced to move.'[34]

Most Corbridge residents today have affectionate memories of Catherine. She could occasionally be seen in the street or having coffee in a local inn, but most people accepted that she was rarely well enough to go out. A large part of the misunderstanding had to do with small-town politics and the resentment caused by what are known locally as 'off-comers' – strangers coming into the community with money and wanting to change things. For this group of people, three new houses built with local labour, bringing more residents and therefore more trade into the town, were to be preferred to Catherine's private garden. Another significant part of the controversy was rooted in Catherine's own complex personality. Although she appeared to be warm, lively and cheerful to other people, inside, 'every thought of mine has a negative side'. When Tom went out shopping and was late coming back she was afraid he had had an accident. She was terrified of being a nuisance and if she wanted to ask a favour from a friend she was sure it would be refused. Using the telephone was an ordeal: 'I immediately hear the reception as hostile, even though no-one, practically no-one is hostile to me, at least now.'[35] She was sensitive to minute nuances of conduct, invisible to everyone else. The slightest criticism or indication of disapproval was shattering to her and in her relations with the outside world she was always braced for a fight. 'No matter how I try I cannot get my innermost mind to run along positive lines where the consequences of a thought will be pleasant and without incident, without retaliation from someone, and without an obstacle of some sort about to confront me.'[36]

Things got worse in Corbridge when a women's magazine began to run Catherine Cookson-related coach tours, visiting Jarrow and some of the more picturesque locations featured in her novels. The itinerary included Corbridge, where fans wandered down the foot-path and stopped outside Catherine's gate to photograph the house. As the gate was only a few feet from the front door and the windows of the house, Catherine felt besieged. The press, both local and national, were also beginning to take an interest in her. One after-noon the Cooksons came home to find a reporter peering through the sitting-room window and on another occasion, when Catherine was undressing in the bedroom, Tom came running upstairs to tell her that there was a man with a cine camera on top of the wall. She was even more upset when she received an obscene telephone call from what she called 'one of those mad sex men'.

The final straw came when the house was burgled in January 1981. Two local schoolboys broke in and stole some of Catherine's possessions – only about £450 in value but including a pair of trea-sured brass candlesticks she had brought from the Hurst. Catherine no longer felt secure in the house and so the Cooksons reluctantly decided to sell it. John Anderson, now with his second wife, was quite keen to buy it back, particularly the field, which still had outline planning permission for houses. Catherine and Tom had spent over £20,000 turning it into a beautiful landscaped garden with trees, bulbs, rhododendrons and azaleas and they were very reluctant to see their work destroyed. Catherine offered to donate the field to the town as a park, but Corbridge Parish Council said they couldn't afford the upkeep. If they had been at all receptive, Catherine would probably have offered them some form of endowment and it would now be a tremendous tourist attraction. But Catherine was repulsed by what she felt was ungenerous negativity on their part and included the field in the sale to John Anderson. Although willing to pay the price of £50,000 for it, John told the Cooksons that he couldn't afford to pay it until the houses were built and sold. Catherine agreed to wait. She felt very bitter when, later, John Anderson went bankrupt still owing her the money.

Through all the upset and controversy, Catherine went on writing, working now on a very broad canvas. The story of *Tilly Trotter* was published between 1980 and 1982 in three thick volumes, and throughout the latter part of 1980 and most of 1981 she was working on *A Dinner of Herbs*. This is one of her longest novels, published in one volume running to more than 250,000 words, and it entailed a great deal of research. The manuscript has been lodged with Newcastle University and it is a good illustration of her working method. She began by reading a number of books on the lead-mining industry in the nineteenth century as well as local history and herbal medicine. There are scraps of paper with pencilled notes – lists of herbs, notes on the historical background, odd snatches of dialogue, the names of characters and fragments of information about their relationships, how they fit into the action, their ages and the colour of their eyes and hair. She used Heslop's *Northumberland Words* as a reference for local dialect, though some of the more outlandish expressions, such as 'Smash me Hoggers' or 'Ah'll gan ti hecklebarny' are used sparingly.[37] Then there are the piles of typescript with Catherine's written corrections and additions in pencil between the lines, on the back of the sheet, sometimes all round the edge of the page. The final, published text differs surprisingly little from the first dictated draft. Catherine's way of writing by dictation resulted in novels that were much looser and more diffuse than the earlier books. There is much more dialogue or internal monologue and less prose description. The tightly written descriptive passages that were such a feature of her earliest novels rarely appear. Her advice to young writers to cut by at least a third has long since been abandoned and the later books have the feeling of being much less worked over.

Given these reservations, *A Dinner of Herbs* is definitely one of the best novels of this middle period. Set in the countryside around Langley, only a few miles from Corbridge, among a lead-mining and farming community, it opens as a young widower returns to the community in which he was brought up, bringing his young son. He is violently murdered because he witnesses a crime and the orphaned boy is brought up by Kate Makepeace, a woman who lives alone on the moors and dispenses herbal medicines. In true Cookson style, the murder causes terrible repercussions through three generations. As one of the characters explains, 'Hate's a deadly thing isn't it? Eats its way through everything.'[38]

There is the usual mix of physical violence and blighted expectation, harsh parents and illegitimate offspring. For the young Mary Ellen, a lively child at the beginning of the novel, life turns out to be bitter, but for her forty-year-old daughter Maggie there is a glimmer of hope in the last pages:

She would have all the embraces she needed in life from now on. And when her child was born, be it male or female, she would see that it was cuddled and held as a baby, and that never in its life would it be starved for affection. So whatever it did in life, good, bad or indifferent, could not be laid at the door of a starved life. Moreover, she would teach it not to hate.[39]

18

I realised that . . . I was the North . . . Its people were
my people. I was Katie McMullen. Resolutely,
unashamedly . . . A child of the Tyne.[1]

Catherine and Tom discovered Bristol Lodge, near Langley, when
Catherine was looking at locations for *A Dinner of Herbs*, though
to some of their friends it seemed a strange choice for an elderly
couple in indifferent health, particularly as Catherine was now a
millionairess who could afford to live anywhere. Langley is a scat-
tered hamlet of farms and houses, with a medieval castle recently
restored and run as a restaurant by one of Catherine's friends. It is
a very exposed and isolated place where the weather is often unkind,
and much further from Newcastle, where Catherine had to travel
for emergency medical treatment, sometimes two or three times a
week. Whereas Corbridge is just off the main trunk road to Newcastle, Langley is reached up twisting lanes that are slow in summer
and sometimes impassable in winter. There is not even an identifiable
village, and the nearest shop is some miles away at Haydon Bridge.
But the house is certainly more secluded than Town Barns, situated
as it is on a remote back road, and visitors have to turn up another
unmarked and muddy lane before the entrance becomes visible. The
driveway is guarded by high iron gates, though round the side it is
easy to gain access through the derelict factory building next door.
Originally the property consisted of a modern bungalow and an
adjoining eighteenth-century cottage looking down towards a small
man-made lake and the moors beyond. At the bottom of the garden
there is a sparse copse of pine trees, all angled away from the prevail-
ing wind that sweeps off the Pennines.

Catherine and Tom set out to redesign the existing buildings at Bristol Lodge, a process that entailed gutting the cottage to make bigger rooms, building an upper storey on the bungalow so that Catherine could have a large study with views out over the lake, and then knocking through to the cottage on the new level. The indoor swimming pool, which Catherine could not use, was converted into a fifty-foot drawing room with a huge bedroom and *en suite* bathroom above it. The resulting sprawl of old and new buildings was unrecognisable to anyone who had seen the original.

Downstairs the two vast reception rooms provided an appropriate setting for Catherine's collection of furniture, including the dining table that had seemed too opulent for Loreto. It now had a massive glass and gold centrepiece, given to Catherine by her publishers to celebrate her twenty-seven and a half million sales in paperback. Guests commented on the profusion of colour and detail in the rooms. Everywhere there were 'rich patterned materials, flock papers and damask, flowered linen, chandeliers and ornaments, porcelain in cabinets, walls thickly hung with seascapes and sunsets'.[2] The paintings were often Catherine's own. Everything was always immaculately tidy. Catherine was a perfectionist, but in deference to Tom, she now had two part-time home helps and a gardener to do much of the work. Ronnie Dalton not only looked after the garden, it was also his job to keep the driveway clear of ice and snow in case Catherine needed medical attention, and he acted as a caretaker and handyman and gave much-needed support to Tom. Catherine was 'strict and straight' – a tough employer; 'if she wanted something done, she wanted it done yesterday'. He felt sorry for Tom: 'She always needed him for something . . . time was always scarce, poor chap. Mr Cookson loved the garden . . . and if he'd been able he would have spent a lot more time in it. But it was the same with everything. He just had to manage five minutes here or there when he wasn't needed.'[3] Tom had become interested in railway modelling and was building a layout in one of the rooms, but he was rarely able to spend much time on it.

Once inside the house, visitors taken up the wrought-iron staircase to Catherine's study found themselves in 'a bright upstairs room, uncluttered . . . with parquet flooring, a wall of bookshelves, a huge desk and views from the windows over lake and trees that would distract any but the most doggedly determined'.[4] Shortly after the Cooksons moved in, a *Times* journalist came up from London to interview Catherine for a feature article to celebrate the publication of her sixtieth novel. In a slightly gushing tone she described Tom as 'a slight, neat man in owl-like glasses' when he met her at the station in Hexham. Catherine, 'in a safe green and lamé suit', was rather more formidable, 'a little like the headmistress of a select girls' school'. She told the journalist that, despite her success, she still kept the old suede zip-up boots she had worn in Hastings to dig the garden – she had even painted a still life of them. They symbolised 'the way we've worked for things'. Catherine seemed bewildered by her increasing fame. 'A best-seller is a miracle,' she told the interviewer, 'but I'm not a miracle worker.' Both her publishers and her readers disagreed with the latter part of the statement. Catherine performed the miracle every time she dictated a new novel, and in 1982, a year after her move to Bristol Lodge, Paul Scherer from Corgi presented her with an award to mark the first million sales of *The Mallen Streak*. She was now published in twenty-three different languages.

In the same year, Catherine was awarded an honorary master's degree from Newcastle University. Catherine said that after her wedding day and being given the freedom of the borough of South Shields, the day that she was presented with her degree was the most important day of her life. Catherine's association with Newcastle University had begun shortly after her return to the north. Newcastle is a centre of medical excellence, and Catherine had been blessed – at last – with good doctors who had quickly referred her to the Royal Victoria Infirmary. There her hereditary condition attracted the attention of the Department of Medicine at Newcastle University, which has one of the leading faculties devoted to genetic research in Britain. Catherine spent so much time in the hospital recovering from episodes of haemorrhage that she used to joke that she had her own room there. Told by the medical staff when she began to bleed profusely from the stomach that she would have to travel to London for an operation, since they did not have the laser instrument necessary to treat her in Newcastle, Catherine asked how much it would cost to buy one. The hospital was astonished when a cheque, signed by Tom, arrived the following day enabling them to order the equipment. Catherine used to make wry jokes about having the fibreoptic device she had bought thrust painfully down her throat. It was the first of many endowments, often for unglamorous causes.

Embarrassed by the amount of money she was earning and unable to spend it, Catherine donated large sums to charities. Education and medical research had a high priority and soon Newcastle University was a regular recipient. Seeing an appeal in the local paper for money to buy an incubator for the premature-baby unit in Newcastle, Catherine sent a cheque to the organisers for the whole amount, thus enabling them to buy two incubators. She gave £50,000 to the Department of Dermatology for research into skin diseases such as psoriasis and eczema. Eventually she gave enough money for the university to construct an entire wing – the Catherine Cookson Building – and establish a Catherine Cookson Foundation.

The link with the university was strengthened by a friendship Catherine developed with the librarian Dr Brian Enright. For Catherine it was a great delight to be able to discuss books with such an erudite man; and Brian was charmed by her personality and had considerable admiration for her talents. It was his idea to establish a special collection of manuscripts and memorabilia in the university library. Unfortunately, many of Catherine's manuscripts had already gone to the University of Boston in the USA. The Americans were much quicker than the British to realise Catherine's importance in twentieth-century literary history. As early as 1970, the librarian from Boston had come to Hastings and taken away every available manuscript – a massive amount of material which included the eight drafts of *Our Kate*. However, Brian Enright was able to acquire several of Catherine's later works, including *A Dinner of Herbs* and a novel called *The Runner* which was eventually published as *The Harrogate Secret*.

Catherine's friendship with Brian led to an invitation to visit the English literature department, where Professor Ernst Honigmann asked her if she would give a talk on autobiography to his students. Catherine was delighted to accept and for those who were present it was a fascinating occasion. As Catherine talked and began to relax, she dropped her façade and became more and more Katie McMullen from Jarrow, the accent more pronounced, the language more colloquial. At one point, when talking about the other children in the street, her face flamed with suppressed anger and students in the seminar noticed that she had subconsciously clenched her fists as though ready to hit out at someone.

Catherine asked Professor Honigmann and his wife to dinner at Bristol Lodge, where they were welcomed very warmly. Ernst Honigmann felt that they were being invited to become friends, but, being a very shy man, he was afraid that their situations were too unequal to make friendship possible. They did, however, keep in touch, though he regrets now that the offer of a closer relationship was not taken up.

Catherine was at first afraid that the honorary degree was being given to her only because she had donated so much money to the university. But she was assured that this was not the case. It was a recognition of her achievements in the field of literature. Ironically the MA was presented to her by the Duke of Northumberland, Chancellor of the University – not the duke she believed had been so rude, but his son – at Convocation. Her citation, read by the public orator, included a recital of her childhood circumstances and described her as the 'most popular European novelist of her day'. She was the only woman among a plethora of formidable men (most of whom got doctorates), which included Quentin Bell, a professor of physics at Texas University, two international businessmen and an official of the National Union of Mineworkers. For Catherine it was a momentous occasion. Her lack of formal education had always bothered her. 'I had a chip on my shoulder that over the years became a plank.' The plank fell off the day Catherine received her scroll from the Chancellor. But, after the euphoria had worn off, she had a secret reservation that she confessed to friends. Why hadn't she been given a doctorate, like other writers; why was it only an MA? Was this because she hadn't been deemed good enough?

The answer was that the university's policy when awarding honorary degrees was to give doctorates to those who already had a first degree and MAs to those who had not. Under those rules Catherine was only entitled to an MA, and the university authorities had been far from unanimous in agreeing even that. Some thought that it was inappropriate to award a degree to a writer of popular mass-market fiction.

Catherine had no time for this type of literary prejudice. By the middle of the eighties her books consistently topped the best-seller lists, and thirty-five of the top hundred books borrowed from public libraries were hers. Other popular writers, such as Dick Francis (next on the list) and Jeffrey Archer, weren't even close. Catherine always donated the money she received under the public lending right to the Royal Literary Fund to help struggling writers and she always received the maximum allowable amount. She was scathing about literary snobbery: 'These highbrow literary people who look down their noses at me – their work doesn't sell, does it?' At the same time, she had no illusions about her own work: 'I don't class myself as a great author, but I am a good story-teller.' The *Sunday Times* referred to her as 'the greatest historical novelist of all time'.

The year 1982 brought other honours. She was one of *Woman's Own*'s fifty Women of Achievement, alongside Margaret Thatcher, Jacqueline du Pré and Sue Ryder. She was also voted Woman of the Year by the Variety Club of Great Britain, but couldn't go to the ceremony because she was too ill to travel to London. Instead they came to her and at Bristol Lodge she was presented with a velvet jewellery case with her name inscribed in a gold heart on the lid.

One of the honours that Catherine most valued came at the end of December, when she was the chosen subject of the TV programme *This Is Your Life*.[5] Apart from worrying about whether she would be well enough on the day, Tom also wondered how he was going to keep the secret from her. However, when Catherine sprained her ankle a couple of weeks before the programme, Tom was able to keep her upstairs and out of the way of the preparations. He had fretted for weeks over how he was going to prepare the guest bedrooms and buy in the extra food that would be needed without Catherine guessing that something was happening. But when the day came she was driven into Newcastle by Tom thinking that she was going to be interviewed by a local television journalist for a programme called *Northern Life*. When Eamonn Andrews appeared with the famous Red Book, Catherine was completely surprised and very moved that anyone had thought her important enough to feature in the series. It was a very emotional evening as relatives and new friends, such as her favourite television personality Russell Harty, were ushered on stage alongside old friends such as Annie Robson.

A year later, Melvyn Bragg elected to devote a *South Bank Show* programme to Catherine.[6] This was quite an accolade, since it seemed to Catherine to indicate that she was at last being taken seriously as a writer. But afterwards she felt that the programme never actually addressed her work at all, merely its autobiographical source. In the introduction Melvyn described her work as coming to the page 'hot from her own life, in a release of energy which is also perhaps a relief from pain ... a way out, imaginatively and psychologically'. In a voiceover Catherine dedicates the film to 'all bairns who own no name'. A young girl from Newcastle was chosen to play Catherine for the flashbacks in the film and many of the scenes were shot at Beamish Museum – one of the few places that could still provide an authentic period background. The kitchen of William Black Street was reconstructed for a short interview between Melvyn and Catherine – much of which is word-for-word recitation of episodes described in *Our Kate*, or reflections Catherine had put down in her journal. For the second part of the programme, Melvyn interviewed Catherine in the comfort of her own home and she talked, movingly, about her breakdown, her illegitimacy and the writing of *Our Kate*. The *South Bank Show* was watched by many people who had never read her novels but who were fascinated by the details of her extraordinary life, and it purported to reveal the inspirational and, it hints, therapeutic 'source of her energy and anguish'.

Like many people who are the subject of biopics, Catherine didn't like the finished programme or the picture of herself that it reflected. She thought that Melvyn Bragg had implied that her family's housing had been 'slummy', though on screen it was Catherine herself who used the word. She also felt uncomfortable with the selected fifteen minutes edited from nearly two hours of 'very tiring conversation' with Melvyn. She thought that the way in which the programme had been edited put the wrong slant on things. In the end it was a different programme from the one that she had expected. It had not given greater literary credibility to her novels – which were scarcely mentioned – and had concentrated instead on the more sensational aspects of her childhood. Privately Catherine told her friends that she felt patronised by what she regarded as the literary establishment. It was a club she badly wanted to join, but she was still one of those whose 'names are never mentioned in the literary lounge; they are not even skimmed over, for their writings tilt the noses of the clique ... Why? Oh, whisper it softly, shamefully; they are best-sellers, each and every one.'[7]

The following year Catherine almost gave up writing owing to ill health. Her eyesight had been growing steadily weaker as she grew older, requiring stronger and stronger glasses, but one day in 1985 as she checked a typescript she found that the print was more difficult to see than usual. Catherine put her hand over her right eye and discovered that she no longer had any sight in the left. Tom took her straight to the hospital in Newcastle, where the ophthalmologist told her that a blood vessel had burst at the back of her eye and there was nothing that could be done. Now with only one good eye, Catherine became very depressed. In March she had a bad attack of laryngitis, followed by bronchitis, which pulled her even further down. She was afraid that it would turn into pneumonia and put her back in hospital again. She had also been bleeding a great deal and was totally exhausted. 'I made the decision to give up writing altogether. Believe me I have to be bad to do that. I was in a desperate state . . . and just wanted to give up and let go.' But, as at other crucial points in her life, in some remote part of her consciousness she heard a voice telling her that she must go on. Tomorrow morning, it told her, she must get out of bed, however ill she felt, she must get out of bed 'and DO something. Start checking what you have written. Get onto the tape.'[8] Catherine argued with the inner voice for about an hour before she fell asleep, but in the morning she managed to pull herself out of bed and into the study to start a new chapter. It was only this combative spirit, this implacable will, that was keeping her alive.

Another goal for Catherine to aim for was her eightieth birthday in June 1986. Heinemann were putting together a 'pictorial memoir' of her life which they planned to publish on her birthday. A young editor, Piers Dudgeon, travelled north to work on it with her. Catherine took to him straight away. She liked his respect for her work. Unlike many others who came to interview her, he had actually read some of her books. Piers found Catherine attractive and transparently honest. Like most of those who met her, he was captivated by the combination of toughness and fragility. The book was to be a collection of old photographs of Jarrow, South Shields and Northumberland at the beginning of the century, with relevant extracts from Catherine's novels and short autobiographical fragments. It was part of a series that had included *Hardy's Wessex* and *Dickens' London* and would be marketed as *Catherine Cookson Country*, anchoring her work firmly in the northeastern landscape, the 'background that had forged her and fostered her talents'. Catherine confessed in her introduction that she wished now that she had published her books under the name Katie McMullen. 'Although that wasn't my name . . . nevertheless, it is the name that holds for me all my early years.' The admission was a big step forward for Catherine.

Her publishers and her agent Anthony Sheil were also planning a big celebration for her birthday. And South Shields Town Council were about to launch a new tourist venture also appropriately called Catherine Cookson Country, the focal point being a recreation of William Black Street in the Shields Museum and Art Gallery, with a Cookson Trail round all the local landmarks that had associations either with Catherine or the characters in her novels. Catherine was, for once, well enough to attend the opening of the exhibition, though she was rather ambivalent about the creation and marketing of Catherine Cookson Country. In the speech she gave, she seemed almost overwhelmed by the fact that the town she had once wanted to get away from for ever should actually want to adopt her name. It was 'embarrassing' but on the other hand it was a very great honour. 'Never did I imagine, when I was leaving the north when I was twenty two that I would become a name applied to this particular part of the North-east – remembering that I hadn't a name of my own.'[9] She told assembled dignitaries and journalists that she wanted to get rid of the Andy Capp cartoon image of the north. 'We have been sold in the wrong wrapping long enough.' She was delighted that her books had brought employment back to the town. Television adaptations of her novels had already created a hundred new jobs, and the council had begun to promote the region in America as a tourist destination. They even took a stand at the Travel Fair in Olympia, among the big tour operators, to promote Catherine Cookson Country as a major tourist attraction. Catherine Cookson was now the area's most flourishing industry and was described satirically in *Private Eye* as 'the last remnant of working heavy industrial plant in the North-east'.[10]

To mark her birthday, Catherine donated another £160,000 to Newcastle University, bringing the Cookson Foundation there up to more than a million pounds, and the university announced that they were to set up a Catherine Cookson lectureship in molecular haematology. Catherine also agreed to give an interview to Professor Honigmann to add to the Newcastle University archive. The taped section of the interview is only part of a much longer talk and listening to it is rather like coming into the room in the middle of a conversation and having to leave before the end. Catherine spoke at length about *Our Kate*. Pressed by Ernst Honigmann, she admitted that she had used her novelist's art to tell a story, rather than simply record the truth, and she revealed that she was now trying to write 'the real facts, not that *Our Kate* wasn't the real facts, but there were one thousand and one things that happened to me' which hadn't been written. She had cut a great deal in order to trim the book 'into readable prose . . . if I had portrayed Kate as she was at times, when in drink, she wouldn't have appeared as good . . . in those times she wasn't the real woman, she was influenced by drink . . . that was the part that caused me suffering and I don't explain that fully in *Our Kate*.' Now she was trying to write it down 'warts and all' with the knowledge that it wouldn't come out until she was dead, 'putting things down as I know they happened – in the raw'.

She told Professor Honigmann that there were ten unpublished novels. This was borne out on another occasion when she indicated a stack of brown parcels on the shelf and told a visiting journalist, 'They didn't pass Tom's eye.' It was her own critical judgement that had withheld them, she told Professor Honigmann. 'I am my own critic and if I think this isn't right it doesn't go.' But she added, 'The publishers will rake them out when I'm gone . . . not perhaps, definitely, they will.' It didn't seem to bother her that what she regarded as substandard work would be published after she was dead.

Catherine was quite pleased with the interview and when Professor Honigmann asked for permission to use the content as part of a paper he wanted to publish on autobiography, she seemed quite happy to allow him to do so. But when he sent her a transcript of it later, she wrote back withdrawing her consent, telling him that he couldn't use it until after her death. Professor Honigmann was disappointed and didn't really know why she had changed her mind. He could only conjecture that perhaps, because she was so relaxed, she had talked more freely than she intended and regretted it when she saw the transcript.

Five days after her birthday Catherine was informed that the Queen had awarded her the Order of the British Empire and she was overwhelmed. Her desk was piled high with cards and presents from friends and well-wishers. Dr Brian Enright gave her a book which had been printed in 1850, containing poetry and coloured plates of flowers and fruit, which Catherine afterwards, despite her failing eyesight, set out to copy. It was very delicate work with a tiny camel-hair brush, but the results show that Catherine had lost none of her skill as an illustrator.

Happiness always had a very positive effect on Catherine's health and when the day of the big celebration arrived she was her usual vivacious self. The publishers had organised a huge party in Corbridge to be held in a peach and white marquee erected on the lawns of the Ramblers Restaurant and festooned with flowers. Catherine was elegantly dressed in a cream dress, buttoned up to the neck, with a matching bow in her hair. Music was provided by an octet from the Northern Sinfonia orchestra which Catherine had recently agreed to sponsor.

In sending out the invitations, almost everyone had been remembered. Dr and Mrs Anderson were there, Professor Honigmann, her medical practitioners, her optician Ian Graves, alongside television personalities such as Bob Langley and Russell Harty and the footballer Laurie McMenemy. Every guest found a copy of *Catherine Cookson Country* beside their plate as a gift from Catherine. There were many speeches and tributes. Heinemann's Paul Scherer said that he didn't 'know anyone who is so positive about life, so direct, so unpompous, so generous and caring'. Catherine herself talked for twenty minutes, at her eloquent best, reducing everyone to tears of laughter. She gave a moving tribute to Tom and thanked him publicly, because 'he has given me his life in order that I have the time to write'.[11]

Shortly afterwards, Anthony Sheil negotiated a £4 million, ten-book transfer deal to Transworld Publishers.[12] Catherine thought it was an obscene amount of money and told a local paper, 'I don't think anyone is worth that sort of money. I'd write if I wasn't paid a penny.' Transworld, through their ownership of Corgi, had been publishing Catherine in paperback for some time. Now they were to publish her novels in hardback under the Bantam imprint. To some people it might have seemed risky to pay £4 million to an eighty-year-old in very fragile health for ten novels that might never materialise, but not only did Catherine have ten unpublished novels already languishing on the shelves of her study, there were other books in the pipeline, held back because Heinemann couldn't cope with her prodigious output. They simply weren't big enough. Two novels a year were their limit and Catherine was sometimes producing three or four. Transworld were happy to stockpile the surplus. In fact, they were to publish another twenty-seven of Catherine's books before she died and still have several more to bring out posthumously to feed the insatiable demand of her fans.

Catherine was getting frailer and having problems with her eyesight. But her spirit was still young. She boasted that although she was over eighty the grey matter above her eyebrows was still only thirty-five or forty. Tom continued to look after her – putting the stamps on the letters, making coffee, looking after visitors, preparing lunch. Photographs taken at this time show him looking strained and anxious. He was very tired. Catherine worked seven days a week and rarely took a holiday. She had begun another book as soon as the birthday celebrations were over, although *Bill Bailey* and *The Parson's Daughter* were about to come out and Transworld had another eight novels waiting to be issued. 'I wasn't working. It was working on me,' she explained. 'I felt, "Don't start another one", and yet I felt if I didn't, I would lose a good story that has been niggling at me.' She told journalists that she had thought of retiring 'but there is something up here that won't let me'.[13] Writing for her was a compulsion and she couldn't give up. If she stopped writing she would stop living. The drive that had kept her going, that had got her to where she was, wouldn't let her stop. She was a workaholic and it was a form of illness. Catherine confided to a close friend that she couldn't stop writing, because if she did she was afraid that all her fears and phobias would fill her head and overwhelm her. She wrote to keep them out.

Shortly after Catherine moved to Bristol Lodge, when she had been interviewed by two young researchers from Tyne Tees Television, she had happened to mention that she occasionally wrote poetry. They had begged her to read some of it and were so impressed by what they heard that they contacted Maxwell Deas, the head of religious broadcasting. He suggested that Catherine put together a series of reflections, including some of her 'prose on short lines', to be broadcast as epilogues later on Saturday evenings. These extracts from Catherine's journals and the fragments of autobiographical insight were very well received and afterwards she was inundated with requests for copies. Catherine's willingness to reveal her vulnerability to millions with such candour touched most people who heard her. In 1987 her publishers suggested expanding these essays to fill a new volume of autobiography and poetry, interleaved with illustrations taken from her collection of paintings and drawings. Putting it together caused Catherine more anguish than any of her novels. It took her six months, and there were several occasions when she almost threw the manuscript on the fire and gave up in disgust.

Just when she thought she had the pieces numbered in the right order, she would give the book to Tom for his comments and he would suggest that she move a poem into another section, or include a piece she had already discarded. There were some lively battles. The climax came 'when, after weeks and weeks of sorting and re-sorting and rewriting ... the schoolmaster husband who had been reading through them once again said, "I really do think that you should alter that line in such and such a poem, it just doesn't scan,"' and Catherine lost her temper and threatened to tear it all up.[14] The following week Paul Scherer and Mark Barty-King of Transworld travelled up from London to look at the results of Catherine's struggle. They found her in such a state of self-doubt, having lost confidence in the book altogether, that they deemed it best to take the existing manuscript away with them as it was. The title was to be *Let Me Make Myself Plain*, and it was published towards the end of 1988. As usual Catherine sent signed copies as presents to all her friends and braced herself for their criticism. The feedback that she got was all positive but, although they would never have dreamed of telling her, knowing how painful it would have been, many of Catherine's friends had reservations about the inclusion of her 'prose on short lines'. They felt that it injured her reputation as a writer and that her poetry should have remained a private emotional safety valve. However, the book pleased Catherine's fans and she received letters 'so touching that they brought tears to my eyes'. Tom actually broke down reading one of them out to her.

By 1988 she was so famous that letters addressed to Mrs Catherine Cookson, Tyne Dock, Hastings, Sussex, North England, still managed to reach her. She was included for the first time in a list of Britain's wealthiest 200 people, entering the list at 187, with earnings of £10 million worldwide. Eventually she worked her way up the list to be among Britain's top twenty richest women. She continued to give most of it away. St Hilda's College, Oxford, received £100,000 to support science studies for women, because, Catherine wrote in her letter, 'I understand how hard women have had to strive for the right to be educated and how much it takes to achieve, even nowadays, particularly when one comes from a disadvantaged background.' She gave £50,000 to Girton College, Cambridge, to fund an archive on women's studies, despite the fact that she was far from a supporter of feminism. Like many self-made women, she was ambivalent about it and suspicious of any kind of feminism that was about 'women wanting to be more like men'. Her years in managerial positions at the workhouses in Tendring and Hastings had given her a great deal of experience of working with members of both sexes, and she could never tolerate having a man as a boss, she said. As she has the heroine remark in *Justice is a Woman*, 'Your dominant male doesn't carry any water with me. Most women could buy a man at one end of the street and sell him at the other.' She hated being patronised by men. 'You go to some committee meeting and there are a lot of men there, all talking across each other to no purpose. Then a woman will put the whole issue concisely and calmly.' Men, she said, were afraid of their own feelings, seeing them as 'unmanly'. 'There's really the thinnest thread of difference between men and women; women aren't afraid to show their determination and strength. Why should men be afraid to show their tenderness?' Her heroes are often 'new men' and their characters owe a lot to Tom, who had always been prepared to put his ego to one side for Catherine because he saw what she was doing as more important. Tom actually said in an interview that if more husbands were prepared to do this for their wives, the world would be a better place.

In 1988 Catherine was voted Best Writer at the annual Women of Achievement awards and interviewed on *Woman's Hour*. But despite her determination and willpower, her health was once again slipping downhill. She developed allergies to chicken, eggs and fish. She couldn't eat sweet things and meat made her nauseous. Her novel *The Fifteen Streets* had been turned into a stage play, but she was in bed suffering from internal bleeding and unable to see the premiere in Newcastle. Locally it was a sell-out and received a rapturous reception. But nationally the play had a rougher ride. The producers were trying to transfer *The Fifteen Streets* to the West End at about the same time as Jeffrey Archer's *Beyond a Reasonable Doubt* was having a successful run and, despite Catherine's name and reputation, they had difficulty in finding backers. An advert appeared in the papers: 'Angels wanted for major west end play by Britain's biggest-selling author. High risk – but high returns possible.' Gritty northern realism was out of fashion among London's smart theatre-goers. The eighties favoured glitzy escapism and jet-set fantasy. When *The Fifteen Streets* finally opened at the Play House Theatre, reviewers remarked sarcastically that it threw in 'not merely the kitchen sink but the grey scum lipping the wash house boiler'.[15] Catherine had always dreamed of having a play put on in the West End, and she was very disappointed when it was taken off after a few months.

However, the play had been noticed by a television producer, Ray Marshall, who saw the possibilities of adaptation. The script consultant was Rosemary Anne Sisson, who had previously had successes with other period dramas such as *Upstairs, Downstairs* and *The Duchess of Duke Street*, and Sean Bean was chosen to play the antihero Dominic. The resulting television film was one of three finalists for an Emmy, and its success led Ray Marshall to adapt another ten of Catherine's novels for the small screen. Catherine was never altogether happy about these adaptations and was critical of the 'bad language' added to the script. In her day, people wouldn't have used these words. She was also unhappy about the explicit sexual content. She failed to understand the sleight of hand necessary to convey the past realistically to a contemporary audience.

In the second half of 1988 Catherine enjoyed just over five months of reasonable health free from allergies and major episodes of bleeding. She was in good spirits and beginning to hope that she was at last being given a reprieve. But as she sat at her desk in her dressing gown early one morning her 'nose exploded in a gush' and Tom had to get her quickly into the car and make the familiar dash to Newcastle to have the bleeding arrested. Catherine hated the process of packing her nostrils with gauze. Anyone who has had a sinus operation will sympathise. It is extremely uncomfortable, and for the two days that the packing was in place Catherine couldn't eat or breathe properly and would become increasingly edgy in anticipation of the painful process of removal. By the eighties she had come to dread it more than anything. Tom told a friend that she sometimes wished she would die rather than have to go through it again. Why me? Catherine asked repeatedly. Why, at eighty-two, couldn't she have some rest? In her journal she was scathing about those who told her that her constant ill health had given her a valuable insight which enabled her to write so well about the human condition.

> Don't say
> It's because it gives me the material to write,
> And the insight into pain;
> And, moreover, look what it's brought me;
> Position, wealth,
> Well, let me tell you; anyone may have it all
> In exchange for one year of health.[16]

Despite her own discomforts, Catherine still had time for other people. Beryl Cotterell, the wife of a close friend, was slowly dying of cancer in 1988, though at first she didn't tell Catherine. 'Her cheerfulness and thoughtfulness put me to shame.'[17] Catherine still didn't know it when she sent Beryl a copy of *Let Me Make Myself Plain* and was worried afterwards that some of the discussion of death in it might have upset her. But Beryl was glad to have someone she could talk to frankly on the subject of 'our earthly demise and future'. They rang each other every day to exchange notes on bodily discomfort and laugh about it. Catherine wrote to Harry Edwards's Healing Sanctuary asking that Beryl should be prayed for, and sent presents to make her last days more comfortable, flowers and fruit and a wool and cashmere shawl to put around her shoulders as she lay in bed. Beryl died on Christmas Eve and one of her last acts was to send Catherine – 'In Memoriam' – a copy of *The Prophet* by Kahlil Gibran, which Beryl said had helped her to come to terms with death.

In 1988 Tom, Catherine's mainstay, suffered a breakdown from the pressure of work. Catherine had always refused to send out standard form letters to the thousands of people who wrote to her about her books or asking for money. She insisted that all letters were answered personally. As her own eyesight and general health declined, this meant that Tom had to do it for her. He was now seventy-six and very tired. He was admitted to hospital suffering from 'exhaustion' in September 1988. Friends begged Catherine to retire, but she went doggedly on. She told reporters that she had more stories in her head than she had years left to live. And the more she wrote, the more deadlines there were to meet. She had become an industry that supported a vast empire, with hundreds of people dependent on her for their livelihood. 'This is a treadmill we are on and you cannot rest.' Catherine would not allow either herself or her husband to stop, but she did agree that Tom should have some help to deal with the letters.

Throughout the eighties, Catherine was very conscious of her own mortality and it made her inward-looking and reflective. Winter, in particular, often brought on the premonition of impending death and the winter of 1988, which was quite severe, saw some poignant entries in her journal. Waking early one morning and pressing her nose to the ice-patterned window to glimpse the sun illuminating the white, frozen garden, she wondered how many more times this would be granted to her.

Shall I remember the glory of it?
This I cannot tell, but vow,
If one wish were mine
Granted when I pass,
There will go with me
A morning as now,
Frost glinting on glass,
Trees silent of rustle,
And stiff the grass.

The knowledge that she had no children to carry on her genes increased her sorrow. She hated the thought that when she died her mind would die with her and that one day even her books would be forgotten. But her greatest fear was that Tom would die before her. Tom was equally afraid that Catherine would die first – after all, he was six years younger and in better health. She tried to joke him out of it with quips such as 'When I die, take all the money and buy yourself a yacht.'[18] They were, by now, so deeply dependent on each other that neither could face the thought of being left alone.

During the winter of 1989 Catherine was extremely ill with flu and began spending all her time in bed. Tom wondered whether she would ever be able to get up again. But even when she was in this depleted state, the tape recorder was beside her bed ready for her to dictate. Occasionally she would pick it up and talk. What she was really suffering from, she recorded, was a renewal of depression, a complaint 'in which the past is a mountain weighing us down'. She was almost ready to give up the struggle and Tom was the last rung of the ladder to which she clung. Both body and mind were so exhausted that she had no desire to write. She felt totally drained, even of the will to live. Only the raw violence of the weather beyond the window had any kind of reality.

The light filters through the trees from the far hill. I lie watching it, my body inert, still . . . How long have I lain here in this state that is like the awaiting of death? Going down: all emotions gone; no looking back in bitterness; no hate, not even love . . . The scene is suddenly wild, the snow, wind-driven has covered the pane. No longer does the light come through the trees, the hill is gone, the room is encased as if in a feathered tick in which I lie, still inert.

Would that storm would rage within my mind and blow away this overpowering lassitude that lies upon me.[19]

While she lay in this condition, she found it deeply galling to read a report in the *Sunday Sun* that she had stopped her chauffeur-driven car to intervene in a brawl outside Macey's Bar in Newcastle. Not only did she not have a chauffeur, it was completely untrue and Catherine could never decide whether the account was fictional or a case of mistaken identity. This kind of misreporting worried Catherine, who was anxious that people whose requests she'd turned down for reasons of ill health might see the news item and think she was prevaricating. 'Here I am supposed to be having a nightlife and it makes me out to be a liar.'[20]

Lying in bed thinking about death and the afterlife renewed many of her old religious fears. Although Catherine had 'told God where to go' years before in Hastings, she was now beginning to doubt the wisdom of what she had done. She felt that she was being punished for it. 'I know now . . . that He has purposely kept me alive and given me a number of complaints by way of expiation for my blasphemy.'[21] Catherine was often visited by Father Thomas Power, priest of St John of Beverley in nearby Haydon Bridge, who made determined efforts to bring Catherine back to the Catholic church. He had even sent to Rome for plaques signed by the Pope to give to Catherine. It was Father Power who told her that the strange perfume which occasionally surrounded her was a spiritual manifestation. Catherine was convinced that this undefinable fragrance was not just hallucination. It had also been detected on one occasion by Tom and on at least one other by the nurses who attended her in hospital. Catherine found it inexplicable. 'Read the life of Saint Thérèse of Lisieux,' Father Power told her. 'The very same thing happened to her.' Catherine's publisher Paul Scherer, now with Transworld, was also a Catholic, and Catherine often joked when he visited her that he and Father Power were part of a conspiracy to get her back into the church.

Confined to bed in the aftermath of flu, debilitated and unable to write, Catherine soon found herself in the grip of a depression she hadn't experienced since her breakdown forty-five years earlier. She became completely withdrawn, lost the use of her legs and her mind was periodically invaded by obscene images and sounds that couldn't be blocked out by the creation of characters or stories. Her imaginative faculties had been totally subverted. The mental torment was so severe that Catherine made up her mind to ask Dr David Harle to admit her to a psychiatric hospital for treatment when he came the following morning. 'I knew . . . I could not fight this alone now, as I had done before, I would have to have help.'[22]

This was a Sunday afternoon – always the worst day of the week for Catherine. But as she lay in bed wondering how she was going to bear the inevitable separation from Tom, she heard a voice in her head ordering her to get out of bed, go into the next room and switch on the television. She knew that, however weak she was, she had to obey. Tom, hearing her stumbling about, came running upstairs fearing the worst. Considerably upset, he led Catherine to a chair close to the television and crouched on the floor beside her, holding her hand. Mesmerised, Catherine kept her eyes on the screen, watching *The Railway Children* and then the beginning of *Songs of Praise*, which was being broadcast that evening from Buckfast Abbey. As Tom went out of the room to make Catherine a cup of coffee, the cameras focused on a stained-glass window depicting the face of Christ. 'The eyes looked into mine [and] I suddenly thrust out an arm and placed my hand flat on his face . . . while I cried from the depth of my tortured being, "HELP ME! PLEASE HELP ME!"'

What happened next Catherine could only describe as a miracle. It was what she had longed for and prayed for all her life. She was suddenly free from fear and filled with an exquisite feeling of absolute peace. The intensity of her experience transmitted itself to Tom who was downstairs in the kitchen. When he came upstairs, Catherine told him that she now believed in God and would never question him again. 'I am afraid of Him no longer . . . I can see Him taking the hand of a much bewildered and hurt little child, once known under the name of Katie McMullen and who still exists just beneath the skin of Catherine Cookson.' In her journal she wrote, 'I was uplifted, freed from all torment; I was, in a way, made whole.'[23]

19

I find that time is galloping away now; it isn't dawn
before it's dusk. The hours leap into days and the
days disappear into weeks . . . When the race is
almost run and the two ends of the circle are
meeting, you see the child coming towards you . . .
The knowledge of [her] magic is fresh before your
eyes . . .[1]

Catherine's newly found peace of mind was short-lived. During 1990
she became increasingly worried about the failing sight in her one
remaining eye. She had four pairs of glasses in quick succession, each
stronger than the last. Soon she could see to read only through a
thick fog and more distant images contained black holes. Catherine's
optometrist Ian Graves once more referred her to a consultant, who
told her bluntly that she was going blind. Catherine had 'macular
degeneration', a condition linked to ageing, which leaves only periph-
eral vision. It was little consolation to be told that she would still
be able to distinguish shapes and light from dark. In the short term
she would be able to read with the aid of a large magnifying glass,
but she would have to face the fact that one day quite soon she would
be unable to read at all. Other drawbacks soon became apparent.
Catherine could not see her plate clearly at mealtimes and became
distressed at not being able to eat fastidiously. The feel of a messy
napkin or damp spots on her clothes would reduce her to tears.
Her sight often played tricks with her – she kept trying to pick up
nonexistent black objects from the bedclothes, only to discover that
they were simply spots in her vision.

At first Catherine felt very bitter and once again blamed God.
'What had God done for me? Hard work and grind all my life,

coupled with most of the illnesses my body could take and the mental torments of shame and rejection!'[2] But it wasn't long before her combative instincts took control. When she listened to a Radio Four programme on blindness – one of the *In Touch* series – it occurred to her that she might be able to use her experience to help others afflicted with the same complaint. She wrote a booklet called 'Coping Again' for the local *Shields Gazette* about dealing with blindness and contributed a humorous piece to *In Touch* about the group of blind men she had nursed at the Hurst during the war.

Catherine now had to devise yet another new way of continuing to write. She could still dictate her novels on tape, but Tom or her secretary had to read them to her for oral correction. Although this process worked well for Catherine, it led to a noticeable decline in the quality of her books. After *The Black Candle* in 1989, her novels are substantially below the standard of her best books. They are still good stories, but none approaches the quality of *The Black Velvet Gown*, the Mallen novels or *The Round Tower*. They gradually become weaker and more formulaic, with repetitions of plot, incident and character.

It was hardly surprising that there was some diminution of her powers. Apart from her failing eyesight, her heart was also struggling to cope. In August 1990, now eighty-four, she was described as 'very poorly' in hospital after a heart attack. But as her health declined, her reputation continued to grow, as did her fortune, estimated at £14 million. Shortly afterwards, as she recuperated at Bristol Lodge, she learned that she had at last been awarded an honorary doctorate of literature, not by Newcastle but from the newly created University of Sunderland. As Catherine was not well enough to go to a public ceremony, the degree was presented to her at Bristol Lodge and there was a party for her closest friends.

During the winter of 1990 there were a number of frightening episodes of bleeding, when Tom had to bundle Catherine up into her old black coat, wrap her in woollen blankets and drive the thirty-odd miles into Newcastle for laser treatment. In one bad week he had to make the journey four times. One night the hill fog was so thick that he could hardly see the verges of the road and the journey took hours. He was afraid that Catherine would bleed to death before they got there. At seventy-eight, Tom was beginning to wonder how long he would be able to carry on driving.

The following year Catherine's heart was in such a critical condition and she was bleeding so profusely from her stomach that the Cooksons were told she might only have weeks to live. She could die at any time. Catherine immediately asked Tom to burn all her diaries, journals, letters and much other personal material, including fragments of the new autobiography she had been intermittently writing. There were other urgent changes to be made. Catherine's doctors advised her to move into Newcastle closer to the hospital, because the thirty-mile trip from Langley could mean the difference between life and death. Ann Marshall, wife of Catherine's consultant Hugo Marshall, quickly found a suitable property close to both their own home and the Freeman Hospital. The bungalow at 23 Glastonbury Grove in Jesmond Dene was in a secluded position, large enough to be comfortable and much easier to manage than the multilevel sprawl of Bristol Lodge. Catherine had to be carried from the hospital to view the property and, while she was there, had to ask for a bowl three times in order to vomit blood. It was painfully embarrassing for someone as fastidious as Catherine. She was afraid she would stain the carpet.

The house in Langley was put on the market for £450,000. Although the new bungalow was spacious, especially after Catherine had an extension built to create an extra bedroom with *en suite* bathroom, there were only eight rooms of average size. Catherine was saddened to realise that she would have to part with many of her treasured possessions. Many of the bigger pieces of furniture and large quantities of bric-a-brac were auctioned in Newcastle. There there many bargains to be had. Bristol Lodge had contained five three-piece suites; four of these were sold off and they had hardly been used. There was also the white gilded kidney-shaped dressing table from her bedroom and the petit point chairs that had sat on either side of the bed. Although her early books had been written on the kitchen table, she later used a small antique lady's desk she had bought at auction with some of her first royalties. It was bought by a fan for £1,300. Later still she had used a massive, more practical, modern desk, which was bought by the Catherine Cookson Museum. The auction realised a total of £42,000. Fans seeking memorabilia were buying small items at silly prices believing that they had belonged to Catherine. The auctioneers were criticised for not making it plain that some of the furniture being sold had come from other sources. One woman paid a fortune for a broken mirror believing it to be Catherine's. Some of the more valuable pieces, beyond the pocket of Cookson fans, didn't fetch as much as expected. The mahogany breakfront bookcase went for about £2,000 less than its valuation.

Once settled at Glastonbury Grove, Catherine left the house on only about three subsequent occasions, except for her visits to the hospital. When well enough, she would receive visitors and journalists in her bedroom, closely guarded by Tom and Ann Marshall, who now acted as Catherine's secretary. She and Hugo looked after both the Cooksons with great devotion for the next seven years.

Catherine continued to give away most of her earnings to charity. She was inundated with letters from people asking for help – not all of them genuine. Often she gave spontaneously to someone whose plight had been mentioned in the local press. One of these was a talented young tenor from Newcastle, whose fees at the Guildhall school of music in London were paid by Catherine. Another was a local teenager who was given money to join Operation Raleigh on a three-month expedition to Japan. An article in the *Newcastle Journal* mentioned that he had found it very difficult to raise the £2,750 sponsorship and might have to relinquish his place. Catherine made up the shortfall. She also donated money so that a little boy with chronic liver problems could go to America for a transplant, and in 1992 gave £118,000 to Operation Lifeforce towards the building of a liver-transplant unit in Newcastle. Catherine was equally generous to friends, employees and associates. Every Christmas Catherine telephoned the Sheil Land agency to ask for a list of people working there, and each one received an envelope containing a number of fifty-pound notes.

On her return to Newcastle, Catherine had been contacted by Father Ken Thorns of St Peter and Paul's in Jarrow and welcomed the re-establishment of a link with her old church. She donated a cheque to the school for computer equipment and gave £6,000 for some much-needed renovation work to the outside of the church. From that time on, Father Thorns and, after his retirement, Father Ian Jackson sent her cards and flowers on her birthday and said Masses for her Intentions. Catherine was very moved by this. When she heard that the church needed a new heating system, she sent a cheque for the whole cost of £26,000. Annie Robson was one of those who came to thank her and was shocked to see how frail Catherine had become. Although she made an effort to talk to the priest and the other two church representatives, Catherine quickly became exhausted and Tom signalled that it was time to leave. Annie was the last to leave the room and had an emotional exchange with Catherine. They were both old women now and realised that this was probably the last time they would meet. Catherine made a joke of it and clutched at Annie's hand as she left. Annie felt something in it, but Catherine wouldn't let her look. She closed her hand over Annie's and gripped it tightly, saying, 'That's for you, Annie. That's for *you*.' When Annie got outside she discovered that she had been given two fifty-pound notes.

Catherine rarely forgot old friends. She was still supporting the Hastings Writers' Group (as it was now known) and giving money each year for a small literary prize for short fiction. Letters to the Cookson Foundation poured through the letterbox in their thousands and Catherine insisted they all had to be vetted by the Cooksons – which meant a great deal of work for Tom. When Tom was admitted to hospital again with exhaustion, Catherine declared that she would close the foundation down rather than employ someone else to sift through the requests. 'Britain has become a nation of beggars,' she complained.[3] Catherine was very naive politically, and it never occurred to her that this might be the result of the crumbling of the welfare state.

During this period Catherine was contacted by a professor of genetics, John Burn, to ask if she would lend her name to an appeal for people willing to participate in genetic research. Her first reaction on the telephone was 'How much do you want?' He replied that he didn't want money, simply the use of her name to bring people forward and give a higher profile to the project. This really impressed both Catherine and Tom, who joked that John was the only doctor they'd seen who hadn't asked for money. Catherine was delighted to lend her name to the appeal if it would bring a better quality of life to people like herself.

When they met, Catherine liked John Burn very much. He was young and energetic, and possessed a brilliant mind coupled with an attractive sense of humour. He had total integrity, which Catherine always valued. She also liked the fact that he came from the northeast, from a working-class background, and had gained his position through scholarships. John Burn's reaction to Catherine was equally positive. When asked if he liked her, he responded simply, 'I loved her.' Quite apart from his admiration for her courage and her literary gifts, John observed that Catherine had that very rare and elusive quality, charisma. She made a tremendous impression on almost everyone who met her.

Later, John Burn asked Catherine if she would be interested in helping to develop a genetic solution for sufferers of haemorrhagic telangiectasia. He gave a rundown of the costs of the research, which he estimated would be about £45,000 a year for three years, and was amazed when a cheque came back, signed by Tom, by return of post. There was a note with it, asking him to let them know when he needed the rest. The result of this research project is the Cookson mouse, which has been successfully bred with the offending gene, which is attached to chromosome 9. John Burn hopes eventually to develop a gene-carrying spray that can be inhaled into the nostrils – the main site of the disease – in order to modify the defective genes within the cells and stop the bleeding.

In February 1992 Transworld announced the creation of the Catherine Cookson Prize for an unpublished novel in the Cookson tradition. The winner would receive £10,000 and publication. It should now have been impossible for anyone in the world of literature to ignore Catherine's achievements. The 'Catherine Cookson novel' was now an established genre, quite distinct from other category fiction. Catherine was featured in an interview on BBC television's *Bookworm* programme as one of the country's foremost authors and was now the eleventh wealthiest woman in Britain, surpassed only by the Queen and a number of shipping and supermarket heiresses. No other living British author could claim to have all their novels still in print in both hardback and paperback, and few had published anything like the total of eighty-four books on Transworld's lists by the mid-nineties. People claimed that her books changed their lives. A Catherine Cookson Appreciation Society had been set up by a young couple, David and Kathryn Higginbottom. Injured in a car crash, both had spent a considerable time in hospital, which had destroyed their dreams of renovating a house to create a bed-and-breakfast business. But when Kathryn read *Our Kate* in hospital and passed it on to her husband, she claimed that it had given them new determination to overcome their difficulties. Reading about the enormous hurdles that Catherine had had to surmount was an inspiration to others.

The Cooksons received more than three hundred letters a week detailing these experiences, each one of which was answered personally until they were both too old to do so. Often the correspondence would develop into a relationship which one friend likened to communications 'between a therapist and a patient'.[4] Catherine's agent Anthony Sheil believes that this ability to connect with people at a very fundamental level may be one of the keys to her phenomenal success as a novelist. 'In primitive societies the person who was almost as important as the shaman and operated on the same kind of level was the storyteller. The storyteller also played a therapeutic role in society; he was society's memory and in a sense could also be the memory of the individual.'[5] He or she could also be the mouthpiece for messages from the spiritual rather than the material world. Certainly Catherine seemed to be able to communicate with her readers in a powerful way that defied rational critical analysis. In using her storytelling art to heal herself, she was delighted to discover that she appeared to be able to heal others. She had always believed that she had some form of psychic perception and came to see herself as a kind of folk philosopher. 'Tom thinks I am a philosopher; that I have some of the answers,' she said on tape.[6] She reached out to touch people through novels, autobiography and letters and succeeded in a way that totally confounded agents and editors, none of whom had initially predicted the enormous sales she eventually had.

In 1993 Catherine was created a Dame of the British Empire, which Catherine regarded as the greatest honour that had ever been bestowed on her. Unfortunately her sight had failed so badly and her health was so poor that she was unable to go to London to receive the order from the Queen. It was presented by Sir Ralph Carr-Ellison, the Lord Lieutenant of Tyne and Wear, as her house in Jesmond Dene.

As a result of her increasing fame, people had begun to want to write Catherine's biography and, understandably, she resisted the idea. Her former agent and friend John Smith, now retired, had been the first to make the attempt. He had begun a biography in the eighties based on his own reminiscences. When the idea was first mooted, Catherine was far from keen on it, but was persuaded that, as someone was bound to write her biography sooner or later, John Smith was the best person to do it sympathetically. So she agreed, and John was given a contract and an advance. Catherine gave him full cooperation and allowed him to record some very frank taped conversations in which she revealed much that had not been in her previous autobiographical essays. She was, at the time, intending to write 'the whole truth' about Nan and Kate herself, and so she talked freely to John. But when the completed manuscript was shown to Catherine, she was horrified and upset. John magnanimously told her that if it was going to disturb her peace of mind so much, he would withdraw the book. It was never published.

A local freelance journalist was the next person to make the proposal and encounter Catherine's ambivalence. Cliff Goodwin had first met Catherine when he went to a press call for the stage production of *The Fifteen Streets*. Then, when he was subediting for the *Newcastle Journal*, he looked at their substantial collection of library cuttings and the amount of interest she was generating in the press and was amazed that there was no biography of Catherine in existence. He wrote to her agents, Sheil Land, about the project. Within a few days he had been telephoned by Anthony Sheil, then by Paul Scherer of Transworld, both of whom tried to dissuade him from doing it. He then received a telephone call from Tom Cookson, who said, 'You'd better talk to Catherine.' She agreed to give him two one-hour interview sessions.

When Cliff arrived at Glastonbury Grove he found Tom very friendly and courteous. Tom said that he liked the proposed title of the book, *To Be a Lady*, which Cliff took to be an indication of approval. But when he went into the bedroom, Catherine said flatly, 'I don't want this biography written.' He tried very hard to convince her that her life was so extraordinary that it ought to be written about, telling her that it was 'a story that deserves to be told'. Eventually she agreed to talk to him but wouldn't allow him to take notes or to use a tape recorder. She did allow him to take out his list of questions and she sat up in bed and began to talk. Catherine talked for more than two hours until she was utterly exhausted and Tom terminated the interview. Cliff had been almost afraid to move in case he interrupted the flow of words.

Catherine was never well enough to be interviewed again, but Cliff sent her lists of questions, which were always courteously answered, and he took this cooperation as tacit acceptance of the book. Catherine cared very much about accuracy. When Cliff gave a radio interview about his biography, she rang him straight away to say that she disagreed violently with two of the things that he had said. Cliff argued that he could prove they were true, but she would not agree. Friends say that Catherine was never happy about the book.

When she heard that Cliff had advertised for people who knew her to come forward, she hated it. Tom spoke for both of them when he said, 'She's eighty-eight, unwell, and doesn't need that kind of hassle.'[7] Cliff's letters in the local papers in Hastings and Newcastle, asking for information about Catherine, produced about twenty-five or thirty replies, many of them from people declining to talk to him on the grounds of their friendship for Catherine. She was someone people either loved or hated. Her terrible fears and insecurities could make her defensive and prickly. But underneath the confident, jokey exterior she was still the vulnerable child that made people want to protect her. Catherine's friends were – and still are – very protective. Few are willing to talk. One journalist talked about having to fight his way through the 'Cookson mafia'. But her friends are right to be reticent. In the last decade of the twentieth century personal privacy is not respected – the more famous someone becomes, the less they are regarded as having any right to privacy, and Catherine was more vulnerable than most. Cliff Goodwin further upset Catherine when he started trying to track down her father. He believed him to have been a footman at Ravensworth Castle, but when an old photograph of the staff was published in the *Sunday Sun*, Catherine rang him, angry and distressed, to insist that her father was not one of those in the photo.

To Be a Lady was published in 1994 and was savaged by Philippa Gregory in the *Daily Telegraph*. Goodwin had failed to 'reveal a hidden Cookson' or to explore connections between her life and work. The style is described as 'flat and boring' and Gregory points out that 'It is a fatal flaw for a biography of a writer to lack critical analysis. Goodwin's plot descriptions inspire confidence neither in him as a reader, nor in Cookson as a writer.' It ends, 'Stolen glimpses of banality serve no purpose but to increase the biographer's bank balance.'[8]

Cliff Goodwin's biography was written in good faith to please her fans and fill in gaps of her life not covered by *Our Kate*, which dealt only with the period up to 1956. It was not meant to be a serious, literary biography. But it failed to explain, even at a very basic level, why Catherine wrote so obsessively; why, in the words of one reviewer, she 'sacrificed her health for mediocre literature'. Reviews of Catherine's books became less adulatory and more critical throughout the nineties. A backlash was definitely setting in. Was Catherine aware that some of her books were better than others?

one reviewer asked. And why are her relationships between men and women 'so gothically black? Her sex scenes so perverse?'

Catherine's answer to the curiosity about her life was to prepare a sequel to *Let Me Make Myself Plain*. Once again she was 'baring my soul, leaving myself naked to the world, and asking myself, Was that a good thing or a bad thing?' Her justification was that her experience appeared to help others to come to terms with difficulties in their own lives. She was not so much relieving her own mind as 'opening doors in others, and in doing so letting them know they are not alone in their fears, and quirks, or in their searching'. *Plainer Still* contains much more poetry than its predecessor and a wide range of occasional pieces from different periods in her life as well as recent extracts from her journal, whose spasmodic entries were now dictated on to tape and typed up. What was kept was very selective. Catherine's previous resolve to leave an account of the truth about Nan and Kate was now abandoned – she and Tom were engaged in a ruthless sorting-out process, whereby as much material as possible was destroyed in order to leave nothing private to be misinterpreted by others after their deaths.

Emergency surgery on her colon in December 1994 seemed to bring the reality of Catherine's demise much closer. She knew that when she died she would be written about. But she did not want an authorised life and forbade her publishers to commission one. However, when Piers Dudgeon proposed writing a book that would link her life with her novels, she cooperated with him, partly because she liked him and thought he'd done a good job as editor of *Catherine Cookson Country* and partly because the proposed book was seen as a serious analysis of her novels rather than a biography. She generously sent him several hours of tapes in answer to his queries and allowed him to quote freely from her novels, but for Piers too there was always a feeling of thus far and no further.

Catherine wanted her own account of her life to stand as written in *Our Kate* and the occasional pieces in *Let Me Make Myself Plain* and its sequel *Plainer Still*. But how accurate a record are they? Catherine's friends regarded *Our Kate* as 'an exercise in ruthless, yet dignified confession',[9] and there is certainly a great deal of emotional truth in it and an almost embarrassing degree of honesty in the two subsequent volumes. But by Catherine's own admission, they are all subjective and highly selective accounts of her life. Several hundred pages of incident and observation were deleted from *Our Kate* alone before she showed it to her publisher, and more than a hundred pages of that draft were edited out before publication. The most damaging episodes of her life were omitted altogether. Catherine really didn't want to dig too deep. Just as she had turned her back on her childhood friends Belle and Cecilia, so she turned her back on the more painful events of her life as she grew older. At some point self-criticism had to stop. Approval and validation were the medicine she needed. She was very flattered when the High Commissioner of Zambia wrote to say, 'will you please not write so many books Mrs Cookson, because I cannot get any work done!'

Catherine's need for positive reinforcement was threatened by the increasingly critical attitude of the literary establishment. The *Sunday Times*, which had reviewed some of her early novels in glowing prose, now posed some hard questions. 'Why did she shift the location of her historical novels back to harder times? Was it to underline the pain of her own childhood?' and 'Why are her books so deliberately style-less?' The reviewer talks about 'linguistic poverty, which alienates intellectuals' and asks whether this was the result of her lack of education or a deliberate decision in order to reach a mass market. And why, another reviewer asks, does she appeal mainly to women? John Carey in the *Sunday Times* books section wrote that 'for literary intellectuals Dame Catherine is an upsetting phenomenon ... disgracefully popular' and wondered whether this was part of the problem. This is the age of mass media and popular culture. Anything that can be sold will be sold – regardless of standards. Catherine Cookson, inevitably, was made into a product to be relentlessly marketed as a brand name. The image of a plucky Geordie girl from the slums winning through against all odds was very commercial. But it did not mean that the product itself was without value.

Professor John Bachelor of Newcastle University defended her prose, but plans to run a course on her work at the University of Leeds had to be abandoned when only one person signed up. Elsewhere, in American universities, Catherine's work is studied as social history. Further afield, in Australia and New Zealand, she is on university curricula as the author of autobiographical fiction. The pluses of her books are that they have strong narrative drive and social realism, and Catherine is not afraid of tackling difficult subjects such as poverty and its results, crime, child abuse, homosexuality, double moral standards, exploitation, hypocrisy and men's abuse of women. Her novels are in some ways more honest than her autobiography. Catherine had no illusions.

> Oh, I know I've got a great following now, but so had so many writers, great writers, men and women much better at their job than I am, and do you hear their names mentioned? ... It's no use telling people that the main thing success has done for you has been to make you wiser to the extent that you realise the ephemerality of it ... in a very short time you will be dead and who will remember you?[10]

Her books continue to sell in millions – a total of 123 million by the end of 1998. They are much better written than some reviewers give credit for – particularly the early novels. Other critics regret the absence of a love of language. But is this fair? There is evidence that language – oral rather than 'book words' – was her great strength. Her characters leap off the page as soon as they open their mouths. 'Geordie' is a rich language, rooted in Old Norse, with a rhythm and music of its own, and it is this spoken language that was Catherine's natural medium. Required to write in classroom English, she was as crippled as any author having to write in a second language they speak only imperfectly.

Many of her detractors have obviously not read her books or they could not state that she never experiments with plot and structure. Her early novels show many attempts to experiment, most of which were curtailed by her publishers, who needed to market her work in a very narrowly defined category. She has consistently been denied real assessment – either savaged by the 'heavies' or sycophantically praised by the devotees. Some of her supporters would argue that this is because she came from the north and the working class, whereas the literary establishment is firmly rooted in the south and the middle class. But her uneven output is also an obstacle for anyone trying to assess her work, though this is probably inevitable with someone who wrote over a hundred novels across almost fifty years. And her literary advisers have not always helped in this respect. Catherine always suffered from low personal esteem, established in childhood, and badly needed the uncritical approval she got from her public. She became so used to ignoring people and fighting her way up that she sometimes made bad decisions. In 1995 Pan Books published *A Feast of Stories* in paperback. This collection of previously published women's magazine stories is very weak and dated and such stories by any name less well-known than Catherine Cookson's would never have seen the light of day again. The *Lady* magazine featured one of the stories from the collection, but 'The Simple Soul' is thin and full of old-fashioned sentiments and moral attitudes, though it has a good plot, like all Catherine's work. On the opposite page Joanna Trollope, Penelope Lively and Robert McCrum all have glossy reviews and the juxtaposition makes an uneasy contrast.

More and more of Catherine's work was being adapted for television, mainly by World Wide International Television in partnership with Tyne Tees. *The Black Velvet Gown* was even screened in America, where it secured a good audience. Catherine was often lucky to have exceptional screenwriters to write the adaptations. *The Man Who Cried* was scripted by Stan Barstow, a writer Catherine particularly admired. He was delighted to work on her novel, describing her as 'a runaway story-teller'. Television adaptations of Catherine's work had tremendous viewing figures: 10,800,000 for *The Black Candle*, rising to almost 13 million for *The Black Velvet Gown* and *The Fifteen Streets*.

After initial suspicions about screening her work, Catherine struck up a good relationship with Ray Marshall, the executive producer and managing director of World Wide International TV, who had originally produced *The Fifteen Streets*. Although she was never entirely happy, Catherine was on the whole pleased with the results of his work. Ray tried to be true to the spirit of her books, knowing that her fans would be intensely critical if he got it wrong. Catherine wanted a lot of control, insisting that she was shown the scripts, and liked to feel that she was consulted at each stage of the process. She didn't like Bob Peck being cast in *The Black Velvet Gown*, but accepted that he was right for the part when she saw the first cuts. Catherine always insisted on seeing both the rough cuts and the fine cuts as long as her eyesight permitted. Her main complaint was an objection to people kissing 'with tongues half way down each other's throats', as well as bad language and explicit sex. 'We didn't do that then.'[11] The film company thought that this was simply Catherine's prudishness. But people of Catherine's generation on Tyneside say that the only way they were able to cope with courting for three, five and sometimes even seven years before being able to marry was by 'keeping off' each other. There was no contraception for most people; intense kissing and 'heavy petting' led to loss of control and its inevitable consequences. In Catherine's books the dangers lie for girls who go out with men who don't know the rules. Christine Winter, the heroine of *Fenwick Houses*, finds herself on the riverbank with a young man innocently undressed after swimming and she sees no danger in close physical contact.

> I felt, not the slightest embarrassment, only an intense joy at the contact of Martin's instep across my foot. Then I could no longer look down at my feet, for he had turned my face towards him again and was holding me close, and there descended on my mind and body and all the world a stillness, and within the stillness I lay awake. What followed was inevitable, nothing could have stopped it, for I had no strength within myself to combat such a force, my religion and upbringing were as useless as if they had never existed.[12]

By 1996 Catherine was fragile, bedridden and almost blind. She was being kept alive with transfusions of two or three pints of blood every couple of weeks, but still dictating. Four novels appeared that year, a combination of old and new: *The Bondage of Love*, *The Bonny Dawn*, *The Branded Man* and *The Upstart*. Catherine was also persuaded to release a tape of songs which included her shaky rendering of Frank Sinatra's 'My Way', one of her own compositions called 'Falling Leaves', and family favourites such as 'Thora' and the Irish ballads old John McMullen had sometimes sung when he was drunk. These songs had been recorded ten years earlier when Catherine was bedridden and experimenting with a new portable tape recorder. During the Cooksons' ruthless clearance of old manuscripts and personal material, the tape was rooted out of the attic by Tom. He happened to be playing it, in order to see what it contained, when Ray Marshall was visiting. Ray quickly realised the commercial potential, and took it to the musician Colin Towns at Abbey Road Studios, where the unaccompanied ballads were given a backing track. Verbal reminiscences were spliced in between to create a product of a reasonable length.

When she made the tape, Catherine had been fulfilling her great desire to sing, to use her voice as an instrument, and many felt that it should have been left in an archive – it was unkind to release it to the general public. Catherine was over eighty when she sang those ballads into the microphone, yet what surprises the listener is the steadiness and musicality of the voice. She had obviously had a beautiful singing voice when younger, which had never been used. By the time she made the tape, it was too late.

In 1997 Catherine gave record amounts to charity, including £250,000 to Newcastle University's Hatton Art Gallery to help it to survive. The University Senate had voted to close it in order to reduce their expenditure by 6 per cent. Catherine gave an initial £50,000 and pledged £200,000 more over four years to keep it open. She donated £100,000 to Bede's World in Jarrow to develop an Anglo-Saxon heritage centre there, a further £200,000 to the Royal Victoria Infirmary for medical research and £50,000 to fund a study of the aftereffects of nuclear tests on British servicemen.

A photograph of Catherine in the *Evening Chronicle* to mark her ninety-first birthday shows her in a red dressing gown with a scarf tucked into the neck looking frail and tragic.[13] By the early months of 1998, it was clear to everyone around her that Catherine could not fight for much longer. The decline was gradual. Catherine knew she was dying and became very troubled about the state of her soul. In April, on Holy Thursday, Father Ian Jackson at St Peter and St Paul's Church received a telephone call from Tom asking him to come and see Catherine. When he arrived, Catherine told him that she had 'had a dream that Jesus was in the garden crying' outside her window. In the dream Father Jackson had been there too and Jesus had had his arm around him. Catherine told Father Jackson of her long spiritual struggle and then said, 'I want to make my peace with God and the church.'[14] She made her confession, received the Anointing of the Sick and Holy Communion. From then on Father Jackson went every week to hear Catherine's confession and give her Holy Communion. For the last three or four weeks she slipped in and out of consciousness. Tom sat constantly beside her bed, relieved only by Ann Marshall and Father Jackson, who was able to give her much spiritual comfort and, eventually, the last rites of the Catholic church. As many of her friends had predicted, she died 'in the faith', on 11 June in the early afternoon, shortly after her fifty-eighth wedding anniversary.

Despite her great age and her ill health, people who had known her were stunned. John Burn, who was about to go on a trip to Sweden, turned back at the airport when he was told. Many other friends also dropped what they were doing and went to be with Tom. Ann and Hugo Marshall were particularly supportive. Her fans wept.

Although Catherine's death had been expected, Tom was shocked and bewildered. He had always told friends that without Catherine 'there would be no life', and it proved to be true. Always a stickler for duty, he initially occupied himself in the organisation of Catherine's funeral and all the legal and financial business that had to be sorted out. Catherine had a private funeral service at West Road Crematorium in Newcastle. Only family and friends were present. Tom was very touched by the avalanche of tributes to Catherine that poured in and pleased that his sister contacted him for the first time in many years. Afterwards, friends tried to make sure that he was not alone, but without Catherine Tom was lost. John Burn invited him round to inspect a new roof garden, but he never came. Tom had made supporting Catherine and looking after her his life's work. After she died, he visibly lost the will to go on without her and crumbled quickly despite all their friends' attempts to help him. A fortnight after Catherine's death, Tom was admitted to hospital suffering from cardiovascular problems and exhaustion. A week later he was dead.

Before she died, Catherine had transferred most of her money to Tom (over £20 million) and to the charitable trust they had established. In her will she left only £8,476,174. Newcastle medical school got £250,000, the Harry Edwards Spiritual Healing Sanctuary £10,000 and Sister Catherine Marie of San Gabriel, California, £5,000. Her friends and advisers were also handsomely rewarded. Her bank manager, now retired, got £10,000 and her three doctors £20,000, £30,000 and £50,000 respectively. Her agent, Anthony Sheil, received a present of £50,000 and Mark Barty-King of Transworld £30,000. After Tom's death the Cooksons' house in Jesmond went to Ann and Hugo Marshall and the remainder of the money to the Catherine Cookson Foundation. Income from Catherine's books means that her charitable donations will go on for a very long time into the future.

An obituary in the *Daily Express* asked whether Catherine's compulsive giving was driven by guilt or a need to be loved and approved?[15] A close friend described it as 'an enigma. In order to understand her, you've got to realise that she was the combination of an illegitimate little girl who desperately wanted to be loved, and a professional writer whose wealth was almost an embarrassment to her.'[16] For Catherine, it was never just about writing cheques.

There were obituaries and tributes to Catherine in all the major papers. Many tried to address what it was in her life that had made her a writer. Was it childhood deprivation? The need to 'show people' what she was made of? The deeply ingrained feeling of difference she had experienced as a child? Laurence Cotterell, Catherine's great friend, quoted a conversation he had once had with Siegfried Sassoon, who said, 'A poet is a poet, is a poet. It doesn't matter what condition a man is born to, poverty or affluence, peace or war; the quality of his poetry, if it is born in him will be constant. Environment and circumstance may colour the content and presentation, but not the quality.'[17] Catherine had always maintained that although her environment gave her the material for her books, the desire to write was born in her. It was the clash between character and environment that made the story.

NOTES AND SOURCES

Unless otherwise attributed, quotations are taken from *Our Kate* by Catherine Cookson, published in 1969 by Macdonald & Co. Where given, page numbers refer to the uniform Corgi paperback edition of her novels. Boston MSS refers to manuscripts held by the Mugar Memorial Library, University of Boston, Mass. Newcastle MSS refers to manuscripts held in the Catherine Cookson Collection, Library of the University of Newcastle upon Tyne. EAH refers to taped interviews with Professor Ernst Honigmann. JST refers to taped interviews with John Smith. ACC refers to the author's own correspondence and interview notes.

Introduction

1. *The Black Velvet Gown*, ch. 1, p. 15

Chapter One

1. *The Glass Virgin*
2. *Fenwick Houses* and *The Fifteen Streets*
3. *The Fifteen Streets*, ch. 4, p. 63
4. *Colour Blind*, ch. 7
5. *Kate Hannigan*, ch. 2
6. *The Fifteen Streets*, ch. 1, p. 15
7. *The Fifteen Streets*, ch. 2, p. 29
8. Carol Chinn, *They Worked All Their Lives*
9. Boston MSS
10. Boston MSS

Chapter Two

1. *Fenwick Houses*, ch. 1
2. *The Fifteen Streets*, ch. 2, p. 42
3. *Kate Hannigan*, 'The Kitchen', p. 29

Chapter Three

1. *Let Me Make Myself Plain*
2. *The Fifteen Streets*, ch. 3, p. 50
3. Boston MSS
4. *The Fifteen Streets*, ch. 1, p. 18
5. *The Fifteen Streets*, ch. 5, p. 79
6. *Kate Hannigan*, 'The Ride'
7. *Kate Hannigan*, 'The Ride', p. 82
8. *Colour Blind*, ch. 6, p. 98
9. *The Fifteen Streets*, ch. 5, p. 79
10. Boston MSS
11. *Plainer Still*, 'Reading', p. 133
12. *Kate Hannigan*, 'Annie', p. 88

Chapter Four

1. *Colour Blind*, ch. 10, p. 191
2. *Catherine Cookson Country*, p. 15
3. *Colour Blind*, ch. 6, p. 101
4. Boston MSS; *Our Kate*, pp. 65, 171, 85–6
5. Boston MSS
6. *Kate Hannigan*, 'Annie', p. 94
7. Boston MSS
8. *Fenwick Houses*, ch. 1

Chapter Five

1. *Catherine Cookson Country*, p. 165
2. Boston MSS
3. *Colour Blind*
4. Boston MSS
5. Boston MSS

6. *Fenwick Houses*, ch. 2
7. Boston MSS
8. *Good Living*, February 1987
9. Boston MSS
10. Boston MSS

Chapter Six

1. Boston MSS
2. Boston MSS
3. Boston MSS
4. *Kate Hannigan*, 'The Ride', p. 82
5. Boston MSS
6. Boston MSS
7. Boston MSS
8. Boston MSS
9. Boston MSS

Chapter Seven

1. *Colour Blind*, ch. 1, p. 19
2. Boston MSS
3. Boston MSS
4. *The Letters of Lord Chesterfield*, Letter CXLII
5. Ibid., Letter CLXXX
6. Ibid., Letter CCXXXIV
7. *The Black Candle*, ch. 2, p. 58
8. *Plainer Still*
9. Boston MSS
10. EAH, Newcastle University MSS
11. Boston MSS
12. Boston MSS
13. JST
14. *The Black Candle*, ch. 2, p. 50

Chapter Eight

1. JST
2. Boston MSS
3. JST

4. Interview with Stuart Nicol, *Catherine Cookson, People and Places*, video, 1998

5. Boston MSS, interview with Annie Robson

6. Boston MSS

7. *Plainer Still*, p. 330

8. *The Obsession*, Pt. II, ch. 7, p. 167

9. Boston MSS

10. Boston MSS

11. JST

12. *Let Me Make Myself Plain*, 'Friendship', p. 95

13. JST

14. Boston MSS

15. Boston MSS

16. JST

17. JST

18. JST

19. JST

20. JST

21. JST

22. Boston MSS

Chapter Nine

1. *The Obsession*, ch. 5, p. 53

2. *Katie Mulholland*, Book 5, ch. 2, p. 427

3. JST

4. *The Obsession*, ch. 1, p. 7

5. *The Glass Virgin*, ch. 1, p. 34

6. JST

7. Boston MSS

8. *Plainer Still*, 'Buying Second-hand', p. 125

9. *Catherine Cookson Country*, Foreword

10. *Plainer Still*, 'From the Opaque to the Agony', p. 318

11. ACC

12. JST

13. JST

14. JST

15. *Our Kate* and Piers Dudgeon, *The Girl from Leam Lane*

16. *Kate Hannigan*, 'The Ride', pp. 82–3

17. Piers Dudgeon, *The Girl from Leam Lane*

18. *Catherine Cookson Country*, Foreword

19. *Catherine Cookson Country*, Foreword

20. *Catherine Cookson Country*, Foreword
21. JST

Chapter Ten

1. 'Our Wedding', *Newcastle Journal*, June 1990
2. JST
3. JST
4. *Catherine Cookson Country*, Introduction, p. 12
5. 'Our Wedding', *Newcastle Journal*, June 1990
6. JST
7. JST
8. *Let Me Make Myself Plain*, p. 110
9. *Plainer Still*, 'Ignorance', p. 114
10. ACC
11. JST
12. JST
13. Piers Dudgeon, *The Girl from Leam Lane*
14. *Plainer Still*, p. 34
15. Boston MSS
16. Boston MSS
17. *Catherine Cookson Country*, Foreword
18. *Plainer Still*, 'Another Odd Happening', p. 199

Chapter Eleven

1. *Let Me Make Myself Plain*
2. Boston MSS
3. Boston MSS
4. *Plainer Still*, 'God Is a Hippopotamus', p. 326
5. JST
6. Boston MSS
7. Boston MSS
8. Anthony Storr, *Human Aggression*
9. JST
10. Catherine Marchant, *The Iron Facade*, p. 5
11. Boston MSS
12. *Maggie Rowan*, ch. 15, p. 326
13. Anthony Storr, *Human Aggression*
14. *Symptoms and Defense Mechanisms in Adult Female Survivors*, University of Oregon, 1995

15. Michele Elliott, *Female Sexual Abuse of Children*
16. Boston MSS
17. *Maggie Rowan*, ch. 15, p. 327
18. Boston MSS
19. Boston MSS

Chapter Twelve

1. *Plainer Still*, 'The Payment', p. 70
2. *Plainer Still*, 'The Experience', p. 190
3. *Let Me Make Myself Plain*, 'Insomnia', p. 88
4. EAH
5. *The South Bank Show*
6. Laurence Cotterell, *Independent*, obituary, 12.6.1998
7. *Let Me Make Myself Plain*, 'Nerves', p. 121
8. ACC
9. *Let Me Make Myself Plain*, 'Bill', pp. 21–6
10. *Mary Ann and Bill*, ch. 2, p. 37
11. Ibid.
12. Let Me Make Myself Plain, 'Spiritual Healing', pp. 155–6
13. *The Fifteen Streets*, ch. 4, p. 70
14. *The Fifteen Streets*, ch. 4, p. 71
15. *Let Me Make Myself Plain*, 'Spiritual Healing', p. 160
16. Ibid.

Chapter Thirteen

1. *Plainer Still*, p. 38
2. EAH
3. *Northern Echo*, 27.9.1988
4. ACC
5. *The South Bank Show*
6. 'My First Novel', *The Author*
7. *Let Me Make Myself Plain*, 'Dreams. What Are We Really?'
8. ACC
9. 'My First Novel', *The Author*
10. ACC
11. 'My First Novel', *The Author*
12. *Let Me Make Myself Plain*, 'The Need for Applause', p. 116
13. ACC
14. *Dillons Newsletter*, 1994

15. Piers Dudgeon, *The Girl from Leam Lane*
16. Ibid.
17. Ibid.
18. *The Fifteen Streets*, ch. 5, p. 76
19. *The Fifteen Streets*, ch. 4, p. 68
20. *The Fifteen Streets*, ch. 7, p. 122
21. *The Fifteen Streets*, ch. 14, p. 219
22. *Plainer Still*, 'From the Opaque to the Agony', p. 317
23. ACC

Chapter Fourteen

1. Richard Jefferies, *The Story of My Heart*, London: 1883
2. Piers Dudgeon, *The Girl from Leam Lane*
3. Boston MSS
4. Boston MSS
5. *The Solace of Sin*, ch. 4, p. 56
6. *Catherine Cookson Country*, p. 12
7. *Catherine Cookson Country*, p. 70
8. Boston MSS
9. Boston MSS
10. *Kate Hannigan* and *Katie Mulholland*

Chapter Fifteen

1. Diane Wood Middlebrook, *Anne Sexton*, Houghton Mifflin, 1991
2. *Catherine Cookson Country*, Introduction, p. 21
3. *Radio Times*, 10.2.1996
4. Boston MSS
5. Boston MSS
6. EAH
7. *The Journal*, 5.10.1983
8. EAH
9. Dr Louise J. Kaplan, *Oneness and Separateness*
10. Dr Louise J. Kaplan, *Oneness and Separateness*
11. Linda Gray Sexton, *Searching for Mercy Street*
12. *Our Kate*, p. 65
13. Linda Gray Sexton, *Searching for Mercy Street*
14. Boston MSS
15. Boston MSS
16. Boston MSS

17. Boston MSS
18. Boston MSS
19. Boston MSS
20. EAH
21. EAH
22. EAH
23. *Katie Mulholland*, Book 3, ch. 2, p. 285
24. *Plainer Still*, 'The Mink Coat', p. 63
25. *Plainer Still*, 'Talking', p. 91
26. *Plainer Still*, 'Talking', p. 91
27. *Plainer Still*, 'Talking', p. 97

Chapter Sixteen

1. *Let Me Make Myself Plain*, p. 81
2. ACC
3. *Plainer Still*, 'From the Opaque to the Agony', p. 317
4. JST
5. *Catherine Cookson Country*, p. 16
6. *Plainer Still*, p. 68
7. *Pure as the Lily*, Book 3, ch. 1, p. 240
8. *Catherine Cookson Country*, Introduction, p. 21
9. *New York Times*, 8.4.1984
10. JST
11. JST
12. JST
13. JST
14. JST

Chapter Seventeen

1. *Plainer Still*, 'The Payment', p. 70
2. *The Journal*, 5.10.1983
3. *Shields Gazette*, June 1998
4. JST
5. JST
6. Boston MSS
7. *Catherine Cookson Country*, p. 186
8. JST
9. JST
10. *Plainer Still*, 'The North East', p. 208

11. Piers Dudgeon, *The Girl from Leam Lane*, ch. 8, p. 197
12. *Ibid.*
13. *Catherine Cookson Country*, p. 48
14. ACC
15. *Plainer Still*, 'God Is a Hippopotamus', p. 325
16. Ibid.
17. *The Journal*, 5.10.1983
18. *The Times*, October 1983
19. *Yorkshire Post*, October 1983
20. *Catherine Cookson Country*, p. 42
21. *Catherine Cookson Country*, p. 190
22. Private correspondence
23. *Plainer Still*, 'Dog Days', p. 84
24. Ibid.
25. *Guardian*, 17.5.1988
26. *The Journal*, 4.10.1983
27. *Shields Gazette*, June 1997
28. *Shields Evening Chronicle*, 29.9.1982
29. Speech by Dr David Harle, memorial service
30. Ibid
31. *Shields Evening Chronicle*, 15.4.1978
32. ACC
33. *Shields Evening Chronicle*, 19.1.1984
34. Ibid.
35. *Plainer Still*, 'The Judge and Jury, p. 77
36. Ibid.
37. Catherine was eventually given a leather-bound copy to commemorate the Catherine Cookson Building at Newcastle University
38. *A Dinner of Herbs*, Pt. 4, ch. 1
39. *A Dinner of Herbs*, Pt. 4, ch. 12

Chapter Eighteen

1. *Catherine Cookson Country*, Introduction
2. *The Times*, 15.8.1983
3. *The Journal*, 21.11.1998
4. *The Journal*, 4.10.1983
5. *This Is Your Life*, 22.12.1982
6. 20.11.1983
7. *Plainer Still*, 'Fame', p. 287
8. *Catherine Cookson Country*, p. 190
9. *Shields Gazette*, 14.6.1986

10. *Private Eye*, 1992
11. *Journal Photo*, 21.6.1986
12. 13.10.1986
13. *Shields Gazette*, 14.6.1986
14. *Plainer Still*, p. 16
15. *Guardian*, 17.5.1988
16. *Plainer Still*, 'Counting Your Chickens', p. 228
17. *Plainer Still*, 'How to Die'
18. *Let Me Make Myself Plain*, p. 48
19. *Plainer Still*, 'Subconscious', p. 24
20. *Sunday Sun*, 9.1.1989, *Shields Gazette*
21. *Plainer Still*, p. 191
22. *Plainer Still*, p. 191
23. *Plainer Still*, 'The Experience', p. 197

Chapter Nineteen

1. *Let Me Make Myself Plain*, 'Time and the Child', p. 32.
2. *Plainer Still*
3. *Shields Gazette*
4. ACC
5. ACC
6. JST
7. *Shields Gazette*, 1996
8. *Daily Telegraph*, 20.8.1994
9. Laurence Cotterell, *Independent*, 12.6.1998
10. *Let Me Make Myself Plain*, 'Success', p. 176
11. *Shields Gazette*
12. *Fenwick Houses*, p. 159
13. 2.5.1997
14. ACC
15. 12.6.1998
16. *Newcastle Journal*, 12.6.1998
17. *Independent*, 12.6.1998

BIBLIOGRAPHY

Carol Chinn, *They Worked All Their Lives: A study of working women 1880–1939*, Manchester University Press, 1997
Piers Dudgeon, *The Girl from Leam Lane*, Headline, 1997
Michele Elliott, ed., *Female Sexual Abuse of Children*, Longman, 1993
Cliff Goodwin, *To Be a Lady*, Century, 1994
Dr Louise J. Kaplan, *Oneness and Separateness*, Simon and Schuster, 1978
Dr Louise J. Kaplan, *Lost Children*, HarperCollins Publishers, 1995
Lisa Lipshires, 'Female Perpetration of Child Sexual Abuse', *Moving Forward* vol. 2, no. 6, 1994
June Price, 'Suffer Little Children: The inner world of abusing mothers', unpublished PhD thesis, 1997
Linda Gray Sexton, *Searching for Mercy Street*, Little, Brown, 1994
Anthony Storr, *Human Aggression*, Allen Lane, 1968
'Symptoms and Defence Mechanisms in Adult Female Survivors', discussion paper, University of Oregon
D. W. Winnicott, *Playing and Reality*, Penguin, 1971

PUBLISHED WORKS BY CATHERINE COOKSON

1950 *Kate Hannigan*
1952 *The Fifteen Streets*
1953 *Colour Blind*
1954 *A Grand Man*
    Maggie Rowan
1956 *The Lord and Mary Ann*
1957 *Rooney*

1958 *The Devil and Mary Ann*
  The Menagerie
1959 *Slinky Jane*
  Fanny McBride (originally called *The Ladies*)
1960 *Fenwick Houses* (originally called *Christine*)
1961 *Love and Mary Ann*
1962 *The Garment* (originally called *Deeds of Mercy*, written in 1959)
  Life and Mary Ann
1963 *Heritage of Folly* (as Catherine Marchant; Katie McMullen in the USA)
The Blind Miller
  The Fen Tiger (as Catherine Marchant, written 1961)
1964 *House of Men* (as Catherine Marchant, Katie McMullen in the USA; written 1961
Marriage and Mary Ann
  Hannah Massey
1965 *Mary Ann's Angels*
  The Long Corridor
  Matty Doolin (for children)
1966 *The Unbaited Trap*
1967 *Mary Ann and Bill* (written 1965)
  Katie Mulholland (originally called *The Steel Heart*)
1968 *Joe and the Gladiator* (for children)
  The Round Tower (winner of the Winifred Holtby Award)
1969 *The Nice Bloke*
  Our Kate (autobiography)
1970 *The Glass Virgin*
  The Invitation (originally called *Bugger the Duke*)
  The Nipper (for children)
1971 *The Dwelling Place*
Feathers in the Fire
1972 *Pure as the Lily*
  Blue Baccy (for children)
1973 *The Mallen Streak* (written 1972)
1974 *The Mallen Girl* (written 1972)
  The Mallen Litter (written 1972)
  Our John Willy (for children)
1975 *The Invisible Cord*
  The Gambling Man
  Miss Martha Mary Crawford (as Catherine Marchant)
1976 *The Tide of Life* (written 1974)
  The Slow Awakening (as Catherine Marchant)
  The Iron Facade (as Catherine Marchant)
  Mrs Flannagan's Trumpet (for children)

1977 *The Girl*
  Go Tell it to Mrs Golightly (for children)
1978 *The Cinder Path*
1979 *The Man Who Cried*
1980 *Tilly Trotter*
1981 *Tilly Trotter Wed* (written 1978)
  Lanky Jones (for children)
1982 *Tilly Trotter Widowed* (written 1979)
  Nancy Nuttall and the Mongrel (for children)
1983 *The Whip*
  Hamilton
1984 *The Black Velvet Gown* (written 1980 as *The Black Velvet Dress*)
  Goodbye Hamilton
1985 *A Dinner of Herbs*
  Harold (originally *Hello Harold*)
1986 *The Moth* (written 1980 as *Thorman's Moth*)
  Bill Bailey
  Catherine Cookson Country (ed. Piers Dudgeon)
1987 *The Parson's Daughter* (written in 1983 as *The Parson's Prig*)
  Bill Bailey's Lot (written 1986)
1988 *The Cultured Handmaiden* (written 1980)
  Bill Bailey's Daughter
  Let Me Make Myself Plain (autobiography)
1989 *The Harrogate Secret* (written as *The Runner*)
  The Black Candle
1990 *The Wingless Bird* (written 1987)
  The Gillyvors (written 1980)
1991 *The Rag Nymph*
  My Beloved Son (written 1984)
1992 *The House of Women* (written 1985)
  The Maltese Angel (written 1988)
1993 *The Year of the Virgins* (written 1985)
  The Golden Straw (written 1989)
1994 *Justice is a Woman* (written 1974)
  The Tinker's Girl (written 1991)
1995 *The Obsession*
  A Ruthless Need
  Plainer Still (autobiography)
1996 *The Bondage of Love*
  The Bonny Dawn (written 1958)
  The Branded Man
  The Upstart
1997 *The Desert Crop*

Lady on My Left
1998 Riley
The Solace of Sin
The Blind Years

INDEX

Campbell, Patrick 220
Candide (Voltaire) 133, 138
Career of Catherine Bush, The
    (Glyn) 94
Carey, John 319
Carr-Ellison, Sir Ralph 315
Carstairs, Dr (Kate's doctor) 218
Cartland, Barbara 4
Catherine Cookson Appreciation
    Society 314
Catherine Cookson Country 12,
    297–8
Catherine Cookson Country 297,
    318
Catherine Cookson Museum 311
Catherine Cookson Prize 314
Catherine Marie, Sister 324
Caufield, Miss (at Tyne Dock
    school) 37–8, 69, 70, 79
Chaplin, Charlie 43
Charrot, John 195
Charrot, Margaret 195, 206, 207,
    213
Chatterbox Annual 40, 47–8
Chester-le-Street 23
Chesterfield, Lord 94–5, 105, 108,
    115, 155
Chisholm, Elsie 99, 119
Chisholm, Mr and Mrs 99, 119
Christian Agnostic, The
    (Weatherhead) 217
Christy & Moore 205, 274
Cleadon 89
Coleridge, Gill 274
Collins, Jackie 4
Colour Blind 37, 87, 211, 214, 230
    Miss Flynn 37; Rose Angela 37,
    48, 215; Bridget McQueen 60,
    254
Comic Cuts 35, 41
Cookson, Catherine
  LIFE: raised as grandparents'
    child 20, 23–4, 26, 29, 30;
    schooldays 30, 35, 37–8;
    childhood shoplifting 40–1,
    150; pawnshop visits 41–2;
    fetching drink 49–50; learns

of her illegitimacy 31, 50–3;
first attempts at writing 67,
97, 136, 144–5, 183; goes
into domestic service 75; pen-
painting on fabric 76;
appointed laundry checker at
Harton Workhouse 85; moves
to Tendring Workhouse
laundry 104; laundry
manageress at Hastings
Workhouse 112; joined by
Nan Smith 119; joined by
Kate 127; buys the Hurst
129–31; meets Tom Cookson
137–8; marries Tom 149–52;
their marriage 4, 138, 187–8,
212, 245–7, 300, 303, 306;
evacuation to St Albans 154;
to Hereford 168; return to the
Hurst 180; taken on by
Christy & Moore 206; first
novel *Kate Hannigan* accepted
by Macdonald 206–7; move
to Loreto 222–3; wins
Winifred Holtby Award 258;
breaks into American market
258–9 260; given freedom of
South Shields 270; moves to
Heinemann 274; moves back
to northeast 279–81;
honorary MA at Newcastle
University 292, 294;
establishes Catherine Cookson
Foundation 293; on *This Is
Your Life* 295; on *South Bank
Show* 295–6; awarded OBE
299; moves to Transworld
300; honorary D. Litt at
Sunderland University 310;
awarded DBE 4, 315; death
323–4
  CHARACTER AND VIEWS: her
    illegitimacy 18–20, 21–2, 31,
    37, 54, 82, 92, 100, 104–7,
    110–11, 116, 144, 166, 172,
    228–9, 232, 248; quest for her
    'gentleman' father 19, 81, 105,